10/01/13
24/01/13
09/02/13

2

15/12/15

CAN

Books should be returned or renewed by the last date
above. Renew by phone **08458 247 200** or online
www.kent.gov.uk/libs

Ian Fleming's Commandos

Ian Fleming's Commandos

THE STORY OF 30 ASSAULT UNIT
IN WWII

Nicholas Rankin

faber and faber

First published in 2011
by Faber and Faber Limited
Bloomsbury House
74–77 Great Russell Street
London WC1B 3DA

Typeset by Palindrome
Printed and bound by CPI Group (UK) Ltd, Croydon

A CIP record for this book
is available from the British Library

ISBN 978–0–571–25062–2

2 4 6 8 10 9 7 5 3 1

This book is for
30
then and now

And especially for the veterans of 30AU who helped me

Mr John Brereton†
Mr Peter Jemmett
Mr John (Doc) Livingstone
Mr Bill Marshall
Mr Paul McGrath DSM
Mr Bill Powell
Mr Sandy Powell MBE, DSM†
Dr A. G. (Bon) Royle PhD
Major Freddie Townsend OBE, RM†
Sir Charles Wheeler CMG†

Contents

Illustrations

15 Sean Connery and Ian Fleming, 1962. © Frank Herrmann / *The Times* / News International Syndication.

16 Ian and Ann Fleming at Goldeneye, 1964. Photograph by Francis Goodman © reserved; photographs collection, National Portrait Gallery, London.

Every effort has been made to trace or contact all copyright holders. The publishers would be pleased to rectify any omissions or errors brought to their notice at the earliest opportunity.

Maps

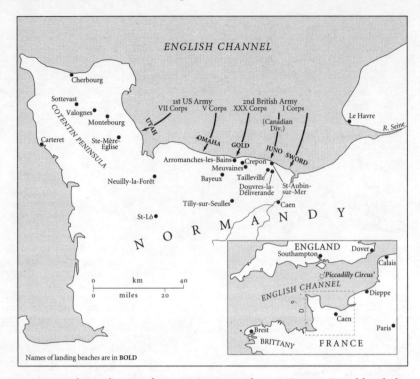

1 30 Assault Unit's area of operations in north-west France. First blooded
at Dieppe in August 1942, they took part in the Operation NEPTUNE
landings in Normandy on D-Day, 6 June 1944, where their targets included
naval bases, midget submarines, radar stations and rocket-launching sites.
30AU was at the spearhead in Brittany and helped to liberate Paris from
Nazi occupation.

2 30AU in Nazi Germany. As Hitler's Third Reich collapsed under assault from Allied forces, small, mobile parties of 30AU men were able to seize key targets: industrial factories, often using slave-labour from concentration camps, major naval bases and experimental workshops developing new weapons of war. In one brilliant coup, 30AU also captured the entire archive of the German navy at Tambach Castle.

Abbreviations and Acronyms

BIOS   British Intelligence Objectives Sub-Committee
CAFT   Consolidated Advanced Field Teams
CIOS   Combined Intelligence Objectives Subcommittee
COHQ   Combined Operations Headquarters
COPPs   Combined Operations Pilotage Parties
DNI   Director of Naval Intelligence (DDNI, Deputy Director;
    ADNI Assistant Director)
FFI   Forces françaises de l'intérieur
FIU   Royal Navy Forward Interrogation Unit
GC&CS   Government Code and Cypher School
IAU   Intelligence Assault Unit
ISTD   Inter-Services Topographical Department
JIC   Joint Intelligence Committee
LRDG   Long Range Desert Group
MI(R)   Military Intelligence (Research)
NID   Naval Intelligence Division
OIC   Operational Intelligence Centre
OSS   Office of Strategic Services
RDF   Radio Direction-Finding
RTU   Returned to Unit
SAS   Special Air Service
SBS   Special Boat Section/Service/Squadron
SHAEF   Supreme Headquarters Allied Expeditionary Force
SIGINT   Signals Intelligence
SIS   Secret Intelligence Service
SOE   Special Operations Executive
TAC HQ   Tactical Headquarters
W/T   wireless telegraphy

Prologue

On 20 September 2010 the Pentagon ordered the entire first print-run of a book written by a US military intelligence officer about spycraft in Afghanistan to be destroyed, because it revealed secret classified information. One of the 200-odd deletions from the second edition of Lieutenant Colonel Anthony Shaffer's *Operation Dark Heart* was the term TAREX, defined in the first edition's glossary as 'TARget EXploitation. Small-unit, up-close, intelligence-gathering operatives. Usually two-to-three man units.'

The gathering of intelligence by small units at the military front may be a secret to Americans; it is not new to the British. This book describes how Ian Fleming, the author of the James Bond books – Lieutenant Commander I. L. Fleming RNVR (Special Branch), as he then was – introduced the idea to Britain's Naval Intelligence Division during the Second World War. *Ian Fleming's Commandos* tells the true story of the commando unit that Fleming founded, known at various times as 30 Commando or 30 Assault Unit, who won their spurs seizing Axis enemy intelligence in North Africa, Italy and France and finally achieved two great intelligence coups in the collapsing Third Reich in 1945.

Fleming's fictional secret agent James Bond is now as well known as Sherlock Holmes. The books (a dozen novels, two volumes of short stories) have sold millions and the films have made billions. Anthony Burgess considered James Bond 'likely to end up as one of the great twentieth-century myths', adding that he is 'a model neo-Elizabethan, a hero we need'. Simon Winder's *The Man Who Saved Britain* argued that Fleming's quixotic hero masked and solaced the UK's drastic post-war decline.

Much of *Ian Fleming's Commandos* is about the secret side of warfare, the codebreaking, the deals and double-dealings, and above all the drive to acquire new, war-winning technologies – things that Fleming learned about in his six extraordinary years working in wartime Naval Intelligence. There he liaised with spies, agents and special forces, and founded his commando unit dedicated to seizing enemy documents, weapons and equipment from the front line. This is the backstory of James Bond, who, like his creator, 'thought nostalgically and unreasonably of the excitement and turmoil of the hot war, compared with his own underground skirmishings since the war had turned cold'.

In a new century, after a gap of six decades, Ian Fleming's groundbreaking idea of a Royal Navy intelligence assault unit dedicated to 'target exploitation' has been revived in the UK. With just a few of its original veterans from the Second World War still alive, 30AU has risen like a phoenix from the ashes.

The inaugural parade of 30 Commando Information Exploit-ation Group Royal Marines took place on a very cold, bright morning, 13 December 2010, at Stonehouse Barracks in Plymouth. The name 30 Commando was chosen in tribute to the forgotten men of Fleming's 30 Commando/30 Assault Unit, and the secretary of the 30AU old comrades' association, Mrs Dianne Fisher, represented them at the ceremonial blessing of their yellow and blue standard.

The revived 30 Commando is part of 3 Commando Brigade, a core component of the UK's Joint Rapid Reaction Force. Under the motto *Attain by Surprise*, but using twenty-first-century technology, the successors to Ian Fleming's intelligence commandos continue as the overt/covert 'information regiment'.

1

Day Trip to Dieppe, 1942

The thud of a big gun woke Ian Fleming from his doze. He found himself in a black leather armchair, still wearing the canvas Mae West life jacket that everyone put on to cross the German minefield at midnight. No longer just a 'chocolate sailor' stuck behind an Admiralty desk, thirty-four-year-old Lieutenant Commander Ian Fleming RNVR was going into battle on board a Royal Navy destroyer, swashing over the English Channel towards the Seine-Maritime coast of occupied France.

It was past 3 a.m. on Wednesday 19 August 1942 and the crowded wardroom that ran thirty feet athwart HMS *Fernie* was blue with tobacco smoke. Over the electric fireplace, on a small wooden shield, hung a fox's brush, the tally-ho emblem of a Hunt class destroyer. A white-jacketed steward deftly slipped his tray of drinks between the officers and the mess table. The crop-headed Texan Brigadier General Lucian Truscott hand-rolled another cigarette and boasted that One Skunk, the full-blood American Indian among his fifty US Rangers, would be using his commando knife to slit, rip and lift the first Nazi scalp.

Three years into the Second World War, Operation JUBILEE was the largest cross-Channel foray so far. This Anglo-Canadian 'reconnaissance in force' aimed to seize Dieppe in German-occupied Europe, to destroy targets, take prisoners and to re-embark, all in a few hours. Ian Fleming had friends at the HQ of Combined Operations and knew a lot about the plan. JUBILEE had evolved into an eight-pronged amphibious assault, carried in thirteen naval groups across the Channel, designed to sweep in on the early morning tide and jab into six colour-coded beaches along a dozen miles of the German-defended French coast. In

1

the sky above, 700 aeroplanes from sixty squadrons of the Royal Air Force (including the three Eagle squadrons made up of US volunteer pilots) were expecting to give the Luftwaffe their biggest thrashing since the Battle of Britain in 1940.

The Dieppe operation was not intended to be the opening up of the long-demanded 'second front' nor, as leaflets in French explained, the hoped-for *libération*. To save the lives (and homes) of French civilians, there was to be no prior bombardment by battleships or heavy bombing from the air, only some shelling by seven destroyers and strafing by aircraft. On the two outer wings, advancing from Orange and Yellow Beaches, British commandos were to knock out the two big coastal gun batteries that threatened the fleet of ships at sea. On the inner flanks, landing on Green and Blue Beaches, Canadian forces would assault the field batteries and the radar station, then seize the high ground commanding the town and spread out beyond to block enemy reinforcements.

Thirty minutes later, according to the JUBILEE plan, with their flanks now covered, the main assault force, more Canadian infantry with Canadian tanks, was to hit the White and Red Beaches directly in front of Dieppe's broad promenade, go over the sea wall and through the wire, and then advance through the town towards the port. At the same time another group of commandos, together with naval demolition parties, would be entering Dieppe harbour by sea in order to assault the docks and cut out the German invasion barges moored there. This second group of commandos was of particular interest to Ian Fleming.

The British Commandos (one of Winston Churchill's pet ideas) were first formed in June 1940, straight after Dunkirk, as a vigorous tonic for defeat and depression. They were an aggressive force of 'Striking Companies' intended to mount 'butcher-and-bolt' or 'hit-and-run' raids against the German forces along Europe's coastline. The original commandos were hand-picked volunteers for hazardous 'Special Service' who could come from any regiment in the British army and kept their own cap-badges. Class or status didn't matter, only their competence as irregular front-line warriors. If they weren't the right stuff, or could not make the grade, they were RTU'd: Returned To Unit. 'Remember that you represent the flower of the British Army,' said one of their lieutenant colonels, a slender Scottish aristocrat, the 24th Chief of Clan Fraser of Lovat, the night before Dieppe. 'I know you'll come back in a blaze of glory.'

The idea of an elite spearhead spread to other services, including the Royal Navy, whose corps of Royal Marines also contributed a commando to the Dieppe raid. The Royal Marines were already one of Britain's oldest military formations, founded in 1664 as the amphibious infantry of the Royal Navy, serving under the motto: *per mare per terram*, by sea and by land. They had won their laurels all over the globe, seeing action in every continent during the rise of the British Empire. The first Royal Marine Commando was formed in February 1942. They were known as 'A Commando', and they too had a role in Operation JUBILEE.

On board the gunboat HMS *Locust*, not far away among the nearly 300 vessels, was the particular platoon of Royal Marine commandos tasked by Ian Fleming with a new experiment for the Naval Intelligence Division (NID). Their job was to enter the Dieppe quayside hotel housing the local HQ of the German navy, the Kriegsmarine, and to seize all German navy cipher machines, code books and secret documents. Although Fleming originated the idea of what he first called an 'advance intelligence unit', then an 'intelligence assault unit', he himself was forbidden to go in with them on their first mission because his wartime job in Naval Intelligence made him privy to many secrets – especially one great one, as we shall see – that could never be allowed to fall into enemy hands. At this time the Nazis were believed to have a truth serum that could make anyone talk. (Another squad of Canadian soldiers who landed on Green Beach at Dieppe, charged with protecting a British radar expert with their own lives, had melodramatic secret orders to kill him if the only alternative was capture.)

In his dark navy pea-jacket Fleming went up the iron ladder and out on deck to see what had woken him. HMS *Fernie's* grey bulk was so festooned with new aerials she could barely traverse her guns. As the reserve headquarters ship to HMS *Calpe*, the escort destroyer was carrying a duplicate Combined Operations staff, sundry observers and the extra signals equipment to coordinate the primitive communications between the army, navy and air force elements who were all meant to be working together in Operation JUBILEE.

The moonless August night felt warm and still. The stars gleamed and you could smell the fresh-cut hay of French meadows. Miles away to port, Fleming saw white star shells, red and green tracer, yellow and violet flashes lighting up the northern horizon. Was the thud a four-inch gun? Something was happening there whose significance he did not yet understand; events were eroding the schedule. But the Allied fleet pressed on into the darkness, carrying 10,000 men towards Dieppe.

One of the lads assigned to work for Ian Fleming in the unit dedicated to seizing intelligence was a forceful Royal Marine called Paul McGrath. Aged nineteen, nearly six feet tall and eleven and half stone in weight, he had the invincible self-confidence of the young, healthy and handsome. Quick with his fists and skilled with his weapons, 'Mac' McGrath was one of the cheerful bootnecks of 10 Platoon, X Company, in the Royal Marines A Commando. They had been practising for this Naval Intelligence mission in Portsmouth harbour. They had to come alongside fast, jump off the motor gun boat and then pound across the wharves past surprised dockies to enter designated buildings to clear rooms and look for papers. Now, very early on a fine summer's morning, they were approaching the real thing. No one had told them where they were, but it certainly wasn't much like the rehearsals in Portsmouth. They had already seen waves of blue-green Hurricanes roaring in low to shoot up the shore defences with stuttering cannons.

Clutching his Lee-Enfield in his right hand, heavy pack on back, lying flat on his belly on the steel top-deck of HMS *Locust*, pressing down against bandoliers chunky with a hundred rounds of .303 ammunition, several spare Bren-gun magazines and an anti-tank 'sticky bomb', McGrath was not able to see much of what was going on overhead. Now there were whining, buzzing dogfights with the creamy silver-coloured Focke-Wulfs of the Luftwaffe, all accompanied by the bang and boom of guns and bombs.

HMS *Locust* was pounding at fifteen knots towards the enemy. Built in Glasgow just before the war as a flat-bottomed gunboat for the River Yangtze in China, and already a shrapnel-scarred veteran of the Dunkirk debacle, she was now captained by Commander Robert Ryder VC. Ryder had won Britain's highest gallantry award just five months earlier, leading the daring Operation CHARIOT that rammed an old American destroyer packed with twenty-four depth-charges into the gates of the graving dock at St-Nazaire, to prevent the huge German battleship *Tirpitz* from berthing there. Now Ryder was hurtling into mortal danger again.

Straight ahead, the mole protecting the narrow entrance to the harbour of Dieppe was overhung with a pall of black smoke, stitched with lines of red tracer. To the right a high cliff like Dover's overlooked the seafront promenade. To the left lower escarpments dominated the harbour. And from both sides German guns were firing at them. A shell struck the *Locust* on the starboard side, twenty feet from Paul McGrath.

The noise of the explosion was gigantic. The shock of it blew all the fuses in my nervous system. I was petrified with such a terror it stunned my mind. I lay on the deck with a sort of premature rigor mortis, immobilized by the awful thought of an immediate and terrible death.

Decades later, in old age, McGrath still remembered it as the greatest feeling of fear in his entire life. A black hole of paralysis.

In the ringing silence the air stank of burnt explosive. There were groaning wounded among the shocked platoon on the deck. Beside him lay their sergeant, twenty-one-year-old John Kruthoffer from Liverpool, also covered in dirt and debris. As the three-striper stirred from stupor, he cursed effusively. McGrath never knew anyone who swore quite as much as 'Krut' Kruthoffer.

Mac then noticed 'Ginger' Northern, a red-haired lad who was due to be married in a fortnight's time, slumped against the bulkhead with a 'sick-bay tiffy' or naval medical orderly kneeling beside him going through his pockets.

'What are you doing?'

'He's dead. I'm taking his personal stuff to be sent back home.'

'Oh.'

'Orders to throw the dead overboard. Here, give me a hand.'

So Mac had a future, and Ginger was all past. HMS *Locust* was now veering away from its suicidal 'bow-and-arrow run'. Facing a blizzard of shellfire Ryder had aborted the landing mission, but ordered all his guns to engage the enemy on the cliffs. Two 4-inch quick-firing guns, a 3.5-inch howitzer, a pom-pom and a pair of four-barrel .50 heavy machine-guns can crack out a hell of a din. The marines crouched on the deck with their hands pressed to their ears.

Ian Fleming was keenly trying to watch *Locust*'s activities from *Fernie*. Amid the aggravating clatter of the Oerlikon anti-aircraft gun swatting off enemy planes, it was hard to work out the bigger picture of events because of the smoke. On this clear day with a blue sky above a calm sea, there was a drifting white bank of artificial fog hanging offshore, and only through the gaps in it could you glimpse flashes. Destroyers dashed back and forth dragging behind them billowing curtains of smoke to hide the ships from the guns on land, and the smaller naval craft were also dropping smoke pots that bobbed on the water like little belching fumaroles.

Others were also trying to make out what was happening and whether it was going well. The chief of Combined Operations, Vice Admiral Lord Louis Mountbatten, who had overall responsibility for the plan, was following what happened by radio from RAF Uxbridge back home. Never shy of publicity and alert to the power of propaganda, Mountbatten had made sure that twenty, mainly North American, newspaper correspondents and photographers accompanied the Dieppe raid. Quentin Reynolds, the influential reporter for *Collier's* magazine, was the only journalist assigned to the HQ ship, HMS *Calpe*, where he met all the senior commanders. A press officer on board also showed Reynolds close-up aerial photos, detailed maps of Dieppe with their intelligence overlays and let him in on the elaborate timetable of the plan. Reynolds later wrote:

Reading it was like reading the script of an exciting play. Reading it, you know it's going to be a hit; the action is terrific, the dialogue marvelous. It's so good you can't wait to see it played . . . This script was foolproof: it couldn't miss. And what a show it would be!

Dieppe seemed a beautiful plan: great in theory, good-looking on paper. But too many cooks were in fact combining to spoil it. 'No battle plan survives contact with the enemy,' observed the German Generalfeldmarschall Helmuth von Moltke. The complex JUBILEE plan that had been evolved, so dependent on surprise, clockwork timing and the cumulative achievements of its sixteen objectives, soon degenerated into chaos.

In his 2005 book *The Dieppe Raid*, the late Robin Neillands suggested that the mainly naval people at Combined Operations Headquarters had not made a proper military 'appreciation of the situation' at Dieppe. Nor did they pay due attention to the geography of the target. Dieppe lay in the notch that the river Arques had cut between cliffs and, if the chalky headlands either side of the town were not secured by troops or battered into submission by bombardment, then the main infantry landing in the middle – a frontal attack on an open beach – was going to be enfiladed from every angle. The original plan, Operation RUTTER, made by Bernard Montgomery before he went off to head the Eighth Army in Africa, called for battleship big guns to blast the way for the attack, but the Royal Navy would not risk losing capital ships to the Luftwaffe. The frontal attack stayed in the plan, but without the suppressive firepower.

The geology of that beach was crucial to an amphibious operation, too. No one in history had ever before tried to unload armoured scout cars and five dozen infantry tanks on to an open beach under enemy fire. It was a daring innovation that foundered on a basic error. The 14th Canadian Army Tank Regiment from Calgary had rehearsed their tank landings on the flat sand and shingle of Bridport in Lyme Bay, on Dorset's Jurassic coast. But the geology of Dieppe was different: it was chalky, like Hampshire, Sussex and Kent. Chalk is a limestone made from the skeletons of ancient sea-creatures forming sedimentary strata of calcium carbonate sometimes hundreds of metres thick. The scouring sea can wash away this soft, white, earthy material, leaving behind the harder bands of silica layered within it. (This why the sea-shore below white cliffs is mostly rounded stones, grinding each other smooth in the rolling action of the waves.) The beach at Dieppe was formed of chert, whose big potato-sized pebbles lay heaped in deeper, steeper banks that made vehicle traction more difficult. As the 38-ton Churchill tanks dug down, slithered and foundered on the great sliding piles of stones, hard round pebbles of a singular infrangibility were able to roll in between the drive sprockets and the tank tracks and so break the track-link pins. Of the twenty-nine Churchill tanks that left the ships at Dieppe, two drowned, but twelve never got off the beach.

N

From the ship's rail of *Fernie,* Ian Fleming looked down into the landing craft alongside, bringing back another group of commandos, the British army's No. 4 Commando from Operation CAULDRON, the most successful part of the whole Dieppe raid. 'In and out – smash and grab' was how their commanding officer, Lord Lovat, described the brutal aggression of this swift Commando attack that eliminated a gun battery at a cost of sixteen British dead and twenty wounded.

Fleming watched the walking injured and the 'cot-cases' from No. 4 Commando being loaded aboard the destroyer from the landing craft. Among them, stretchered back from the battle on a broken door, was Major Pat Porteous, twice shot and later awarded the VC for his courage and leadership. Wet and filthy, with their faces under knitted comforter caps streaked with black and poisonous green camouflage paint, the elite warriors were exultant and exhausted after their battle, wild with delight to be alive, but dog-tired as the adrenalin receded. The 250 men of No. 4 Commando – who fought without helmets, armour or heavy kit, some of them in gym shoes for extra speed – had just managed to destroy the German coastal battery of six guns at Varengeville-sur-Mer, covering the western approaches to Dieppe. Fleming was taken with the enthusiasm of the commandos in the aftermath of battle. One of them showed him letters he had taken from a dead German. The commandos had gone in hard, killed many and taken some prisoners from the battery. But a written British order, captured by the Germans at Dieppe, saying that German prisoners should be shackled, plus a Commando attack on Sark in early October where German prisoners were tied up and shot, led to Hitler's infamous order of 18 October 1942 that 'all enemies on so-called Commando missions in Europe or Africa . . . whether armed or unarmed, in battle or in flight, are to be slaughtered to the last man'.

↗

The Canadian Army Overseas was having a desperate day. Although they had been the very first British Empire troops to come over to defend 'the mother country' in December 1939, the Canadians felt the frustration of being the last to fight. By the summer of 1942 soldiers from Australia, New Zealand, India, East, West and South Africa, and even tiny island colonies and far-flung protectorates had all seen hostile action and won combat medals before any men from the Dominion of Canada. When the Canadian Prime Minister Mackenzie King visited his compatriots serving in the UK in September 1941, Winston Churchill said: 'We have felt very much for them that they have not yet had a chance of coming to close quarters with the enemy.' So it was politically important that the untried young men got the opportunity to prove their courage in what Churchill called 'a hard, savage clash' at Dieppe on Wednesday, 19 August 1942.

But the intelligence for the raid was flawed. It was over-reliant on daytime photoreconnaissance, which missed both the caves and tunnels the Germans had camouflaged in the cliffs and the 3.7-cm PaK anti-tank cannons and heavy machine-guns they held there on rails, ready to run out. It was inaccurate about the calibre of the German Fifteenth Army – which was both efficient and effective – and overconfident about the enemy's power of resistance. Forewarned and ready, the infantry defending Dieppe had rehearsed just such an enemy invasion the day before: a Canadian colonel found the German mortar teams' ranging stakes still hammered in at precise, paced-out distances along the beach where his men lay dying from their expertise.

On the bit of shore below the cliffs and gully at Puys, the Royal Regiment of Canada was almost completely destroyed. The Canadian reporter Ross Munro, who went in (late, in daylight) to Blue Beach with the second wave of men from Winnipeg, described how he crouched, horrified, at the back of the landing craft among blood and bodies as accurate firing from machine-guns, snipers, mortars and artillery turned the attack into a shambles. On the next beach along, Red Beach, his friends in the Essex Scottish were decimated: they lost not one in ten but an incredible 90 per cent of their men killed, wounded or captured. Padre Foote, Chaplain to the Royal Hamilton Light Infantry, won the VC for tending casualties of the abattoir carnage on White Beach.

Command cannot control a battle without communications. These were not good at Dieppe in 1942. Wet sets that failed, garbled signals, different systems, messages that were not passed on in time or to the right person, all thickened the fog of war. Major General 'Ham' Roberts, the divisional commander on the HQ ship HMS *Calpe*, was passed a true message that Canadian soldiers were now inside the Dieppe Casino and clearing rooms, but deduced from a small heroic action that the whole attack on Red and White Beaches had succeeded. So he ordered in his floating reserves to consolidate. That meant the Canadian Fusiliers Mont-Royal and the British Royal Marines, including Ian Fleming's group, who were to land on Red Beach and then head left towards the port, their original objective, a mile away.

As the news filtered down to Fleming's men on HMS *Locust* that they were going in, one young marine turned to his platoon commander.

'For Christ's sake, sir, where the fucking hell are we?'

'I suppose I can tell you now. That is Dieppe. And I want to see you in my office tomorrow morning for using improper language.'

The officer was twenty-three-year-old Lieutenant Huntington-Whiteley, who had been christened Herbert Oliver, but his family and friends called him Peter (and behind his back the men nicknamed him 'Red', for his red hair).* Tall and languid-looking, Huntington-Whiteley came from the establishment. His father's father was a Conservative MP who got a baronetcy in 1918 and

---

* He is also the great-great-uncle of the model Rosie Huntington-Whiteley.

his mother's father was the former Conservative Prime Minister Stanley Baldwin. He was educated at Eton, which may explain why Ian Fleming – another Old Etonian – asked him to use his 10 Platoon to raid the Kriegsmarine HQ.

Locust disgorged its Royal Marine commandos into landing craft. 10 Platoon, helmeted and heavily burdened with kit, clambered down rope scrambling nets into a tank landing craft with the Commando HQ party. The mechanised landing craft (LCM) was a flat-bottomed vessel designed to land two lorries or a single tank and was about forty feet long and twelve feet wide with a ramp at the front that dropped down on the beach like the old horse boats. It was made of bullet-proof steel, and a flange at the top of the four-foot-high side gave some protection from shrapnel to men crouching below it. There were two Ford V8 diesel engines and a small wheelhouse at the back with a crew of three to run it, two ratings and a Royal Navy sub lieutenant in a dirty white roll-neck pullover, blue trousers and white plimsolls.

Other companies trans-shipped from minesweepers provided by the Free French into smaller assault landing craft (LCA) which could hold a fully armed platoon, organised in three rifle sections of either ten or twelve men. Some of these vessels had already made at least one landing already. A few of the boisterous bootnecks noticed how quiet and grim their crews were. 11 Platoon, commanded by twenty-one-year-old Lieutenant Derrick Over, joined the same tank landing craft as 10 Platoon. Now there were about seventy men on board. Paul McGrath cheerily greeted his mate 'Lofty' Whyman, a tall nut-brown fellow with flashing white teeth. McGrath was at the starboard rear, next to the adjutant, Captain Alan Comyn, and A Commando's commanding officer, the lean and wiry Lieutenant Colonel Joseph Picton Phillips RM, who was nicknamed 'Tiger' for his aggressiveness. He used to prowl round the barracks at Deal in the early hours trying to catch sentries offguard. One surprised man who instinctively struck back (thus giving his commanding officer a great bruise on the collarbone) was summoned the next morning. He expected to face a charge but was instead promoted to lance corporal 'for being fully alert whilst doing his duty'. Jock Farmer of X Company called Picton Phillips 'as daft as a halfpenny watch', but revered his memory.

McGrath could see two of his platoon's Bren gunners, 'Brad' Bradshaw and 'Alex' Alexander, where they were of most use, up at the front of the landing craft, but the rifleman 'Jock' Finlayson was also with them, now holding a Bren gun with its distinctive curved box magazine and conical muzzle. The stunning shell that hit *Locust* earlier had taken the left leg off 'Pusser' Hill, the third Bren-gunner, as well as blowing Finlayson's rifle over the side, so he had borrowed Hill's light machine-gun.

Shells were falling. 'Cast off!' said the skipper. The flotilla of landing craft formed up 2,000 yards from Dieppe's main beach, revving their engines for the haphazard charge through choppy water towards an opposed landing. It was about 8.30 a.m. The Free French minesweepers were on the flanks to give close up fire-support with their Hotchkiss heavy machine-guns, and the marine gun crews on *Locust* and two destroyers were ready for counter-battery work, firing at the flash of German big guns. The flotilla also had with them some vessels that were in use for the first time: Landing Craft, Flak (LCF), which were gun platforms with four 20-mm Oerlikon cannons that hammered out bullets the size of half a fat finger and eight 40-mm 'pom-pom' guns that quick-fired 2-pounder shells.

The flotilla of landing craft disappeared into the smokescreen. When they came out on the other side the men could see Dieppe's promenade and sea wall and its steeply sloping beach 200 yards before them. The shore was now a weird rock garden of busted tanks and landing craft, with orchids of fire sputtering from bromeliads of twisted metal and the khaki dead lying about like bits of wood on the pebbles.

A storm of shot and shell greeted the first landing craft as its marines led by Major Robert Houghton dashed out for cover behind a stuck tank. Bullets were hitting men below him as Picton Phillips scanned the apocalyptic scene ahead. He had been misinformed: the Canadians held neither beach, the assault was smashed, the enemy strong. To go on was to take his men to their deaths. Don't reinforce failure.

Pulling on white string gloves to make him more visible, the commanding officer scrambled on top of ammunition boxes by the wheelhouse and gestured boldly, palms out, pushing both hands away, signalling to his Marines in the other landing craft: *Go back, go back, go back!* Six craft obeyed; a few carried on.

Marine James Spencer of 11 Platoon remembered Picton Phillips giving the order to 'make smoke'. Smoke pots were set on fire and tossed overboard to produce billows of smoke that drifted landward. But a German cannon had found the range. With a hideous screech and crash, the landing craft was hit. Comyn the adjutant fell forward. A splinter had removed his helmet and the back of his head. The injured colonel glared about belligerently. The landing craft was holed aft, going down at the stern. Shrapnel had also pierced the diesel tank and an iridescence spread over the rising seawater. Someone set off a smoke pot too soon and the gasoline ignited, engulfing the wounded in flames. According to Spencer, Picton Phillips clutched his belly in agony as a burst of machine-gun bullets dropped him to his knees. Flames singed away his hair and eyebrows. Men surged forward to help but he waved them away. 'Leave me. I'm done for. Look out for yourselves.' In Spencer's book, *The Awkward Marine*, Picton Phillips lay back quietly in the lap of fire, resigned, 'dying with his boots on: dying terribly: dying without any show of fear, without any fuss: dying like the brave man he was'.

McGrath remembered no such romantic death scene. In his account Picton Phillips was swiftly cut down soon after he made the signal to go back and Comyn was killed on taking command. The landing craft hit an underwater obstacle that slewed the vessel to port, broadside on. The RNVR skipper was striding along the portside flange in his tennis shoes to try and free his craft when he was shot and fell in the sea. 'Get the Bren guns working!' ordered the sergeant major. Bradshaw and Alexander leapt up among the whooshing shells and whizzing bullets to return fire up at the cliffs. Bradshaw was to win the Military Medal; Alexander was shot through the head and killed. Young Ken Finlayson on the starboard side fired gamely from the hip.

Sergeant Kruthoffer of 10 Platoon remembered isolated jigsaw pieces of the flip from discipline to chaos:

A group at the front trying to kick the ramp down. The C.O., the crewman and others hit and falling about, and a scrum at the back end trying to dodge small arms fire coming down amongst them. Those looking over the shore side or trying to climb out getting it in the head or chest and crashing back onto those behind them. Some Bren gunners at work – one immortal bawling for new magazines – another enthusiast firing from a sitting position and threatening to decapitate anyone moving sideways.

All accounts agree that a shell hit the craft and that the diesel caught fire.

'Christ Almighty, Nutty, what the hell do we do now?'

'It's no use, we'll all be killed, we'll all be killed!'

Lieutenants Over and Huntington-Whiteley were the only officers left. One shouted, 'Every man do the best he can! Off kit and swim for it!' Kruthoffer made sure everybody alive got off the burning ship. McGrath tore off his webbing, pouches and boots, and puffed up the canvas-covered Mae West life jacket strapped to his chest. The scabbard of his fighting knife jammed him briefly, terrifyingly, as he rolled over the metal lip of the hull. It was safer crowded in the cold water behind the body of the craft because grenades were cooking up in the flames and going off.

'Let's go for the beach!' The shore was only thirty yards away.

'Come on. Let's make for the ships!' They were on the horizon.

Men chose, and moved. Lofty Whyman was a strong swimmer; he and Kruthoffer were the first to head out to sea. Bradshaw,

Finlayson, McGrath and 'Spike' Watson were among the Royal Marine commandos of 10 Platoon who followed them.

So Ian Fleming's little band, far from triumphantly seizing secrets from the Kriegsmarine headquarters, ended their first mission with their hands full of water, paddling and splashing away from a burning landing craft and Dieppe's standing columns of smoke. Sporadic bullets zipped after them; twenty-one-year-old Over was hit in the head and sank quietly. The others swam on, the sun mounting hotter in the sky. Shrapnel dust, falling from air bursts, pattered sharp and stinging on the glistening water.

Kruthoffer reckoned he crawled and breast-stroked two and half miles before being picked up. A flak craft that had downed nine German planes and one Spitfire rescued Huntington-Whiteley and others who were so cold they didn't notice the burns on their legs. McGrath had managed to kick off his trousers but was slowly drowning and choking, his life jacket deflated, when a small boat laying smoke picked him up and dragged him over the gunwale. This craft headed straight back in to Red Beach. While McGrath lay vomiting half-naked, more wounded and bleeding Canadians piled on top of him.

Nor were they out of danger on board *Calpe*. The redoubled fury of the German air force pursued them as the HQ ship, still shelling German positions, lingered to try and help the last men off the beaches. The air battle was going badly too. Dieppe's distance from England meant that the RAF fighter-bombers had only about ten minutes flying time over the town, while the Luftwaffe, taking off from closer airfields, had more scope and range. The German air force shot down twice as many Allied planes (106 for 47 losses), and bombed and sank the destroyer *Berkeley*. When a Focke-Wulf 190 bombed the *Calpe*, the men either side of Quentin Reynolds were killed, and his escorting press officer, who had eagerly showed him the plan in advance, received shrapnel wounds in the head and neck as his twenty-first birthday present. More German fighters dived through anti-aircraft fire and Spitfires to strafe the destroyer, and injured men lying on the decks smoking Sweet Caporals and hoping they were out of it were hit again as bullets ricocheted off steel. McGrath was in a cabin full of wounded when they bought in a shot-up boy moaning with pain and laid him on the table.

'Oh God, don't let me die. Oh God, I'm only nineteen, please don't let me die. Please God, don't let me die.'

His voice trailed away and soon he was taken out of the cabin.

N

Nearly 5,000 Canadian soldiers set off on the round trip to Dieppe and most of them did not return that day. Over a quarter of the 2,200 Canadians who did make it back on 19 August 1942 were wounded. Survivors were packed in the destroyer HMS *Garth*, where the doctors could barely cope with the traumatic injuries for lack of transfusion equipment. The Combined Operations staff officer Goronwy Rees listened to 'the oaths and blasphemies, the cursings and revilings, with which men speak of leaders by whom they feel they have been betrayed and deceived'.

More than 900 Canadians never returned to their homes. Of these, 807 men were killed on 19 August and a hundred more died of their wounds or as prisoners of war later. Over 1,800 Canadians were captured, nearly a third of them wounded, and they did not get back till the end of the war in 1945, after suffering all the depressions and privations of dreary PoW camps.

One can write of Dieppe as though it were one of the stupid frontal attacks of the previous world war, a pointless, futile, suicidal squandering of men's lives. One can call it a disaster, a debacle, a tragedy, and point the finger of blame. But at the time, three years into the Second World War, when thousands of civilians had been killed in the Blitz, when hundreds of men were dying every day, and many more hundreds of thousands were being buried by the German juggernaut in Russia, that was not how it was reported and perceived. *Keep Calm and Carry On* was the sort of slogan the Ministry of Information wanted. British propaganda suppressed the casualties of the raid and boosted the positive.

In time the Canadian view came to be that the lessons learned from Dieppe gave the appalling blood-sacrifice its value and meaning; those men laid down their lives and limbs so that others would not be killed and maimed. But only the eventual victory could justify it. Ross Munro, who witnessed the utter massacre on Blue Beach, was once again with the Canadian 2nd Division on the day in 1944 when they liberated Dieppe, without firing a shot, two years and thirteen days after the raid. Munro went back to the very place at Puys, picking his way through landmines, and said it felt like walking into a tomb. But he wrote in chapter XIII of his 1945 book *Gauntlet to Overlord: the story of the Canadian Army*:

Without condoning any of the mistakes made at Dieppe, I'm convinced that if the raid had not been carried out as a prelude to the North African landings, the combined operations in the Mediterranean and the Normandy invasion, these might have been so badly bungled that the war there could have been prolonged for years.

'The Duke of Wellington said Waterloo was won on the playing fields of Eton. I say that D-Day was won on the beaches of Dieppe.' Mountbatten's mantra became his post-war justification. But others shared the thought nearer the time. Two years after Dieppe, when Winston Churchill and the chiefs of staff first visited the Normandy bridgehead on 12 June 1944, six days after the greatest amphibious invasion in human history, they sent a cable to Mountbatten at South East Asia Command in Ceylon, signed with all their names – ARNOLD, BROOKE, CHURCHILL, KING, MARSHALL, SMUTS:

Today we visited the British and American armies on the soil of France. We sailed through vast fleets of ships, with landing-craft of many types pouring more men, vehicles and stores ashore . . . We wish to tell you at this moment in your arduous campaign that we realise that much of this remarkable technique, and therefore the success of the venture, has its origin in developments effected by you and your staff of Combined Operations.

N

19 August 1942 was a long and nerve-racking day for Ian Fleming. 'It was difficult to add up the pros and cons of a bloody gallant affair,' he wrote for the NID's *Weekly Report*, adding, rather less frankly, that 'one thing was clear: intelligence, planning and execution had been faultless. The machinery for producing further raids is thus tried and found good. But the fortunes of war (*vide* that damnable mischance on our left flank) must be with us next time.'

'The fortunes of war . . .' Ian Fleming associated war with the gaming table: 'The grass-green baize battle-ground would soak up the blood of its victims and refresh itself,' he would write in his first novel after the war. Whether he is near the real casino at Dieppe or in the fictional *Casino Royale,* the serious player must not brood on loss. '[Bond] set his mind to sweeping away all traces of the sense of complete defeat which had swamped him a few moments before.' In *Goldfinger,* too, the hero cannot afford to dwell on his mistakes. 'Bond never worried too long about his bad or stupid shots. He put them behind him and thought of the next.' He had to be cool about the business of killing, too: 'If it happened, it happened. Regret was unprofessional – worse, it was death-watch beetle in the soul.'

Ian Fleming rocked no boats after Dieppe. He needed to keep in with Combined Operations if he wanted to develop his idea for an intelligence assault unit further. But he had already managed to convince the single most important person of its merits. This was his boss, the extraordinary Director of Naval Intelligence (DNI) Admiral John Godfrey, who in time would become the fictional James Bond's boss, M, also an admiral, with the 'keen sailor's face' and 'the clear, sharp sailor's eyes', – the older man with the 'tranquil, lined sailor's face that he loved, honoured and obeyed'.

2

The Godfather

Three years earlier, in January 1939, John Godfrey, former captain of HMS *Repulse* and promoted to rear admiral for his new job, had assumed command as DNI. War had not yet broken out, but vigilance was certainly needed on the bridge. Great Britain may have been leading the world in the peaceful manufacture and export of bicycles, but Nazi Germany was making more gun barrels and blast bombs. Walking to Whitehall, you could still see evidence of the 'precautionary measures' left over from the Munich war scare at the end of September 1938: scars of trenches in the leafless parks, sandbags beside sentry boxes. People had given up carrying gas masks in cardboard boxes, but officialdom remained jumpy and the country dithered between hope and fear.

The initial 'thrill of relief' when Premier Neville Chamberlain flew back from Munich with his piece of paper from Hitler promising 'peace for our time' had been replaced by what the First World War Prime Minister Lloyd George called 'a sense of shame'. At the end of October 1938 he had mused aloud about appeasement: 'China, Abyssinia, Spain, Czechoslovakia – we have descended during these years a ladder of dishonour rung by rung. Are we going, can we go, any lower?' That autumn, Germany started expelling Polish Jews, dispossessing between ten and twenty thousand people and dumping them on the border, and on 9 November 1938 Kristallnacht, a Nazi-sanctioned orgy of violence and destruction, was unleashed against Jewish people, property and synagogues across all Germany.

Meanwhile the involvement of Hitler and Mussolini in Spain and the Mediterranean, where General Franco's Nationalists were winning the Spanish Civil War, was worrying the Royal Navy. The Mediterranean was foremost in Godfrey's mind when he arrived at the Admiralty as DNI.

N

What exactly was 'Naval Intelligence'? At its most basic, it was any information that gave advantage to His Majesty's Royal Navy in its operational security and effectiveness. 'Operational' is the key word. The Admiralty – located in the heart of Whitehall, founded in the reign of Henry VIII and encrusted with four centuries of tradition – was the *operational* headquarters of the Royal Navy and in direct control of the fleet. (This differentiated it from the War Office, which was merely the *administrative* headquarters of the British army.) In the summer of 1939 the Royal Navy had 129,000 officers and men, 73,000 reservists, and 317 warships dotted around the world. A *Navy List* volume from 1939 gives a sense of the hierarchy. Below the Board of Admiralty and its secretariat, the Naval Intelligence Division appears as the very first among the divisions of the Naval Staff. The NID was not enormous: the Director (DNI), Deputy Director (DDNI) and Assistant Director of Naval Intelligence (ADNI) are among only twenty-five Naval and Royal Marine officers, supported by some forty-two civil staff, including clerks and draughtsmen.

The NID was originally formed in the 1880s to gather data on foreign navies: 'to collect, classify and record with a complete index all information which bears a naval character . . .' In peacetime this easily declined into passive librarianship. Geographically organised sections had neither incentive nor budget to share information. The single 'Movements Officer', who wrote ships' names by hand into large dusty ledgers, did not even subscribe to the essential shipping information of *Lloyd's List*. Officers were not encouraged to think strategically or to evaluate emerging threats.

This had begun to change in August 1937 after General Franco asked Benito Mussolini to help stop ships in the Mediterranean supplying his opponents, the democratically elected Republican government. Fascist Italy then had the largest fleet of submarines in the world – eighty-three as compared to Britain's thirty-eight – and Mussolini covertly unleashed two dozen submarines which torpedoed merchant shipping without warning in violation of the submarine warfare protocol that Italy had signed. The Royal Navy knew perfectly well who was carrying out these attacks because they were picking up Italian naval messages through naval wireless interception in the Mediterranean, which had been started by Lord Louis Mountbatten on Malta. What if the fighting in Spain escalated into a world war? British Empire shipping would have to be protected, as would the strategic naval base of Gibraltar. Admiral Sir William James asked Naval Intelligence to give him a better picture of the disposition of potentially hostile forces, and in early June 1937, Lieutenant Commander Norman Denning was appointed to this vital task.

'Ned' Denning, who came from a clear-minded family – his eldest brother Reginald became a general who planned the details of D-Day and his elder brother Tom ended up as a famous Law Lord – started setting up, within the NID, the elements of the Admiralty's Operational Intelligence Centre (OIC), the brilliant organisation that would later help win the battle of the Atlantic. Through his interviews with First World War intelligence veterans, Denning realised that his embryonic OIC had to evolve a new corporate brain for the Royal Navy, capable not only of taking in the right kind of information but also pushing it out in good time to the right people. There was a flood of incoming data to handle, sort and organise. Some of it was signals intelligence: the Royal Navy maintained fixed wireless interception stations (Y stations) listening to enemy radio signals near Scarborough and Winchester, sending on any coded signals to the Government Code and Cypher School (GC&CS) for decryption and analysis, whence it came back to the OIC. Come the war, Denning's OIC would process a vast range of intelligence – sightings of ships and aircraft by friendly observers and coast watchers (rewarded from 1940 onwards by payments ranging from £1 to £1,000), secret reports by Secret Intelligence Service (SIS) agents arriving from the Foreign Office in red-bordered files known as 'Scarlet Pimpernels', information from prisoners of war, censored letters and captured documents, merchant marine data from the Baltic Exchange or Lloyds of London, and reports from the BBC and the Foreign Office, who perused all enemy press and propaganda. All through the war, in the reinforced concrete citadel of the Admiralty, the OIC would be putting all this information together so they could track submarines and battleships on giant maps, share the latest information with Operations and swiftly transmit it onward to the Royal Navy fleet.

Despite Denning's new initiatives, the NID was still something of a backwater. Bill Cordeaux, who joined the geographical section covering Italy and the eastern Mediterranean in March 1938, remembered 'shocking inefficiency'. Admiral John Godfrey arrived early in 1939 with the right temperament and experience to transform the NID. Vigorous, balding, rubicund and clean-shaven, with a cleft chin and pale blue-grey eyes, he was disciplined and exacting. He drove hard for excellence and used his volcanic temper to frighten people, but he also had liberal and forward-looking ideas. His wife, Margaret, a cousin of Neville Chamberlain's, was a very intelligent woman who had left Newnham College, Cambridge, early to marry; she later worked at Bletchley Park and then helped run the Inter-Services Topographical Department (ISTD). Godfrey himself subscribed to the *New Statesman*, kept books and pictures and music in his cabin and had no interest in public school games. Like many great English admirals, he was the product of a grammar school – the famous King Edward's School, Birmingham – and rose through merit, not birth. He devolved responsibility to his officers and trusted them, keeping an eye open without fussing officiously. He cared for the welfare of his men because that way you got the best out of them.

Godfrey had sailed the seven seas. He had been at the Dardanelles in 1915 and helped put the Lancashire Fusiliers ashore at 'W' beach where they won six VCs before breakfast. In the Aegean he had heard the 'distressing eerie sound' of men from the torpedoed *Goliath* drowning in the darkness. He had been up in the observer's seat of a sea-plane submarine-spotting, dropped four twenty-pound bombs on the Turks, crash-landed in the water and found it all 'exhilarating'. In the Red Sea he had walked on deck with Lawrence of Arabia; he worked with the Japanese, American, Greek, French and Italian allied navies during the First World War, and later with the Germans and the White Russians. He had served in the Plans Division of the Admiralty as well as in Polynesia and on the China Station. In 1935 he was finally given command of the 35,000-ton Renown class battlecruiser HMS *Repulse*, a vast castle of steel with a crew of nearly 1,200 men that was happy and efficient under his captaincy.*

In June 1936, soon after arriving on the Mediterranean Station, John Godfrey and HMS *Repulse* were caught up in the Spanish Civil War. The British government subscribed to the policy of non-intervention, but when the Republicans began bombing Palma de Mallorca, Godfrey took his ship in to evacuate British subjects and other foreign nationals who wished to escape. HMS *Repulse* removed 194 men and 309 women and children to Marseilles and then made for Valencia so that crisp white uniforms could escort more Britons safely through the anarchic militias. Godfrey was still in the Mediterranean when Mussolini began his covert

---

* In chapter 20 of *On Her Majesty's Secret Service* (1963), James Bond visits M's bachelor home on the edge of Windsor Forest and finds the bell outside the front door is 'the brass ship's-bell of some former HMS *Repulse*, the last of whose line, a battle-cruiser, had been M's final sea-going appointment'.

submarine attacks, and when he became DNI during the first years of the war, submarine warfare by the Axis would be one of his chief concerns.

✐

Despite the improvements in information-gathering and communication at the NID, there were deeper problems at the heart of the Royal Navy in 1939 when Godfrey took up his new post. British strategic sea-power had been eroded by the Washington Naval Conference of 1922 (in which the British were restricted in building new vessels so the USA had parity) and the London Naval Treaty of 1930 (in which the Labour government cut the number of capital ships). There had been problems with morale and discipline as well. After the brief Invergordon 'mutiny' about pay in 1931, there had been a massive run on the pound, and the British Empire abandoned the Gold Standard. By the time Godfrey came to the Admiralty, the navy that Lord Halifax had boastfully called 'unchallengeable' was actually massively overextended trying to police the worldwide British Empire, including Singapore and Hong Kong, now being eyed by Imperial Japan. This meant Britain was failing to respond appropriately to the German threat in Europe.

After the scuttling of the Imperial German High Sea Fleet at the end of the First World War the British had become rather complacent about the German navy (Reichsmarine). Persuaded by smooth-talking German diplomats that Nazi Germany's naval interests were solely directed against communist Russia, Britain had signed the Anglo-German Naval Agreement in 1935, under which Germany could continue rebuilding its fleet as long as it was limited to 35 per cent of the size of Britain's. But the Germans only pretended to conform to this requirement, and did not permit anyone to check. Of course, the Royal Navy still outnumbered the Germans in aircraft carriers, battleships, cruisers, destroyers and smaller vessels, but there was one extraordinary omission in the treaty. A let-out clause gave Nazi Germany 'the right to possess a submarine tonnage equal to the total submarine tonnage possessed by the members of the British Commonwealth of Nations'. The fact that German U-boats (*Unterseeboote*, submarines) had almost brought island Britain to its knees in 1917 seems to have been completely forgotten. Straight after signing the Anglo-German Naval Agreement, the Germans gave their Reichsmarine a belligerent new name, Kriegsmarine (or 'War Navy'), and began constructing its full quota of U-boats.

On the surface all seemed well with the Royal Navy. After the dramatic abdication of King Edward VIII, the coronation of his brother King George VI on 12 May 1937 was conducted with great pageantry, and a week later HMS *Repulse* was one of eleven great British battleships gleaming with fresh paint in the huge coronation review at Spithead. The royal yacht bearing the new king and queen sailed past eight lines of warships from eighteen nations (including the German pocket battleship *Admiral Graf Spee*), while a million people watched from the shores of the Solent. This was the pinnacle of national pomp. But four of those great British battleships (including *Repulse*) would soon go down in flames – torpedoed, shelled, bombed from the air. In a dozen years all the rest would be scrap iron; hundreds of the proud crewmen and thousands of the happy spectators at Spithead would not live to see the next coronation.

As newly appointed DNI Godfrey was right in the heart of the security establishment. This was clear from the NID telephone switchboard in Room 19. Two secret landlines led directly to the Cabinet Office and the prime minister's office at the Treasury. Other direct lines went to the Foreign Office, and the intelligence directorates of the War Office and the Air Ministry. A subcommittee of the Committee of Imperial Defence called the Joint Intelligence Committee (JIC) had been set up in 1936 to collate intelligence for the chiefs of staff at the Admiralty, the War Office and the Air Ministry and Godfrey was soon attending, getting to know his service equivalents, the Director of Military Intelligence and the chief of Air Staff (Intelligence). Yet more direct lines linked the NID to Scotland Yard and Sir Vernon Kell's British Security Service, MI5. Godfrey was responsible for all aspects of naval security, including prevention of sabotage and subversion as well as counter-espionage, so he met staff at Special Branch of the Metropolitan Police and at MI5 on the top floor of south block, Thames House, Millbank, overlooking Lambeth Bridge. There he found a competent organisation with an excellent registry of file cards; he learned that forty-three British sea ports each had a dozen men and an officer working under the direction of MI5, keeping a close eye on foreign vessels and their crews. Of course, Godfrey also had a direct line to the SIS and to its signals satellite, the GC&CS.

Nazi Germany was deliberately provoking confrontation. On 30 January 1939, not long after Godfrey arrived at the NID, Adolf Hitler had made a speech at the Reichstag referring openly to 'the annihilation of the Jewish race in Europe'. Public threats were accompanied by personal insults. MI5's good inside information on Nazi Germany meant that soon after the Munich negotiations they were able to sting Neville Chamberlain's vanity by telling him that Adolf Hitler had privately called him 'an arsehole' (*Arschloch*). On 15 March 1939, when the Germans invaded Czechoslovakia, Hitler destroyed Chamberlain's proud diplomatic achievement, the Munich Four-Power Agreement. This struck at the core of the British prime minister's self-belief. Two days afterwards, on the eve of his seventieth birthday, in a quietly angry speech in his home town of Birmingham, a gaunt Chamberlain started drawing a line in the sand. A fortnight later, he gave a cast-iron guarantee in the House of Commons. Should anyone violate the territorial integrity of Poland, said Chamberlain, both Britain and France would lend the Poles 'all support in their power'. Only three days later the German High Command directed the German armed forces to prepare for the invasion of Poland.

On 27 March 1939, a fortnight after the Nazis invaded Czechoslovakia, Godfrey received a visit in the Admiralty from an old man with a face like a bird of prey. This bald magus with eagle eyes and a mouth like a trap was his most illustrious predecessor as DNI, Admiral Sir Reginald Hall, who had run Naval Intelligence during the First World War. The reappearance of the famous 'Blinker' Hall in his old Admiralty offices was further proof that NID's winter of discontent was over.

Hall's motto was 'boldness always pays'. His father had been the Admiralty's very first Director of Intelligence in 1882, and Hall was a master of subversion and trickery who had operated at a high strategic level in the First World War. He had almost managed to avert the bloody Gallipoli campaign by bribing the Turks for passage through the Dardanelles, and had started the Arab Bureau, the intelligence centre in Cairo that sent T. E. Lawrence into Arabia. Above all, it was Hall who first set up Room 40, the signals intelligence centre, in the Admiralty Old Buildings in London. Known as OB40, it located, intercepted and analysed cable and wireless traffic and decrypted German naval, military and diplomatic coded messages. 'Blinker' Hall's skilful use of the infamous German Zimmerman telegram had helped bring the USA out of neutrality in 1917, thus ensuring victory over the Central Powers, in what one knowledgeable writer described as 'the greatest Intelligence coup in history'.

Hall swooped on Godfrey in 1939 as a mentor, not a meddler. 'To no one am I more indebted than Reggie Hall,' Godfrey wrote later. '[He] very unobtrusively offered me full access to his great store of knowledge and judgment on this strange commodity, Intelligence, about which I then knew hardly anything.' Hall met with Godfrey frequently, and even lent him his comfortable first-floor flat on the other side of Green Park at 36 Curzon Street, next to the Curzon Theatre. Hall's efficient housekeeper Dulcie continued to shop, cook, serve and clean for the admiral, who lived and entertained there, largely alone, while his wife Margaret got on with her war work in the country. Godfrey had a direct telephone line installed from his Curzon Street bedroom to the duty officers in Room 39 and the OIC.

Hall stressed the importance of bright people and good contacts for Naval Intelligence. As DNI Godfrey would have to create his own trusted team, picked for their range and readiness to contribute and criticise ideas. The novelist William Plomer said of his five and half years in the NID, 'I learned anew, every day, that . . . several heads are as a rule better than one.' Hall made sure that Godfrey met the key members of his old Admiralty code-breaking team in OB40 – including their chief, Commander Alastair Denniston OBE (schoolmaster) and Alfred Dillwyn 'Dilly' Knox (classical scholar), clever men who were still doing the same work but now with the GC&CS. Hall also told Godfrey he would need contacts in the financial world of the City of London. Plugging into the powerhouse of capitalism made good sense, because bankers and investors need to know what is going on around the world in order to make money. So Godfrey lunched with Grenfells and Rothschilds, the banking Smiths and the chairman of Barings. He met Sir Charles Hambro, an Old Etonian merchant banker who was to rise high in a new secret service, the Special Operations Executive (SOE), and recruit many men from the bowler-and-brolly brigade.

Godfrey had already brought in his old friend Edward Merrett, an intelligent and emollient solicitor who had been with him on HMS *Repulse*, as his private secretary (a civilian post), but Hall suggested that the DNI could also do with an additional personal assistant, or 'fixer', in uniform. A smooth and well-connected Old Etonian stockbroker called Claude Serocold had been one of his two personal assistants in the First World War, and Serocold now helped by putting out the word. One spring day Godfrey received a telephone call on Admiralty extension 743. The Governor of the Bank of England himself, Montagu Norman, was on the line from

Threadneedle Street.

'I think we've got your man.'

'Should I come and see you?'

'No, sir. Your time is more valuable than mine. I shall call on *you*.'*

So the next morning, chauffeured in his black Lincoln, nervy Montagu Norman, who looked like a melancholy Spanish grandee with his pointed beard and hat, arrived by the statue of Captain Cook on the gravel of The Mall, and at ten sharp was shown into Room 38 at the Admiralty. 'Admiral, I think we've found the man you want. He is a junior partner in the firm of Rowe and Pitman, stockbrokers in the City of London. His name is Ian Fleming.'

On 24 May 1939 Ian Fleming walked into the downstairs Grill of the Carlton Hotel, at the bottom of London's Haymarket where it met the eastern end of Pall Mall. The debonair thirty-year-old, smoking a Morland Special cigarette, looked a natural denizen of St James's, 'someone out of a Wodehouse novel' as Cyril Connolly once noted when he bumped into Fleming in his blue suit and Eton Ramblers' cricket club tie in Brook Street. Fleming's club was Boodle's, because White's was too noisy, and he often ate in Scott's just up the road. Someone extremely important whom he had never met before had invited him to lunch, but the polish of Eton College and a brush of Sandhurst had given Fleming the social aplomb to deal with such an event effortlessly. He was good at charming older men and senior officer types: the trick was not deference but confidence. Tall, dark and handsome (a

---

* In chapter 5 of *Goldfinger*, M tells Bond that he dined with the Governor of the Bank the night before. 'Hadn't occurred to me that the Bank of England knew so much about crooks. Suppose it's part of the Bank's job to protect our currency.' He gets Bond an appointment with the Bank's research department. 'From what the Governor told me, that's nothing more or less than a spy system.'

broken nose gave him an interesting gladiator look), the chain-smoking, smooth-haired Ian Fleming was an easily bored *flâneur* and gambler who had yet to find his niche, a late starter and a dabbler who feared that he might be a failure. Because he was amusing and posed as a cynical romantic, he had little trouble getting women into bed, though he dumped them afterwards rather too quickly. The primrose path towards alcoholism was already looking attractive.

Sitting at the luncheon table were two admirals in dark suits. Fleming had already met the first, white-bearded Aubrey Hugh-Smith, one of the two nautical brothers of the senior partner in Rowe & Pitman, the stockbroking firm that gave him an annual income without engaging his energies. (He had chosen not to go into his grandfather's merchant bank, Robert Fleming & Co.) Smith introduced him to their host, Admiral John Godfrey, with his air of a stern Roman senator; previously Fleming had only spoken to him once, on the telephone.

They ordered; Fleming talked pleasantly in his worldly, well-informed way. Shuffling the cards of his CV to best advantage, he had plenty of foreign experience to convey to the men scoping him out. He had spent time in Austria and Germany and in Switzerland at the University of Geneva, and was fluent in French and German. He spoke some Russian too, and had recently returned from a trade mission to drab Soviet Moscow, which he had reported for *The Times*. The Soviet Foreign Minister Litvinov had just been touting an 'anti-aggression front'; in Parliament Lloyd George, Churchill and Eden were all urging a revival of the old First World War entente alliance of Britain, France and Russia as the best way of containing Germany and Italy, who had just signed the Axis military pact. Fleming had picked up the taste for vodka in Moscow in 1933, covering a Stalinist show trial as a correspondent for Reuters. He saw the strategic value of the Soviet Union and the toughness of its soldiers, but reckoned it would make a treacherous ally. Perhaps they touched on other topics of the day, like the conscription which had been introduced in Britain in April 1939. Fleming was ahead of the game here too, already a reserve subaltern in the Black Watch.

At such encounters it may not be what is talked about that matters, but what is unspoken; the gut feeling or the first impression. Godfrey liked the cut of Ian Fleming's jib and suggested that the younger man might like to come in to the office for a few afternoons next week, if he had the time. With hindsight we can see the lunch at the Carlton Grill as a crucial turning point. Without this entrée to Fleming's six years in the NID there would be no 'Double O Seven', and the immortal James Bond would never have been born.

John Godfrey and Ian Fleming chimed because their curious, connective minds were similar: both read more widely than you would expect on first impression. But at a deeper, unconscious level, perhaps the fifty-one-year-old admiral and the thirty-one-year-old stockbroker were drawn to each other as surrogate family. Godfrey had three daughters but no son; Fleming had three brothers but no father. Val Fleming was killed eight days before his son Ian's ninth birthday. Now, four days before his thirty-first birthday, Ian Fleming had found his patron.

A sentence on the first page of Duff Hart-Davis's biography of Ian's eldest brother Peter says a lot about the Flemings: 'The family, though recently established, was rich and powerful.' The boys got into the establishment through the singular money-making skill of their Scottish grandfather, Robert, born in poverty on the outskirts of dour Dundee in 1845. Robert Fleming the Scottish financial genius is in some ways reminiscent of Robert Stevenson the Scottish engineering genius and lighthouse builder, not least because both had a world-famous writer as a grandson. 'We rose from obscurity at a clap,' wrote Robert Louis Stevenson of his own family. Just as harbours and lighthouses cushioned the early years of the author of *Treasure Island*, so did investment trusts and the financing of foreign railroads privilege the upbringing of the creator of James Bond.

Robert Fleming started out as a clerk and book-keeper in the jute industry but became interested in the stock market as new joint stock companies emerged in the 1860s. Although he was hit hard by the crash of 1866, he started investing shrewdly in the American railways that were laying more track after the Civil War. In 1873 he set up the Scottish American Investment Trust to offer collective investors selected American railway mortgage bonds 'at the minimum of trouble and with the maximum of security and profit'. In 'exporting' Scottish capital, he essentially took British Empire wealth and bet it on the industrialising USA. (His grandson would mirror the process in his novels, exporting British Second World War warrior prestige to Cold War America.)

In the 1880s Fleming's Dundee syndicate invested in Texas cowboy country. Their 'Matador Land and Cattle Company' was one of the few to survive the dreadful winters of 1885 to 1887. By the 1890s, married and with four children, Robert and Kate Fleming had moved south to England. After that they only returned to Scotland in the summers, renting large sporting estates to enjoy strenuous exercise (rowing, swimming, golf, long walks) and prodigious deer-stalking, grouse-shooting and trout-fishing. By 1900 he had personal capital of £810,000 (the equivalent of £40 million today) and his income from dealing, dividends, interest and commissions was around £115,000. In 1903, as a wealthy Edwardian gentleman, he purchased the 2,000-acre Nettlebed estate in Oxfordshire and built a lavish mansion called Joyce Grove. A squire and lord of the manor in the country, big-chinned, white-moustached Robert Fleming was also the doyen of the investment trust movement in the City of London.

In 1906 his first-born son Valentine Fleming (educated at Eton and Oxford) married the wild but attractive Evelyn Sainte Croix Rose. Val became a barrister, and in 1910, at the age of twenty-eight, was elected Conservative MP for South Oxfordshire. Val and Eve Fleming had four sons: Peter was born in 1907, Ian in 1908, Richard in 1911 and Michael in 1913. Valentine Fleming was in C Company of the Queen's Own Oxfordshire Hussars, the same regiment as his friend Winston Churchill. In 1914, soon after war was declared, they went off to France. On 20 May 1917 the War Office telegram came with the news that he was dead. He was thirty-seven years old, and was awarded a posthumous DSO. His death changed the lives of his sons.

It was eleven days before Peter's tenth birthday. Later he wrote in a fragment of memoir:

Somebody grabbed me and bustled me away upstairs. Behind me in the hall were the terrible sounds of grief. I knew that my father had been killed. For some reason I was put to bed on a sofa in the school-room . . . I fell asleep. Before I did so, I heard from somewhere in the house the sound of a man crying, loudly and uncontrollably. I assumed it was my grandfather. It was a sort of bellowing noise. Life had become a nightmare. I was completely out of my depth.

Little Peter Fleming had to grow up fast. 'You must be very good and brave, Peter, and always help your mother: *because now you must take your father's place*.' This sensitive boy who had suffered from all kinds of mysterious illnesses, stunting his growth and totally destroying his sense of smell and taste, now put on the mask of control. He would never really take it off again. Later in life, he completely understood the Chinese concept of 'face' because he shared its English version, 'the façade of nonchalance' as his biographer, Duff Hart-Davis, put it. Etonians tended to be very good at understatement and emotional concealment, the classic defences of the English public-schoolboy.

Peter's younger brother Ian was always rather different, more *soigné* and sybaritic. As a child he used to bribe the servants to bring him breakfast in bed. He soon eschewed the hearty Fleming habit of foot-slogging over brae and glen and the dreariness of wet rhododendrons in Scotland. Motoring was swifter than walking; golf on the links was better than guns on the moor. Indoor pleasures like smoking, drinking and gambling were very agreeable. But there was always another side to Ian Fleming. He had an interesting mind and an intellectual life that he tended not to display, burning his volume of early (and rather precious) poetry, *The Black Daffodil*. Aged seventeen, at school, he had written a fan letter to the poet William Plomer, whose daringly sexual first novel of racial miscegenation in South Africa, *Turbott Wolfe*, had just been published by Leonard and Virginia Woolf's Hogarth Press. They forwarded the note to Tokyo, where the homosexual Plomer was living with a Japanese companion. When he returned to England in 1929, he and Fleming became life-long friends; Fleming would get Plomer a job in Naval Intelligence, and Plomer would later edit all the Bond books at Jonathan Cape from 1953 to 1964.

Fleming was a wide reader with an interest in fine printing and a subscription to a journal on typography. In 1952 he would help found *The Book Collector*, which remains the leading English-language journal for bibliophiles. A decade later he wrote that if he were ever stranded on a desert island, an essential item would be '*The Times Literary Supplement*, dropped to me each Friday by a well-trained albatross'.

Secretly he wanted to write himself, though in May 1939 few of his London acquaintances thought of him as an author. He mixed with braying City types who liked gin, golf, cars and cards. The Fleming brother who wrote seemed to be the brilliant Peter, already author of *Brazilian Adventure*, *One's Company*, and *News from Tartary*, whom Vita Sackville-West described as 'a modern Elizabethan'. Peter was like the dashing, recondite hero Sandy Arbuthnot in the Buchan books; he wrote amusing fourth leaders for *The Times*, and was married to Celia Johnson, the luminous star of *Brief Encounter*. It seemed everyone thought Peter Fleming was wonderful – which was not very easy for Ian.

On the one hand, Ian hero-worshipped Peter. On the other

hand, he didn't. It was gall and wormwood to have a better-looking brother almost exactly one year older who was an effortless star at absolutely everything he did. At Eton Peter was in the exclusive 'Pop' society, was captain of the Oppidans (in effect the head boy of the school), won all sorts of prizes and edited the school magazine; at Christ Church, Oxford, Peter shone in the Bullingdon Club, was president of Oxford University Dramatic Society and editor of *Isis*; later, out in the real world, he became a best-selling man of letters who sucked up all the oxygen of publicity. Ian, on the other hand, 'Fleming (minor)' at school, had run his heart out and been Victor Ludorum at athletics twice – but athletics didn't really matter at Eton; he wasn't thought bright enough to go to Oxford or Cambridge, had to leave Sandhurst early under a cloud, failed to join the diplomatic service and only got into journalism because his bossy mother Eve knew the wife of the man who had bought Reuters. And now he seemed to be the world's worst stockbroker. How could poor Ian ever compete with someone like Peter?

When W. H. Auden and Christopher Isherwood met Peter Fleming in China in 1938, they found him 'a subtly comic figure – the conscious living parody of the *pukka sahib*'. Smooth-haired and tanned, with his pipe clenched in his teeth, uttering clipped expressions ('useful' and 'effective' were favourite adjectives), obsessed with the shooting of game, mortifying himself through hard travel, the puritanical Peter Fleming affected the unshakeable urbanity and drawling imperturbability of the 1920s pulp-fiction hero Captain Hugh 'Bulldog' Drummond, DSO, MC. The Old Etonian bookseller C. E. H. P. Warner once made a comment that illustrates the role Peter played in his younger brother's imaginative life: if you crossed Sapper's fictional creation Bulldog Drummond with Peter Fleming, you got James Bond.

Ian and Peter Fleming seemed very different but shared a common core. Both were born under the sign of Gemini, the

Twins, with their birthdays three days apart.* Both were haunted by the spectral presence of their absent father. Major Valentine Fleming MP was thirty-seven years old when he was killed by shellfire in the First World War while doing his patriotic duty; Winston Churchill wrote his obituary in *The Times* and the cutting hung framed on Ian Fleming's bedroom wall all his life. 'Please, God, make me like father' was the prayer dunned into the boys. There was absolutely no question that both Colonel Peter Fleming and Lieutenant Commander Ian Fleming would serve King and Country in whatever capacity was asked of them, without cynicism. Ian said his own need for heroes 'all started from hero-worshipping my elder brother Peter, who had to become the head of the family at the age of ten, when our father was killed in 1917'. Both Fleming brothers consistently sought father figures in older military men.

Early in 1939 a semi-secret branch of the War Office called Military Intelligence (Research) or MI(R) contacted Peter Fleming. On 31 January, after an interview with the Deputy Director of Military Intelligence, he wrote in his diary: 'MI are going to give chaps like me a preliminary canter soon.' Five months later, in June 1939, Ian Fleming was making his first probationary visits to Godfrey's NID offices. At almost the same time, both brothers were stepping closer to the adventurous world of 'shilling shockers' like those by William Le Queux, inventor of Duckworth Drew of the Secret Service, heroic staver-off of Britain's (somewhat implausible) enemies. Such First World War-era fantasies had nourished all their generation – though Ian Fleming also enjoyed the somewhat subtler thrillers of John Buchan, including the Richard Hannay/Sandy Arbuthnot adventure *Greenmantle* (1916)

---

* Ian Fleming the novelist also gave his birthday, 28 May 1908, to one of his principal villains, Ernst Stavro Blofeld, the head of SPECTRE, who described agent 007 as 'a common thug, a blunt instrument wielded by dolts in high places'.

in which the American agent John S. Blenkiron says that 'If I had a big proposition to handle and could have my pick of helpers I'd plump for the Intelligence Department of the British Admiralty. Yes, sir, I take off my hat to your Government sleuths . . . '

When Ian Fleming first entered the crowded office of Naval Intelligence with its windows looking out across Horse Guards Parade to the back garden of No. 10 Downing Street, it was not the stuff of romantic fiction. The banal reality of Room 39 was men at desks with telephones, filing cabinets full of dockets with impenetrable initials, coal scuttles by the fireplace and endless cups of tea. This 'secret service' was just like the civil service, occupied with systems of administration and organisation, trying to turn efficiency into effectiveness as war loomed ever closer in the summer of 1939. Room 39, housing section 17, was the brains trust, talking shop and co-ordinating centre of the NID.

Fleming was not the only new boy. At the time he arrived in June 1939 Bill Cordeaux felt that 'a new inspiration was [being] breathed into everyone in the Division' by John Godfrey's 'drive and brilliance', and the NID was recruiting fresh people, young and old, at home and abroad. Naval Intelligence did not have spies but it did have uniformed officers called naval attachés stationed at embassies and legations abroad who sent back information that might be of interest. Among several good appointments, Godfrey knew just the man needed for naval attaché in the western Mediterranean: in the spring of 1938 he had met the British consul in Majorca, Alan Hillgarth, a retired lieutenant commander who wrote thrillers, had been wounded in the Dardanelles and was a friend of Winston Churchill. Hillgarth was fluent in Spanish and good at dealing with Franco; earlier that year, as Franco's Nationalists emerged the winner of the civil war, Hillgarth had helped broker the peaceful surrender of Minorca. Now Godfrey got Hillgarth promoted to commander and secured his appointment as naval attaché in Madrid, where he would do an outstanding job helping to keep Spain neutral.

After his month's probation, on 26 July, Ian Fleming was commissioned as one of eight lieutenants in the Special Branch of the Royal Naval Volunteer Reserve or RNVR. The RNVR Special Branch was mainly for shore service: administrators, specialists and experts 'above the age of thirty and under the age of forty'. New boys took the 'Junior Staff Course' at the Royal Navy College, Greenwich, which inducted them into Admiralty traditions. Lieutenant Ian Fleming could be identified as RNVR (SB) from the cuffs of his dark blue No. 1 uniform, which had an emerald green strip of cloth running between the two undulating 'wavy navy' gold stripes of his rank. (Royal Navy had straight stripes, Royal Naval Reserve had chain-braided stripes.) The wearing of a uniform mattered; Admiral Godfrey never wanted his NID representatives to be disadvantaged by appearing in civilian clothes, especially at important meetings with the other armed services.

In Room 39 at the Admiralty, Fleming was put at a desk near the green baize door that led to Admiral Godfrey's office, Room 38, sitting with Godfrey's old friend and secretary Ted Merrett. Merrett did not really like Ian Fleming; he thought him unhappy, withdrawn and typically Etonian in his determination to establish ascendancy from the start. He also quietly resented Fleming's favoured status with the admiral and hated his 'filthy' cigarettes, which seemed to give the Etonian a permanent cold; he was a snuff man himself. But Fleming was good at his job and imperturbable; his favourite remark was a dispassionate, 'Well, there it is.' Fleming and Merrett would become the explosive DNI's filters and valves: for the next six years, they would get the first blast and be the last stop.

3

Technology and War

By August 1940 Winston Churchill could see that the Second World War was different from the First. It was 'a conflict of strategy, of organization, of technical apparatus, of science, mechanics and morale'. The problem was that the Germans seemed to have stolen a march on the British in many of these fields. But the newly inducted naval lieutenant was already attuned to a more technological war.

As any reader of the James Bond books will know, Ian Fleming loved gadgetry and technical know-how. In the mid 1930s, having done well on a Stock Exchange deal, he had given a Marxist book dealer called Percy Muir an initial payment of £250 to search out and acquire a most unusual collection of books. He wanted anything that marked milestones of progress, discovery, invention and ingenuity since 1800, when ships had sails and light came from candles. In the end there would be more than a thousand items. Fleming collected the first editions of books or periodical articles recording seminal events in science, technology, thought and culture, from airpropellers and finding bacilli to X-rays and zip-fasteners. This astonishing collection on the practical advances of Western civilisation (in their original languages, too) was in its day unique, and the Lilly Library of Indiana University bought the collection in 1970 for US$150,000. In the catalogue there are eclectic and original contributions to aeronautics, archaeology, atomic theory, biology, chemistry, cinema, the *Communist Manifesto*, criminology, economics, electricity, engineering, evolution, explosives, fingerprints, games and sports from baccarat and bridge, billiards and bicycling, to ping-pong, racquets and swimming, government, india-rubber manufacturing, machine-guns, mathematics, *Mein Kampf*, optical instruments, photography, physics, psychology and psychiatry, railways, scouting, sociology, telegraphy, telephony, television, and the wondrous world of valves and wireless. Ian Fleming's commandos would also later put a lot of energy into hunting down new German inventions and technologies.

Fleming kept his books in his bachelor flat at 22A Ebury Street, a former chapel that had once belonged to Oswald Mosley. He had all sorts of books, including '*vice anglaise*' spanking pornography that he liked to try out on prospective girlfriends. But this special technological collection was stored in custom-made, fleece-lined, black buckram boxes with IAN LANCASTER FLEMING gilded on the side under a goat-like device from the Fleming coat of arms granted his grandfather in 1921, with the new family motto 'Let The Deed Shaw' (Scottish for 'show').

As the Nazi storm-clouds brewed over Europe, pressure was on to start breaking the German secret codes, a prime example of the enemy's technological superiority. On the brink of a world war, British code-breakers could not crack a single German naval or military message. By contrast, German code-breakers in the *Beobachtungsdienst* of German naval cryptology were reading most Royal Navy and Merchant Navy messages within days.

The German Armed Forces or *Wehrmacht* were encrypting all radio messages for security, using Enigma machines – electro-mechanical polyalphabetic cipher-generating Geheimschreiber machines made by the Enigma company, which looked like typewriters in wooden boxes. Patented by the engineer Arthur Scherbius in 1918 and first purchased by the German navy in 1926, variants of this machine were eventually used by all the German armed services, police and diplomats. The Enigma had an apparently standard Continental QWERTZU keyboard, but if you pressed a letter – let us say E – you saw a different one lit up by a tiny bulb in the 'lamp board', which was an illuminated QWERTZU panel on top of the machine. No matter how many times you pressed down the letter E, E was the one letter that would never light up in the lamp board. (This clever-seeming characteristic was actually a flaw that helped the cryptographers to break in later.) The Enigma machine scrambled the letters of the alphabet through a series of rotors, wheels that rotated with every depression of a key, thus making different electrical contacts light up the bulb. In later models, a plug board that took old-style telephone jacks was added at the front. Plugging different letters together with cables made even more complex synaptic connections inside the box. Unless you knew how the rotors and the plug board were configured for each week or each day, the machine-generated cipher with its billions of possible combinations seemed unbreakable.

But the French and the Poles, like the British at the GC&CS, had been working hard on the problem, and they had managed to intercept wireless traffic indicating German troops massing for an imminent invasion of Poland. This inspired the Polish code-breakers to invite their British counterparts to meet and share information, a courageous gesture which broke the normal rules of the nationally competitive world of cryptography. It was agreed that Dilly Knox, veteran of Reginald Hall's First World War OB40 and an expert in the German Enigma enciphering machine, would go with Alastair Denniston, head of GC&CS.

In mid-July 1939 John Godfrey turned up on Knox's doorstep in full admiral's uniform with gold braid and cap to ask Knox to take the NID's Commander Humphrey Sandwith to Poland with them. Sandwith was the man who ran the Admiralty Y service and passed on German naval Enigma messages to GC&CS. Denniston and Knox took the boat-train from Dover on 24 July and met Sandwith in Warsaw. On the day that Ian Fleming received his naval commission, Wednesday 26 July 1939, they met French colleagues and the Polish cipher people at Pyry in the woods south of Warsaw and were shown the 'bombes', electro-mechanical machines which the Poles had devised to break into Enigma. The next day Knox met the three Polish mathematicians who had somehow managed to work out how the wiring of a *Wehrmacht* Enigma machine went from the keyboard to the wheels; their leader was the brilliant Marian Rejewski from the University of Posnań. Knox was eager to find if the 'diagonal' (the entry connection from the keyboard to the wheels of the Enigma) was wired randomly, a fearful prospect to crack. '*Quel est le QWERTZU?*' he asked straight out. 'A, B, C, D, E, F, G, ' replied Rejewski. It was so obvious that Knox hadn't thought of it. 'There's no question that Knox grasped everything very quickly, almost as quick as lightning,' remembered Rejewski years later, 'It was evident that the British really had been working on Enigma.' Not long after the British visit to Pyry and before war actually broke out, the Poles gave replicas of the Enigma machine to the French and the British so that the cipher bureaus of all three nations could get on with the work.

But August 1939 brought a political bombshell. Because the French and the British had failed to do a deal with them, the Russians made a Non-Aggression pact with the Germans instead. Signed in Moscow on 23 August by Ribbentrop and Molotov, the Nazi–Soviet pact was a classic gangsters' alliance. In a political volte-face the twin tyrants Hitler and Stalin ignored their ideological differences, agreed not to turn their guns on each other, and instead began planning to carve up the European map in the old way, ignoring the new nations created by the Versailles Conference. Polish independence was only twenty years old: Germany and Russia had been dividing its territory for two centuries. But on 24 August Neville Chamberlain reiterated Britain's obligation to defend Poland.

Ian Fleming's easy confidence and lack of what Godfrey called

'Very Senior Officer Veneration' quickly made him one of his trusted representatives. Section 17 was the co-ordinating section of Naval Intelligence, and as '17F' it became Fleming's duty to liaise with SIS and MI5, GC&CS, as well as the War Office, the Air Ministry and the Joint Intelligence Committee. In his 1968 book *Room 39: Naval Intelligence in Action 1939–45* Donald McLachlan said that, though perhaps not 'the wisest' of the staff working for Godfrey in Room 39,

Ian Fleming was the most vivid and became the best-known personality. His gift was much less for the analysis . . . of intelligence than for running things and for drafting. He was a skilled fixer and vigorous showman . . . His judgements could be vehement and might give offence; a paper specially addressed to the Director would be intercepted by him and come back with the remark 'Absolutely of no consequence 17F'.

'Well, Quacker,' Fleming would say in his bantering way to the older and more senior Commander Charles Drake, sitting across the way from him. 'Now what is it? What's the trouble? Paper for the Joint Intelligence staff? Let's get Miss Cameron in and start drafting. The great thing is to get something down, get it started.' And Fleming the journalist would start fluently dictating copy that would be typed up in an hour by Joyce Cameron, the DNI's secretary. Drake would read it and say, 'But my dear Ian, you've got hold of completely the wrong end of the stick; this is all the wrong way round.' And Fleming would simply reply, 'All right. Take out the first paragraph altogether and then change the rest as you want.'

Fleming started recruiting civilians that he knew from the world of books for Naval Intelligence. The antiquarian book collector Simon Nowell-Smith (a future Secretary and Librarian of the London Library) was plucked from the back page of the *Times Literary Supplement* to work with William Plomer on a Naval Intelligence news digest, the *Weekly Intelligence Report*. Also involved was the Hawthornden Prize-winning novelist Charles Morgan, whose first book, *The Gunroom* (1919), reflected

his experiences as a Royal Navy midshipman, and the thriller
writer and journalist Hilary St George Saunders, later librarian
of the House of Lords. Fleming worked all his social contacts,
networking ruthlessly, 'a giant among name-droppers' as Donald
McLachlan put it. Fleming had met the *Daily Express* journalist
Sefton Delmer on his overseas trade trip to Russia. Hearing that
Delmer had been in Poland in September 1939, he invited him
into the office to describe it to Naval Intelligence. A few years
later, Delmer would be running a black propaganda station,
Atlantiksender, beamed at the German navy, for NID.

Photography was a modern technology that Fleming wanted for
Naval Intelligence's watch on the German navy. As Lewis Mumford
had observed in his 1934 cultural study of the machine, *Technics
and Civilization*, 'The mission of the photograph is to clarify the
object.' A maverick Australian photographer called Sydney Cotton
had virtually reinvented aerial photographic reconnaissance,
working for the SIS's air section; just before the war, he hid three
Leica cameras in the fuselage of a Lockheed 12 executive plane
and took secret photographs all over Germany. But Cotton was
not happy with the top brass at the Air Ministry, whom he found
stuffy and obstructive, so he kept up contacts with other potential
clients. He had a flat near the Dorchester where he kept open house
for Admiralty and defence people. One of them was Ian Fleming,
who began to give him commissions. '"Oh Sydney, we want this
or that." And prontissimo, the stuff would be on Ian's desk next
morning.' Fleming had the gift of charm: Cotton said that 'When
Ian rang up to thank me he would always say "Amazing, Sydney.
Amazing."' But after Cotton took photographs of some German
ships at Emden, a dispute broke out because the Air Ministry gave
Cotton 'very strict instructions' that the pictures were not to be
shown to the Admiralty. Nevertheless, the next morning Cotton
showed up in Room 39 at the NID and announced that he had 'a

very important parcel' for Fleming. When the Air Ministry found that the Admiralty had made sense of the pictures three days before they did, they were furious.

Fleming seems to have enjoyed needling the 'Brylcreem boys' of the air force. The Air Ministry insisted that their 'listening systems' gave effective warning against enemy aircraft; Cotton doubted it because he had never been challenged when he himself made unauthorised flights. When Fleming was told about this, he saw an opportunity of scoring a point. He took Cotton to see Admiral Dudley Pound and gained permission to fly with Cotton on a photographic trip over Portsmouth and Weymouth. He then sent a message to the Air Ministry saying that 'We have heard on reliable authority that yesterday between the hours of eleven and twelve there were enemy [aircraft] over the area Portsmouth, Weymouth.' The answer came back that not only had there been no enemy aircraft, there had been no British aircraft either. Pound used the film Cotton had taken to prove that the Air Ministry were wrong.

But it was possible to be too clever. F. W. Winterbotham, head of the SIS air section, says that in August 1939 Ian Fleming made a 'back-door approach' to Cotton, offering him the rank of captain if he came over to the Admiralty as well as 'all the assistance and cash he wanted'. This caused what Winterbotham called 'a violent row' between the chief of the Naval Staff and the chief of the Air Staff. It was partly a matter of the way Fleming had approached Cotton, which was thought 'underhand', but also because, according to Winterbotham, 'There was a definite agreement between the services that the RAF alone were responsible for aerial photography.' Cotton never joined the NID, but his battles with officialdom illustrated what Lewis Mumford called 'the paradox in technics: war stimulates invention, but the army resists it!'

On Sunday 3 September 1939 Prime Minister Neville Chamberlain informed the nation via BBC wireless that 'this country is now at war with Germany'. The air-raid sirens started wailing and people went to the shelters and braced themselves for the Luftwaffe. But no bombs fell on Britain that day, and this false alarm marked the start of the first eight anti-climactic months of the Second World War, called by impatient American journalists 'The Phoney War'. At sea, however, hostilities began immediately. Chamberlain spoke before Sunday lunch, and by suppertime people were drowning in the Atlantic. Naval Intelligence was soon on full alert.

The immediate strategy of both Britain and Germany was economic warfare by strangling each other's supply lines at sea. There were laws of war about this: cargo vessels could be sunk or disabled only after capture and their crews' evacuation to 'a place of safety'; unescorted passenger ships were in theory exempt from attack. In the first action of the war at sea, off the coast of Uruguay in the south Atlantic, the British light cruiser HMS *Ajax* stopped the German merchant vessel *Olinda*, bound for Hamburg with a cargo of grain and beef. The British played by the rules of warfare, ordering the crew into their lifeboats before shelling the ship till it sank. But soon, thousands of miles to the north, the first submarine attack of the war took a different turn.

Kapitänleutnant Fritz-Julius Lemp, commander of *Unterseeboot-30*, fired two G7 torpedoes at what he took in the darkness to be an armed merchant cruiser, thus a legitimate target. As the ship slowly sank, Lemp consulted his boat's copy of *Lloyd's Registry* and was shocked to find that he had attacked an innocent liner, the SS *Athenia*, carrying 1,400 people from Britain to Canada. The passengers had been at dinner when the torpedo detonated at about 7.30 p.m. *U-30* slunk away quietly from the screaming chaos and the captain only confessed what he had done when he got back to Wilhelmshaven three weeks later. To protect morale Konteradmiral Karl Dönitz, the head of the German submarine service, lied about the incident. Cock-up soon turned into conspiracy: Joseph Goebbels's Nazi propaganda claimed that Winston Churchill had secretly ordered a British submarine to sink the passenger liner in order to sway public opinion in the neutral USA against Germany.

British propaganda presented the *Athenia* incident as an outrageous reversion to the all-out submarine warfare of the First World War. In fact it was just a mistake. But increased vigilance against U-boats led to another tragedy the following week. At night, off the coast of Norway, the British submarine HMS *Triton* torpedoed what looked like a German U-boat. The captain rescued two lone survivors; he went white on finding he had actually sunk another British submarine, HMS *Oxley*.

On 18 September 1939 *U-29* torpedoed HMS *Courageous,* which sank in the Western Approaches, south-west of Ireland, taking the captain and over 500 of his crew to a watery grave. (The last recorded words of Captain W. T. Makeig-Jones were 'What a damned fine shot!') And in the night of 14 October Günther Prien's *U-47* daringly struck at the huge British battleship HMS *Royal Oak*, in the heart of the supposedly safe Scottish anchorage Scapa Flow in the Orkneys. When the 33,000-ton battleship rolled over and sank, 833 officers, men and boys died in the icy water.

Now technology became crucially important. From the start of the war, the British were on the back foot with regard to the latest German torpedoes and mines, and the capabilities of the German submarines that carried them. They needed to get hold of examples as soon as possible in order to counteract them. On 3 September 1939 Winston Churchill, who understood the power of submarines, had come back to office as First Lord of the Admiralty. In *The World Crisis,* his 1927 history of the First World War, he had called the struggle between British sailors and German U-boats 'in scale and in stake the greatest conflict ever decided at sea', and he remembered all too clearly the dreadful choke-hold of the 1917 German submarine blockade. Now *Courageous* and *Royal Oak* had been spectacularly destroyed. British merchant shipping was also being sunk at an alarming rate: a cargo ship a day went down in September, and twenty-one more in the month of October.

The British had to work out what weapons were achieving these formidable successes. Hitler had warned on 19 September that 'the moment may come when we use a weapon which is not yet known and with which we could not ourselves be attacked'. Did the word *Waffe* (weapon) refer to the *Luftwaffe* – the German Air Force – or was there a German secret weapon?

As ships started being blown up in the mouths of British estuaries, the Admiralty got moving. Ashe Lincoln, a Jewish junior barrister who was now a minesweeper lieutenant in the RNVR working out of HMS *Vernon*, the Royal Navy's Torpedo and Mining Establishment in Portsmouth, found himself summoned to London one November morning. He was told that Winston Churchill had ordered the formation of a team to tackle the problem of an unknown type of German sea mine that was blocking Britain's harbours and rivers. The Tees and the Tyne were virtually closed to shipping and 185 ships were held up in the approaches to the Thames; so many ships were being lost or delayed that at this rate Britain would starve in six weeks. Lincoln was to apply his lawyer's forensic mind to sifting the evidence of these sinkings for clues.

He went through the reports from ships that had survived such explosions. None happened in deep water and none seemed to have been caused by actually hitting a floating or a tethered mine. The explosion did not make a big hole like that of a conventional contact mine, although it was capable of breaking a ship's back or even blowing it clear out of the water. The British speculated that it might be a magnetic mine. Then Lincoln saw the 10,000-ton tanker *James Maguire,* which had a massive 140-foot dent running fore and aft along her bottom. He posited a cone-shaped blast seventy feet beneath the ship. Now they knew the new mine was untethered, on the seabed, and must be magnetic. Despite the fact that the British had themselves deployed an earlier type of magnetic mine in the First World War, Winston Churchill thundered that the new German weapon was 'about the lowest form of warfare that can be imagined. It is the warfare of the IRA, leaving the bomb in the parcels office at the railway station.'

On 22 November Admiral Erich Raeder reported to Hitler that German destroyers had laid 540 mines off the Thames and the Humber, German submarines had ejected 150 from their tubes off the east and west coasts, and German aeroplanes had dropped 77 more: 45 British and neutral ships had been sunk in two weeks. But on the very night that Raeder made his report to Hitler, luck favoured the hard-pressed British. Coast watchers in east Essex on the northern lip of the mouth of the Thames saw an enemy He-115 sea-plane dropping a parachute in the darkness, and whatever it carried landed in the tidal mudflats beyond the salt-marshes at Shoeburyness.

The Admiralty was alerted and before midnight Churchill and Pound were talking to two mine experts from HMS *Vernon*, Lieutenant Commanders J. G. D. Ouvry and R. C. Lewis, who were soon in a car heading for Southend. As the tide went out at 3 a.m., they examined the new kind of mine by torchlight. It was a heavy metal cylinder about six to seven feet long. Then they found another one about three hundred yards away. Ouvry made sure there was no metal in his clothing and, carrying non-magnetic brass tools, tackled the first mine, removing one detonator in the sticky mud. A booby trap would have meant kingdom come. They removed a second detonator and after three hours' work the mine was safe. It was driven to Portsmouth and within eighteen hours the Admiralty knew exactly how it worked. The mine experts (who got medals) were luckier than they knew: those mines could not have been salvaged if they had worked as intended, because they were deliberately designed not to be retrieved. If they fell in shallow water or were hauled up above the depth of five metres again, the spring-loaded plunger in the clockwork mechanism should have withdrawn, detonating the mine.

The British had to use improvisation and ingenuity in tackling the problem of German magnetic mines. It was possible to degauss the ship by girdling it with coils of electric cable, or to 'wipe' a ship's magnetic field by passing it through a temporary coil that had a powerful electric current sent through it. Or you could change the ship's polarity: if the south pole of the ship pushed down instead of the north, the mine would not explode. There were other technical fixes, but the magnetic mine problem was only overcome because British experts got hold of an actual device and took it apart. The same happened with torpedoes. After Günther Prien sank the *Royal Oak* at Scapa Flow, Royal Navy divers brought up one of the unexploded seven-metre-long 'eels' from the murk, and Admiralty scientists discovered that the Germans had now developed a weapon that left no wake. Instead of the alcohol-fuelled steam torpedo, which trailed a widening track of bubbles, the G7e was propelled swiftly, and almost invisibly, by two electric motors.*

You needed to get hold of the other side's technology. Perhaps it was at this stage that certain trains of thought began forming in Ian Fleming's mind.

Back in Whitehall, the chief of the Secret Service was dying. (The head of the Secret Intelligence Service is always called C, after the initial of its first head in 1909, Manfield Cumming.) Old Admiral Sir Hugh Sinclair had feasted and roistered and smoked many a fat cigar, but his sixty-sixth birthday in 1939 was to be his last. Cancer clawed him that August. But who would take C's crown? There were two internal candidates. Claude Dansey and Stewart Menzies were both colonels and long-time members of SIS. Dansey, fifteen years older and based in Zurich, was more the rough diamond ('an utter shit; corrupt, incompetent, but with a

---

* This explained the noise 'like an electric sewing machine' that three crew members of SS *City of Mandalay* heard just before their ship blew up on the Humber on 17 October 1939.

certain low cunning' according to Hugh Trevor-Roper) who ran the covert Z network of agents and sometimes used Alexander Korda's film company as a front. Menzies, already Sinclair's deputy, was a smoother man from the courtier class who had come out of Eton and the Household Brigade and never discouraged the rumour that he was the illegitimate son of King Edward VII. Admiral John Godfrey was also asked to put his name forward: according to his wife he declined, feeling his naval career would otherwise be at an end. How shipshape SIS might have become had Godfrey been appointed! But the insiders prevailed. Dansey the bruiser got second place and became the kind of deputy who secretly dominates his superior, and Menzies, the establishment man, got the top job with the bottle of green ink by tradition reserved for the sole use of C.*

The first big operation on Stewart Menzies's watch went spectacularly wrong. In October 1939 SIS in the Netherlands began negotiations with figures in the German armed forces who were part of a conspiracy to remove Hitler and make peace. On 9 November two SIS men, Major Richard Stevens and Captain Sigismund Payne Best, went to Venlo on the Dutch–German frontier to meet a Luftwaffe general. But in a shoot-out by the Café Backus, opposite the customs house in the no-man's-land of the border zone, their Dutch escorting officer was killed and the two British secret agents were kidnapped and frogmarched a few yards across into Germany. 'Our number's up, Best,' said Stevens. The whole charade had been an elaborate sting by the Nazi security service or *Sicherheitsdienst*. There was no peace-loving general, and their regular contact, who called himself

---

* James Bond's fictional chief is called M, from the initials of his name, Admiral Sir Miles Messervy. In *Moonraker* we learn he also writes in green ink. 'Major Dansey' in *From Russia With Love*, 'a tall, quiet Englishman with a black patch over one eye', is Kerim Darko's predecessor as SIS Head of Station in Istanbul. Colonel Daintry in Graham Greene's 1978 espionage novel *The Human Factor* is also based on Claude Dansey.

'Major Schaemmel', was actually Major Walter Schellenberg, head of German counter-intelligence, who later tried to kidnap the Duke and Duchess of Windsor in Iberia. The captured SIS men spent the next five years separated in various concentration camps and, according to Nigel West, told the Germans a good deal about British secret intelligence.*

Around the same time the British made another mistake that was almost a reverse image of the Venlo one: this time they were too sceptical, rather than too credulous. Many senior people in the war effort were not yet as aware as Churchill of the importance of science and technology; and thus they were more receptive to the gentlemanly idea of 'decent Germans' than they were to an offer made by an anonymous German scientist to the naval attaché in Norway in early November. This letter told Rear Admiral Hector Boyes that if the British were interested in learning some German scientific and technical secrets they had only to alter the preamble to the BBC eight o'clock news on Monday 20 November 1939 from '*Hullo, this is London calling*' to '*Hullo, hullo, this is London calling.*' (A similar intervention on the BBC German Service on 11 October had been the preamble to the Venlo incident.) Soon after this was done, Boyes received a small packet containing seven pages of German text which came to be known as 'The Oslo Report'. The British Legation translated it into English and forwarded the packet to SIS/MI6 in London, and the head of the air section passed it on to the enthusiastic physicist who had been attached to them for scientific intelligence, twenty-eight-year-old Reginald Jones. The future Professor R. V. Jones gingerly opened the parcel and found the letter and a small glass tube. This looked like an electronic valve but was in fact a proximity fuse for an anti-

---

* Two journalists who went to investigate the incident at Venlo narrowly escaped capture at the Café Backus. The American Pat McGroarty was safer because he was a neutral, but Ralph Izzard of the *Daily Mail* was a Briton critical of the Nazi regime. He was on the point of flushing his British passport down the lavatory when the landlady got rid of the German soldiers.

aircraft shell, designed to trigger the explosion when it detected another metal body nearby. It did not need a direct hit to work, and was far more advanced than any such device the British then had.

Jones studied the accompanying seven-page typewritten letter. Clearly composed by someone with a good technical and scientific background, it revealed other German developments. Radio-controlled, rocket-driven, explosive gliders to be used against ships were being tested at a place called Peenemünde. There was a Luftwaffe experimental station at Rechlin working on a wireless beam method of measuring a plane's exact distance from base in order to aid accurate bombing. There were details of German radar (RAdio Detection And Ranging) including the duration of pulses and the wavelength used. There were revelations about new kinds of radio-guided and acoustic homing torpedoes being used by the German navy, with microphones in the head that could pick up engine noise and steer towards it. Other torpedoes had the submarine variant of the proximity fuse and just needed a magnetic signal from a ship's steel hull to trigger a devastating explosion under the vessel. The author of the Oslo Report also suggested a remedy for this (which the British were already working out for themselves): change the ship's magnetic field.

In late 1939, however, R. V. Jones could not get people in the Admiralty and the Air Ministry to believe this extraordinary Oslo report was genuine. Older experts there pooh-poohed the new techniques described and thought the report was a Hunnish deception seeded with a few plausible half-truths. Jones kept the Oslo report in a drawer and over the years of the war took it out occasionally to tick off all the technical items as they came on stream and into Allied consciousness.

Years later Jones discovered 'the Oslo person' was Hans Ferdinand Mayer, a leading electronics scientist from Siemens, the great German company that was founded at the time of the invention of the telegraph and expanded through the age of electricity and radio. Born in Pforzheim (a city that RAF bombs would later devastate utterly), he had 'betrayed' his country's secrets because he detested Hitler and the Nazi dictatorship, and also because he admired the courage and integrity of an Englishman in GEC he had befriended, a Lancastrian by the name of Harry Cobden Turner. Hans Mayer was arrested by the Gestapo in 1943 for listening to the BBC and survived five concentration camps including Dachau and Buchenwald before he escaped, eventually making his way to America where he became a professor of radio astronomy at Cornell. Mayer only told his family he had written the report in 1977, three years before he died.

Ashe Lincoln, the former lawyer briefed to investigate new German weapons, received the King's Commendation in 1942 for his work 'rendering safe the new type magnetic mines', and told the story of another message that came from behind enemy lines in that year. One of his officers was disarming a German mine when he found that the internal works had already been sabotaged. The explanation was on the inside of the mine casing, where someone had written, in English, 'We are with you', under a drawing of a six-pointed Star of David. 'Clearly this was the work of a Jewish forced labourer . . . used as one of the slave labourers by the Nazis . . . The risk that he or she had taken was enormous because quite clearly, to deliberately sabotage a weapon . . . involved the risk of execution.' When Lincoln reported the finding to Winston Churchill, the latter ordered that complete secrecy about the incident be observed, because if it ever came to public knowledge a 'wholesale massacre of slave labourers' would doubtless ensue.

By the end of 1939 the Oslo gift of scientific knowledge had been offered and stupidly turned down, but the men in Naval Intelligence had learned from the successes with magnetic mines and torpedoes that they could deal with German technological superiority if they got hold of their kit and found out how it worked. When Churchill made his prescient observation that the Second World War was a conflict 'of technical apparatus, of science, mechanics', he could not foresee how good the British would eventually become at stealing such things from the enemy, or that Naval Intelligence and Ian Fleming's commandos would lead the way in theft.

4

The Philosophy of the Pinch

PINCH, *noun* 1. Action of obtaining by covert or any available methods secret official documents, esp. cryptographic documents, of another state or of any organisation. 2. Any secret document or collection of secret documents so obtained, esp. when of cryptographic value. Bletchley Park 1944 *Cryptographic Dictionary*

In the First World War, British code-breaking gained an early advantage through three covert captures – early examples of the so-called 'pinches' in which Ian Fleming's assault unit would specialise. A week after war was declared in August 1914, a copy of the *Handelsverlehrsbuch* (HVB), the German mercantile signal book, was taken at pistol-point from the cargo-ship *Hobart* in Melbourne harbour. In October 1914 came the second windfall, described by David Kahn as 'perhaps the luckiest in the whole history of cryptology' – a copy of the *Signalbuch der Kaiserliche Marine*, the German navy's code book, was retrieved from the wrecked cruiser *Magdeburg*. Then in early December 1914 a British trawler dredged up a lead-lined iron box with a third German code book, the *Verkehrsbuch*, ditched overboard after the battle of the Heligoland Bight. Such finds became prized, and First World War British divers who slipped into sunken U-boats where dogfish and congers were gorging on the dead crew could win a handsome £100 reward for bringing up secret material.

At the beginning of the Second World War, British code-breakers at Bletchley Park were crying out for just such bounty. Bletchley Park, or 'BP' as its inhabitants knew it, was being turned from a hideous manor house into a highbrow mini-university. In the spring of 1938 Admiral Sir Hugh Sinclair, C, had selected the

58-acre heart of an old estate and purchased it out of his own pocket as the 'dispersal location' or 'war station' for both the SIS and the GC&CS. Bletchley Park was fifty miles away from the expected bombing of the capital but very well connected by trunk telephone cables. 'Bletchley itself was a desperately awful place,' remembered Margaret Cordy, who joined in the summer of 1942. 'It had a cinema and one mouldy café with a depressing notice saying "Regret no toilet". At least it was easy to get out of, with plenty of trains to London, Oxford, Cambridge, Rugby and Birmingham.' Bletchley Park was walking distance from the railway station. With the main house, stables and cottages occupied for living-quarters and other staff billeted in private homes and pubs like the Eight Bells and the Shoulder of Mutton, additional single-storey wooden huts had to be built in the grounds as work places.

Dilly Knox, the First World War code-breaking genius who had gone on the mission to meet the Poles at Pyry even though, as it turned out, he was already ill with lymphatic cancer, set up his headquarters for Enigma research slightly apart from the administrators, in a curious cottage meant for a groom in Bletchley Park's stable yard. According to Mavis Batey, Ian Fleming would visit him regularly, every two weeks or so, on naval business. Two huts, Hut 4 and Hut 8, were dedicated to deciphering naval Enigma messages and sending them back to the Admiralty.

The Bletchley Park site (which at its peak in January 1945 had a staff of 9,000 men and women working in shifts around the clock) was ringed by barbed wire, guarded by the RAF Regiment and kept incredibly hush-hush. Its inhabitants just said, if asked, that they worked 'in the country'. Further enquiries went to 'Room 47, Foreign Office', post to 'Box III, Bletchley, Buckinghamshire'. When the Whitehall 'Man of Secrets' Lord Hankey made his report into SIS and MI5 in March 1940, even he averted his gaze from Bletchley Park: 'At the beginning of my inquiry I visited the 'war station' of the GC&CS. Because of the extreme confidentiality of this area of secret intelligence, it is not appropriate for me to commit anything about the current work of this organisation to paper or even to express an opinion about its current state . . .'*

For all Bletchley Park's best efforts, however, and despite the gift of the cloned Enigma machine from the Polish code-breakers, by the end of 1939 no encrypted German messages had been decoded. They needed some luck.

*

Early on Monday 12 February 1940, the minesweeper HMS *Gleaner* hunted down and depth-charged the German submarine *U-33* in the Firth of Clyde. *U-33* had laid many mines and sunk a dozen cargo-vessels and trawlers, and the skipper of *Gleaner*, Lieutenant Commander Hugh Price, was awarded a DSO. Secretly the award also acknowledged an excellent pinch.

When the damaged *U-33* was forced to surface, Kapitän Hans Wilhelm von Dresky tried to destroy his secret material before exploding the scuttling charges. All radio messages from German U-boats to HQ at Wilhelmshaven were encrypted using the naval version of the Enigma machine. This *Schlüsselmaschine M* (cipher machine M) had more rotor wheels than the German army model, on the principle that the more complicated you made the enciphering, the greater the security – a belief that in the end would lead the Germans into overconfidence. Von Dresky had distributed all eight metal wheels from his Enigma machine among three crew members, with strict orders to ditch them in the sea as soon as they abandoned boat. Two remembered, but in the emergency evacuation Stabsobermaschinist Fritz Kumpf forgot. When *Gleaner* rescued some of the shivering German submariners from the cold black Clyde, three metal and plastic wheels that looked like customised chain rings from a pedal bicycle

---

* This classified document was purloined from Hankey by his clever Marxist civil servant John Cairncross and delivered to the latter's real masters in the Soviet NKVD.

were found and handed to the skipper. Lieutenant Commander Price sent the rotors down to the Admiralty and the NID made sure they soon reached Bletchley Park, where they turned out to be most useful to the men unriddling Enigma.

They were, in fact, Enigma alphabetic rotor wheels or *Walzen*. Enigma machines had rotors numbered I to VIII, cogged wheels of metal and black plastic that looked similar on the outside, but the Roman numeral indicated that each had different internal wiring. By great good luck, two of the Enigma rotors recovered from *U-33* were previously unknown wheels, numbers VI and VII.

Even the basic Enigma machines depended on a huge number of possible settings. Readers allergic to technical explanations may safely skip to the next section, but even a quick glance will show the order of difficulty that British code-breakers were facing.

One layer of the rim of every wheel, 'the alphabet tyre', had the twenty-six letters from A to Z marked around its 'tread'. Both faces of each wheel were circled by electrical contacts, two per letter, twenty-six copper plates flush with the left face of the wheel, twenty-six spring-loaded copper pins protruding from the right ('left' and 'right' because the wheels would eventually be placed vertically in the machine). A maze of insulated wires inside each wheel connected each contact plate to a different contact pin on the other side. All this was part of the scrambling: a signal coming in at contact plate A might go out at contact pin X, and returning the other way come in at pin B and go out at plate J. Although the wiring was fixed inside the wheel, the correspondence of contacts to letters wasn't, because the alphabet tyre could be rotated around the core of the wheel to an index mark (either a red line or two white dots). This setting was known as the *Ringstellung*.

The wheels themselves then had to be assembled in a particular order on a central hub or axle before being fitted into the basket of the unlocked and opened Enigma machine. With three wheels to choose from there would be six possible orders of wheels and faces, but with eight wheels there were 336 permutations. When a hub loaded with the three wheels was inserted into the machine, the protruding finger ring of each rotor could be turned around so that each wheel started at a different letter of the alphabet, yielding 16,900 possible combinations of settings.

To send a message, a three-wheel Enigma on any particular day of the month had to be set up according to instructions with, say, wheels IV, III, I inserted from left to right, the *Ringstellung* set at, say, B, Z, G from left to right, and then each individual wheel clicked round on the wheel adjuster so that, say, the letters K, C, L, were showing in the little windows from left to right. This was the starting position or *Grundstellung*. That was the easy bit! When a message was being enciphered on the Enigma, each physical depression of a letter on the keyboard engaged a pawl on the cogged edge of the right-hand wheel and clicked the wheel round one place, before sending an electrical signal from the 4.5-volt battery through that wheel. When a certain 'placement' notch – the turnover position – on this 'fast' right-hand wheel was reached, it engaged another pawl, which also clicked round the wheel to its left one place. After a certain number of clicks the second wheel's placement notch also engaged to click round the third wheel to its left one place. Whenever the first two wheels' placement notches aligned, they also clicked the third wheel round, and so on. Only after 16,900 letters did the three wheels return to their original position.*

To scramble the letters further, some Enigmas also had an alphabetic plug board or *Steckerbrett* on the front with a set of double-ended telephone jacks. These *Stecker* plugs connected the keyboard and the lamp board to the plate where the electrical

---

* The turnover notch for wheel I came after the letter R, for wheel II after the letter F, for wheel III after W, for wheel IV after K and for wheel V after the letter A. So 'Royal Flags Wave Kings Above' became the notch mnemonic for the code-breakers at Bletchley Park. This would actually read through the window on the cover of the Enigma machine as one letter earlier, Q E V J Z.

current entered. So in addition to the wheel order and ring-setting, the month's list of daily instructions for Enigma operators might indicate up to ten *Steckerverbindungen*, or cross-pluggings of letters, say A to N, C to Z, E to M, G to Q, H to L, J to S, T to F, which would swap those letters both before entering.the rotors and before reaching the lamp board. With ten pairs of plugs there were 140 million million possible *Stecker* combinations. Nevertheless, there were ways through this maze for the code-breaker. The reciprocal nature of 'steckering' was important: if A was plugged to N, then N was plugged to A. It was also known that the Enigma machine was 'non-crashing', i.e. no letter could ever encode as itself – if you pressed A on the keyboard, the one letter you would never get on the lamp board was A.

So the electrical signal triggered by the pressing of a letter key on an Enigma machine flowed through the plug board, then through the clicking wired wheels from right to left and, after bouncing off the *Umkehrwalze* or reflector which also had twenty-six contacts wired randomly in pairs, travelled back from left to right through the wheels, thus going through seven additional substitutions before dodging through the plugs again to light up a different letter in the lamp board. Thus the possible ways to jumble the twenty-six letters of the alphabet to encipher a message were being multiplied from mere hundreds and thousands into millions, billions and even trillions: the realm of the mathematician.

Alastair Denniston, head of the GC&CS, understood cryptography was moving from wordplay to a numbers game. He began trying to recruit chess players and mathematicians in place of Classics dons and crossword wizards. Yet it wasn't easy; only three out of the first twenty-one code-breakers taken on in September 1939 had a background in science rather than the humanities. Denniston put the word out in Oxford and Cambridge. Peter Twinn from Brasenose College, Oxford – later the first code-breaker to read a German Enigma message – was among the early recruits, and there were Cambridge men like Gordon Welchman, who later wrote a book about his time at Bletchley, *The Hut Six Story*. They all went on the one- or two-week Territorial Army training courses offered at SIS HQ, Broadway Buildings in London. A fruitful source of 'the professor type' required was King's College, Cambridge, from which had come such veterans of Room 40 as Dilly Knox, Frank Adcock and Frank Birch. At Bletchley Park Birch administered the Naval Section in Huts 4 and 8.

In September 1939 a code-breaker of genius arrived, a twenty-six-year-old Fellow of King's who is now recognised as the father of modern computer science and artificial intelligence, Dr Alan Mathison Turing.*

At the time 'the Prof' was only known as the author of a brilliant 1936 paper that posited an abstract mathematical machine controlled by a 'programme' in its memory. This 'universal Turing machine' was the forerunner of the first electronic digital computer, which Turing would formulate in 1945. At Princeton University Turing had grasped that the machine could be used in codes and ciphers, and when he returned to England in 1938 he went on his first course at GC&CS. On the outbreak of war, Turing reported immediately to Bletchley Park, where the code-breaking teams were assimilating what the Poles had learned about Enigma ciphers.

This was to be the war work for the next months and years. 'We're breaking machines. Have you got a pencil?' were the first words

---

* In September 2009, following a successful petition on the No. 10 Downing Street website, British Prime Minister Gordon Brown apologised for Alan Turing's 'utterly unfair' treatment by the authorities after the war: convicted in 1952 of illegal sex acts with another man, Turing was offered a stark choice between imprisonment and chemical castration by hormone injection. Turing accepted the chemicals, which made him grow breasts, and in June 1954 killed himself by eating an apple dipped in cyanide. In *Zeroes & Ones* Sadie Plant says this is for ever remembered in the bitten-fruit logo of Apple™.

that Mavis Lever heard when she arrived at Bletchley Park seven months later. The outlook seemed gloomy. But Turing had the ideal mind to help crack an ultimately computable system. As an inky, untidy fifteen-year-old he had found a new method of working out π to thirty-six decimal places without using elementary calculus. Still schoolboyishly scruffy and shy, with yellow teeth and black fingernails, Turing often behaved eccentrically. He buried silver bullion in the woods, but then lost the enciphered map of its whereabouts; he wore a gas mask as he bicycled the three miles from the Crown Inn at Shenley Brook End to Bletchley Park to protect him against hay fever from pollen, and he chained his tea mug to the radiator with a combination lock to keep it safe from his colleagues. (The notoriously absent-minded Dilly Knox was once seen pondering a problem as he drank a cup of tea on the lawn by the ornamental lake; an idea struck him and, wanting to hurry back to his desk, he simply threw his cup and saucer into the water.) Fortunately Bletchley Park was run on collegiate rather than military lines. If Turing did not want to come down from the attic of the cottage for meals, a basket on a pulley could be rigged to send coffee and sandwiches up to him. The task of managing such brilliant but eccentric people must sometimes have been as thankless as herding cats, made harder by the fact that the workforce had undergone a sudden wartime expansion. Yet the intellectual camaraderie there, with women working alongside the men, made days congenial.

In *The Hut Six Story,* Gordon Welchman describes how he began noting the timings and frequencies of intercepted German messages, particularly the opening call signs, groups of letters that were sent before the message itself. Like Marian Rejewski, the Polish mathematician who first broke the Enigma, Welchman saw that the sender's very first letters indicated to the receiver how the machine was set up. Welchman asked for a complete register of all intercepted Enigma traffic to be sent to Bletchley Park for later, detailed scrutiny. The Y Service interceptors at Chatham were happy to oblige and Station X and the Y service began cooperating closely. Complete accuracy mattered because those opening letters gave a key to the settings.

Much enciphered radio traffic was utterly routine and banal. If the interpreters could guess correctly what a standard phrase might be, it became what was known as a 'crib'. Given at least twenty letters of plain text, plus its encipherment, and knowing how the Enigma worked, it was theoretically possible to run through many settings of the machine and work out which sequence had produced it.

Useful information came from prisoners of war. The revelation by a captured enemy Funkmaat (radio petty officer) called Meyer in November 1939 that the German navy always spelled out numerals in full meant that *EINS* (one) became the commonest tetragram in German Naval traffic – at least one *EINS* featured in 90 per cent of messages. An *EINS* catalogue could be made by enciphering *EINS* at all the 16,900 positions of the machine on the keys of the day in question, and then comparing it with other messages of the day for repeats. At first this process of comparison was done manually by moving perforated sheets, but later Turing developed a 'bombe' or electronic computing machine, which was then built by Harold 'Doc' Keen of the British Tabulating Machine Company, a firm at nearby Letchworth. Essentially this device stacked thirty or more Enigma systems into an iron-framed cabinet six and half feet high, seven feet long and two and half feet deep. It weighed a ton and contained ten miles of wire and a million soldered connections. The prototype bombe, 'Victory', was installed in Hut 1 at Bletchley Park on 18 March 1940. It functioned like a computer, using algorithmic techniques to try out all the possible combinations of wheel settings and *stecker* pluggings that would match the enciphered 'crib'. It was still painfully slow. 'Running a single crib in all wheel orders took a week,' says Stephen Budiansky in *Battle of Wits*.

Dilly Knox's Research Unit in the Bletchley Park stable yard broke the first German air force Enigma message on 20 January 1940. By the time the rotors from *U-33* came in February, Turing was the head of Hut 8, working on the more difficult naval Enigma, which he liked because 'I could have it largely to myself.' But things needed to speed up. John Godfrey wrote to Frank Birch, Head of the Naval Section, to say he was 'setting up an organisation to arrange "pinches", and I think the solution will be found in a combined committee of talent in your department and mine who can think up cunning schemes'. Ian Fleming's trips to Bletchley Park continued.

The battle for Norway, the first major grapple of Allied and Axis forces, was about to get serious. Already in the first seven months of the war, fifty-four ships from Norway had been lost to bombs, mines and torpedoes, and both the Royal Navy and the Kriegsmarine were violating the neutrality of Norwegian waters. Open warfare in 1940 began almost accidentally, as if two bands of robbers, intent on burgling the same house, bumped into each other in the dark, triggering a chaotic sixty-two-day struggle over the rugged kingdom.

The First Lord of the Admiralty, Winston Churchill, had become fixated on striking strategic blows to cripple the enemy's war economy. Scandinavia at the time provided Nazi Germany with 80 per cent of the high-grade iron ore it needed for guns, tanks, and warships. The Kiruna/Gällivare region of northern Sweden alone supplied Germany with around ten million tons of iron ore every year, shipped in summer from Luleå to German Baltic ports, and in winter, when Luleå was ice-bound, sent overland by train to the ice-free port of Narvik and thence to Germany.

The German assault on Norway was a terrific gamble, full of risks, but the military professionals of the three armed services cooperated well. U-boats carried volatile loads of 130 tons of bombs and aviation fuel for the German air force, and the entire functioning German navy, from battleships and cruisers down to patrol craft, helped to deliver six divisions of army infantry, artillery, tanks, fuel and supplies, supported by a thousand Luftwaffe aeroplanes, the largest air armada to date in warfare.

At this time the British had still not broken a single German naval Enigma message, whereas the German *Beobachtungsdienst* – literally 'Observation Service' – under Wilhelm Tranow (who followed every British battleship, tracking enemy forces) had cracked the five-digit naval code and was reading 50 per cent of Royal Navy and Merchant Navy wireless telegraphy traffic without delay, and up to 80 per cent within days.

'Traffic Analysis' of signals at Bletchley Park was then a rudimentary new art, in the youthful hands of a twenty-year-old Cambridge history undergraduate called F. H. Hinsley. Frank Birch, head of the Naval Section, had set Hinsley to studying radio intercepts and D/F (direction finding) fixes so he could map German navy signal networks and their patterns of W/T (wireless telegraphy) use. When Hinsley noticed a spike in radio signals 'without precedent' emanating from west of Denmark and in the exit to the Baltic on the night of 6/7 April 1940, he cranked the handle of the direct telephone line to tell the OIC at the Admiralty in London.

Catastrophically, this warning was ignored. Perhaps it was understandable because it was the first ever from GC&CS to naval operational intelligence in the Second World War. But the Home Fleet missed the opportunity to destroy a major German expedition at sea. According to Hinsley, who later became the official historian of British Intelligence in the Second World War, 'prevailing opinions and lazy assumptions' ruled British thinking. On 4 and 5 April 1940 the British Prime Minister, Neville Chamberlain, and the head of the British army, General Sir Edmund Ironside, had both been heard crowing loudly that Hitler had 'missed the bus'. Thus with everyone unable to see the big picture, the Germans moved on the dark night of a new moon and invaded Denmark and Norway by surprise in the early morning of 9 April.

There was an element of bad luck in all this, as the British had nearly been in Narvik three weeks earlier. An Allied expedition to help Finland fight the Soviets (then allied with the Nazis) had been planned to go via Norway, but, when the Russo-Finnish 'Winter War' ended on 13 March, the two divisions gathered to seize Narvik were dispersed. Among those stood down while they were actually loading their ships to embark from Glasgow were the winter-trained 5th (Supplementary Reserve) Battalion Scots Guards, led by the British bobsleigh champion Lieutenant Colonel J. S. Coats with the veteran polar explorer Martin Lindsay as assistant adjutant. Lindsay would later marry Loelia Ponsonby, after whom Ian Fleming named James Bond's 'delectable' secretary, and one of the colour sergeants in 5th Scots Guards would in time lead Ian Fleming's commandos. He was a stocky, fair-haired explorer called Quintin Riley, who had been with Lindsay on the British Arctic Air Route Expedition of 1930–1 and been the meteorologist on the British Graham Land Expedition to Antarctica of 1933–7. (A British army regular NCO was puzzled by Riley's Polar Medal with Antarctic clasp: 'How can you get a medal for playing *polo*?' he asked.)

Naval Intelligence in London was forced to improvise its response to the German invasion of Norway. On 9 April William Todd, who had worked for the travel agents Thomas Cook & Co before he joined NID, scurried round the major passenger liner companies – P & O, Orient, Royal Mail, Blue Star – gathering up tourist brochures and maps as well as photographs of Norwegian harbours, jetties and landing places taken during cruises. Tourist maps of a summery Norway, the land of fiord and folk song, were all the advance information that some luckless soldiers ever got.

On 11 April 1940 another young man who would later be a notable character in Ian Fleming's commandos, an RNVR lieutenant called Patrick Dalzel-Job, found himself on board the light cruiser HMS *Southampton* in Scapa Flow, headed for Norway with the 24th Guards Brigade. Make it up as you go was the order of the day; no one seemed to know anything about Norway or about winter warfare. (Clement Attlee was said to have shown Churchill the empty War Office file on Norway which had the letters SFA written on it. 'I suppose it means Sweet Fanny Adams,' said the deputy prime minister. 'I sincerely hope,' remarked the prime minister, 'that there is no other interpretation to be placed on those letters.') April was springtime to the English, so Dalzel-Job's production of his own photographs of Arctic Norway in April, showing deep snow, caused consternation – there were no skis, snowshoes or white camouflage material on board.

Like Ian Fleming, Dalzel-Job had lost his father in the First World War (Machine Gun Corps, the Somme) and had spent time in the Alps learning to ski. Brought up by his mother and largely self-educated, he was obsessed with sailing and in his early twenties had helped build a sixteen-ton topsail schooner called *Mary Fortune*, sailed to Norway in it and fell in love with the country. In the late 1930s he offered himself to the Admiralty to chart all the Norwegian fjords northward to the Russian border, looking in particular for places where small boats could hide. Back in England the Admiralty at first showed little interest in his Norwegian experiences, but six months later changed their tune.

Two other British expeditionary forces, MAURICEFORCE and SICKLEFORCE, were rushed to Norway in mid-April 1940. Ian Fleming's brother Peter, now Captain Fleming of MI(R), was in the vanguard. He was one of the first British soldiers to land openly in Norway, arriving in an RAF flying boat on Namsos fjord, 'wounding the still, dark surface of the water with that wonderful arrogant swish that a Sunderland makes'. Fleming, together with Martin Lindsay and two signallers, formed No. 10 Military Mission, whose job was to make radio contacts with Norwegian forces and assist the landing of MAURICEFORCE.

The British hid themselves from the German aircraft, but

Namsos turned into a shambles after the French swift deployment unit, the Chasseurs Alpins, arrived and noisily opened fire on the first Luftwaffe aeroplanes they saw. In response the Germans bombed the town and burned its wooden houses, leaving only their stone chimneys sticking up like blackened totem-poles. MAURICEFORCE, advancing on Trondheim from the north, were beaten back.

Peter Fleming flew back to Britain for further orders on 26 April and, having missed the night train from Inverness, with Etonian aplomb ordered a 'special' train from the stationmaster to take him down to London. Delivering his dispatches to the War Office early in the morning, he saw Winston Churchill, the First Lord of the Admiralty, in his silk pyjamas, smoking a cigar before breakfast. About to light his own pipe, Fleming asked Churchill if he minded and got the retort 'Yes, I bloody well do!' Back in Norway on the 29th, with a bagful of MI(R) explosives for last-ditch demolitions, Fleming remarked, 'You can really do what you like, for they don't know what they want done.'

The German air force dominated the entire Norwegian campaign, keeping the Royal Navy at a safe distance, destroying British airplanes on the ground and strafing terrified British troops. German warplanes, working with the army, pushed back the other British expeditionary force, SICKLEFORCE. At the morning meeting of the War Cabinet on 1 May, Churchill listened to Prime Minister Neville Chamberlain summarising an eyewitness report by MI(R) technical expert Major Millis Jefferis that told how 'low-flying attacks with bombs and machine-guns' by the Luftwaffe's Stukas had scared the raw Territorials of SICKLEFORCE:

the moral effect of seeing the aircraft coming, of being unable to take cover, of being able to observe the bomb dropping, and of the terrific explosion, had been overwhelming.

Chamberlain concluded that it was 'quite impossible' for land forces to withstand complete air superiority. Once again technology was deciding the course of the war. Two days later, in the British evacuation under fire from Namsos, the British destroyer HMS *Afridi* was fatally dive-bombed by Stukas. Jack Haslam, a soldier from Wakefield watching the attack, saw 'yellowish coloured rats' scurrying across the deck of his own bomb-damaged ship, 'pushing us out't way to jump over the side . . . They say rats always leave a sinking ship, so we were getting worried then . . . '

The 1940 Norwegian campaign saw Britain's first tentative use of what would become known as 'Special Forces', a grouping that would eventually include Ian Fleming's 30AU. In mid-April 1940 ten 'Independent Companies', each made up of 270 volunteers and twenty officers, were recruited from Territorial and Regular units. Each company was armed and equipped to operate independently for a month. Four were combined as SCISSORSFORCE under the command of the extraordinary professional soldier, Lieutenant Colonel Colin Gubbins MC, who would later go on to lead SOE.

Colin Gubbins's English father was a fluent Japanese-speaker in the diplomatic service and his mother's family were McVeans from the Hebridean Isle of Mull. Gubbins had won his MC as a gunner in the First World War, fought against the Bolsheviks in revolutionary Russia and against Sinn Fein in the Irish Civil War of 1922–3, and spoke French, Russian and Urdu. In peacetime he seemed like a typical reserved clubland type, with a carnation in the buttonhole and smooth suede gloves. In uniform he was 'slight, dapper full colonel with a small moustache'. But war made him into a fighting chieftain. A naval officer who met him during the 1940 Norway campaign described a brute in a khaki shirt with the sleeves cut off, snoring prodigiously in a twenty-minute squirt of sleep, then waking up alert and talking coherently, 'an extraordinary man, very short and thick, with vast hairy arms that looked as if they could crush rocks and hung down almost to his knees'.

When Colonel Gubbins sailed from Glasgow to Norway on 4 May with his Independent Companies, one of his two intelligence officers was Quintin Riley, whose earlier attempt to come to Norway with the 5th Scots Guards had been aborted, and the other was Riley's good friend and future brother-in-law Captain Andrew Croft. The two men were both veterans of Greenland.*

The two young intelligence officers became guerrilla fighters based in Bodö, in a bay backed by snow-capped mountains, going on small raids up the fjords in a sixty-foot diesel-engined Norwegian 'puffer' fishing boat. In the shortening nights the 'Gubbins flotilla' blew up bridges and destroyed petrol dumps, but in the end they had to assist the Independent Companies' retreat. Norway was a defeat, not a victory, for the British and they were evacuated in June.

Croft and Riley were lucky not to be on board the British aircraft carrier HMS *Glorious,* which was hurrying back from Norway to the Orkneys. Just as had happened two months earlier at the start of the Norwegian campaign, the OIC was not paying enough attention to alerts from Bletchley Park. Young Harry Hinsley of Traffic Analysis warned them of wireless indications that big German ships were leaving Kiel and the Baltic on 4 June. But once more he cranked the telephone handle in vain; his message was noted but never passed on to the fleet. The German battle cruisers *Scharnhorst* and *Gneisenau* surprised HMS *Glorious* and her escort destroyers, *Ardent* and *Acasta,* on Saturday 8 June 1940, bombarding the British ships with hundreds of six-inch and eleven-inch shells. *Glorious* was fatally stricken and blazing, *Ardent* was sunk, and *Acasta* could have used her smokescreen to escape safely, but Commander Glasfurd came back and fired a torpedo into the *Scharnhorst* that killed two officers and forty-

---

* In 1934 Andrew Croft and Martin Lindsay took part in the longest-ever recorded dog-sledge journey carrying all its own provisions – an incredible 1,080 miles.

six men and caused flooding and a shutdown of its main engine. The *Gneisenau* then pounded the *Acasta* with shellfire and sank her. Charles Glasfurd remained at his post on the bridge of the dying destroyer and was seen by the sole survivor taking out his cigarette case and lighting up a final gasper.

Over 1,500 British sailors and airmen died because of this particular failure to connect the naval brain with the operational hands. According to Hinsley, however, the Admiralty and the OIC responded to these appalling losses 'with alacrity', and thereafter seriously improved relations with Bletchley Park's Naval Section and Traffic Analysis.

N

One small consolation for the British was that Enigma signals between the German army and air force in Norway, code-named 'Yellow' by Bletchley Park, started being broken from the middle of April 1940, even though at this stage the systems to get the data back to the right people in the field were not yet in place. Another achievement of the Norway campaign was a brilliant pinch that greatly improved the code-breakers' chances thereafter.

After the British destroyer HMS *Arrow* was rammed by an enemy Q-ship camouflaged as a Dutch trawler, British vessels were ordered to find other disguised fishing boats in Norwegian waters. HMS *Griffin* chased a suspicious boat called *Polares*, apparently flying Dutch colours, which gave up without a fight. As the boarding party was rowing towards the trawler, Lieutenant Alec Dennis noticed that the boat at its stern was a canvas mock-up probably concealing a Q-ship's gun. The Germans managed to throw two canvas bags overboard. One, which probably contained the ship's Enigma machine, plummeted, but the other was spotted still floating. A gunner called 'Florrie' Foord whipped a line round his body and dived off the *Griffin* to grab the slowly sinking sack. The line parted and Foord went under several times, but he came up again still clinging on. Eventually he was hauled out of the ocean with his sodden load of secrets: the ship's confidential books, ciphers and charts.

Griffin's crew were gleeful at their prize. *Polares*, in reality the German patrol boat *VP 2623*, had been carrying to Narvik (in addition to the torpedoes) three artillery pieces, four magnetic mines, sundry depth charges and explosives and a Browning .50 calibre machine-gun for use against aircraft. Alec Dennis steered the *Polares* back to Orkney with the German stokers working under guard while the Bavarian chef cooked them huge meals of fresh eggs with Danish bacon. *Polares* entered Scapa Flow triumphantly (if thoughtlessly) flying the White Ensign over the Swastika, and was filmed doing so by a Universal News crew. The film was seized and the news suppressed, because 'the Narvik pinch', as it came to be known, could only be an intelligence coup if it was kept secret so the Germans would not change their codes on hearing they were compromised.

Admiral Godfrey sent Lieutenant George Pennell of NID to Orkney to take possession of the documents. The Narvik pinch helped Bletchley Park open a brief window into German naval Enigma in May 1940. Among the papers were the keys for April 22–27 and the plain text and cipher text of messages sent on April 25 and 26, which acted as a crib. There were also two days' worth of *Stecker* or plug board settings scrawled on a bit of paper, and a guide to the bigram or 'two letter' tables that the German navy employed to make their enciphered messages harder to crack. The Narvik pinch had not yielded the bigram tables themselves, but Alan Turing was now able to start reverse-engineering them. Thanks to the pinch identifying that day's right-hand and middle wheels, he could also now reduce the number of wheel orders that had to be put through the bombe. The technique involved the use of large, specially printed sheets of paper with letters of the alphabet, set a quarter of an inch apart, that could be punched out so the sheets slid over each other to get correspondences 'in depth'; Turing called it 'Banburismus' after the Oxfordshire town,

Banbury, where the sheets were manufactured. But this was just the first window, not yet a door that they could walk through to explore the whole house.

↯

Soon the pinches involved whole countries rather than documents. On 4 May, the same day that Lieutenant Pennell arrived at Scapa Flow to retrieve the Narvik pinch documents, the intelligent and meticulous Major Humphrey Quill of NID 4, the future senior officer in 30 Assault Unit, was ordered to Iceland. (By Churchillian command, naval staff officers always had to write out the geographical name clearly as 'Iceland (c)' – this was because someone once sent a ship to *Ireland* by mistake.) Iceland seemed an odd destination to Quill, as he was in the Japanese section of NID, having just returned from two years as an intelligence officer in Singapore, but a Royal Marine is used to obeying orders. Quill was to accompany a scratch force of 750 raw Royal Marines on Operation FORK. Their mission was to pinch the entire island of Iceland, all 39,000 square miles of glaciers, hot springs and volcanoes.

Iceland was a sovereign state, but also a dominion of Denmark. After the German invasion of Denmark on 9 April, the island declared a temporary independence. In order not to cause further provocations, Iceland refused the British offer of 'protection' against the German plan to occupy the country, code-named IKARUS. Churchill told the House of Commons on 11 April, 'No German will be allowed to set foot there with impunity.' There were no Danish troops on Iceland, only a hundred or so policemen. As breaching neutrality was a legally contentious matter, Quill was assigned 'Pen' Slade, a barrister from the geographical section of NID, swiftly kitted out in naval uniform hired from Moss Bros. Admiral Godfrey opened up his safe and gave Quill £500 sterling in notes for bribes and sundries, including paying his 'interpreter', Lionel Fortescue. This French teacher from Eton spoke not much more Icelandic than a salmon-fishing tourist, but was reporting to C, the head of SIS.

At 5.00 a.m. on 10 May 1940 the destroyer HMS *Fearless* docked at Reykjavík. Operation FORK was not exactly a surprise after a Supermarine Walrus flying boat or 'Shagbat' had blundered noisily over the city at dawn, waking people up. A small crowd of curious Icelanders, some in eighteenth-century-looking national costume, watched the Royal Marines disembark down gangplanks. Quill was supposed to capture the German consul general and round up 120-odd German sailors living on the island. The British consul general, Sir Francis Shepherd, indicated where his German counterpart lived and Quill marched there with a platoon.

He banged on the front door and rang the bell insistently. Herr Werner Gerlach stuck his head out of the upstairs bedroom window and harangued the men with guns about the Hague protocols of diplomatic immunity, but eventually he opened the front door and was formally arrested. Someone smelled burning and the escort dashed upstairs to find the German consul general's wife and children busily burning papers in the bath. A ship's fire extinguisher quenched the flames, and the marines picked through soggy ash and scorched pulp looking for something legible.

The Icelandic government resigned itself to *force majeure*. Quill spent some of Admiral Godfrey's money buying stockings and perfume to bribe hospitable Icelandic women into telling him where the German sailors were hiding.

Pen Slade's legal worries about invading a peaceful neutral nation soon dwindled into insignificance. A far more serious pinch was under way in Europe, and not by the British. That same day, 10 May 1940, news came over the wireless that the German armed forces had once again breached international law by invading Belgium, Holland, Luxembourg and France. Cities like Rotterdam were being smashed and firebombed, even after they surrendered. Enemy troops were dropping from the air by parachute or from gliders, destroying fortresses. Tanks and armoured vehicles supported by Stuka dive-bombers were rolling over the Low Countries, ready to chew up and spit out the British Expeditionary Force at Dunkirk. Hitler's 140 divisions had begun smashing the French army, bombing and strafing French civilians, utterly humiliating *la belle France*. The Narvik and Icelandic pinches were as nothing compared to this, one of the biggest land-grabs in European history.

Ian Fleming was a good linguist, and by June 1940 was on his way to France.

5

Doing Deals

The Republic of France had been Britain's principal ally and, as the scale of the French military and civil collapse became clear, the Admiralty began to worry about the reliability of the French navy. If the 270 warships of the Marine Nationale Française came over to Britain all would be well, but what if their battle fleet instead fell into the hands of the German Kriegsmarine? The British naval attaché in France did not think the French were absolutely trustworthy, and nor did Admiral Godfrey. When he became DNI, Godfrey had gone to Paris to strengthen links with the French navy, but the commander-in-chief, Admiral Jean Darlan, seemed to him a proud man tinged with anglophobia, jealous of the Royal Navy and still resentful of the death of his great-grandfather by English gunfire at the battle of Trafalgar.

Now the French government, having quit Paris as the Germans advanced, was already squabbling about whether to fight on or give up. In the Allied conference at Briare on 12 June 1940 after the Dunkirk evacuation, Winston Churchill, barely a month into his premiership, wrung from Darlan a promise that he would never let the Germans get the French fleet. Churchill thought the French government largely defeatist, with the exception of the young undersecretary for war, General Charles de Gaulle. The French Naval Staff had abandoned their Paris headquarters and retreated to Montbazon near Tours, making the Admiralty's teleprinter link to the British embassy in Paris useless. On 13 June Godfrey sent his personal assistant Ian Fleming to restore communications with Darlan and clarify the French navy's intentions for their ships in the event of surrender.

Fleming picked up a fat bundle of cash from the SIS Paris office in the avenue Charles Floquet, acquired an RAF wireless operator, and drove south-west to Tours. His fluent French was useful on 15 June when he passed on to Darlan an official message urging him to bring his fleet over to Britain, saying that all preparations were being made to receive him and his ships. Darlan temporised, claiming that 'The Germans are only in the south of Paris . . . For the moment the war at sea will go on as before.' Patrick Beesly was the radio operator when Godfrey had a direct half-hour wireless conversation with Ian Fleming in Tours. Fleming told him France was collapsing and offered to stick to the evasive Darlan as he moved further south-west to Bordeaux where the whole French government had now decamped. Godfrey reiterated the British government's position that France could only negotiate peace terms with the Germans *after* the French fleet came over to Britain. Fleming's suggestion was simple but bold: let Darlan have the whole Isle of Wight as French territory in which to keep his ships.

German forces had already taken Paris when Churchill, in desperation, offered the Republic of France a complete political union and joint citizenship with the United Kingdom. (This would also in its way have been a brilliant pinch for Britain.) But the French government in Bordeaux fell apart, and Prime Minister Paul Reynaud resigned and dissolved his cabinet on 16 June. Marshal Philippe Pétain, the eighty-four-year-old French soldier recently returned from a fawning ambassadorship to General Franco's Falangist regime in Madrid, formed the new government, appointing Admiral Darlan minister in charge of the navy and the merchant marine. Crusty, white-moustached Pétain wanted an armistice with Germany: '*Il faut cesser la lutte.*'

Churchill now sent the First Sea Lord, Dudley Pound, down to Bordeaux in a last-ditch attempt to persuade Darlan to remove all French warships, if not to British waters then to the French West Indies or even neutral America. Before they left, Admiral Godfrey passed on a warning from his friend Lord Tyrrell, who had been

Ambassador to France from 1925 to 1933: 'Darlan is a twister.' But on 17 June Jean Darlan reassured his anxious British visitors that he would never surrender his fleet to the Germans.

✕

Ian Fleming saw chaotic scenes in Bordeaux that summer. Six million refugees fleeing the German invasion had clogged the main roads of France with every kind of wheeled vehicle. Many had been bombed and machine-gunned ruthlessly from the air. Now thousands wanted to escape from the mouth of the Gironde estuary, one of the last pick-up places in Operation ARIEL. Everyone remembers Operation DYNAMO, which lifted 338,000 men from Dunkirk, but ARIEL was the other great evacuation organised by the Royal Navy from north-western and western France in the summer of 1940, lifting thousands of Belgian, British, Canadian, Czech, French and Polish troops from Cherbourg, St Malo, Brest, St-Nazaire, La Rochelle, the Gironde and even as far south as St Jean de Luz. Operation ARIEL, like DYNAMO, was a 'miraculous deliverance', rescuing 190,000 fighting men, hundreds of guns and thousands of vehicles. This too was shadowed by disaster: perhaps 4,000 men died when the overloaded Cunard liner/troopship *Lancastria* was dive-bombed out of the sun, set ablaze and sunk, all in twenty minutes off St-Nazaire.

The same day, Monday 17 June 1940, General Charles de Gaulle, now no longer French undersecretary for war and national defence, arrived in London in an RAF aeroplane sent by the British prime minister and met Churchill at 10 Downing Street. The tall Frenchman in exile said he would not give up: *la lutte continue*. This was the upbeat message that Churchill wished the news media to put out to the world, not the loss of *Lancastria*, which was quietly suppressed for several years. Duff Cooper arranged for de Gaulle to write and broadcast a statement in French on the BBC the following evening. It was the start of a PR campaign to rebrand a nation corroded by defeatism. De Gaulle admitted that the enemy's tanks and aeroplanes had overwhelmed France. 'But has the last word been spoken? Should hope vanish? Is the defeat final? NO!' France was not alone, he declared; the battle of France was part of a world war. Inviting French officers and soldiers, engineers and weapons technicians to join him, De Gaulle declared that the flame of French resistance would not go out.

Bordeaux in mid-June 1940 was pullulating with French government bureaucrats, their families and hangers-on, men in every sort of uniform, diplomats, expatriates, the international press and civilian refugees. Most of the British embassy from Paris were there, and King Zog turned up with the Albanian crown jewels. Commander Ian Fleming found himself with Captain Edward Pleydell-Bouverie RN, the new British naval attaché who had also been tracking Admiral Darlan. New orders came crackling over Fleming's radio from NID: make sure that several dozen crates of new aeroplane engines and spare parts get shipped out. In their trim dark-blue uniforms and white caps, the naval officers got busy. At Verdon, the port sixty miles north-west of Bordeaux, they bribed, cajoled and commanded.

One of the vessels diverted to help the evacuation was the British India Steam Navigation Company's SS *Madura,* a 9,000-ton cargo vessel carrying 180 passengers, which had been at sea two months since leaving Mombasa. Now at Bordeaux 1,500 extra people were being packed on board, including the *Sunday Times* reporter Virginia Cowles, who listed

bankers, officials, cabinet ministers, wives, children, soldiers, nurses, business men, invalid ladies, retired colonels, maiden aunts, and fifty or sixty journalists . . . there were several hundred French people: many of them climbed on board weeping convulsively at the parting from their relatives and the uncertainty as to whether they would ever see their native land again. There in the harbour, with the sun streaming down and the peaceful outline of the French coast in the distance, it was hard to realise that France had come to an end.

On 22 June 1940 in the Compiègne forest north of Paris Adolf Hitler, surrounded by the Nazi top brass, triumphantly delivered Germany's armistice terms to defeated France. The momentous event was carefully stage-managed. Hitler took Marshal Foch's old seat in the very same wooden railway carriage where Germany had been humiliated by signing its armistice on 11 November 1918. The carriage had been taken out of a museum and placed in the exact same spot, though all signs and symbols of earlier French victory were now draped in swastikas. Article 8 said that all French navy ships not on colonial duties were to be 'demobilised and disarmed under German or Italian control'. All of France's important naval bases on the Atlantic – Brest, Lorient, St-Nazaire, La Rochelle, Bordeaux – were in the Occupied Zone and were now at the Germans' disposal to wage war on the maritime convoys supplying Britain. Indeed, Admiral Dönitz's U-boats would be deployed there from July 1940, cutting their run to the battle of the Atlantic by seven days.

Marshal Pétain publicly accepted Nazi terms and moved his government to the new capital, Vichy, the spa town in central France whose many hotels were now turned into ministries and offices to rule the Free Zone. It was a come-down from Paris: Latin American diplomats posted there described it as 'a banana republic with no bananas'. In London on 22 June General de Gaulle spoke again, at greater length, on the BBC, rejecting Pétain's surrender for three reasons: honour, common sense and the national interest. In a world war between freedom and slavery, what good would it do France to be on the side of slavery? The free French had to continue the fight wherever they were:

I, General de Gaulle, undertake here, in England, this national task . . . I invite . . . all French forces on land, sea and air, wherever they are now, to join with me. I invite all French people who want to stay free . . . to follow me. Long live free France with honour and independence!

So Frenchmen had to choose: Vichy or France Libre. At Sousse in Tunisia, the officers and crew of the ocean-going French submarine *Narval* decided unanimously *not* to obey orders from Vichy to demobilise. Captain François Drogou rallied to De Gaulle's appeal and sent a signal, 'Betrayed right down the line, I am making for an English port', setting off in *Narval* just before midnight on 24 June for the British-held island of Malta. His maverick act was particularly important because he took the French naval codes with him.

Churchill decided he could not trust Darlan's word and set in motion Operations GRASP and CATAPULT, the seizure or disablement of the French fleet. On 3 July 1940 the Royal Navy overcame French ships and submarines in the harbours of Portsmouth, Plymouth, and Alexandria in Egypt. (A fight broke out on the world's biggest submarine, the 110-metre *Surcouf*, at Plymouth, in which three Britons and a Frenchman died.) But the Algerian port at Mers-el-Kébir, near Oran in North Africa, was where the French navy held its most powerful squadron of four battleships, a seaplane carrier and six destroyers. The British Admiral Sir James Somerville spent the day in a desperate attempt to achieve the cooperation of the French Admiral, Marcel-Bruno Gensoul.

The British had a card up their sleeve thanks to François Drogou, captain of the *Narval* submarine, now safely docked in Malta. The Free Frenchmen could not be expected to betray their countrymen's codes, but the officers allowed themselves to be distracted ashore while the British lifted the ciphers from the captain's safe. These were then sent by flying boat to NID and Bletchley Park, so that Admiral Somerville could get intercepts of all Darlan's messages, and track the movements of the French fleet.

Somerville's emissary to the French admiral, Captain Cedric Holland, carried the message that it was 'impossible for us, your comrades up to now, to allow your fine ships to fall into the power of the German or Italian enemy'. An ultimatum with a time limit was refused, partly because of delays and misunderstandings in communications between the two sides. Against his will Somerville had to comply with the 'disagreeable and difficult' order from Winston Churchill's Cabinet which left him feeling 'thoroughly dirty and ashamed'. Just before 6 p.m. the Admiral opened fire on the ships of the French, Britain's recent allies. The United States got the news on Independence Day 1940 and it certainly made an impression: 'The British mean to win,' wrote the new US military attaché to London. The hail of British shells that sank the *Bretagne* and heavily damaged the *Dunkerque* killed 1,297 French *matelots* in ten hellish minutes, and made for bad blood. Harold Nicolson recorded in his diary: 'The House [of Commons] is at first saddened by this odious attack but is fortified by Winston's speech.' At the end there was an ovation, but Churchill was 'sitting there with the tears pouring down his cheeks'.

Ian Fleming was not evacuated from Bordeaux at the end of June 1940, but contrived to get himself into Portugal, from where he boldly wangled a seat on the regular German-run Lufthansa flight from Lisbon to Madrid. Nazi triumphalist propaganda bellowed from all the Spanish newspapers he saw. On 13 June, just days before Fleming landed on the grass airstrip at Madrid, the Franco regime had changed its war status from 'neutrality' to an undefined 'non-belligerence' with what the Falangist newspaper *Arriba* called 'ardent sympathy' for the Axis. Mussolini's Italy had entered the war three days earlier on Nazi Germany's side and everyone expected Spain to follow suit soon. The Spanish military's 'provisional' occupation of Tangier, the 'international zone' in Morocco, on 14 June, seemed like a first step towards it.

One trick that a hungry and impoverished gentleman in the Spanish Golden Age might use was to walk in the street ostentatiously picking his teeth, hoping to fool social inferiors that he had just enjoyed a large lunch. In 1940s Spain there was the same kind of gap between rhetoric and reality. The country was exhausted by three years of civil war: many people were near starvation, there were a million dead, half a million people in exile and as many in jail, a corrupt centralised economy and a thriving black market. General Franco had come to power in Spain largely thanks to financial and military assistance from Nazi Germany and Fascist Italy, and the debt had not yet been repaid. In the world war Franco was expected to support those who had helped him to power, as well as supplying iron and tungsten/wolfram, copper, lead, pyrites and zinc for their military industries. On 27 March 1939 Franco joined the Anti-Comintern Pact and four days later signed a Treaty of Friendship with Germany. His speech in León on 22 May 1939 was full of fraternal bombast about the heroic German soldiers and their great Führer. But Franco's cautious cunning (*astucia hábil*) held him back from total commitment to the Nazis in case he risked wedding his country irrevocably to the losing side. Better to send out secret feelers while waiting to see who would win 'the Battle of Britain'.

The British offered the Spanish government generous loans and shipments of Canadian bread-wheat in return for staying neutral. Churchill's new government asked Sir Samuel Hoare if he would go as ambassador extraordinary to Madrid in May 1940 with the specific remit of trying to keep the Spanish out of the war. The deputy chief of the Naval Staff, Vice Admiral Tom Phillips, reminded Hoare of the vital importance of the British naval base at Gibraltar to the control of the Mediterranean. If German U-boats could regularly set out from Spanish bases in the Canaries and Cádiz they would imperil all the Allied convoys across the Atlantic, and 'I do not know how we shall carry on.'

At this interesting moment in June 1940, Ian Fleming came to Madrid to see Captain Alan Hillgarth, the novel-writing vice consul in Mallorca whom Godfrey had appointed naval attaché in 1939. The imaginative Hillgarth was proving a great success for NID. Unlike most British naval officers, he really understood how things worked in Spain, and he retained an unusual and direct access to his friend, the British prime minister, Winston Churchill.

In one of his admirably clear reports on his role Hillgarth wrote, 'The naval attaché is not a spy and must never do any snooping. But circumstances in 1940 made it imperative for the naval attaché to engage in covert intelligence through others.' The 'circumstances' were that Franco's Spain was restocking and refuelling German navy ships and submarines in violation of its privileged neutral status. Hillgarth had to draw attention to (and plug) the most flagrant breaches without alienating the Spanish authorities. Hillgarth and his Gibraltarian assistant naval attaché, Salvador Gómez-Beare, attacked the problem from both ends of the hierarchy, getting the British ambassador to protest formally at the very top, but also leaning on the 'conscientiousness of minor officials at the harbours'.

What did Hillgarth mean by 'covert intelligence *through others*'? During the civil war, he had got to know the millionaire Juan March Ordinas, who was born in Mallorca and was said to own half of the principal Balearic island. Largely self-taught and the son of a peasant, Señor March had started out tobacco smuggling and then made a fortune from neutral Spain by doing all kinds of business with, and between, both sides in the First World War. Colonel Charles Thoroton RM, based in Gibraltar and one of Admiral Hall's best agents, won him over to work with the NID. By 1939 March was the richest man in Spain. He had his own bank, held the complete cigarette monopoly (still moving contraband tobacco where it was profitable) and controlled almost all the country's oil supplies. To some March was 'a scoundrel of the deepest dye', to others he was 'the Rockefeller of Spain'. His long life began in piracy and ended with charitable foundations, following the arc of the great tycoon who finds that nobody likes him very much in life and settles for the gratitude of posterity.

It was almost certainly through Hillgarth that this mysterious millionaire had come to London in the third week of war. When fifty-eight-year-old March arrived at the Foreign Office in London on 22 September 1939, he looked like a banker, not a buccaneer: tall, bald and stooping, with horn-rimmed spectacles above a beaky nose, and a fresh handkerchief sprouting from the top pocket of his dark, double-breasted suit. Speaking through his own interpreter, he announced that he came to offer his services to the British and French governments without remuneration. March restated that he had been of great use to the Admiralty in the First World War and said that out of respect for British institutions he now wanted once again to help Britain win the war. As chief shareholder of Trans Mediterranean Shipping Company, March said his network of agents could supply maritime intelligence, watch for German vessels and ensure that no German U-boats refuelled at Spanish ports. But March also professed himself General Franco's intimate friend, having bankrolled him from the earliest days, and so claimed all his actions would have the tacit support of the Spanish government.

The next day, March spoke to the DNI, Godfrey, and suggested that he could make life very difficult for the Germans. (Nothing was specified then, but in a letter dated 15 December 1939, Hillgarth told Godfrey that March 'has already had two German agents shot in Ibiza, though I did not ask him to do so and knew nothing about it till afterwards'.) March said he wanted to help England with intelligence but naturally also wanted to help himself by, for example, selling arms to Yugoslavia. March now proposed to buy all the German ships currently impounded in Spanish ports, fifty-five altogether, with covert British financial assistance, and use them in ways helpful to the Allied cause. The Foreign Office suspected this was just a scam, and moreover would provide the Germans with lots of hard currency. Straight after the session with Godfrey, Winston Churchill met March and immediately warmed to the old smuggler. 'This man is most important,' he minuted. Churchill wanted March to purchase those German ships and vigorously defended him. Ian Fleming was asked to work behind the scenes with his former contacts in the city, including Sir Edward Peacock, managing director of Barings Bank, to see how the thing could be managed. A Spanish company was set up to buy the ships, and then Ian Fleming had the difficult task of driving the fat docket for the transaction through the bureaucratic mill race of various ministries. In the National Archives you can still see Churchill's pugnacious comments in red ink over an acerbic letter from the minister of transport, Sir Andrew Duncan: 'Juan March was pro-German (Churchill: *Why should not he be?*) and later pro-Nazi, (Churchill: *Why not?*) and he is a clever, self-seeking rogue (Churchill: *double tick of approval*). He would certainly double-cross us if he could (Churchill: *Not certain*). He has made a lot of money (Churchill: *Why not?*) and moneymaking is his main interest (Churchill: *Quite untrue he was ready to sacrifice everything for Franco*).' Churchill concluded, 'I think we shall be nearer the mark in assuming that J. M. was a shrewd and honest patriot to Franco Spain than a self-seeking gangster.' Four days later, on 27 September 1939, Juan March met the then British Ambassador at San Sebastian, Sir Henry Chilton, who subsequently parroted the Foreign Office line, 'It would be a mistake to trust him an inch.' Fleming finally got frustrated with the misgivings of mandarins and wrote to Godfrey, 'I think we should quickly get the matter out of the docket stage and see if it will fly. Otherwise let it die. It is already half-throttled with paper.' According to Fleming's biographer Andrew Lycett, 'Ian's decisive intervention did the trick. Secret funds to buy up the German ships were released.'

Memos from Godfrey in the early months of 1940 are much concerned with March. 'I feel fairly sure that, if [Señor March] were given a *quid pro quo*, he would be able to establish at Vigo an organisation that would make the use of a port by German submarines extremely difficult, if not impossible.' Churchill personally approved another scheme cooked up with Hillgarth whereby March was the conduit for 'sweeteners' to certain Spanish generals to help keep the senior military neutral. Much of the money went through a Swiss bank in New York in US dollars. But March also supplied the local currency, pesetas, and was repaid with gold bullion in London. A post-war record from the Finance Division of HM Treasury noted:

Juan March was of service to His Majesty's Government during the war in connection with some irregular activities which were carried out in Spain. There was a need to establish a pool of pesetas to draw on for financing payments which could not be passed through normal clearing channels . . . There was also part of a debt outstanding to Juan March himself for pesetas put up by him in 1941 when a shipping company was bought on behalf of HMG – to prevent Spanish ships falling into German hands if things went wrong. To cover these needs, Juan March in 1942/43 put pesetas at the disposal of HM Embassy in Madrid in return for which gold was deposited for him in the Bank of England in the name of a Swiss company he controls, Società Financière Genova SA.

The gold was blocked for the duration of the war but afterwards March was free to export it, to sell it for sterling – for use without restriction in the sterling area – or to convert it into US dollars. The 1942 price of the gold was stated as £2 million sterling, but the real value of the deal lies in the fact that what HMG deposited was not paper money but 236,686.391 ounces of fine gold. That much bullion is worth over US$307,000,000 today.

Gold retained lasting allure for Ian Fleming, as the names and titles 'Goldeneye', *Goldfinger* and *The Man with the Golden Gun* attest. James Bond (whose surname also has a financial meaning) gets an interesting disquisition on the economic and cultural history of gold from Colonel Smithers of the Bank of England early in *Goldfinger*, originally entitled *The Richest Man in the World*. The shiny precious metal with its singular qualities is described, in an arresting and accurate phrase, as 'the talisman of fear'. In uncertain times, when paper currencies are shaky, individuals and nations buy and hoard gold. Fleming understood ordinary people's fascination with gold, and its atavistic appeal as the prime symbol of wealth. His villains desire it too, whether planning to knock off the USA's gold stocks at Fort Knox (*Goldfinger*), or demanding a hundred million pounds' worth of bullion from the prime minister as ransom for two British atom bombs (*Thunderball*).*

✄

The collapse of France in 1940 altered the wider strategy of the Second World War. The USA could no longer expect the Franco-British alliance to defeat Hitler on its own. If Britain, now isolated, were also invaded (and the US Ambassador to London Joseph Kennedy predicted that this was imminent) and if the ships of the Royal Navy ever fell into the hands of the Kriegsmarine, the USA might find itself threatened by Nazi Germany from the Atlantic and by Imperial Japan from the Pacific. And so, even though in the summer of 1940 the majority of the American people were still against involvement in a European war, the political elite began to think that it was probably in the USA's national interest to support Britain.

Now it was time for the Americans and the British to start doing deals. A fifty-seven-year-old Republican lawyer and soldier called Colonel William J. Donovan, also known as 'Wild Bill' Donovan, came over to England on a mission in the summer of 1940. Donovan was a big man and a war hero who, at the age of thirty-five, had won the Congressional Medal of Honor – the USA's 'highest award for valor in action against an enemy force' – for leading an attack in October 1918 against a strongly defended German position, rallying his men among heavy casualties and refusing to leave them when himself wounded by machine-gun bullets. Donovan had been sent to the UK by the Secretary of the US Navy, Frank Knox, former publisher of the *Chicago Daily*

---

* Fleming later named his house in Jamaica 'Goldeneye', and *GoldenEye* was the villain's weapon of mass destruction in the first Bond film with Pierce Brosnan.

News, and was accompanied by a journalist from that paper, Edgar Ansel Mowrer. Donovan and Mowrer would later write a series of articles alerting Americans to the need to be on guard against their enemies, published in a booklet with an introduction by Knox, *Fifth Column Lessons for America*.

The aim of their mission was to report back on the UK's state of morale and its defences. Would the British resist? In quest of an answer, between 19 July and 3 August 1940 Donovan saw everybody who was anybody, from the King and Queen down. It was Admiral John Godfrey, keen to encourage closer relations with America, who arranged much of Donovan's schedule of social, military and industrial visits, and everyone Donovan saw was eager to demonstrate that Ambassador Kennedy's defeatism was hopelessly wide of the mark. Donovan spent time with C, Colonel Stewart Menzies, but hit it off better with the DNI.

Donovan spent his last evening with Godfrey at his flat in Curzon Street. Godfrey, like Frank Knox, was openly in favour of closer collaboration, and argued for direct liaison between the British and American DNIs as well as British access to US consular reports from French and North African ports. The British urgently needed more destroyers, he said, as well as the US Navy's superb gyroscopically stabilised (and jealously guarded) Norden bombsight. Donovan and Mowrer carried back the message that the British had guts and spirit and the Royal Navy could hold off any seaborne invasion, but that the armed forces were in sore need of replacements for all the weapons and equipment lost in France.

In the much-publicised Lend-Lease scheme of September 1940, President Roosevelt agreed to lend Britain fifty old US destroyers in return for a ninety-nine-year lease on eight air and sea bases in Newfoundland, Bermuda, the Bahamas, Antigua, St Lucia, Jamaica, Trinidad and British Guiana, which extended the US navy's range eastwards into the Atlantic. Later the president extended the loan to more guns and ships, describing the moneyless deal, in a folksy simile for suspicious US isolationists, as being like lending a hose to a neighbour whose house was on fire.

The first US destroyers were waiting in Canadian waters to sail to Britain in early September 1940 when the RMS *Duchess of Richmond* arrived from Liverpool carrying the British crews who would man them. Hidden among the Royal Navy personnel on the *Duchess* were an unannounced group of British men in plain clothes. They were, in fact, the scientists and engineers, civilians and servicemen who made up what became known as the 'Tizard Mission' after Sir Frank Tizard, the scientist who led it. What followed between 9 September and 1 December 1940 was, according to the Canadian historian David Zimmerman, 'the most far-reaching and comprehensive technical and intellectual exchange of military secrets that had ever taken place'. The group, which included the Nobel laureate Sir John Cockcroft, boffins like E. G. Bowen from the secret research station at Bawdsey Manor near Orford Ness and serving officers with hands-on experience of technology in war, set out to share British inventions with the Americans in exchange for industrial mass production from 'the arsenal of democracy'. Initially some senior Americans were sceptical, believing the British were far too backward to have anything worthwhile to offer the high-powered USA, but others were keen to learn practical lessons from the Brits about the way vessels, vehicles, weapons and technical kit stood up in actual combat.

British technicians revealed all their advances in sonar and radar. This made the Americans sit up and listen. Both technologies essentially work on the principle of echolocation. This means sending out a sound wave through water, or a radio wave through space, and then locating, through a signal on a screen like a cathode ray tube, the moving target that the pulse bounces back from – perhaps a submarine under water, a ship on the horizon or an aeroplane in the sky. A series of tall transmitting and receiving radio aerials had been set up in the UK for air defence. By the outbreak of war this chain of nineteen stations, known as 'Chain Home', covered the air space facing Europe from the Orkneys to the Isle of Wight and was able to detect aircraft up to an altitude of 15,000 feet and 140 miles away. Even before Chain Home was fully effective, the Royal Air Force Fighter Command began adapting their tactics to this new technology, using a network of landlines specially laid by the Post Office. The ground-controlled interception system (GCI) took continuous plot and track data from the radar stations and passed the information on to the RAF Operations Room HQ at Bentley Priory, where women from the Women's Auxiliary Air Force (WAAFs) in headphones converted it into visual form by pushing little model aeroplanes with croupier rakes over the grid squares of large map tables of the UK. Staff viewing from above guided the response from the nearest air station. It was partly thanks to radar and the GCI system that the Hurricanes and Spitfires of sixty-eight RAF fighter squadrons won the Battle of Britain in summer 1940.

The Royal Navy, however, needed smaller radar equipment to fit on ships and compact aerials suitable for masts. In order to detect tiny targets like submarine periscopes sticking out above the waves or low-flying aircraft, they also required shorter electromagnetic wavelengths than current technology could achieve. (Radio waves have a shorter wavelength, or gap between successive crests of waves, than light waves, which can be up to 20,000 metres apart. Radio broadcast long waves are around 1,000 metres apart, medium waves 100 metres and short waves about 10 metres, while the wave lengths of television go down to single figure in metres.) What was needed for advanced radar was a narrow pencil beam of pulses that could radiate and reflect without picking up a lot of random clutter. This required wavelengths only centimetres apart, but at that time there were no vacuum valves powerful enough to concentrate the pulses and pick up an echo from very small targets. The answer to the problem came from Professor Marcus

Oliphant's Physics Laboratory at Birmingham University where Dr John Randall and Harry Boot developed early in 1940 a new kind of cylindrical valve called a resonant cavity magnetron. This fist-sized device used a magnetic rather an electric field to spin electrons around a cathode, producing the oscillations of a high-frequency radio field in eight resonating chambers or cavities, which then generated pulses of microwaves around ten centimetres apart.

When it was demonstrated to them in September 1940, the Americans were astonished by the transmission power of the small cavity magnetron because it was a hundred times more powerful than their very best thermionic vacuum valve, the klystron tube. This device heralded a microwave revolution that would transform the war effort. Most of the military technology that came to America with the Tizard Mission was divided up among the three armed services, but because nobody had foreseen this particular development in electronics, it was scooped up by Vannevar Bush's new scientific agency, the National Defense Research Committee (NDRC). The NDRC could subcontract research and development work to civilians in universities and corporations, so microwave applications were worked on by the best minds of MIT (Massachusetts Institute of Technology) and Bell Telephone Laboratories.

Lord Lothian's original aide-memoire to President Roosevelt on 9 July 1940, suggesting an 'interchange of secret and technical information . . . particularly in the ultra short wave radio field', had also hoped 'to employ the full resources of the radio industry' in the USA, and this is exactly what happened. Microwave radar sets, producing a sharp beam from a small aerial, now started to be produced in quantity for British and American ships and planes. Airborne Interceptor (AI) radar and an improved Air to Surface Vessel (ASV) radar gave new eyes to aircraft, and the IFF (Identification Friend or Foe) system installed in all planes made pilots less likely to be shot down by their own side in a so-called 'blue-on-blue' incident. On ships, naval-type 281 radar sets could now warn of approaching aircraft, and U-boats would no longer be able to escape submarine sonar at night by hovering on or just below the surface (where the signal was noisy with clutter), because 10-centimetre radars enabled ships to detect submarines on the surface at night, even if they were four miles away. Microwave radar could also be used to help guide artillery, from monstrous 15-inch naval guns to smaller anti-aircraft cannons like the 40-mm Bofors gun, which the Americans took to enthusiastically. Both the US army and the US navy, themselves ferocious rivals, were extremely pleased with what the Brits of the Tizard Mission brought.

The British had other electronic breakthroughs to explain and share. Britain's long expertise in radio manufacture and the government's establishment of the Communication Valves Development agency in 1939 had enabled Marconi-Osram Valve to produce a subminiature electronic valve that was rugged enough to withstand being shot from the barrel of a quick-firing anti-aircraft gun. The CV122 could be fitted inside the nose cone of a 3.7-inch shell, because it was about the size of a .380 revolver cartridge, a little over an inch long. This cylindrical glass proximity fuse was in essence a tiny radar set transmitting and receiving pulses, with the body of the shell acting as its aerial. When its receiver/amplifier got back a large enough signal from a nearby metal target, it triggered the thyratron or 'gateway' valve, which discharged a capacitor to detonate the shell's explosive. No longer did the ack-ack gunner have to achieve a direct hit: misses could also wing a bird. The Americans went on to produce twenty million proximity fuses, enabling British anti-aircraft batteries to shoot down 79 per cent of the V-1 rockets they engaged in 1944, and the US Navy to down so many enemy aircraft in 1945 that the Japanese were forced into kamikaze suicide tactics.

The British mission to the USA had been a great success, and proved once again the validity of Churchill's observation of the importance of technological and scientific know-how and industrial production to the waging of world war. As important, perhaps, as the technical exchange was the beginning of British and American collaboration in the secret world of signals intelligence, which began at the time of the Tizard exchange and has lasted until today. The FBI had enquired about sharing information on the communications of German agents in July 1940, but the first major suggestion for a cryptanalytical partnership was made on 31 August 1940, when General George Strong of the US army proposed 'a free exchange of intelligence'. On 5 September 1940 Strong cabled the US chief of staff, George Marshall, from London: 'Are you prepared to exchange full information on German, Italian and Japanese code and cryptographic information?' On 11 September 1940 Secretary of War Henry Stimson approved the sharing of 'cryptanalytic information' with the British. The first official American visit to GC&CS, the Sinkov mission, took place in February 1941.

The vital importance of America's economic might is encoded in the very first James Bond novel, *Casino Royale* (1953). James Bond and René Mathis, representing the *entente cordiale* of British and French Intelligence, are confronting the gangster Le Chiffre over the 'battlefield' of the green baize baccarat table. Le Chiffre (whose name means 'Cipher') is a former displaced person with murky Nazi/Soviet antecedents. At the moment of crisis, when Bond is 'beaten and cleaned out' by the turn of a card and sits, 'silent, frozen with defeat' at the start of chapter 12, a squat anonymous envelope arrives for him, 'as thick as a dictionary'. The wads of banknotes that rescue Bond come with a message in ink: 'Marshall Aid. Thirty-two million francs. With the compliments of the USA.' The money comes from 'the CIA chap from Fontainebleau', Felix Leiter, whose name means 'Happy Leader'. Fleming could give no clearer nod of gratitude to the Americans who helped save Europe.

N

In 1940 Spain and Gibraltar were a continuing concern. The Germans had a plan, ISABELLA-FELIX, to thrust through Spain and seize Gibraltar in order to choke off the Western Mediterranean. The Rock of Gibraltar was the only toehold that the Allies had on the continent of Europe, and if it fell, Churchill intended to retaliate by taking Spain's Canary Islands with an aircraft carrier full of planes and 10,000 Royal Marines and commandos. If the Germans attacked peninsular Spain, the Royal Navy had plans to escort Spanish shipping to North African ports, and there would be sabotage operations on land. Many of the preparations to counter FELIX came under the code name GOLDEN EYE, and the docket on the subject became one of Ian Fleming's babies at the NID.

Spain, where the first indigenous 'guerrillas' had fought on the same side as Wellington's regular soldiers in the Napoleonic wars, was full of spies in the 1940s. SIS had helped set up MI9, the escape and evasion network which ran underground 'lines' in and out of Spain, including the 'Pat O'Leary' route across the Pyrenees from Marseilles to Barcelona, Madrid and then down to Gibraltar. The 'Comète' route, further west, used old Basque smuggling trails to move a new kind of contraband: persecuted Jews, shot-down airmen, abandoned soldiers, escaped prisoners of war. On the Rock of Gibraltar itself, MI5 regularly photographed and kept files on the short-haired, fit-looking Europeans in plain clothes and their Spanish subagents in Algeciras and Tangier who were zealously poking around Gibraltar's defences, docks and airfields and monitoring all ship movements through the Straits. In Madrid the counter-espionage section of SIS, section V, kept close tabs on all German secret agents passing through Spain, using information from Bletchley Park decrypts. Kenneth Benton, the intelligence officer in charge of the Madrid SIS office, used the network of twenty-two British consuls, vice consuls and their assistants around Spain to obtain all ship, train and aeroplane passenger lists. It seems likely that no German agent ever got from

Iberia to the UK undetected, and many others were taken off transatlantic liners at Bermuda before they could get to the USA.

Admiral Wilhelm Canaris, head of the German armed forces foreign intelligence service, the Abwehr, and another friend of the entrepreneur Juan March, spoke good Spanish from his time in South America and running agents in Spain in the First World War. His Abwehr branch in Madrid was the biggest outside Germany. Canaris led the first German military team to Algeciras in July 1940 to study the Rock's defences and to plan the FELIX assault which grew in the end to involve 65,000 men, 210 big guns and fleets of dive-bombers. In September 1940 Luftwaffe General Wolfram Freiherr von Richthofen flew to Spain to urge Franco to join in the attack on Gibraltar. They knew each other of old: von Richthofen's Condor Legion had fire-bombed Guernica and many other towns on Franco's behalf during the Spanish Civil War. The Nazis had their feet under the table in Franco's Spain. The Gestapo's man, Paul Winzer, had been in place since 1936 and stayed there till his death in a Lufthansa plane crash in 1944. Everybody kept an eye on the opposition: Winzer's deputy lived in the flat underneath the Bentons' in Madrid. Winzer's boss, SS chief Heinrich Himmler, visited Spain a few days before Franco's encounter with Hitler in October 1940. He enjoyed junkets and hunting parties but his real purpose was to ensure German and Spanish police collaborated in counter-espionage and the capture of anti-Nazis. Subsequently the Franco regime drew up a list of 6,000 Spanish Jews to give to the Gestapo if Spain fully joined the Axis alliance.

General Franco came to meet Adolf Hitler at the railway station in Hendaye, the most south-westerly town in France, just across the river frontier from Spain, on 23 October 1940.*

---

* The newsreel footage of Caudillo meeting Führer is reminiscent of the scene in Charlie Chaplin's contemporaneous film *The Great Dictator* where Benzo Napaloni and Adenoid Hynkel comically cannot quite synchronise their handshakes and fascist salutes.

Admiral Canaris had given advance warning that the German leader would be disillusioned by meeting the Spanish one, who was 'not a hero but a pipsqueak'. Franco looked tubby and complacent in his legionnaire's uniform, sporting a cap with a silly tassel. After inspecting a deplorable Spanish Guard of Honour with rusty rifles, the two dictators mounted Hitler's private armoured train, *Amerika*, for talks which were completely at cross-purposes.

As Paul Preston has shown, Franco later repackaged his only meeting with Hitler for Allied consumption, portraying himself as a noble patriot standing up to a threatening megalomaniac, single-handedly preventing the Nazi invasion of Spain. In fact Franco overplayed his hand with Hitler. Drunk with power and convinced that he and Hitler saw eye to eye, Franco demanded a Spanish empire in North Africa as his price for joining in the war. This 1,700-mile arc, embracing the entire coastline of north-west Africa from south of Spanish Sahara as far east as Oran, would have meant ceding all French Morocco and a chunk of French Algeria to Spain. Franco also asked for all French Cameroon, as well as more supplies of foodstuffs, fuel and armaments.

Hitler had to endure nearly nine hours of the 'Latin charlatan', as he called him, whose reedy voice sounded like a muezzin wailing in a minaret. Hitler later told Mussolini that he would rather have 'three or four teeth pulled' than go through it again. Hitler's special train was soon travelling back through France for another meeting with Marshal Pétain; keeping Vichy France sweet was more important than humouring Franco. Frustration with Franco's 'greed and obstinacy' (the phrase is Trevor-Roper's) prompted Hitler's War Directive No. 18, issued on 12 November 1940, three weeks after Hendaye. This proposed the exact opposite of the deal Franco wanted: Vichy France was to secure all its African possessions and Germany would invade Spain early in 1941, moving south from France to capture Gibraltar in a swift four-week campaign.

According to Alan Hillgarth, however, 'If that happened (and

Juan March was very firm about this) the Spanish government would resist and British aid in guerrilla and denial operations would be acceptable.' So from late 1940 and through 1941, the British had to work out two different sets of plans for when the balloon went up: to assist the Spanish military with regular forces if they resisted the Germans (Operation SPRINKLER), and to blow things up and infiltrate guerrillas if the Spanish collaborated with the Germans (Operation SCONCE). SOE recruited a mixed bunch of fifty Spanish-speakers and trained them at Camusdarach, ten miles from Inverailort, 'to interfere with German communications' in northern Spain.*

The British officers who trained in Scotland as area commanders for guerrilla and sabotage work in Spain arrived in Gibraltar disguised as Royal Engineers, while another 250 sappers and pioneers were prepared to start demolitions of Spanish oil facilities, ports, cranes, road bridges, and so on.

Early in 1941 Ian Fleming flew to Lisbon and Madrid and then travelled by road down to Gibraltar. For his journey south through Spanish territory, he was issued with an elaborate 'courier's passport', valid for a journey to Gibraltar and return to Madrid dated 16 February 1941. (This single-page document sold for £15,525 at Sotheby's early in 2000.) Fleming spent a week touching base with all the naval, military and intelligence people he needed to see in Gibraltar. The limestone Rock was a hive of amazing secret tunnelling activity, building underground

---

*   One participant was the exiled medical doctor E. Martínez Alonso, who had helped the British embassy in Madrid smuggle Axis escapees to Portugal. *Adventures of a Doctor* (1962) mentions his time training on Scottish moors at night on operations 'to teach us to blow up things, kill the enemy from behind with knives, hand grenades, Tommy guns, traps, kicks on the most delicate parts of a man's anatomy, and other disgusting manoeuvres . . .' See also *La clave Embassy* (2010) by his daughter Patricia Martínez de Vicente.

supply and ammunition dumps, offices and workshops, including Eisenhower's future headquarters. There were nearly thirty miles of tunnels and caves you could drive vehicles into, and the extracted rubble was used to extend the aerodrome into the sea, so it could take up to 600 aircraft.

One of the most extraordinary schemes devised by Admiral John Godfrey, was Operation TRACER. If the Germans ever occupied Gibraltar, half a dozen naval men (two doctors, three signallers and an executive officer) were to be left behind, walled up in a cave high in the southern ridge of the Rock, with 10,000 gallons of water and enough supplies for a year. They would spot ships and planes from tiny windows and radio the information out to the Admiralty via an eighteen-foot aerial. (Vigorous bicycling was needed to recharge the battery of a transmitter and receiver selected and approved by the heads of naval and SIS secret communications.) Great attention was paid to the calibre and stamina of the stay-behind party who would have to live cheek-by-jowl in a chamber forty-five feet by sixteen feet by eight feet. Surgeon Commander George Murray Levick, who had survived an Antarctic winter in an ice cave, advised on the psychology and physiology of confinement. There was no way out: anyone who died would be embalmed and cemented into a tomb in the wall. Godfrey believed such hidden cells should also be set up in Malta, Aden, Trincomalee and Colombo.*

On Monday 24 February 1941 an RAF Short Sunderland flying boat touched down in Gibraltar harbour bringing the American Colonel William J. Donovan on the last stages of his second journey to Europe on behalf of the US government. This time his brief was to investigate fully the scope of 'the economic, political

---

* In Ian Fleming's short story 'From a View to a Kill' (1960) the assassins' hideout, which was dug underground by 'gypsies' in the forest of Saint-Germain, is elaborately camouflaged with brambles and briars to look wholly natural.

and military standpoint of the Mediterranean area' and report back to President Roosevelt. He had left the USA on 6 December 1940 and would not return home until mid-March 1941. In London he had seen Winston Churchill and been given SIS funding and Lieutenant Colonel Vivian Dykes from the Cabinet secretariat as his escort and factotum for the trip. Together Donovan and Dykes visited Greece, Bulgaria, Yugoslavia, Albania, Turkey, Cyprus, Palestine, Iraq, Egypt, Libya, Malta, Gibraltar, Spain, Portugal and Ireland, saw kings and prime ministers, dictators and diplomats, soldiers and spies. Donovan was very interested in commandos, the SAS, the Long Range Desert Group and all the British organisations waging unconventional warfare or gathering intelligence.

That Monday the two men lodged at Government House in Gibraltar. Because Donovan needed a minor procedure for a cyst inside his eyelid, he stayed in bed and missed dinner with Captain Alan Hillgarth and Commander Ian Fleming. The next day, the party set off in two cars for Madrid. In his diary for Tuesday 25 February 1941 Vivian Dykes recorded: 'I sat with Ian Fleming much of the way. He is a brother of Peter Fleming and was on Reuter's staff before the war. He told me some interesting experiences as a Reuter's man and was a bit inclined to knock it back too much.' Donovan tried to secure a meeting with Franco by indirectly suggesting the USA might be able to offer economic aid. This did not happen, but Donovan had several meetings with Sir Samuel Hoare in which the British ambassador emphasised that American economic aid to Spain would be a powerful way of 'undermin[ing] German influence'. Then Donovan flew on to Lisbon to try to get the same message across to the Portuguese dictator Salazar.

At this stage, the real possibility of a Nazi invasion of Spain meant that the fledgling SOE, then known as SO2 and originally the sabotage section of SIS, were sending many people to Iberia, some of whom were intriguing with the Left in Spain. Hoare, however, was always anxious that the British should observe the proprieties of living in a neutral state so as to protect the embassy and Foreign Office from embarrassment. Hoare, though he came from SIS, was no longer keen on the spying business and, like most people of SIS extraction, was even more alarmed by SOE sabotage. Alan Hillgarth was also worried by the 'dangerous amateurish activities' of SOE. Vivian Dykes records a conversation in the car with Ian Fleming back in February, which makes it clear that Fleming thought SIS and SOE were on a collision course: 'He [Fleming] agrees "C" [head of SIS] and S.O.2 are a pretty fair crash-out.'

Fleming himself was the sort of man who liked action, which must have made it hard for him to accept the need for quiet diplomacy. Dykes had noted that he liked to 'knock it back too much' – drink a lot – and the next time Fleming was back in the region in July 1941, he got trumpeting drunk in Tangier with the NID agent H. L. Greenleaves. Catching the active spirit of the BBC's recently started 'V for Victory' campaign and ignoring Hoare's anxious desire for caution, they marked out a giant V-sign in the sand of the bullring.*

In 1942 SIS and the Admiralty discovered that the Germans were secretly installing infra-red bolometers or 'Bodden beams' either side of the straits of Gibraltar. This would enable German technicians to detect and measure the size of all ships passing through the straits, by day or night, by the heat signature of their funnels. NID's Room 39 produced a full report on these German observation posts in March 1942, and according to Donald McLachlan, some in the Admiralty favoured immediate Commando raids to blow them up. Ian Fleming 'played a leading part' in pressing for direct action to stop what he called the Germans' 'detailed and deadly watch' on shipping. Godfrey seems

---

* So says Andrew Lycett, but an earlier biographer, John Pearson, says the symbol was on the international airstrip.

to have backed him. But once again those pressing for commando raids were 'bridled and delayed', and the diplomatic route was taken. In May 1942 in a face-to-face interview with Generalísimo Franco that lasted more than an hour, Sir Samuel Hoare began presenting detailed evidence of Spanish military collusion in the infra-red scheme. This finally embarrassed Franco into telling the German Admiral Canaris to close the electronic operation down. The beams were dismantled by October 1942, before the Allied TORCH landings in North Africa, though vigorous spying continued. This was yet another occasion when deals rather than direct action won the day, but it left Ian Fleming straining at the leash.

6

The Commandos Get Cracking

'Wars are not won by evacuations,' the Prime Minister had growled on 4 June 1940. The collapse of the French Republic, the terrible defeat of its army – 90,000 killed, 200,000 wounded, 1,900,000 missing or captured – and the narrow escape of the British Expeditionary Forces in the debacles of France and Norway shook up UK military thinking. Two days later, to regain the offensive, Churchill authorised the founding of the Commandos, what he called 'butcher-and-bolt' 'Striking Companies' made up of 'specially trained troops of the hunter class, who can develop a reign of terror down these coasts'. He hoped they might also boost British morale after 'colossal military disaster'.

Churchill's Commandos were initially drawn from Colin Gubbins's Independent Companies back from Norway and from other army volunteers for 'hazardous service'. Their first two amphibious raids were near Boulogne on 24 June and against German-occupied Guernsey on 14 July 1940. The aggressive symbolism of these attacks was much greater than their effectiveness. One participant in the Channel Island raid described it as 'a ridiculous, almost a comic, failure'. Three men who had lied about their swimming ability had to be left behind to become prisoners of war because they could not swim back to their boats. Churchill said, 'Let there be no more silly fiascos,' and on 17 July 1940 appointed his old and admired friend Admiral Sir Roger Keyes, the Tory MP for Portsmouth, as Director of Combined (meaning 'amphibious') Operations. Keyes took his small staff out of the Admiralty, set up headquarters for Combined Operations (COHQ) in grander offices at 1A Richmond Terrace, directly across Whitehall from Downing Street, and thought himself answerable only to the PM.

Churchill had a soft spot for the aggressive old sailor primarily because Keyes retained a loyal belief that Churchill's bold but disastrous scheme for the forcing of the Dardanelles in 1915 could have worked. Moreover, Keyes had led the daring Zeebrugge Raid on St George's Day 1918, and his intervention in the House of Commons (in full naval uniform) had helped bring down Neville Chamberlain in May 1940. On appointment as prime minister, Churchill had straightaway sent Keyes as special liaison officer to King Leopold in Belgium,* where, in the Blitzkrieg in 1940, the old salt discovered that 'the German modern war machine' was better equipped and more unified than the British.

July 1940 was a key month in Britain's reorganisation for total war. Two days after Keyes's appointment, Army Order 112 formally authorised the British army's Intelligence Corps, which set up its depot in Oxford University. On the same day, 19 July, the Cabinet established another new organisation, SOE, 'to co-ordinate all action, by way of subversion and sabotage, against the enemy overseas'. 'And now, set Europe ablaze!' Churchill told them.

Ian Fleming felt the effects of this reorganisation because of his key role in 'NID 17', the section set up by Admiral John Godfrey at the NID early in 1940 'to co-ordinate intelligence' internally and to liaise between NID and other intelligence bodies. As well as his daily job as Godfrey's personal assistant, his responsibilities for JIC work and the daily NID situation reports, Fleming now had to keep in touch both with C and with SOE.

SOE, as the bastard child of the SIS, never succeeded in wholly freeing itself from the constraints of its parent, as was evident in Spain. Though a lot of SOE staff came from the ranks of the SIS, the heads of the two organisations couldn't stand each other. The

---

* 'Silly old Roger Keyes', 'stupid, sentimental and quite inarticulate', infuriated clever Alec Cadogan of the Foreign Office. The mandarin raged in his diary: 'Why use these ridiculous unofficial busybody "emissaries"? They don't know the background, so they don't understand and they can't report correctly because they're not trained to it.'

smooth courtier Colonel Stewart Menzies, who had become C in the autumn of 1939, hated the highland warrior Brigadier Colin Gubbins, head of SOE, and the feeling was mutual. This helped to poison the relations of organisations whose field aims already conflicted. Spies (SIS) needed peace and quiet, but saboteurs (SOE) wanted noisy explosions.

Menzies's deputy, Claude Dansey, was the SIS liaison with SOE, and sat and read all SOE's wireless traffic at a desk at 64 Baker Street. Dansey and Menzies set the rules that bound SOE, as well as their codes and ciphers. Intelligence produced by SOE had to be passed directly to SIS rather than being shared between its own country sections. There was always a great shortage of RAF planes for inserting and extracting agents, but in any clash, SIS had absolute priority. Ian Fleming's social skills were useful amid such hostility. He was good at watertight compartments, could keep friends apart, separate his head from his heart, be discreet if need be, or gossip when he wanted.

Fleming was still making regular visits to Bletchley Park, where the British code-breakers were finding German naval Enigma codes difficult to crack. Frank Birch, head of Bletchley Park's Naval Section, passed on to Admiral Godfrey Hut 8's view that 'a successful pinch of a month's keys with all appurtenances (such as bigram tables) offered the best chance . . .'. Accordingly, Godfrey sent Ian Fleming to talk to Dilly Knox.

Nigel West has asserted that 'Ian Fleming was almost certainly never indoctrinated into the valuable cryptographic source distributed as ULTRA during his wartime service in the NID'. But it is scarcely credible that Ian Fleming, as personal assistant to the DNI throughout the war, liaising with C and regularly visiting Bletchley Park to talk to Knox, did not know at least in outline what was going on in the code-breaking field. He learned from Knox that the acquisition of the final wheel VIII in August 1940 meant there was no need to pinch actual Enigma machines, but the paperwork was still urgently required: the books, pads and sheets with the monthly keys that indicated the complicated daily settings of the machine.

Fleming now had another of his imaginative brainwaves. The German navy had fast motor torpedo boats called *Schnellboote* whose duties included air-sea rescue, working in conjunction with the Luftwaffe. Fleming reckoned that if they could capture one of those S-boats intact they would find the keys to the Enigma settings. On 12 September 1940 he minuted Godfrey:

I suggest we obtain the loot by the following means: 1. Obtain from the Air Ministry an airworthy German bomber (they have some). 2. Pick a tough crew of five, including a pilot, W/T operator and word-perfect German speaker. Dress them in German Air Force uniform, add blood and bandages to suit. 3. Crash plane in the Channel after making SOS to rescue service in P/L [plain language]. 4. Once aboard rescue boat, shoot German crew, dump overboard, bring rescue boat to English port.

The memo was circulated in NID; Rear Admiral J. W. Clayton of the OIC saw 'a chance to get what we want' and so Fleming elaborated his plan. The fake German bomber was to take off before dawn on the tail of a big raid on London (the Blitz had started on 7 September 1940), cut out one engine, lose height with smoke pouring from a firework in the tail, send a distress signal and then pancake into the sea in a grid square patrolled by a single German boat. The equally fake crew would sink their plane and take to a rubber life-raft. Once rescued by the *Schnellboot* from the sea they would overpower the crew and make for England. Fleming added a story in case they were caught: 'It was done for a lark by a group of young hot-heads who thought the war was too tame and wanted to have a go at the Germans. They had stolen the plane and equipment and had expected to get into trouble when they got back.'

Perhaps it was the notion of killing their Good Samaritan rescuers that gave the operation its code name: RUTHLESS. Frank

Birch, with his background in theatre, thought it was a 'very ingenious plot', with 'the enormous advantage of not giving anything away if it fails'. He entered into it enthusiastically, supplying a three-page memorandum on the signals, markings and activities of all the German naval units in the Channel. Admiral Godfrey pulled strings with Lord Beaverbrook, the Minister of Aircraft Production, to get hold of a Heinkel-111 bomber that had been shot down near Edinburgh and repaired at Farnborough. The plane had to have its perspex nose strengthened lest it collapse on crashing into the water and drown the crew. The Air Ministry cooperated, providing authentic captured German flying kit from an RAF store hangar. Fleming volunteered himself as the German speaker in the mission but was turned down. He still went with his group to await events in Dover, and on the way visited his brother Peter who was organising the covert Auxiliary Units of the Home Guard for guerrilla warfare and sabotage in Kent.

But two RAF Coastal Command reconnaissance flights and careful listening by the Y service revealed no suitable German *Schnellboot* in the Channel or North Sea. On 16 October, Operation RUTHLESS was postponed; Vice Admiral Dover suggested they try nearer Portsmouth. The Bletchley Park Naval Section codebreakers were bitterly disappointed, and Birch wrote to Callaghan of NID on 20 October:

[Alan] Turing and [Peter] Twinn came to me like undertakers cheated of a nice corpse two days ago, all in a stew about the cancellation of *Operation Ruthless*. The burden of their song was the importance of a pinch ... if they got a pinch – even enough to give a clue to deciphering one day's material, they could be pretty sure, after an initial delay, of keeping going from day to day from then on; nearly up-to-date if not quite, because the level of traffic now is so much higher and because the machinery has been so much improved. The 'initial delay' would be in proportion to the pinch. If the whole bag of tricks was pinched, there'd be no delay at all.

N

The kind of men Ian Fleming wanted for Operation RUTHLESS were the kind of men who were joining the new Commandos – active, self-reliant soldiers who would not shirk danger. Such infantrymen were an elite, hand-picked from volunteers from all fighting units and support services who responded to the call for men up for 'special service' or 'hazardous work'. They had to be able to swim and drive, be ready to parachute and not suffer from seasickness.

Churchill at first wanted 5,000 men for small-scale, hit-and-run amphibious operations against the Germans along the coastline of occupied Europe. But the Commando selection process always started with one man, an experienced warrior who could became the chieftain of a small band. One example was a vigorous rugger-playing, pig-sticking gunner called Captain John Durnford-Slater, who was made a Lieutenant Colonel and told to raise 500 men from across Southern Command. His new 'No. 3 Commando' had to be ready to operate in a fortnight.

Durnford-Slater set off on 28 June 1940. First he travelled to his region's headquarter towns, giving ten-minute interviews to officer volunteers with a view to picking some thirty-five first-class leaders. 'I wanted cheerful officers, not groaners. A good physique was important, but size was not. I looked for intelligence and keenness.' He checked their service records and rang their previous civilian employers, always looking for signs of success and initiative. The ten best he made troop leaders with the rank of captain, then sent them out in teams of three to look for Other Ranks. 'I always avoided anyone who talked too much . . . We never enlisted anybody who looked like the tough-guy criminal type, as I considered that this sort of man would be a coward in the battle.' By 5 July 3 Commando had ten troops of fifty, each with three officers and forty-seven men.

One officer Durnford-Slater picked was jug-eared Second Lieutenant Peter Young, who had joined the Bedfordshire and Hertfordshire Regiment in 1938, survived Dunkirk and enjoyed it. (He would end the war a Commando brigadier with a DSO and three MCs.) Young was sent out with two other officers to raise H troop. They were looking for fit young men, trained in the services, not necessarily with experience of fighting, blokes with gumption who could finish a job on their own. One officer favoured bandsmen because they could already do several things at once. There were no tests, just a talk and a swift intuiting of character. About one in six was selected.

From the start commandos like these were seen as irregulars who did not require a fixed establishment. They got a ration book and special pay of 6/8d a day for men, 13/4d for officers, but they had to fund their own food, lodging and travel from that. If they saved the money by enterprise or skill, then bully for them and more for beer. Commandos did not live in army camps but were billeted in 'digs' or lodgings in private houses, where they were cosseted by landladies and tended to behave better than in barracks. Having no drill hall or gymnasium, they improvised meeting places and outdoor exercises. Some took to bicycles. The first commandos drew their weapons and equipment from stores as available, and gathered for operations that lasted less than twenty-four hours, using tip-and-run tactics. They route-marched at seven miles an hour, fully loaded. The whole idea was to train for speed, surprise and offensive spirit.

One of the men Young picked from the 5th Northamptons was Private George Herbert, who had won the MM for courage in the retreat to Dunkirk. But he was soon up in front of the colonel, with another soldier, on a charge, 'conduct to the prejudice of good order and military discipline, i.e. fighting in billets'. In a dispute over £2, Herbert had stuck a knife in the other man. Durnford-Slater thought them both decent-looking men, and without any evidence, it was one man's word against another's.

'I'll have to send you both back to your units.'

'Give us whatever punishment you think fit, but don't send us back to our units.' (Being RTU'd was the worst fate for any commando.)

Peter Young spoke well of both men's characters, and so the colonel made his Solomonic judgment:

'Well, divide the money; the next small charge against either of you and out you go.'

Herbert was still with 3 Commando four years later, as a commissioned officer. ('You owe me a pound' he used to chide his CO who was by now a friend.) Two days after D-Day, while leading a section attack in Normandy, Bren gun blazing, Lieutenant George Herbert was shot through the heart. The bullet that killed him cut the crimson and blue ribbon of his DCM.

The particular flavour of the first commandos permeates the last novel by Robert Quixano Henriques, who came from a long-anglicised Sephardic Jewish family. *The Commander*, published posthumously in 1967, opens in June 1940, after Dunkirk. David Lamego (the name surely a nod to Evelyn Waugh's character Guy Crouchback) is a brigade major in the Royal Artillery quartered in an agreeable Georgian country house. As a motor mower purrs across the large lawn outside and the brigadier complains about the lack of a butter knife, it all seems ridiculously far from the war. Lamego, a thirty-four-year-old Jew, suddenly remembers a 'neither well-phrased or succinct' official letter calling for *Volunteers for Special Service*, 'only on fighting duties which will require the best types of officers and men'.

Lamego is a physical weakling and remembers the humiliations of being a 'wormlike schoolboy'. Motivated by a desire to redeem himself, he puts his name forward. 'He became the British Jew anxious to repay the three centuries of hospitality and emancipation enjoyed by his family in Christian England – and, to be frank, to be seen doing so. He was showing off, if only to himself.' Lamego has to get the agreement of his divisional commander, who is appalled by his volunteering. 'Childish! Literally childish . . . I thought you had more sense . . . you'll get the misfits and rejects, the regular defaulters, the scruffy types of soldiers who can't take discipline, or won't.'

In London, Lamego ends up in the War Office and makes his way

to a very small room where a solitary officer, a Lieutenant-Colonel, going a bit bald, plumpish, with a pink face and sagacious if dissolute expression, sat in a tilted chair, his feet on the desk. He was reading *The Times*. 'Well, whatever next?' he said.

'Dudley!'

'None other.'

This is the real Dudley Clarke of MO9, the founder of the Commandos. They go off to the bar of the Ritz Hotel, on the corner of Green Park, and after a deal of gin and wine, Lamego persuades another officer to accept him as a troop commander. He then has ten days to 'rustle up a Troop'.

Lamego picks his first officer, Joe Ryan, at the airport in Ulster, just because he likes his looks and alert manner. With the second, an untidy, unmilitary bear of a man called Philip Pinckney from the Berkshire Yeomanry,

It was not exactly clear who was interviewing whom.

'I'd like to come, if you can do with me.'

'I can do with you.'

'In that case, there are some chaps of mine would like to come along.'

Pinckney goes outside and mutters, 'I think it's alright boys.'

Thus Lamego ends up with a curiously assorted troop, 'an organic group' of men feudally loyal to Pinckney and ready to follow him anywhere. *The Commander* may be a novel, but it brilliantly catches the improvisatory, sometimes impetuous, way in which commando units were put together, and the bonds of friendship and loyalty which linked these small, tough bands. These would be the kind of men who joined Ian Fleming's commandos, the kind who responded to Churchill's 'backs to the wall' oratory after Dunkirk:

Even though large tracts of Europe and many old and famous states have fallen or may fall into the grip of the Gestapo and all the odious apparatus of Nazi rule, we shall not flag or fail. We shall go on to the end . . . we shall defend our island whatever the cost may be, we shall fight on the beaches, we shall fight on the landing-grounds, we shall fight in the fields and in the streets, we shall fight in the hills; we shall never surrender . . .

✐

In early May 1940, just a month before that famous speech, the Scottish laird William Stirling returned home to Stirlingshire after an unsuccessful jaunt to Norway called Operation KNIFE. Bill Stirling had gone to Norway as part of a six-man MI(R) special operation team, leaving on 24 April aboard HM Submarine *Truant* and carrying arms, ammunition and explosives to supply the Norwegian resistance and to blow up bridges. Not long out into the North Sea, *Truant* set off a German magnetic mine and was forced to return. On the 27th, the MI(R) saboteurs tried again on HM Submarine *Clyde*, but this boat developed engine trouble.

Setbacks can be fruitful. The would-be sabotage party now repaired to drown their sorrows in good whisky in the Stirling ancestral home, Keir House, south of Dunblane. Guerrilla warfare was the topic of the day. At Keir they had guns, ammunition, plastic explosives with new contact switches and a 15,000-acre estate to play with. Wouldn't it make an ideal training ground for unconventional warfare? Stirling and CO Bryan Mayfield took their idea down to London, where they found it was just what MI(R) needed. As Bill Mackenzie later recorded in his history of SOE: 'The Director of Military Training's approval for a centre for guerrilla warfare training for up to 500 men was given on 9 May, and the centre opened on 3 June: instruction was first provided by the MI(R) officers who had been trained for the abortive "Knife" expedition to Norway.'

William Stirling recruited as an instructor the youngest of his three brothers, David, six feet five inches tall, a wild and reckless Second Lieutenant in the Scots Guards whose ambition before the war had been to be the first to climb Mount Everest. Andrew Croft recalled congratulating David Stirling at Inverailort on his promotion to captain, and David's insouciant reply: 'Don't bother about those pips, Andrew. There's so much brass around in this place that I put them up myself.' David Stirling later joined 8 Commando and sailed with the ad hoc formation 'Layforce' to the Middle East, where in 1941 he famously founded the SAS, or Special Air Service, as it was named by Dudley Clarke.

Bill Stirling had also recruited his cousin Shimi, whom he bumped into in White's club. Bill's mother was a Fraser, from the aristocratic Catholic Highland family. Her brother, Brigadier General Simon Joseph Fraser, the 14th Lord Lovat, had founded the famous Lovat Scouts (recruited from Highland ghillies, stalkers, shepherds and gamekeepers) who had beaten the Boer commandos at their own game. Shimi Lovat (the Stirling boys' school-fellow at Ampleforth) was now the fifteenth lord, an aggressive soldier, good with sabre and bayonet, and at a loose end in early May 1940 because he had just resigned from the Lovat Scouts after quarrelling with their inept commanding officer. Lovat lived up to the family motto of readiness, *Je Suis Prest*, and leaped at the chance to join the new training school. He reckoned that Lochaber, the traditional country of the feuding Clan Cameron, would be an even better training place for irregular warfare because it had access to the sea, and he selected Inverailort Castle as the best site. Under the draconian Emergency Powers Act (1939) the War Office requisitioned Mrs Christian Cameron-Head's family home. (She was dead by the time they paid post-war compensation.)

Situated some twenty-five miles west of Britain's highest mountain and ten miles south of Scotland's deepest loch, 'the Big House' at Inverailort stood on the south side of a sea loch, not far from Lochailort station on the spectacular final stretch of the West Highland line that would later provide a surprise introduction to the two-week irregular warfare course. Unsuspecting new officer candidates would be dozing on the last leg of their journey after a day's travel from London, rattling through the tight curves and gradients of 'the Mallaig extension'. Suddenly the steam train would screech to a halt, throwing the passengers back and forth in their blacked-out teak carriages. Thunderflashes, gunfire, urgent yells: 'Get off the train!' In a rush of adrenalin, they would have to run with all their kit down the unmade road to the big house, live rounds cracking overhead in the darkness.

Special Training Centre Inverailort became the first of a network of training schools for special forces in what is now called 'Commando Country' in Scotland. Royal Marine commandos who joined Ian Fleming's 'assault unit' would for the most part train at Achnacarry, twenty-five miles away, but the principles of commando training were first laid down at Inverailort. One of the first instructors, back from guerrilla fighting in Norway, was Quintin Riley, who would later lead 30AU. Other instructors included some remarkable eccentrics. After early-morning cold-water ablutions by the Nissen hut, the candidates would gather in the hall of the Big House. Two middle-aged officers in uniform, Captains William Ewart Fairbairn and Eric Anthony Sykes, would then appear at the top of the staircase and proceed to roll and tumble swiftly right down the stairs, emerging at the bottom in a fighting crouch with a pistol and a knife in each hand. These two officers had both served in the Shanghai police and now taught 'all-in fighting' and gruesome methods of silent killing with bare hands or impromptu weapons; they invented the double-edged, razor-sharp, 7½-inch Fairbairn-Sykes Fighting Knife, designed to pierce a sentry's thickest greatcoat or slash the toughest gizzard, which Wilkinson Sword began manufacturing in 1941 as the 'Commando dagger'. They also taught close-quarter pistol shooting at pop-up targets in the 'Mystery House' at STC Inverailort.*

---

* Such training certainly paid off for Norwegian SOE agent Knut Haugland. On 1 April 1944 a hundred Germans trapped him in the Oslo hospital where he was operating a secret radio hidden in a chimney. When eight Germans came pounding up the stairs, Haugland crouched in a dark corner and then made a dash for it. 'Two other Germans emerged, whom he shot and killed. He made his way down to the cellars where he encountered four more Germans;

George Murray Levick, who had been part of Captain Scott's fatal last expedition to Antarctica and got through the entire winter of 1911/12 living off seal and penguin in a snow cave, came out of retirement to teach the men endurance among clouds of maddening midges at Inverailort. The zoologist and writer Gavin Maxwell taught the art of walking into a room backwards so the occupants thought you were walking out. Captain Wally Walbridge, an expert with the .303 Bren, probably the best light machine-gun of the war, did weapons training. Sappers Jim Gavin and 'Mad' Mike Calvert ran demolitions and explosives, teaching students about primers, detonators, switches and fuses, mines, incendiaries and simple booby traps. Sandy Wedderburn taught rock climbing and rope work and took parties to the top of Ben Nevis. Peter Fleming visited, and his wireless equipment, safely brought back from Norway, was used to teach signals and morse code, although Fleming himself soon slipped away to help Lovat with the fieldcraft that he found more agreeable.

Shimi Lovat also features in Robert Henriques's novel. David Lamego endures the course at Inverailort in what seems like never-ending rain in the late summer of 1940. In one exercise two students are picked to play escaped prisoners of war and the rest of the group have to hunt them down. Lamego is partnered with Courtney Brocklehurst, a real-life fifty-two-year-old ex-Royal Flying Corps pilot and former game warden in the Sudan. Brocklehurst has a wild tracker's skill of freezing invisibly, whereas

one he killed, another he fired at, and two others fled. A fifth appeared and Lt Haugland shot him at 30 yards with the last shot in his magazine. He put in a fresh magazine as he emerged from the cellar down into the grounds. He was fired on as he did so, but was not hit; he scaled a 9-foot barbed wire fence and dropped 15 feet into a quiet roadway from the rocks. He took off his overalls, washed his face in the snow and walked leisurely about the streets while the Gestapo prosecuted a search of the whole neighbourhood. His look-out came through the controls in a car, picked him up and they drove quietly away. The place from which Lt Haugland transmitted in the chimney was not discovered, and the W/T set was recovered several weeks later.'

civilised Lamego is found out vainly imitating a telegraph pole. Another exercise finds Lamego retching with exhaustion on steep scree while the lordly Lovat looks back down at him and sneers 'Not exactly fit, are you Lamego?'

The Royal Navy also took part at Inverailort. Black-bearded Commander Sir Geoffrey Congreve came to lend a hand at the end of June 1940. He was eager for glory partly because his father had won the VC in South Africa and his brother Billy had died winning one in the Rifle Brigade in 1916, whereas Congreve had so far only managed to get the DSO, leading the converted fishing boats of the 16th Anti-Submarine Striking Force to Norway in April 1940. A popular figure at Lochailort, he set up a course in handling small boats, teaching raiders to get ashore and back quickly from ships and boats. It became an axiom of commando work that they should train with the actual men who were to ferry them ashore. But Congreve never did get to win his VC. While observing Operation CHESS, a tiny raid on the Pas de Calais, in the early hours of 28 July 1941, he was hit by a stray German machine-gun bullet and died in a landing craft off Ambleteuse.

A fortnight into his new job as Director of Combined Operations, sixty-eight-year-old Admiral Sir Roger Keyes came up to Scotland to watch one of the early night landing exercises on Loch Morar in early August. He looked frightful but was still game. The exercise started at one in the morning and he settled down with a flask of coffee and was soon fast asleep. At dawn the admiral awoke to find himself captured by two noiseless figures, the Polar pals Andrew Croft and Quintin Riley. 'Splendid attack!' said Keyes. Lovat thought Keyes a leader of genius:

The admiral believed in leading from the front. I have seen him in London clothes, wet to the skin, struggle to the wrong beach in a high running sea, and then call for a repeat performance. Nor did he quit until the last man was back aboard his ship; more than once I helped to change his clothes, for his feeble hands were too cold to undo hooks and buttons on a duffel coat.

Keyes brought his old friend Admiral Sir Walter Cowan out of retirement to help. 'Tich' Cowan was now sixty-nine years old and kept fit by riding to hounds in Warwickshire. Both elderly admirals could be seen in foul weather on wet beaches, shouting, 'Far too much noise, you must do it again.'

September 1940 was the month of the great panic about the planned German invasion of Britain, Operation SEELÖWE or SEA LION. In the emergency Commandos and Independent Companies were removed from Keyes and given to the commander-in-chief Home Forces to help defend the British Isles. It was a good opportunity for training. 11 Scottish Commando warned one airfield that they would raid it as an exercise between certain dates; the Home Forces defenders were issued with live ammunition. The commandos achieved their aim by deception, just like the exercise in the Lee Marvin film, *The Dirty Dozen*.

One morning a staff car drew up at the airfield's main gate and an angry major got out and berated the 'slovenly' guard. He barked out orders and they grounded their arms, which the major's batman then picked up and locked in the guardroom. A rather tall, masculine WAAF and a very butch charlady now strolled through the gates with baskets of dummy grenades, which they began chucking through office windows. Then a busload of 'workers' (armed to the teeth) also drove in. Along the perimeter, other parties of commandos snipped the wire and rolled into the defender's slit trenches, ready to machine-gun the pilots as they ran from their huts or to riddle their fighters as they took off. In half an hour the entire airfield changed hands.

Others said all this was just playing at soldiers. Guerrillas and underground resistance fighters, etc., were all very well in occupied countries, but they were irrelevant against the armoured juggernauts of the Third Reich; the established regular forces should get all the resources. An absurd decision came down from on high that the romantic South African name 'Commando' should go, to be replaced by 'Special Service Battalions' in a 'Special Service

Brigade'. But top brass had a tin ear: for most people, the lightning-flash letters 'SS' stood for Hitler's stormtroopers. The units used their famous initiative and simply carried on calling themselves 'Commandos' until authority changed its mind again in 1941.

In the spring of 1941 there were some major commando raids in the north. In March 500 commandos successfully swooped on the wintry Lofoten Islands, eighty miles west of Narvik, inside the Arctic Circle. Ostensibly this raid, Operation CLAYMORE, was driven by the Ministry of Economic Warfare's desire to destroy the Norwegian fish factories because the Germans were converting their fish oil into glycerine for munitions and vitamins for troops. There was little resistance from the German occupiers and great enthusiasm from the Norwegian fishermen who had gathered there for the cod run. The commandos cut the communications, then parties of sappers set about demolishing and burning eighteen fish-meal factories and tanks containing 800,000 gallons of fish oil, bunker fuel and petrol. Dismal photos show thick palls of choking pollution curdling and unfurling blackly from the snow-blotched islands. They sank eleven ships, capturing 216 German prisoners and 60 quislings, brought back 315 Norwegian volunteers (eight of them women in sweaters and ski pants) and rescued the English manager of Allen & Hanbury's cod liver oil plant. A randy sergeant managed to get his leg over and earned the nickname 'Thirty Kroner Jack' for what he paid the obliging woman. The commandos looted useful German kit – pistols, cameras, wristwatches, binoculars, sunglasses, jackets, boots, etc. – as well as cases of schnapps to celebrate. Signallers looked on in despair as beautifully made Siemens radio sets were smashed.

But all this was just the cover story. The real reason for the Lofoten raid, 'concerted between the NID and the GC&CS' according to Hinsley, was a covert pinch of 'the Enigma machine and its settings' from the German harbour defence vessel *Krebs*, which A. P. Mahon in his *History of Hut Eight* called 'one of the landmarks in the history of the [naval] section'. Hugh Alexander confirms in his *Cryptographic History of Work on the German Naval Enigma* that the Lofoten raid was 'planned with this end in view'.

The fight in the Vestfjord off Svolvaer early on 4 March was fast and bloody. The *Krebs,* though only an armed trawler, bravely took on the much bigger British destroyer HMS *Somali,* but three shells killed the captain and the trawler ran aground on a small island and eventually surrendered. The boarding party found a trove of cryptographic material on *Krebs,* most importantly the complete German naval Enigma 'Home Waters' keys for the month of February 1941, which in theory should have been destroyed by March. The failure to do so revealed to the British the Enigma wheel orders, settings and *Steckerverbindung* cross-pluggings for four weeks' worth of intercepted material. At last, this was the pinch that Ian Fleming's aborted Operation RUTHLESS had envisaged.

The Lofoten commando raid and the subsequent reading of naval Enigma really mattered because in the spring of 1941 the Battle of the Atlantic was entering a new and more deadly phase, with an increasing number of German submarines operating in 'wolf packs' to attack convoys from North America and ships supplying Britain with food and munitions. The war was spreading into the mid-Atlantic too, and even though new technologies like radar helped, there was a burning need to read all coded messages. As soon as the keys arrived at Bletchley Park on Wednesday 12 March 1941, Alan Turing got to work on them, reading all of February's back traffic. The keys also helped him to reconstitute the bigram tables and so read April and May's traffic more quickly.

Then Hinsley of Traffic Analysis had a brilliant idea for another pinch. Among the decrypts were messages from German weather ships. These were trawlers sent north of Iceland or into the mid-Atlantic to report conditions and help German meteorologists draw up accurate weather maps for Luftwaffe operations. Hinsley thought them an excellent target. The German 'Short Weather Cipher' condensed weather observations (time, place, barometric readings, temperatures, wind-speeds, cloud-cover, visibility) into single letters for ease and speed of transmission before the messages were encrypted using the Enigma. Hinsley reckoned that since these vessels went out for long periods they might have two months' worth of keys on board, so a pinch would be really worthwhile.

The OIC took up the idea. The Royal Navy then committed three cruisers and four of its fastest destroyers to the capture of a weather ship somewhere north-east of Iceland. The flotilla caught *München* on the afternoon of 7 May 1941. The crew managed to throw their Enigma machine and the current keys overboard in a lead-lined bag before they abandoned ship and surrendered, but Captain Jasper Haines RN came aboard the captured ship in plain clothes and, in an officer's cabin, found some dull maroon folders which contained the inner and outer Enigma settings for June 1941. It was exactly what Hinsley had been hoping for.

Two days after the successful attack on *München*, there was another crucial pinch, this time from the German submarine *U-110*, south-west of Iceland. *U-110*'s commander was Fritz-Julius Lemp, the man who had accidentally sunk the passenger-ship *Athenia* on the first day of war. Lemp had just fired three torpedoes at a merchant convoy when a British corvette from its escort group, HMS *Aubretia*, spotted the German submarine's periscope and swiftly dropped depth charges, forcing the German crew to abandon ship under fire – some were killed and wounded, others, like Kapitänleutnant Lemp, drowned. The commander of the British 3 Escort Group, Captain Joe Baker-Cresswell, knew enough history to remember the *Magdeburg* pinch in the First World War and sent a boarding party from his ship HMS *Bulldog*. Sub Lieutenant David Balme rowed over with six seamen, a stoker and a telegraphist in a wooden whaler, equipped with gas masks in the event of a chlorine leak. In a heavy swell, they clambered aboard the enemy submarine and then up the iron ladder of the shrapnel-scarred conning tower. It was a strange experience to open the alien hatches and go down into an enemy warship with its signs and notices in a foreign language, not knowing if anybody was waiting inside to kill them or if the scuttling charges were about to blow them all to kingdom come. The humming sub was lit up but eerily deserted, an abandoned chaos of unmade beds, unfinished meals, scattered possessions. Down below the waterline, it was disconcerting to hear the clangorous thud, thud, thud of British depth-charges vibrating violently through the hull as destroyers tried to bomb the other U-boat they thought was lurking nearby. Balme started gathering books, charts and papers while Long the telegraphist began dismantling signal equipment, including what seemed to be an electric typewriter in a box. The sailors formed a line to shovel the stuff up the conning tower and into the boat. Once again the British were amazed at the craftsmanship that had gone into the U-boat and the quality of German navy kit: sextants and Zeiss binoculars, leather clothing and boots, tinned food, beer, cigars and cigarettes. Over several hours they stripped the U-boat of everything removable.*

Back at Scapa Flow in the Orkneys, Lieutenant Allon Bacon from the OIC was on hand to dry and sift the papers from the drowned submarine, take them down to London and deliver them triumphantly to Bletchley Park, waving them over his head as he carried them into Hinsley's office at Hut 4.

Captain S. W. Roskill RN, the official historian of the war at sea, tells the story of *U-110* in his 1959 book, *The Secret Capture*. Although he indicates the Admiralty's delight at their seizure, he

---

* Able Seaman Arnold Hargreaves, one of the eight who went aboard *U-110* with David Balme, told me when I met him by chance at Bletchley Park in 2009 how he dumped a bag of souvenirs on a mess-room table for his lower-deck shipmates to pick over.

is reticent about the contents of the two large packing cases in Captain Baker-Cresswell's cabin because, at the time of writing, signals intelligence was still a taboo topic. Admiral Godfrey told Sir Dudley Pound that their haul included a complete Enigma machine with rotors and various important keys, and Pound cabled, 'The petals of your flower are of rare beauty.' Bletchley Park would now be able to read German officer-only or *Offizier* messages, which had a further layer of encryption and often contained special information about changes to Enigma procedures. Together, the *München* and *U-110* pinches reduced the decryption of enemy intercepts from days to hours.

At the end of June the Royal Navy sent another flotilla of four warships out to the far North Atlantic and seized another weather ship, the *Lauenberg,* east of Jan Mayen Island. This time Lieutenant Allon Bacon was with the flotilla, and found among the *Lauenberg*'s papers the Enigma plug-board connections and inner ring settings for August 1941. Bacon got them back to Bletchley Park in three and a half days flat.

Information came from captured prisoners as well as captured documents, some via direct face-to-face interrogation and some via the secret bugging of the rooms where high-ranking or important German prisoners met, followed by transcription and translation of their conversations.*

In June or July 1941 Ian Fleming and two other NID officers,

---

* In *From Russia With Love* Bond imagines what will happen to the Soviet defector Tatiana Romanova: 'Probably at Dover she would be taken away to "The Cage", that well-sentried private house near Guildford, where she would be put in a comfortable but oh so well-wired room. And the efficient men in plain clothes would come one by one and sit and talk with her, and the recorder would spin in the room below and the records would be transcribed and sifted for their grains of new fact – and, of course, for the contradictions they would trap her into.'

Eddie Croghan and Dick Wetherby, took a pair of captured German sailors out to dinner at A L'Ecu de France in Jermyn Street, London, and then on to an MI5 safe house near Sloane Square full of listening devices. The two Germans were Burkard Baron von Müllenheim-Rechberg, third gunnery officer on the battle-cruiser *Bismarck*, who had survived its sinking on 27 May 1941, and Hans Joachim Eichelborn, the chief engineering officer of *U-110*, which sank after the pinch by HMS *Bulldog* on 9 May. The interrogator Ralph Izzard later told John Pearson: 'The idea behind "mating" Rechberg with a U-boat engineer officer was as they both came from different branches of the navy they would be inquisitive about each other's experiences and thus talk usefully in a "bugged" cell.' Alas, in the event, everybody got very drunk and talked rubbish rather than secrets.

Ralph Izzard was last seen on page 53 of this book hiding in a lavatory at Venlo. He was in fact a first-rate foreign correspondent who spoke fluent German because his father, the *Daily Mail*'s gardening correspondent Percy Izzard, had got him a job as the tea boy in the *Mail*'s Berlin office in 1931, two years before Hitler became chancellor. Izzard rose to head of bureau and witnessed the rise of the Nazi state. Because his first wife was the daughter of a Prussian general, Izzard had some difficulty enlisting in the British forces. Eventually he managed to join the navy as a 'Hostilities Only' ordinary seaman in 1940, and manned an Oerlikon gun on merchant vessels crossing the Atlantic. Probably on the advice of Sefton Delmer, who knew Izzard when he was Berlin correspondent on the rival *Daily Express*, Ian Fleming plucked Izzard off the deck and into Naval Intelligence, where he would write the official history of the sinking of the *Bismarck* and specialise in interrogating captured U-boat crewmen.

The philosophy of the pinch was not confined to the British, and neither was the use of commandos. The enemy was making strides in these areas too. In the summer of 1941 Admiral Godfrey was interested to learn that when the Germans were on the offensive, the head of the Abwehr, Admiral Canaris, had 'reconnaissance detachments' right up in the front line, military units of about forty men including linguists, cipherers, radio operators, drivers and soldiers, ready to seize intelligence documents and equipment and to capture and interrogate key personnel. These *Abwehrtruppen* or intelligence commandos were first used in the German invasion of the Balkans on 6 April 1941. On the northern front in Yugoslavia, near Zagreb, they took the Yugoslav Fourth Army HQ intact, seizing plans of all defences and making use of the Yugoslavs' own ciphers and signals to feed false information to Yugoslav officers in the field that their government had capitulated, and so they should lay down their arms. An Abwehr unit of intelligence commandos was first into Athens Naval HQ on 27 April, and intelligence commandos on motorcycles were swift to fossick the British HQs at Maleme and Heraklion when Crete fell in May 1941.

'Abwehr-Truppen were especially successful in the Balkans, under a man named Obladen,' wrote Ewen Montagu, formerly a colleague of Fleming's in the Naval Intelligence Division, in his book *Beyond Top Secret U* (1977).

They kept up with the front-line troops, linked with fifth-columnists and agents, guided, directed and reported and, at times, had the only W/T sets operating in the front line so that the military had to use them. The speed and accuracy of their reports was most impressive, especially in Athens and Greek ports, and they gave their HQ (and us) much valuable information.

A man called Trevor James Glanville brought confirmation of the *Abwehrtruppen* activities to London in the summer of 1941. 'Sancho' Glanville, also known as 'Trevor' or 'Buster' or 'Jim', would play a key role in Ian Fleming's Commandos and write its first history after the war. His identity as a solid chartered accountant working for Price Waterhouse in Zagreb, a British vice consul who knew about steam trains and butterflies, covered up more secret activities. On outbreak of war he got 'the tap on the shoulder' from section D of SIS and was later absorbed into the SOE. Glanville spoke fluent Serbo-Croat, French, German and Russian (his wife Zlata Mionchinsky was Russian). Secretly commissioned as a British army captain on 26 March 1941, he was liaising with the Yugoslav secret services when the Germans invaded ten days later. Arrested by pro-Nazi Croats, he was later exchanged for some Italian prisoners with the rest of the British military mission.

When he got back to London, Glanville told SOE about the new German intelligence commandos. Why should not the British do something similar? He was informed this was not within the SOE or SIS terms of reference. John Godfrey and Ian Fleming, however, pricked up their ears and filed away the idea for their future use.

Back in the Mediterranean, Admiral Keyes had a plan to make use of one of the newly formed Commando brigades, Colonel Robert Laycock's 'Layforce'. This was Operation WORKSHOP in the Mediterranean. Winston Churchill had wanted to seize a key island from the Italians and use it as an airbase to command the central Mediterranean. Pantelleria, a quarter of the size of the Isle of Wight, lies 140 miles from Malta, in the middle of the 100-mile channel between Tunisia and Sicily. Keyes was keen to lead the expedition himself. Three large converted Landing Ships (Infantry) carrying 2,000 commandos were to attach themselves to a convoy bound for Malta, then peel off to storm the island with its bunkers and airfields. But on 29 January 1941 the operation was cancelled, and Laycock's commandos were instead sent to Egypt. Keyes was frustrated and angry and did not stint in expressing his fury; he was subsequently largely excluded from other operations, and by mid-October 1941 he had been sacked, much mourned by the commandos. The following month, his son Geoffrey was killed leading a raid on Rommel's HQ in Libya and was awarded a posthumous VC.*

As the new 'Adviser on Combined Operations' Churchill chose Lord Louis Mountbatten, a great-grandson of Queen Victoria, and a dashing handsome figure (though seen by some as an ambitious schemer) whose destroyer HMS *Kelly* had been sunk during the evacuation of Crete in May 1941. 'Dickie' Mountbatten was addicted to speed – Andrew Roberts entitled his beady-eyed essay on him in *Eminent Churchillians* 'Lord Mountbatten and the Perils of Adrenalin' – and he certainly upped the pace at Combined Operations after he took command in late October 1941. But Mountbatten was careless with other people's lives, and his charisma was not always matched by competence. He was a fluent re-writer of history and a deft blame-shifter. Sir Gerald Templer once told him, 'You're so crooked, Dickie, if you swallowed a nail you'd shit a corkscrew.' One of Mountbatten's nicknames in the Admiralty was 'the Master of Disaster'; under him, COHQ at Richmond Terrace was dubbed 'HMS *Wimbledon*', because it was 'all rackets and balls'. According to the historian of Combined Operations, Brigadier Bernard Fergusson, who considered the appointment 'odd', Churchill's verbal briefing of Mountbatten 'ran something like this': 'Up to now there have hardly been any commando raids. I want you to start a programme of raids of ever-increasing intensity. *But your main object must be the re-invasion of France.* You must . . . bend all your energies towards this great day.'

The last commando raid in 1941 was in fact against Vaagso and Maaloy in Norway on 27 December. This raid yielded useful

---

* Bob Laycock himself managed to escape from the raid on Rommel, and with a sergeant made it back for Christmas dinner after six weeks in the desert. The sergeant thanked the Almighty that he did not have to listen any more to Laycock reading aloud from their only book, Kenneth Grahame's *Wind in the Willows*.

documents and was a landmark because the RAF managed to provide continuous air cover for seven hours and protect all the Royal Navy's ships. It was not an easy pinch, however; the fighting in the long snowy street was fierce and 2 and 3 Commandos took 98 prisoners and killed 120 Germans, themselves suffering 20 dead and 59 wounded. John Durnford-Slater, smeared with blood from a wound in the hand, his tunic scorched by fire and with grenades stuffed in his Mae West, found a handsome young German lying in the gutter, dying from a chest wound. 'He smiled at me. When he beckoned, I walked over and spoke to him. He could speak no English, but indicated that he wished to shake hands. We did. I think what he meant, and I agreed, was that it had been a good, clean battle.'

In February 1942 training for such encounters reached a new professional level with the setting up of the Commando Basic Training Centre at Achnacarry, which put the experiences of nearby Inverailort into mass production. Charles Vaughan, once a regimental sergeant major in the Coldstream Guards but now one of the few colonels with a Cockney accent, was in charge. He devised a ferociously testing course that ended with an adrenalin-charged opposed landing exercise. Small boats stealing across a quiet loch by night were suddenly met with a blaze of tracer, flares and explosions. On completion of the intensive Achnacarry course, commandos earned the coveted green beret.

In the first six months of 1942 there were ten commando raids, large and small. The most spectacular was at St-Nazaire, where the only graving dock in France capable of taking German battleships was blown up, but the most brilliant was at Bruneval, on the night of February 27/28. Operation BITING shines in surrounding gloom. In the first half of 1942 there were military disasters in North Africa, military catastrophe in the Far East as the Japanese overran British possessions and an embarrassing escape of three

German cruisers right through the Straits of Dover. Yet here was a daring raid – dropping a hundred Scottish commandos by parachute on to a French cliff-top and then evacuating them by sea – which succeeded brilliantly. It was a scientific raid whose sole aim was an intelligence pinch: seizing a German radar set. Slowly but surely Dr R. V. Jones, at first unable to persuade his superiors to believe in the 'Oslo Report' (see chapter 3), had managed to convince them that the Germans did indeed have the radar system it referred to, which enabled them to track and shoot down RAF planes. The raid was an opportunity to find out exactly how it worked.

Bruneval was the Parachute Regiment's first battle honour, and only the second time ever that the British used parachutists on operations. Things happened very fast for one man, radar mechanic Flight Sergeant C. W. H. Cox, who discovered on 1 February that he had been 'volunteered' for a dangerous job that began with a two-week parachute course at Ringway, Manchester. A cinema projectionist in peacetime, Cox trained with a party of Royal Engineers for the job. There was a bagpiper to see the Scottish commandos off, and Cox and the others had drunk so much cocoa or rum-laced tea at Thruxton airfield that the first thing he and everyone else did after landing was to relieve themselves. Their blissful piss steamed on the frost and snow of enemy territory.

The Würzburg radar set on the cliff-top field was a disc about ten feet in diameter, with a container of three feet by two feet by five feet behind it holding the units. Bullets were still zipping as Cox started dismantling the pulse gear and amplifier. The German set was beautifully made, but he and Royal Engineer Lieutenant Vernon had to wrench out the transmitter with its entire holding frame because they couldn't reach the screws. This turned out to be a stroke of luck because the frame contained the aerial switching unit. Amid explosions and gunfire they made it down to the beach and waded through cold water to the landing craft carrying the precious gear. A Telecommunication Research Establishment scientist was waiting on board the big ship to grill Cox.

'Now Flight Sergeant, I want a description of everything you saw before memory becomes clouded.'

'Permission to be sick, sir.'

'You can be sick later. At the moment, greater issues than your physical comfort are at stake.'

Cox was awarded the MM.

The success of Bruneval, a daring airborne pinch from right under the noses of the enemy, was probably the final element prompting Ian Fleming to suggest a unit that could do something similar for the Royal Navy. His seven-point Most Secret minute –PROPOSAL FOR NAVAL INTELLIGENCE COMMANDO UNIT – signed 'F. N.I.D (17)' is dated 20 March 1942, three weeks after Operation BITING. It does not mention the British raid explicitly but concentrates on the need to keep up with the Germans (whose Abwehr commandos he had of course learned about from Sancho Glanville and others in the previous year). It begins:

One of the most outstanding innovations in German Intelligence is the creation by the German N.I.D. of special intelligence "Commandos". These "Commandos" accompany the forward troops when a port or naval installation is being attacked and, if the attack is successful, their duty is to capture documents, cyphers etc. before these can be destroyed by the defenders . . . I submit that we would do well to consider organising such a "Commando" within the N.I.D . . . The unit would be modelled on the same lines as its German counterpart and would be placed under the command of C.C.O. [Chief of Combined Operations] perhaps a month before a specific objective is attacked.

Fleming envisaged the unit's duties as finding out exactly what different sections of the NID required from the particular enemy port that had been targeted, 'e.g. cyphers, specimens of material (including enemy oil fuel and food, for instance), charts, enemy fleet orders, mines, R.D.F. [Radio Direction Finding] gear, photographs etc. etc.'; obtaining all intelligence available about their whereabouts; training with the main raiding force and then proceeding 'with 2nd or 3rd wave of attack into the port, and make straight for the various buildings etc. where the booty is expected to be found, capture it and return'. He identified Operation SLEDGEHAMMER as 'a typical example of an objective which might yield valuable fruit if tackled by such a unit'.

The USA had only joined the war in December 1941 but SLEDGE-HAMMER was the plan for a cross-Channel attack that the new-boy Americans were favouring early in 1942. Its aim was to seize either Brest or the Cherbourg peninsula and gain a toehold on the continent of Europe, thus helping to take some pressure off the Russians battling the German invasion of their homeland. The British were far less keen: Alan Brooke, the chief of the Imperial General Staff, grumbled in his diary about 'Russia, USA and the Press all clamouring for a "Western Front" without thinking what it means . . . One might think we were going across the Channel to play baccarat at Le Touquet, or to bathe at Paris Plage!' But now Fleming and Godfrey were seeing a new way of taking part in a cross-Channel attack. Fleming proposed to submit his plan in greater detail with suggestions for organisation and personnel. Godfrey wrote 'YES, most decidedly' in pencil at the bottom of the memo, but also pounced on a bit of wording that seemed weak, striking out the final sentence suggesting that the principle be 'submitted' to the chief of Combined Operations (Mountbatten) for his 'covering approval', pencilling instead, 'The principle be *worked out in detail in collaboration with* C.C.O.' and adding, 'but we won't "*submit*".

Others in NID 'strongly' concurred with the proposal when it circulated among them for their comments. Sir Henry Oliver, who had been Churchill's DNI at the beginning of the First World War, also approved. He pointed out that a basic qualification for the unit should be an ability to speak German and/or the language of the country they were raiding in, and that bomb and mine disposal experts must also be included. 'Yes, let's get on with this,' pencilled Godfrey. Within the week Fleming had 'put up' a docket suggesting organisation and personnel to COHQ. On 1 April he heard back from the chief intelligence officer of Combined Operations that Mountbatten liked the idea and wanted a conference to discuss it fully. Ten days later John Godfrey had second thoughts about handing over 'the working out of an "Advance Intelligence Unit"' to Combined Operations. He deplored the notion that Mountbatten's intelligence staff was any better than his, and now wanted it developed in-house by Ian Fleming and Charles Drake.

By 29 April 1942 Fleming was hitching his 'Intelligence Assault Unit' to the rising star of Operation SLEDGEHAMMER. NID's Commander Murphy was appointed intelligence officer to SLEDGEHAMMER's commander-in-chief, and Fleming suggested that Murphy and two other lieutenant commanders choose suitable intelligence targets. Charles Drake said that the wireless specialist who had boarded the *München*, Captain Jasper Haines, should also be consulted about possible pinches. Godfrey pencilled, 'Yes & with Capt Haines & go ahead'.

It was a disappointment for Fleming when SLEDGEHAMMER was cancelled in May 1942, but the NID team did not give up. Fleming asked the DNI's permission to put Commander Arnold-Forster of MI6 in the picture too. On 2 June 1942 Godfrey sent under his own name a two-page memo, headed INTELLIGENCE ASSAULT UNITS, to his colleagues on the JIC: Brigadier Sidney Kirkman from Military Intelligence, Air Vice Marshal Charles Medhurst from Air Intelligence, Brigadier Stewart Menzies of SIS, Brigadier Sir David Petrie, head of MI5, and Denis Capel-Dunn, the JIC secretary. This largely followed Fleming's copy but Godfrey added that he wanted to develop the idea on inter-service lines, to start planning without delay, and asked 'that an effort should be made to include an Intelligence Assault Unit in Operation

RUTTER'. (This was the initial Combined Operations plan for the Dieppe raid, devised in April, approved in May, rehearsed twice in June, cancelled on 7 July. The Dieppe raid did of course finally go ahead, renamed Operation JUBILEE, on 19 August 1942, as we saw in chapter 1.)

On 12 June 1942 the JIC submitted a memorandum for consideration by the chiefs of staff. Headlined COLLECTION OF INTELLIGENCE DURING RAIDS, this mentioned the German formation of 'Intelligence Commandos' to accompany forward troops 'to capture documents, cyphers, etc. before these can be destroyed', and recommended that

a detachment composed of suitable intelligence personnel should accompany further [British] raids and operations on the Continent. The main task of this personnel, during the raid or operation, would be to deal with such intelligence targets as were recommended by the various Departments and Services and accepted by H.Q. Home Forces or C.C.O.

Godfrey circulated this memorandum through the Admiralty, asking different departments what targets among German weapons and matériel they might have in mind for Intelligence Assault Units. 'The officer particularly concerned with this matter in the N.I.D. is Commander I.L. Fleming, R.N.V.R, Ext. 991, and he will be available to give any further information required on the machinery of Intelligence Assault Units as described in the attached paper.'

By mid-July Fleming was deluged with requests for more information on German mines, hydrophones, Asdic equipment, depth gauges, U-boat tactics from logbooks or war diaries, booms and nets, automatic and anti-aircraft guns and ammunition, predictors, sights and RDF for guns, torpedo pistols, all kinds of wireless sets and valves, aids to navigation and recognition signalling, radio frequencies, procedures and orders, wireless control for light buoys, boats, explosives or jamming, anything to do with infrared or untraviolet rays for signalling or detection, all beach defences, (offshore, onshore, above or below water), warning devices and oilfire defences, illuminants, scorched earth schemes, blockships and all kinds of books, documents, maps, charts and papers that could be found.

N

On 22 and 27 July 1942 two meetings were held at COHQ to discuss the formation of Special Intelligence Units. Those present at both meetings were Colonel Robert Neville of the Royal Marines, Commander Arnold-Forster of MI6, Ian Fleming of NID, Major W. G. Cass of MI5 and MEW (Ministry of Economic Warfare), Major Williams-Thompson of Combined Operations Intelligence and the former German-speaking journalist, Captain Ian Colvin RM. Fleming put the case at the first meeting that there was an urgent requirement for personnel to be intensively trained for special naval intelligence duties. The others agreed that they should be selected and kept together as a unit, and be a permanent body. The MI5 and MI6 representatives were in agreement that this would be more trustworthy from a security point of view. The meeting decided that the chief of Combined Operations should initiate a small-scale trial with a special unit of around twenty men, including a high proportion of officers. Fleming estimated that for the immediate future and the following year the Admiralty would find one platoon of specially trained Royal Marines sufficient.

At the second meeting on 27 July 1942 the meeting agreed the title 'Intelligence Assault Unit' (IAU), and said it should be a permanent body under the command of the chief of Combined Operations that would not be disbanded without the agreement of the JIC. It had to be based near London so SIS and SOE instructors could reach it without difficulty. Ian Fleming said the 'Naval Section' would be given naval intelligence courses; he wanted two officers, Royal Marines, five NCOs and ten marines to be found as soon as possible from the Royal Marine Commando and trained by the DNI. Four officers and twenty-four 'Other Ranks' (of whom six should be NCOs) would be required for the

'Military Section'. The meeting agreed that all officers should speak German with French, Dutch or Flemish as a second language, and one officer should speak Norwegian. It was desirable that Other Ranks and NCOs should know languages, but they could also qualify through special technical and mechanical aptitude.

At this point Robert Laycock, by now the brigadier running the Special Service Brigade, joined them. With a degree of chauvinism the meeting agreed that all volunteers selected for the IAU should be of British nationality – this meant that for example the personnel of 10 Commando, recruited from citizens of occupied countries, would not be suitable. Those selected would wear the commando flash. Though for obvious reasons they could not be told the full nature of their duties in advance, they would not lose pay or opportunities by joining the IAU.

The minutes of the second meeting on 27 July 1942 concluded:

17. Brigadier Laycock undertook to obtain volunteers for the unit as required, and to inform Lt Col [Picton] Phillips, R.M. (Officer Commanding Royal Marine Commando) of the requirement stated by Commander Fleming.
18. It was most urgent that the unit should begin training forthwith.

Three weeks later, on 19 August 1942, the first Intelligence Assault Unit was blooded in the abortive raid on Dieppe. Failure taught them hard lessons. The need for better intelligence could no longer be denied.

7

Mapping the Future

One of John Godfrey's greatest contributions to the eventual success of the Allies was his insistence on the importance of accurate mapping and detailed local knowledge. Godfrey once said, 'Somewhere in or near London can be found *the* great authority on *any* subject – the problem is to find him.'* In February 1940 he knew that Professor Kenneth Mason of the Oxford University School of Geography was just the man to help him set up a new geographical facility for the armed forces, which would become the Inter-Services Topographical Department (ISTD).

When Godfrey and Fleming met Professor Mason they asked for three immediate confidential reports on Finland and the USSR (the Winter War against Russia was still on, and Britain wanted to help the Finns via the Arctic Circle). Mason quickly supplied them, with the help of geographer colleagues including some who worked for Cambridge University's Scott Polar Research Institute. Other detailed geographical reports on strategic areas that caught Winston Churchill's fancy as locations for sabotage attacks – German inland waterways, Russian Black Sea ports, Italian oil refineries, and so on – soon followed.

The ISTD began with one civilian liaison officer in NID 6 in

---

* Godfrey was good at this because he read widely. When British cities were blitzed in 1940–1 and Godfrey was concerned that Home Front anxieties might affect the morale of those serving in the fleet, he got in touch with Tom Harrisson, the anthropologist founder of the organisation Mass-Observation, who pioneered social survey research among ordinary people and later won the DSO in Borneo, leading head-hunters against the Japanese for SOE. Godfrey commissioned Harrisson to send out lay observers in Southampton, Portsmouth, Plymouth, Swansea, Cardiff, Liverpool, Clydebank and Hull and report their findings to him.

March 1940, grew to take over all of Manchester College, Oxford, and by 1945 was employing more than 700 Allied personnel. Many who worked there were women, chief among them being John Godfrey's own wife, who became the assistant to ISTD's chief editor, Professor Freddie Wells. Margaret Godfrey had a formidable, hard-working brain: when she left the ISTD they needed a whole section to replace her. At the end of 1940, learning from the muddled information about Norway and from his own memories of the geographical blunders of Gallipoli in the First World War, Godfrey set up another section of naval intelligence in Oxford (NID 5) to create a new series of Admiralty geographical handbooks. This extraordinary intellectual exercise involved the Universities of Oxford and Cambridge in the production of fifty-eight scholarly volumes, written by 170 (unpaid) volunteers, containing all the useful background information about twenty-nine regions or countries that commanders and others might possibly need, in war or peacetime. Never again would a landing party have to scrabble for tourist brochures and maps. The volumes covered Norway, Denmark, Germany, Luxembourg, the Netherlands, Belgium, France, Spain and Portugal, French West Africa, Belgian Congo, Morocco, Algeria, Tunisia, Corsica, Italy, Albania, Yugoslavia, Greece, the Dodecanese, Turkey, Syria, Persia, Palestine and Transjordan, Western Arabia and the Red Sea, Iraq and the Persian Gulf, Indo-China, China proper and four compendious volumes on the Pacific Islands.

Total war demanded total intelligence to assist in gaining footholds in enemy territory. Terrain intelligence overlapped with the navy's sea charts. Once again it mattered to get the right individuals from the widest range of professions. Working out the gradient of landing beaches required the co-operation of RAF photographic reconnaissance pilots, civilian interpreters at Medmenham, Royal Engineer modellers to put the mosaic of photographs together and Royal Navy hydrographers for tidal charts. There were consultations with geomorphologists and special night raids by the canoeist/divers of Combined Operations Pilotage Parties (COPPs) to bring back samples of mud, sand or shale from enemy beaches so scientists could evaluate their bearing capacity for landings. Even cinema people came in: a small film crew ostensibly scouting locations for an Alexander Korda historical epic movie actually expended much stock on choice landing beaches in Morocco and Algeria.

Ports, harbours, navigable rivers, geology, soils, vegetation, landscape, quality of roads, gauge of railways, sites of airports, industries, workshops, barracks, availability of water, sources of food, electricity, communications, oil and petrol, type of climate, seasonal weather and winds, flora, fauna and insect life, local diseases, medical services, the culture and religion of the inhabitants, their totems and taboos, etc. – all these became relevant to the naval and military planner as the Second World War progressed. This was war work for bibliographers, textual scholars and learned professors. Information had to be researched and compiled from newspapers, journals, official statistics, books in university libraries and learned societies, and from the experience of knowledgeable people: explorers, businessmen, contractors, engineers, scholars and scientists, expatriates and refugees. (A massive 'Contact Register' comprising around 70,000 names and details were kept and organised by a palaeobotanist from the Natural History Museum.)

Much visual information had to be pieced together from aerial reconnaissance photographs and other sources. In 1941 the Admiralty appealed on the BBC Home Service for private holiday photos of beach scenes in Europe, which produced 80,000 replies. These holiday snaps, duly catalogued, graded and sorted, were the basis of a huge and expanding intelligence collection, stored in the basement of the New Bodleian. Data had to be edited and sifted, collated and double-checked, the raw material boiled down and cooked for presentation to service clients in an attractive and easily digestible form. ISTD's ISIS

(Inter-Service Information or Intelligence Series) publications were always beautifully laid out, and they also developed single-sheet Forms-At-A-Glance (FAAGs) that displayed information clearly and graphically with a minimum of prose. Mountbatten once took a Sardinian example to show Churchill, who brandished it happily at Cabinet as a shining example of clarity. ISTD also made scores of two-dimensional geographical models. It was from these rich resources that Ian Fleming got detailed information for his IAU.

Admiral Godfrey loved the intellectual scope of the ISTD and visited Oxford every Wednesday on his day off to nurture his special baby. The academic life appealed so much to Godfrey that after the war he stood unsuccessfully for Chichele Professor of Military History. The American General 'Wild Bill' Donovan also admired ISTD, and the Research and Analysis (R&A) branch of his Office of Strategic Services (OSS) in the USA owed much to Godfrey's ideas. ISTD's close relationship with Oxford University Press (OUP, who also printed the Royal Navy codes and ciphers in great secrecy) enabled them to help when Admiral Sir Andrew Cunningham, Eisenhower's deputy for TORCH, the successful Allied landings in North Africa, asked OUP to print all the operational orders for the naval manoeuvres to land thousands of men on beaches in Morocco and Algeria. The complicated TORCH plans were proofread by Freddie Wells and Margaret Godfrey in one long autumn night. They corrected many inconsistencies and errors that might have caused damage, delay or death. Of their painstaking work Donald McLachlan, the historian of Naval Intelligence, wrote in *Room 39*: 'I know no more striking instance of how the arts scholar can stand guard as effectively as the scientist over the fighting man.'

The ISTD was of great importance to TORCH as well as all subsequent landings on foreign shores. They would vindicate

Godfrey's ideas about the value of 'topographical intelligence'. Yet by the time TORCH succeeded, Godfrey was gone, sacked after three and half years as the best DNI ever, and Ian Fleming had lost his patron and mentor. The First Sea Lord, Sir Dudley Pound, who was beginning to get dozier and more erratic with the undetected brain tumour that would kill him the next year, was the man who delivered the blow, but its real originator was the prime minister, Winston Churchill.

Godfrey had made many enemies. Impatient, irascible, often maddened into bad temper by haemorrhoids that he refused to have operated during the seven years of war alert and warfare, he was bluntly truthful and never ingratiating. Even Ewen Montagu, who disliked him personally, respected his refusal to tell authority only what it wanted to hear. But Godfrey annoyed the chiefs of staff by disbelieving Alan Brooke's theories and by sending intelligence directly to Admiral Sir Andrew Cunningham in Washington DC when he wasn't supposed to, aggravated his fellows on the JIC by never being emollient when criticising shoddy work or demolishing feeble arguments, and infuriated the RAF by frankly disbelieving their claims about the accuracy of their bombing. Dr Joan Saunders, who worked in NID along with her husband Hilary St George Saunders, later told Ian Fleming's biographer John Pearson: 'Of course Godfrey was sacked. He was too good.'

Worst of all, though, Godfrey had annoyed Winston Churchill when he was First Lord of the Admiralty by not accepting the wildly exaggerated figures of the numbers of German submarines sunk that he cooked up to boost public morale in 1939. In private, Godfrey disliked Churchill's 'malignant' strategic thinking and found him 'an unmitigated pest and bully, interfering without knowledge and throwing spanners into wheels'. As General Wavell and others learned, Churchill could be vindictive in his sackings, and was lacking in magnanimity after the event. After forty-three years' loyal service, Admiral John Godfrey was the only naval officer of his rank to get no honour at all for his war work.

Captain Edmund Rushbrooke, who later admitted frankly to John Pearson that he hadn't wanted the job and didn't enjoy it, replaced Godfrey as DNI. In practice this meant that his team in the NID carried on as before, running the smooth and effective machine that he had created. Among them Ian Fleming stayed on as the new DNI's personal assistant, at the heart of things. Joan Saunders said that

Ian [Fleming] did know an awful lot of what was going in NID. He was virtually the man who kept it going after Godfrey went. Old Rushbrooke was no good, and if it hadn't been for Ian the whole thing would have run down. But Ian was determined that it wouldn't. He was a great administrator. Every file went through his hands and he must have known a very great deal.

She added that Fleming was an arrogant man who knew his value and had great social skills. 'He was a flatterer, a bit of a tease. You never knew quite which was which.'

The axe fell in September 1942, just as Godfrey was about to leave on a second important trip to the United States and Canada with Ian Fleming. The two men went ahead anyway.

The year 1942 was crucial for the intelligence relationship of the British and American navies as they joined together to prosecute the Battle of the Atlantic. In the first phase the commanders of five long-range German U-boats had enjoyed what was to them 'the happy time' on the Atlantic seaboard of the USA, sinking twenty-five ships in ten days. Scores of other U-boats combined to sink some two million tons of Allied merchant shipping in the first six months. America did not seem to be seriously at war in those early months; lights still blazed from eastern cities, silhouetting the coastal ships and making them perfect targets for submarines to torpedo or shell. Many were tankers carrying vital oil and petrol from the Caribbean and the Gulf of Mexico to the UK, and their shocking immolation could be witnessed from the shore. America only slowly woke up to the need for an 'Interlocking Convoy System', which they organised from May onwards with Canada and the UK.

The Allies had had problems with Signals Intelligence (SIGINT), too. On 1 February 1942 the Kriegsmarine had introduced a new, four-rotor Enigma M-4 machine for use by their fleet. This integrated two so-called 'Greek' rotors with a unique circuitry known as BETA and GAMMA, and made it harder for Bletchley Park to break into the Atlantic U-boat radio communication network that the Germans called 'Triton' and the British 'Shark'. The Allies effectively suffered a SIGINT blackout from German U-boats for most of 1942. This coincided with the period when the *Beobachtungsdienst*, the German equivalent of Bletchley Park, was regularly reading up to 80 per cent of Allied messages sent in the Royal Navy's Cipher No. 3 (the code used by the American, British and Canadian warships protecting the Atlantic convoys). This information haemorrhage helped the German wolf packs to scent their prey, and let them sink seven million tons of shipping in the Western Atlantic. The wound was not staunched until 10 June 1943 when the improved Naval Cipher No. 5 came on stream.

Though U-boat signals could not be deciphered during this period, their traffic could still be analysed and the direction from which they were sent could be found. In April 1942 Godfrey sent two of his best people to North America to explain how naval intelligence could help win the battle against submarines. The first man, Captain Humphrey Sandwith, was one of the team of three who had travelled to Pyry to meet the Polish cryptographers in 1939. Sandwith was the head of Diplomatic Signals Division, DSD/NID 9, the combined signals and intelligence section that fed information to the OIC. Sandwith described how the British system of Y and D/F (listening and direction-finding) worked, and explained 'huff-duff', H/F–D/F or high-frequency direction-finding, which could get a fix on a submarine radioing a message back to headquarters at Kernéval. He also talked to officers at the US Navy's code-breaking branch (OP-20-G) about Bletchley Park's cryptanalysis and OIC's onward transmission of intelligence to help antisubmarine warfare operations. Sandwith urged both North American countries to set up their own operational intelligence centres as well.

The next British visitor from NID demonstrated what to do with SIGINT data. Since January 1941 Commander Rodger Winn RNVR had been head of the Submarine Tracking Room in the OIC, where information about hostile forces was displayed visually on a large table and wall charts deep inside the windowless Admiralty Citadel on Horse Guards Parade nicknamed by its denizens 'Lenin's Tomb'. Winn, a barrister by profession, now spent his time trying to read the mind of the U-boat supremo, Admiral Dönitz. Winn had a subtle mind that could both grasp his own brief and think like the opposing counsel, and he was also extremely good at handling cantankerous old judges without annoying them. This came in handy in America with Admiral Ernest King, since March 1941 both commander-in-chief, US Fleet, and commander of naval operations, who distrusted the British almost as much as he disliked the US army. King was not an easy man (his own daughter wittily described him as 'even-tempered: always in a rage'), and he thought American ships ought to concentrate on fighting the Japanese in the Pacific.

In Washington DC Winn managed to persuade the crusty admiral of the validity of operational intelligence, and set him on the path to setting up an American Submarine Tracking Room, F-21, which came into being at the end of 1942 under the command of Kenneth Knowles. (Winn also got the Canadians to set one up in Ottawa under John B. McDiarmid.) When Knowles came to London in July 1942 to study the British OIC and the Submarine Tracking Room, he was indoctrinated into ULTRA 'special intelligence' and struck up a close friendship with Winn. Both men were prevented from active service by a physical disability, in Winn's case a limp from childhood polio, in Knowles's case short-sightedness. From the spring of 1943 there was an efficient and secure direct signal link between F-21's 'Secret Room' and the Admiralty's Operational Intelligence Centre that only Winn and Knowles and their deputies were permitted to use. In May 1943 the US COMINCH-CNO, Admiral Ernest King, established the US 10th Fleet, a division of 'hunter-killer' forces mandated to ambush and attack U-boats, and Knowles's intelligence gave them vital guidance. Naval Intelligence on John Godfrey's watch had been at the core of the UK–USA 'special relationship'. When the US War Department and British GC&CS signed the BRUSA agreement to share all 'special intelligence' in June 1943, they were really only ratifying a marriage that had already been consummated by the two navies.

John Godfrey was still promoting Anglo-American cooperation when he accepted his new job in late September 1942. It was a form of exile as flag officer commanding the Royal Indian Navy, then waging war against the Imperial Japanese Navy. He was gone from the NID by the end of November 1942.

Ian Fleming, meanwhile, had travelled from Washington DC at the end of September to visit the British West Indies for a five-day naval intelligence conference about the U-boat threat in the Caribbean; Axis submarines sunk over 330 ships there that year, mostly between May and September. The Anglo-American conference was held at the Myrtle Bank Hotel in Kingston, Jamaica, and one of Fleming's oldest friends, Ivar Bryce, accompanied Fleming on the trip.

Bryce was a full-lipped lothario who had done 'dirty tricks' deception work for William Stephenson in British Security Coordination (BSC), a secret operation set up in New York by MI6. One of Bryce's best ruses was fooling the Americans about

German ambitions in South America, passing off an ordinary German Lufthansa airline map showing their aviation fuel distribution system as a secret political map revealing the Nazis' plans to create what Roosevelt in a thundering speech called 'five vassal states' in the USA's backyard. 'I have in my possession a secret map, made in Germany . . . by planners of the new world order . . . ' roared the President, whipping up popular feeling five weeks before the USA entered the war.

Bryce and Fleming stayed above Kingston in Bellevue, a decaying coffee plantation house owned by Bryce's rich wife, 1,500 feet up in the Blue Mountains, where Horatio Nelson was said to have slept in 1779. It was the Jamaican rainy season and Fleming ate stringy jerk chicken with yam and banana and drank grenadine, staring out from the dripping verandah into the downpouring darkness. He had never been in the tropics before, and it was a revelation. He knew he was about to lose his father figure in Godfrey, and the war would not go on for ever. What would his life be afterwards? He must have been quieter than usual, because Bryce thought that Fleming was not enjoying his stay, and was startled when, on the plane, Fleming put down his conference notes and said:

You know Ivar, I've made a great decision. When we have won this blasted war, I am going to live in Jamaica. Just live in Jamaica and lap it up, and swim in the sea and write books. That is what I want to do and I want your help . . . You must find the right bit of Jamaica for me to buy. Ten acres or so, away from towns and on the coast. Find the perfect place; I want to get it signed and sealed.

Bryce later found a fourteen-acre strip on the north coast of Jamaica, an old donkey racetrack near the village of Oracabessa in St Mary parish, which Ian Fleming bought for £2,000 in 1946. On the Rock Edge promontory above a hidden, dazzling white beach, Fleming built the plain, low-roofed bungalow he called 'Goldeneye'. Noël Coward called it 'a perfectly ghastly house', but it had a vast living room with big windows that had no glass, just slatted louvres, so the moist tropical air could blow through. Ian Fleming the writer put his big roll-top desk in the bedroom. After the war, between 1952 and 1964, he wrote all the James Bond novels there. In 2011 the nearby Boscobel Aerodrome was renamed Ian Fleming International Airport.

8

Mayhem in the Maghreb

Sunday 8 November 1942. Two British warships, HMS *Broke* and HMS *Malcolm*, zigzagged across the moonless Bay of Algiers, carrying Ian Fleming's Commandos into action. Marine Paul McGrath lay cradling his Tommy-gun behind a three-quarter-inch-thick steel plate welded to the deck rail, wondering whether this new invasion of French territory was going to be a re-run of the disastrous Dieppe raid.

On board HMS *Malcolm* with McGrath were other survivors of their unit's first outing three months earlier: Sergeant John Kruthoffer, Corporal Leslie Whyman, Marines Leslie Bradshaw, Ken Finlayson and Jack Watson, all volunteers for this new 'hazardous' mission in French North Africa. The cover name for Fleming's IAU this time was the 'Special Engineering Unit', and the stocky officer in charge of the party, Lieutenant Dunstan Curtis, DSC, RNVR, was a former lawyer decorated for commanding the leading gun boat in the successful raid on St-Nazaire. Blue-eyed, golden-bearded (and another Old Etonian), Curtis was the first of Ian Fleming's new amphibious hybrids, wearing army khaki battledress with Royal Navy shoulder flashes and a naval officer's dark blue peaked cap with detachable khaki cover. Curtis's weaponry wasn't quite British regulation either: he carried a Colt .45 automatic and an American M1 carbine.

HMS *Malcolm*, the elderly destroyer, shuddered beneath them, the white bow wave like a bone in her teeth. Black smoke billowed like a banshee's hair. The bow was armoured with reinforced concrete to help the ship crash through the Algiers harbour boom, and there were hundreds of American soldiers in uniform lying on deck. Their arrival seemed expected: street lights were going out along the coast, and searchlights appearing. After a word with *Malcolm*'s skipper, Dunstan Curtis told his marines to move from the port to the starboard side of the funnel to get off quicker when they reached the mole. Never mind Dieppe, they should remember the last big success against a Vichy-controlled colony, in May 1942, when fifty Royal Marines raced off the destroyer *Anthony* to take control of Diego Suarez in Madagascar.

'Algiers', wrote Alan Moorehead once, recalling rows of white buildings up the hills above the African bay, 'is a beautiful sight from the sea.' But now, ominously, searchlights from the whitewashed city were starting to wander over the dark waters like the torches of householders startled by burglars. A sparkle of gun flashes, spouts of spray – the first shell bursts. Before dawn on Sunday 8 November 1942, the Anglo-American landings right across Vichy French North Africa were under way, and in trouble.

HMS *Malcolm* was a British ship flying the Stars and Stripes in the hope that the Vichy French would not shoot at Americans (the British were of course hated for sinking the French fleet at Mers-el-Kébir in 1940). Relations with the Free French were uneasy; De Gaulle was not quite trusted. A hoped-for French leader of the expedition, General Henri Giraud, an escapee from the Nazis, was sulking in Gibraltar because he had not been given supreme command above US General Dwight Eisenhower. Allied radio and leaflet propaganda for the landings blared messages of friendship for the French people, faith in *liberté, égalité, fraternité*; and enmity only to the Italian and German forces in North Africa. The Vichy officials in the French colonies of Morocco and Algeria were supposed to have been squared by the Americans, but then everything had been complicated by the unexpected arrival in Algiers of Admiral Jean Darlan, visiting his polio-stricken son. Darlan, once the hero of the French navy, now commanded all Vichy France's armed forces and had the power to order resistance to the Anglo-Saxon invasion of French North Africa, *l'Afrique Française du Nord*.

The blond farm-boys from the mid-West lying on the vibrating warm deck of HMS *Malcolm*, soldiers from the 34th Infantry Division, did not speak a whole lot of French. These 'Red Bulls' formed from the Minnesota and Iowa National Guard had been the first American troops deployed to the European theatre of operations, the first to set foot in Northern Ireland in May 1942 and the first to volunteer for the Rangers, the US equivalent of the Commandos. Young men of Scandinavian ancestry who had signed up in places like Ortonville, Minnesota, were now going to be among the first to land in North Africa, putting into action what they had rehearsed in the Belfast docks, disembarking fast from a destroyer.

The American soldiers' job in TERMINAL Force was to hold the port of Algiers and to prevent dock-sabotage and ship-scuttling until the infantry landing on other beaches came in to take over the city (projected to become Allied Force Headquarters). The IAU's job was to get into the French Admiralty building at the head of the Grand Môle, blow the safes and take the papers. The British marines had tried to impress the doughboys on the early stages of the voyage by flaunting their shooting skills, riddling tins in the sea with semi-automatic fire and showing off their muscles with callisthenics and commando unarmed combat. Paul McGrath remembered that the GIs 'reckoned [the IAU] were pretty rugged fellows and were glad we were on their side'.

The plan went awry because, in the darkness, *Malcolm* and *Broke* could not find the boom floating across the narrow entrance to Algiers harbour. Belching a smokescreen, HMS *Broke* swerved away from the sea wall. HMS *Malcolm* tried again to find the gap between the wall and the jetty, failed, and was turning seaward when the searchlights pinpointed them. The guns of the Batterie des Arcades, sited 300 feet up and with a clear line of fire, scored several direct hits amidships. Sparks and steam exploded from the wrecked boilers of the British destroyer as French guns avenged the sinkings at Mers-el-Kébir.

'It is hellish lying still under point-blank shellfire, unable to shoot back,' remembered Ken Finlayson.

The white glare of the searchlights, the crash, crash of the shells, the groans of the wounded, bits of shrapnel flying about and a fire amidships seemed a repeat performance of our experience at Dieppe. I felt something warm and wet under my body and thought 'My God, I've been hit!' but felt no pain. Closer examination revealed it was only warm water from a fractured pipe.

There was carnage on *Malcolm*'s main deck, with ten men dead and twenty-five wounded. Able Seaman Robert Miller looked down from his anti-aircraft gun and in the searchlight glare saw an American gripping the convulsing stumps of his blown-off legs, trying to stop the blood-gush with his bare hands. More shells screamed overhead; men yelled for medics and battled flames; the ship slowed down, listing to starboard. Lost in a muslin curtain of acrid smoke, *Malcolm* crawled out to sea at four knots.

Paul McGrath had sat through a lecture on 'Escaping' the month before. Now there was no escape: the *Malcolm* experience was as terrifying as being shelled on the *Locust* at Dieppe. But this time there was someone in his head saying 'You'll be all right, you'll be all right.' Then he heard British naval voices outside yelling: 'Let's shoot back at the bastards!' and 'Throw that fucking ammunition overboard!' Turning, McGrath saw ammo boxes scattered across the deck and crates of mortar rounds whose cardboard packing was now on fire. He and Lofty Whyman cut the lashings with their fighting knives and heaved the smouldering boxes over the side before they could explode. As fear ebbed and the tension relaxed, Finlayson fell fast asleep on the warm steel.

At the fourth attempt, HMS *Broke* did burst through the Algiers harbour boom and berthed at a different mole. The American troops were so shaken up by the shelling and machine-gunning from the port that they were 'a little slow in getting underway to disembark'. It was around 5.30 a.m. on a Sunday morning. They occupied the southern part of the commercial port to the tolling of church bells, but at 8.00 a.m. heavy firing by the Vichy French began. *Broke* shifted moorings twice to avoid the artillery but was finally forced to leave, abandoning most of the American soldiers. (Hit again on the way out, the damaged destroyer later sank at sea.) Outnumbered and surrounded, menaced by tanks, with five dead, eight wounded and no sign of Allied rescue, Lieutenant Colonel Edwin T. Swenson ordered his 200 men to surrender. Operation TERMINAL was *terminé*. Grinning Senegalese relieved the white boys of their wristwatches, rings and wallets, but a French officer made them give them back. Swenson's Americans were briefly imprisoned (a role reversal for him – he was a prison warden back home). They were lucky not to have been on Operation RESERVIST, the simultaneous Allied attempt to storm the port of Oran. Two coastguard cutters of American 'Ranger' commandos were met by point-blank Vichy gunfire and suffered 90 per cent casualties. Over 300 soldiers and seamen were killed and another 250 wounded.

Meanwhile in Algiers the IAU were still a long way from achieving their aim of raiding the Algiers Admiralty. They had transferred to the HQ ship of the Eastern Task Force, HMS *Bulolo*, a converted liner full of cipherers and signals equipment. Dunstan Curtis was trying to get permission from US Major General Ryder to attach his group to an American 'combat team' (these were groups of mixed infantry and artillery). Skill at finessing senior officers from other services or nations was all part of a commando leader's ability to bluff, improvise and act fast.

Ashore on Beer Green beach, about twelve miles west of Algiers, the IAU set off on a hot and sweaty march through the dust towards another target Ian Fleming had supplied them with, the Italian Armistice Commission HQ at Cheragas. Curtis recalled later being astonished at how much [Fleming] knew about Algiers, how extremely detailed his intelligence was, and how much thought he had given to our whole show. He had organised air pictures, models, and given us an exact account of what we were to look for once we got to the enemy HQ.*

The men spent an uneasy night in a garage with a bellyful of French beer and the next morning took the Italian Armistice Commission HQ in a villa high above the city, capturing seven Italian Other Ranks. The Italians wanted no trouble and gracefully surrendered their functioning W/T set and weapons – McGrath pocketed a Beretta M1934 pistol. Their chef cooked pasta and tomatoes for the hungry invaders. In the pocket of an officer's abandoned greatcoat, Dunstan Curtis found a notebook with particulars of an Italian code.

The Vichy French police then turned up for *un petit contretemps*. Crafty Admiral Darlan in his built-up shoes had negotiated the surrender of Algiers, but denied he had the power to do so more comprehensively throughout Algeria and Morocco. He did not order a general ceasefire until two more days of desultory killing and wounding had elapsed. The Algiers surrender terms gave the Italian Armistice Commission diplomatic status, so they now came under police protection. Curtis (who spoke fluent French) did not argue with this, but hung on to the Italians' weapons and personal documents.

Now it was Keystone Kops in the *kasbah*. Searching Algiers, the commandos found blind alleys and slim pickings, as well as the sudden animal excitements of war. John Kruthoffer was shot up by a Luftwaffe fighter-plane in the street but dodged its bullets. Paul McGrath emptied two thirty-round magazines from Bradshaw's Bren in long, pleasurable bursts of tracer at another German plane 'stooging' over the villa, and saw it dive down into a hail of Oerlikon machine-gun fire from assembled ships in the

---

* In *Casino Royale*, James Bond tells Vesper that his 'pernickety' fastidious-ness about meals comes 'from a habit of taking a lot of trouble over details'.

harbour. The aircraft were a reminder that the enemies whom Operation TORCH was supposed to be driving out of North Africa were not just half-hearted French colonial conscripts. The real enemy were the professional German soldiers and their Italian allies, now busily reinforcing Tunisia, 500 miles to the east, with 17,000 extra troops.

The Americans did a pragmatic deal, a 'temporary arrangement' to save lives, with Admiral Darlan. They agreed to make him High Commissioner for North and West Africa in exchange for his promising to support the Allies. Darlan signed 'in the name of the Marshal [Pétain]'. The deal recognised that Darlan still commanded allegiance: 120,000 Vichy troops, as well as the petty officials who ran the local government of North Africa, would obey the Admiral and carry on doing the bureaucratic jobs that the USA, as occupying power, could not. As Churchill explained later in a Secret Session (unrecorded) speech to the House of Commons on 10 December, 'The Almighty in His infinite wisdom did not see fit to create Frenchmen in the image of Englishmen.' A French officer's obedience to the commands of his lawful superior (or whoever he believed to be his lawful superior at the time) had become paramount in French administrative thinking, because it conferred immunity to any charges of treachery after the regime changes so common in French history. To maintain order and continuity in the current crisis (and to keep the Arabs in their place), the wisest thing for a Vichy colonial official to do was support the legitimate Darlan, rather than a rebel leader like Henri Giraud in Gibraltar, or a deserter like de Gaulle.

The Allied deal with the man whom one newspaper described as 'America's first Quisling' managed to annoy everybody. It disgusted the Free French and shocked liberals in Britain and America who pointed to Vichy's Nazi-style race laws that persecuted Jews. On the other side, it infuriated Pétain and his prime minister, Pierre

Laval, who promptly denounced Darlan as a traitor and broke off diplomatic relations with the USA. And it angered Nazi Germany so much that, despite Pétain's repudiation of Darlan and his pact with the Allies, German troops occupied parts of Vichy France. On 27 November, in further retaliation, the Germans tried to seize the French fleet at Toulon. The French navy was forced to blow up and scuttle all its remaining battleships, cruisers and destroyers. Darlan (true, in the end, to his promise that the Germans would never get the French warships) loftily declared that the vessels should have come over to him in Algiers instead. He reminded his compatriots that it was now everyone's duty to 'crush Germany and Italy and deliver our country'.

On 1 December 1942 Darlan grandly pronounced himself head of state throughout the French Colonial Empire, as well as commander-in-chief of all French armed forces. He was now claiming in the press that much of what he had done in Vichy was against his will: here, in Africa, he was all for the Allies (except the Free French, who were to be rounded up as the usual suspects). In short the Admiral was a great embarrassment. As Churchill pointed out on 10 December, Darlan's position rested

comfortably upon the fact or fiction – it does not matter which – that the Marshal is acting under the duress of the invading Hun, and that he, Darlan, is still carrying out [Pétain's] true wishes. In fact, if Admiral Darlan had to shoot Marshal Pétain he would no doubt do it in Marshal Pétain's name . . .

After drawing the short straw among a band of anti-Vichy resisters, a young French monarchist lieutenant in the Corps Franc d'Afrique called Fernand Bonnier de la Chapelle assassinated Admiral Jean Darlan at the Summer Palace in Algiers on Christmas Eve 1942. This is a murky story, replete with ironies. Bonnier was helping train Corsican guerrillas for the British secret mission near Algiers code-named 'Massingham', run jointly by the Office of Strategic Services and SOE. He shot Darlan with a pistol said to be from SOE stores, issued by SOE's Douglas Dodds-Parker, authorised by SOE's David Keswick, and given to Bonnier because of his SOE duties. Yet both SOE men denied putting him up to it, as did his OSS instructor, who distanced himself from ownership of the .22 semi-automatic Colt Woodsman which some accounts say was the weapon used. The head of SIS, Stewart Menzies, who also happened to be in Algiers that month, claimed to be there on other business entirely. The German press attributed Darlan's death to 'Winston Churchill' and the 'British Secret Service', and the Italians thought it 'a tragic episode of rivalry between French traitors'. (General Henri Giraud finally arrived to weep crocodile tears at Darlan's funeral before stepping into his boots.) The chief long-term beneficiary, Charles de Gaulle, was far away in Scotland, on a charitable visit to wounded French sailors by the Clyde. Bonnier pleaded patriotism; he believed he was doing right by his country. Yet he was swiftly court-martialled by senior French officers, convicted, pardoned, re-condemned, and then put before a beachside firing squad at 7.30 a.m. on Boxing Day. A priest gave extreme unction just before the execution. 'They will not shoot me', the prisoner assured him, with tragic trustfulness, 'They will be using blank cartridges.'

Political imbroglios were the concern of higher ranks staying at the Hôtel St Georges; down on the ground in the anthill of Algiers, Ian Fleming's tiny IAU was clashing with its own immediate rivals. US army intelligence (G-2) were also after secret stuff, as were the Field Security Police of the British Army Intelligence Corps. On his way to HMS *Bulolo* to try to wangle air passage to Gibraltar, Dunstan Curtis made the mistake of telling a man from Field Security Police (FSP) about some suitcases from the German Armistice Commission offices that the American staff intelligence officer had earmarked for him, and was furious to find out later that the FSP major had promptly swiped them himself and dispatched them to London.

But further rummaging yielded a greater treasure. Spike Watson had only been told they were looking for 'typewriters', but what they discovered was, in fact, a special kind of Enigma machine.*

The German Armistice Commission, not surprisingly, had also been a front for the Abwehr. In their offices Curtis found what Mavis Batey later described as 'a "KK" rewired multi-turnover Abwehr machine'. The Abwehr Enigma machine was different from the one used by the German armed services: it was smaller and had no *Steckerbrett* plug board at the front, so the code-breakers did not have to worry about cross-plugging, but its rotors 'turned over' far more often, not once every 26 letters, but 11, 15 and 19 times respectively on the three different wheels. Moreover, on this Abwehr machine the *Umkehrwalze*, which on most other Enigmas was a fixed plate on the left-hand side, also 'turned over', functioning as a fourth rotor wheel. It was these multiple turnovers that proved a headache for the British code-breakers; they were deeply grateful that the Abwehr did not use cross-plugging as well.

The Abwehr intelligence service employed two kinds of cipher. German secret agents in the field were given simple systems you could work out with pencil and paper (sometimes called manual or hand ciphers) to scramble the messages they sent by wireless to their controllers. These were the twigs and branches of secret communications. The 'ham radio' signals of these secret agents were first picked up by the voluntary interceptors of Britain's Radio Security Service (RSS) and cracked quite easily by Hugh Trevor-Roper and Walter Gill of MI8 early in 1940. When passed on to Bletchley Park they became the speciality of Oliver Strachey

---

* The plot of *From Russia With Love* (1957), which Fleming thought was his best book, turns on obtaining '... "the brand new Spektor machine. The thing we'd give our eyes to have." "God," said Bond softly ... The Spektor! The machine that would allow them to decipher the Top Secret traffic of all.' The Spektor itself is 'a grey japanned metal case with three rows of squat keys, rather like a typewriter'.

(Lytton's brother) and were known as ISOS traffic, which stood for Illicit or Intelligence Service Oliver Strachey. However, when Abwehr offices communicated the agents' messages onwards to Berlin or got replies from HQ, they were mechanically enciphered using the Abwehr-modified Enigma machines. This more difficult and more important trunk system of secret communications was first broken by Dilly Knox on 8 December 1941 (the day after the Pearl Harbor attack), and its traffic became known as ISK, or Intelligence Service Knox.

ISOS and ISK traffic (sometimes bunched together under the general cover name ISOS) was the holy grail of secrecy. The fact that it had been penetrated by the British had to be fiercely guarded because it was used to 'play back' false information to the central German intelligence brain. All the Abwehr agents that parachuted into or were landed in wartime Great Britain were captured and 'turned' between 1941 and 1945 – in other words, the messages they continued to transmit were all controlled and composed by MI5. This was the famous Double-Cross System, run by the Twenty or XX Committee, which its chairman, Sir John Masterman, first revealed in his 1972 Yale book, *The Double-Cross System in the war of 1939 to 1945*.

The pinch of the Abwehr Enigma machine in Algiers filled in another piece of the ISOS jigsaw and completely vindicated the IAU's existence. After it was flown from Blida airfield to Gibraltar and then back to England, it yielded the reading of six weeks' back-traffic from an unknown Vichy link, which pleased both Dilly Knox of Bletchley Park and Ian Fleming of NID. His commandos also escorted two tons of other valuable documents from Algiers when they were shipped back to UK on HMS *Black Swan* and HMS *Bulolo*.

Fleming nurtured his intelligence commandos even when his trip to America with Godfrey prevented him taking part directly.

Commander R. E. D. Ryder VC was appointed by Mountbatten to see Fleming's syllabus through, supervising 'the creation and training of a Naval Intelligence Assault Unit consisting of personnel from the Royal Marine Commando'.

The divisions of early training reflected the apartheid of rank in the Second World War. Only officers seem to have got instruction from Captain Jasper Haines and Lieutenant Commander Bacon on what SIGINT material to look for; only they were told the little tricks of cipher clerks, hiding scraps of paper with cribs that made their hard-pressed lives easier under blotters and inside crevices. Even these lessons were very restricted: the IAU trainees were not allowed to take notes, to visit Bletchley Park or to know about progress in breaking enemy ciphers. The thinking seems to have been that IAU personnel should not be 'indoctrinated' (the term then used for 'let into the secret') in case they were taken prisoner in the field and revealed what they knew.*

Meanwhile Other Ranks did the muscular stuff: basic demolitions, dealing with mines and booby traps, house-breaking, lock-picking and safe-blowing, or a street-fighting course in bombed-out Battersea with a visit to Scotland Yard's Black Museum as a treat. There was basic German, study of German armed services insignia and organisation as well as recognition of German terms on documents, like *Geheim*, secret, and *Geheime Kommandosache*, top secret, eyes of brass only. On 16 September 1942, before he left for America, Fleming also wrote a memo saying that 'officers and men should be encouraged to read novels and books on Intelligence work'. The choice of the three authors he recommended as 'good ones' throw interesting light on Fleming's own reading:-

Out of the Night by Jan Valtin

---

* 'Bond didn't know much about cryptography, and, for security's sake, in case he was ever captured, wished to know as little as possible about its secrets.' *From Russia With Love.*

The American Black Chamber by Herbert O. Yardley

The German Secret Service by Colonel W. Nicolai *

The 'Special Engineering Unit' returned from North Africa to find they were no longer experimental, but established. They were now 30 Commando, with headquarters at Amersham in Buckinghamshire, fifty minutes from Baker Street station in London. They were reorganised into a Naval troop, a Military troop and a Technical troop composed of RNVR officers specialising in secret documents, submarines, wireless and radar, mines and torpedoes.

The returning heroes of 'the Algiers job' impressed the new recruits. One of six new Royal Marines selected by 'Red' Huntington-Whiteley in November 1942 for 'hazardous service' in his Naval Section, 33 troop, 30 Commando, was Allen G. Royle. Born in Manchester and a school-leaver at sixteen, 'Bon' Royle had been working as an industrial chemist and studying science at night school before he joined up. At the age of eighteen, just past basic training, he was a big lad with practical hands, still very green. He reported with the other marines to COHQ in Whitehall ('Holy smoke! I'd never seen so many red tabs and pips and

---

* Jan Valtin, real name Richard Julius Hermann Krebs, was a well-travelled German Communist triple agent for the Soviet foreign intelligence service OGPU, who pretended to be a double agent for the Nazis. The Gestapo held his wife as a hostage and killed her when he defected to the USA in 1938. His fictionalised autobiography, published in 1940, caused a sensation. Herbert O. Yardley was America's pioneer codebreaker, head of a secret cryptanalytic bureau called MI-8 that acquired and cracked the diplomatic telegrams of foreign nations. After it was closed down by US Secretary of State Henry Stimson in 1929, on the grounds that 'Gentlemen do not read other people's mail', Yardley wrote his best-selling book in 1931 revealing what he had been doing. Colonel Walter Nicolai was the Prussian officer who led the German General Staff's intelligence branch, Abteilung IIIb, in the First World War. His book was translated into English in 1924. He helped set up Turkish intelligence in the 1920s and at the end of the Second World War he was arrested by the Soviet NKVD and taken with all his papers to Moscow, where he died under interrogation, aged seventy-three.

crowns and crossed batons in my whole bloody life! Very heavy brass in that place') and was then sent out to Amersham with a commando daily allowance of 6s 8d. The 30 Commando base was a derelict farm on the outskirts called Cold Morham, with fields and hedges for night exercises and outbuildings stored with explosives, time-delay fuses, phosphorous and fragmentation grenades, small arms and ammunition of all nations, as well as close-quarter killing kit: spring-loaded coshes, knuckleduster knives, pistols with silencers. New boys like Bon Royle learned all they could from training manuals and courses, but they got a lot from the experienced men who had been under fire and done the business. Though initially awed by the tremendous figures who had done 'the Algiers job', Bon Royle found that they 'weren't putting on the dog at all, and were bloody good blokes'. Soon he would be going back to North Africa with them himself.

In January 1943 the British prime minister and the American president met in liberated Morocco. Churchill's and Roosevelt's parties took over some luxurious villas in Casablanca for meetings that agreed the immediate military strategy: first, defeat the enemy in Africa, and then (on the basis of a hastily baked plan) invade Sicily. At the final press conference Roosevelt surprised everyone by demanding 'unconditional surrender' from the Axis powers. To clear North Africa, the First Army, with a large American corps, was to advance eastward from its landing places in Morocco and Algeria. Meanwhile, the Eighth Army was to continue pushing west from Libya and Egypt after its victory at El Alamein. When they joined up in Tunisia, both armies would expel the Germans and Italians.

The IAU of 30 Commando that sailed for North Africa in January 1943 on the liner *Durban Castle* had three officers, Dunstan Curtis, George McFee and Peter Huntington-Whiteley, and fifteen Other Ranks, Sergeant Kruthoffer, Corporal Whyman,

Marines Ken Finlayson, Dave Halton, Hicky Hickling, Harry Lund, Paul McGrath, Jerry Prince, Bon Royle, Don Thurman, Harry Underwood, Spike Watson, Curly Wilkins, and the two Smiths, James and Henry. Among their kit they also shipped two BSA M20 500cc motorcycles and three brand-new jeeps.

Three years of fighting across arid parts of Egypt and Libya was now entering its final bloody phase among towns and fields. General Rommel had called the war in the desert *Krieg ohne Hass* – war without hate. Though dust and sand grimed and gritted everything, some people had still talked romantically of a 'clean' war, perhaps because civilians were few and far between in the Western Desert, and in the empty spaces matters of life and death were starker. The American journalist Ernie Pyle commended life at the front precisely for its 'magnificent simplicity', while his Australian equivalent Alan Moorehead thought 'the desert was a wonderful place for clarifying the mind'. Thousands of square miles of dry desert behind the sparsely populated Mediterranean coastal strip had also made 'a small raiders' paradise', according to Lieutenant Colonel John Hackett, who from late 1942 coordinated raiding activities for the British, who led the way with 'irregular' forces in the desert. These included Ralph Bagnold's Long Range Desert Group (LRDG, alias 'Libyan Taxis Ltd'), the Indian Long Range Squadron, various Commandos with Robert Laycock's 'Layforce' and Middle East Commando, Roger Courtney's Special Boat Section, David Stirling's 1 Special Air Service Regiment and 'L' Detachment SAS Brigade, the Free French SAS and Popski's Private Army.

Vladimir Peniakoff – nicknamed 'Popski' by men in the LRDG because people couldn't pronounce his name – was a restless Russian Jew, who had settled in Upper Egypt working in the manufacture of sugar. In the 1930s, bored, he started exploring the desert in an old Ford Model 'A'. In 1940, aged forty-three and a lieutenant in the British army, he formed a 'Libyan Arab Force Commando' to go on operations with the LRDG. In the autumn of 1942 Hackett gave Peniakoff independent command of a small 22-man unit called, officially, 'No. 1 Demolition Squadron (PPA)', its remit to cause damage behind enemy lines. The name Hackett gave them, 'Popski's Private Army', caught people's imagination. Many a regular soldier felt he would rather be in a private army, in what he imagined as a small, elite unit of friends, far away from HQ, bureaucracy and administrative bumf, doing daring and exciting things at the sharp end. The 'private armies' for their part often felt they had to stick together for mutual support against the big battalions who disapproved of smaller special forces as 'disorderly'.

Early in 1943 a lot of these British irregular forces met up on the Algerian coast. Members of 30 Commando, still under the cover name of 'Special Engineering Unit (Naval Section)', came to join in. While they were waiting in Algiers for their transport to arrive on another ship, Red Huntington-Whiteley sent some of the men on a diving course at the submarine depot ship HMS *Maidstone*, moored nearby. The idea was to train them to search shallow wrecks they might find along the coast. They went down to about twenty feet in Algiers harbour using a Davis Submerged Escape Apparatus rig, wearing goggles and a nose clip and breathing through the mouth into a rebreather bag with an oxygen canister and a CO_2 scrubber. The course seems to have taken place near the main Algiers sewage outflow and Bon Royle was eager to find a shower afterwards. Luckily *Maidstone* had all facilities for washing: as mother ship to nine submarines, its workshops could provide everything from heavy engineering to fresh bakery. There was a cinema, a chapel, a hospital, a laundry and even a small prison.

On 14 December 1942 *Maidstone*'s Captain, Barney Fawkes, told General Eisenhower's naval aide, Harry C. Butcher, that:

thirteen of the Italians who had placed 'limpets', five-pound mines, on ships in Algiers harbour recently were captives on his ship. They succeeded in sinking one ship and damaging two, which were run ashore. Seems they came from a sub, four miles off shore, wore light diving-suits, rode astride torpedo-like, self-propelled devices with just their heads showing above water, and slipped through to the ships without being observed. Submerging, they quietly fastened their mines to the ships, preferably along the 'backbone'. One was detected, hauled on deck, and, when he refused to tell just where he had fastened his mine, was hung by the neck over the side until he confessed.

These prisoners were men from the Decima Flottiglia Mezzi d'Assalto (10a Flottiglia MAS, or the Italian 'Tenth Light Flotilla Assault Craft') whose activities would later occupy Ian Fleming's intelligence commandos. Italy's most original contribution to the technology of the Second World War was sub-aqua, pioneering midget submarines and producing many daring frogmen who rode the two-man machines known as 'human torpedoes'. It was Italians who planted the underwater mines that blew a hole in the British flagship HMS *Queen Elizabeth* and her sister battle-ship HMS *Valiant* in Alexandria harbour in December 1941, and also waged a three-year submarine guerrilla war against Gibraltar, sinking or damaging fourteen Allied ships. One story about the Italian frogmen in Gibraltar made a great impression on Ian Fleming when he heard it from Alan Hillgarth. The Decima Flottiglia MAS men were hiding inside a derelict Italian tanker, the 4,900-ton *Olterra*, moored within the breakwater at Algeciras. The Italian 'care and maintenance' crew on board were discreet, and fat envelopes kept the Spanish police off their backs. Crates of apparent 'spares' that arrived actually contained disassembled '*Maiale*' two-man human torpedoes with their limpet mines, and the Italians cut a hatch five foot by eight foot, below *Olterra*'s waterline, so the mini-subs could slip out from a flooded bow compartment, wreak their sabotage and destruction in Gibraltar, and return undetected. In chapter 13 of Ian Fleming's novel *Thunderball,* James Bond tells Felix Leiter of the CIA that the failure to spot what was going on in the *Olterra* was '[o]ne of the blackest marks against Intelligence during the whole war'. The Italian 'gentleman crook' in the novel, Emilio Largo, has a treasure-hunting hydrofoil motor yacht in the Bahamas that conceals miniature submersibles ('a two-man underwater chariot identical with those used by the Italians during the war') used to steal two British nuclear weapons from an RAF V-bomber sunk and camouflaged on the seabed.

By the beginning of March 1943 the 30 Commando IAU had established their HQ in a villa with some tents by the sandy beach of a lovely bay at Bône, 400 miles east of Algiers. Bône had been taken during TORCH by British paratroops racing there to beat the Germans, parachuting from 400 feet, laden with extra weapons and ammunition. One officer hit the ground so hard he was unconscious for four days, occasionally murmuring things like 'I'll have a little more of the turbot, waiter.' When the commandos arrived, Bône's busy port and airfield made it still a war zone and divers were exploring a sunken U-boat offshore. One night the unit helped capture some Italian limpeteers from Decima Flottiglia MAS who had swum ashore, wearing tight rubber suits, flippers and breathing apparatus. They carried mines and clamps in a bag and had money belts stuffed with notes. When German bombers attacked, the commandos left their tents on the golden sands and went into caves in the low cliffs of what had once been Hippo Regius in the times of St Augustine. Across the bay Bône gleamed in the sunlight against the dark mountains behind. You could see fields of green wheat and buy oranges and tangerines for a pittance from poor Arabs who lived in hovels outside the town. The RAF posted guards to stop them stealing the wiring and aerials from No. 381 Wireless Unit, the Y station of SIGINT at Bône, quietly listening to the R/T (radio telephony) chatter of lonely Luftwaffe pilots over the Mediterranean. The nights were cold and the stars glittered like ice. 'We had regular and very rummy visitors at Bône,' remembered Bon Royle, 'including Colonel Stirling of the SAS, members of Popski's Private Army who wore black flashes round their shoulder straps with the letters PPA on them, the Long Range Desert Group, and some of Colonel Patch's (US) paratroops. They went into huddles with

Dunstan Curtis, Red [Huntington-Whiteley] and George McFee.' 'Colonel Stirling' was Colonel Bill Stirling, the man who started Commando training back in 1940, now of 2nd SAS Regiment, based at Philippeville, along the Algerian coast. The Germans had just captured his younger brother, Colonel David Stirling, in Tunisia. Two navigators who escaped from that SAS foray were among the first people from Eighth Army to manage to get through to First Army, along with 'Popski' himself.

Learning that a few special forces' vehicles had got through from east to west, Ian Fleming's commandos reckoned they could make it back the other way. They drove to a US army engineering workshop and got the three jeeps modified for the desert, fitting racks to carry spare wheels and extra petrol in German-designed 'jerrycans', and installing a mount for a 30-calibre, belt-fed M1919 Browning machine-gun on one of the jeeps. With the two motor bikes as well, the eleven men made a remarkable 1,200-mile journey in early April, travelling over 200 miles down through scrubby semi-desert to Tozeur on the north side of the Chott el Jerid, a shallow salt lake in winter, and then 120 miles eastward towards Gabès. The going was terrible from Tozeur, like driving over solid beehives, with the jeeps bouncing over tussocks of tough plants on hummocks of hard sand, banging the passengers about bruisingly, and the bikes juddering, slewing and stopping. They crossed the narrow neck of the Chott el Fedjadj at the eastern end but travelling just a few miles southward took all day, as they kept breaking through the crust into wet salty sand.

When Bon Royle embedded his lead jeep, 'the Pompey Privateer', Huntington-Whiteley suggested laying down a camouflage net to give some grip in the alkaline mush. The whirling tyres promptly wrapped the net tightly round the wheels and drive shaft, stalling the engine and locking the jeep solid. They spread out for the chilly night by their camouflaged vehicles. Frost rimed their bedding. Bon Royle worked till late with his knife, cutting away the net. At first light, he decided to *burn* out the final wodge, jammed between the drive coupling and the engine block, to the alarm of the others. But it worked; they unloaded the jeep, lifted it clear, repacked and went on. Ernie Pyle drove jeeps like that thousands of miles, and liked everything about the vehicle except the handbrake: 'It did everything, went everywhere, was as faithful as a dog, as strong as a mule, and as agile as a goat. It consistently carried twice what it was designed for, and still kept going.'

Eventually the 'sailors in jeeps' ran into patrols of friendly forces, the 2nd New Zealand Division who had come round west of the Matmata hills and through the 'Plum' Gap. The lean and laconic Kiwis, unsurprised to find dusty Royal Marines led by a naval officer in the semi-desert, fell on their State Express 555 cigarettes with joy. The commandos drove on through the aftermath of battle at Wadi Akarit, seeing dazed and confused Italian prisoners, eyes rolling from shellshock, being driven away in trucks, past bits and pieces of the dead. It was Bon Royle's first battlefield, five weeks after his nineteenth birthday, and he was startled by the casual, random scattering of bodies, 'broken dolls to be put in the bin', lying among the poppies and wild flowers starting up in the spring sunlight.

30 Commando joined in the van of the Eighth Army heading north in pursuit of General von Arnim's retreating Germans. At the fishing-port of Mahares, on the road to Sfax, a grizzled warrior in an old greatcoat, Major General Douglas Wimberly of the 51st Highland Division, demanded to know who the interlopers were. 'Royal Marines, sir,' said Huntington-Whiteley, delivering his smartest salute. 'And where the hell have you come from?' 'First Army, sir.' '*Have you?* Have the two armies joined together at last? Royal Marines, eh? Where do you want to go next?'

The two armies were like different tribes, meeting among the olive groves and cactus hedges of Tunisia. The pallid Americans of First Army drove out of winter snow in the Atlas mountains in grey-green vehicles with stars on them. They had steel helmets with the strap buttoned, thick woollens under mackintosh wind jackets, baggy trousers tucked into gaiters and boots. All the officers of US II Corps wore ties because General Patton fined those who did not. Monty's men, coming from the desert and the delta, looked shabbier in their bleached lorries and yellow vehicles with the Red Jerboa insignia, but were cockier in spirit. Two journalists travelling with First Army, Ernie Pyle and Alan Moorehead, noticed the difference. Pyle described the Eighth Army men as 'brown-skinned and white-eye-browed' and *Daily Express* reporter Alan Moorehead thought a typical Eighth Army soldier looked like 'a rather rakish and dishevelled boy scout' in dirty shirt and shorts. Scruffy officers in stained corduroys and neckerchiefs wore an assortment of hats. Neither army quite 'got' the other's lingo.

To keep up with the regular army you sometimes had to get ahead of it. Dunstan Curtis's band began to get the full measure of their jeeps, reversing out of trouble or charging into it with disconcertingly noisy firepower to frighten people into running away and leaving valuable things behind. In those circumstances disconsolate Italians abandoned by their retreating German allies were less likely to put up a fight. If there was resistance, Curtis would jump out of the jeep and shout to Huntington-Whiteley, 'Your show, Peter!' and the marines would do the business. The commandos entered the wrecked and evacuated town of Sfax on 10 April. A later 'Recommendation for Decoration' form stated that Curtis 'rode into the town on the back of a tank, receiving a slight wound'. The harbour area had been badly bombed. Uprooted palm trees blocked semi-shattered streets. Avoiding piles of ammunition that might have been booby-trapped, the unit of 'authorised looters' went into German and Italian HQs, looking for papers. There was so much of interest they 'acquired' an Italian five-ton diesel truck to carry their finds. They entered nearby Sousse, also badly damaged by Allied bombing, on 12 April, and scavenged more pickings. With the hard-core Germans now dug in at Enfidaville, fifty miles south of Tunis, ready to fight the Eighth Army again, the 30 Commando IAU headed back to Bône, getting their haul of intelligence to Algiers on 17 April.

↗

The grand finale of the North Africa campaign took place in early May 1943. The First and Eighth Armies had now combined to form the Eighteenth Army Group, and the men from 30 Commando were back with them south-west of Medjez-el-Bab, where General Alexander was ready to launch the armoured divisions' surprise final assault on Tunis. The IAU were now mixed in with 'S-Force', a mixed bag headed by Colonel David Strangeways from the Middle East Intelligence Centre in Cairo, which was going to take various navy, army and air force intelligence people down into Tunis. But primary loyalties still counted: at their encampment near the Byzantine fortress of Ain Tounga, an RAF technical intelligence officer could not help noticing the large Royal Navy White Ensign that Dunstan Curtis and George McFee were flying in the olive grove in contravention of camouflage regulations, and he later saw it again at the back of a column heading into the wrecked naval base at Bizerta.

All the same, 30 Commando was learning to split up into smaller units and to be adaptable in order to reach more targets. They had only jeeps now and no motorbikes. One jeep drove straight past a German airfield and got down into Tunis not long after the 11th Hussars and the Derbyshire Yeomanry on 7 May. They parked in a building with a courtyard that was safe from the Germans still milling about outside. But the sudden collapse of the German and Italian forces turned northern Tunisia into a madhouse: over 250,000 enemy eventually surrendered, wandering about with no one to take charge of them. There was no great Axis evacuation (fewer than 700 escaped, including Rommel), but with the string of command cut, Afrika Korps morale suddenly went. But not everybody gave up at the same time, and the unit was never quite sure what it would run into – Bon Royle said it was 'grope as you go'.

From the signals centre at La Marsa one unit drove eighty miles up to Cape Bon where the Germans were making their last stand. On the way they were briefly caught in a firefight between British and Germans and sheltered in a large farmhouse. Curly Wilkins found a safe upstairs and thought he'd have a go at opening it. He blew all the tiles off the roof and got a bollocking from Huntington-Whiteley. Then they drove south-east to the airfield at El Hammamet looking for gear. Everybody else was at it in one way or another. You could take your pick of enemy clothes, weapons and vehicles, Fiats, Lancias, Volkswagens, select sausages and sundried tomatoes from the piles of excellent German and Italian rations, and liberate their copious stores of drink.

On 12 May 1943 the fighting was all over but the jubilation and junketing continued. As General Harold Alexander cabled Churchill, 'We are masters of the North African shores.' The writer Norman Lewis, then in Field Security, saw

thousands of unconscious British soldiers – I counted over fifty lying on the steps of a single church – a Goyaesque muddle of bodies, and bottles, and wine vomit.

9

Testing the Waters

The Italian island of Pantelleria lies in the middle of the Sicilian Channel between north-east Tunisia and south-west Sicily. Its military code name was HOBGOBLIN and American journalists dubbed it 'Benito Mussolini's Gibraltar'. Pantelleria had long been one of Winston Churchill's obsessions. He had originally wanted 'Layforce' to capture it in 1940 (see page 129) and now, in the run-up to the invasion of Sicily, he saw another chance. At Churchill's meeting with General Eisenhower and other senior Allied officers in Algiers on Saturday 29 May 1943, Pantelleria was the very first item on the agenda.

The island was just over eight miles by five miles square, but its radar could detect planes taking off from North Africa and its airfield could accommodate medium bombers and fighter planes. The cliffs bristled with batteries of big guns; motor torpedo boats and submarines used its harbour, and 10,000 Italians were defending it, equipped with tanks, mortars, machine-guns and flame-throwers. Operation CORKSCREW proposed to capture Pantelleria on 11 June. Heavy bombing from the air and naval bombardment from the sea would be a prelude to landing troops at the only harbour (there were no beaches). Churchill saw the operation partly as 'a very useful experiment' to see how far 'coast defences could be neutralised by air attack'. Would it 'admit practically unopposed landings'?

Also at the meeting with Eisenhower was Air Chief Marshal Arthur Tedder, a former head of RAF Research & Development who had become commander of American and British air forces in the Mediterranean. Earlier that year Tedder had struck up a friendship with British biologist Solly Zuckerman, who was becoming an expert on the damage that bombing and other weapons of war did to people and objects. Tedder now asked Zuckerman to help make Operation CORKSCREW a research experiment. In essence, using all the aerial photographic reconnaissance and intelligence available, his team should work out how many bombs the Northwest African Air Forces would need to reduce Pantelleria's defences to zero: bomb it: then analyse 'the relation of effort to effect'.

The blitz on Pantelleria slowly grew in intensity from 30 May to 11 June. 26,000 bombs were dropped on the island, more than half of them in the last two days. Heavy, medium and light bombers – Flying Fortresses, Wellingtons, Mitchells, Marauders, Bostons – struck at the eighteen coastal batteries, the town of Pantelleria and its harbour, the aerodrome by Gelkhamar and the light defences, in waves that gave no time for repair or maintenance. Of the 6,278 tonnes of high-explosive dropped on Pantelleria 70 per cent came in the form of US-made 500-lb and 1,000-lb General Purpose (GP) bombs and 19 per cent were US-made 20-lb fragmentation bombs. (Only 10 per cent of the ordnance was British.) The island blossomed with explosions; the wind made long hedgerows of smoke and dust. P-38 Lightnings strafed the new ruins that were jumbled up with the remains of ancient Cossyra. Eisenhower and Cunningham themselves arrived by sea to pump naval shells into the hazy inferno from offshore. Throughout the morning of Friday 11 June, a party from 33 Naval Troop of 30 Commando, which included Bon Royle, watched from their wallowing landing craft as more explosive shells from cruisers and destroyers helped to pulverise the industrially bludgeoned cliffs. Then, by the clock, the military-scientific experiment stopped. As after tremendous fireworks, an enormous shroud of smoke hung fading and decaying in the air. At H-hour, twelve noon on the same day, the landing craft went in to Pantelleria's only harbour, carrying men of the British 1st Infantry Division, and were not opposed. 'The town of Pantelleria was, practically speaking, wiped out,' wrote Solly

Zuckerman in his compendious report for Lieutenant General Carl Spaatz in July 1943. 'No single house, either within the town or within the area south of it to the slopes of Mt. Elmo had not suffered bomb damage.' 'What a mess it was,' remembered Bon Royle, 'just piles of volcanic rubble from smashed houses, dust and smoke. The dust was acid volcanic stuff, hard on the throat and thirst.' Stupefied survivors of the bombardment placed a large white cross of sheets on the cratered airfield and flew a white flag from the wrecked harbour to indicate the garrison's surrender. The 12,000 Italians were only too glad to give up.

'Italian casualties were very light,' reported Zuckerman. 'The total number of killed was between 100 and 200 and the total number of wounded was 200. Most people in the northern half of the island fled to the central hills or to the south, and Italian battery crews failed to remain at their posts.' But blockaded by sea, bombed from the air, its two main wells destroyed, Pantelleria had become a thirst-tormented and pestilential misery. 33 Naval Troop picked up more fleas than intelligence from Italian quarters and Bon Royle found the tumbled down place literally sickening: filthy dust and contaminated rainwater gave him dysentery. He had no medicine save atabrine and mepacrine anti-malaria tablets, which turned him yellow. Exhausted from chasing a terrified baggage mule whose fellows had been machine-gunned by a Messerschmitt, Royle, Hickling and Lund slogged in the heat through stony fields up to a high-spot of desolate Pantelleria in the blue haze of the Mediterranean. Their maps were useless and the quest futile, for the supposed gun battery on Montagna Grande had long since been abandoned. When at last Bon passed out on a rusty old bedstead, the naked springs welted his skin like a python. Solly Zuckerman was congratulated for his clever calculations. A thousand tons of bombs per square mile had done the trick; the lab experiment had worked. It was 'the first time in history that an air force had forced the capitulation of a strongly fortified enemy territory before land forces had gone in'. Yet the Bombing Survey

Unit on the ground reported a prodigious wastefulness. Of eighty guns that were bombed, only ten were rendered unserviceable and another thirty-three damaged. Nearly all the bombs failed to get within 200 square metres of the guns that were their target – 96.7 per cent of those dropped by heavy bombers, 93.6 per cent of ones dropped by medium bombers and 97.4 per cent from light bombers missed. Zuckerman argued that smashing a gun was only one of the ways that bombing reduced defences. The human casualties of bombing also contributed to the collapse, as did the destruction of rangefinders, predictors and searchlights, control posts and ammunition stores, communication trenches and roads, barrack buildings and personnel shelters, food and water supplies. Harry C. Butcher wrote in his contemporaneous diary that 'only two' of the fifty-four shore batteries on the island were 'completely knocked out', but the essential thing was that the 'central control system for aiming the guns had been hit'. The landlines from Admiral Parvesi's battle HQ were buried two and a half feet down and mostly ran alongside the main roads; when the roads were smashed, all three communication cables were damaged as accidental by-products. In any case, bombs worked not just because of the material damage they did – they were aimed at people's minds. Zuckerman wrote that 'demoralization may play as big a part in the silencing of a battery as any other single factor . . . The morale of the civil population was shattered by the bombardment and the nerves of the garrison also broke.' (This was not a universal truth. Despite 878 bombs falling around Battery No. 20 by Point Guardia, Captain Edwin Tietz never left it for thirty-three days and nights and was captured at his post.)

What the British began seeing in 1943 was the awesome industrial power of the USA. Less than a month after entering the war, on 1 January 1942, US President Roosevelt signed a declaration, agreed between twenty-six countries including China, India, USSR, UK and the British Dominions as well as eight European and nine Latin American countries, that they would all use their full resources to fight together against 'the Tripartite Pact' of Germany, Italy and Japan, and that none would sue for a separate peace. FDR struck out the term 'Associated Powers' for the Allied countries and coined his own name for them, 'the United Nations', the first time this phrase was used. But only the USA really had the industrial resources to lead what Roosevelt called 'the struggle for victory over Hitlerism'. Five days later, in a stirring State of the Union speech to the 77th Congress, Roosevelt again exhorted the USA to raise military industrial production and become 'the arsenal of democracy'.* He offered 'a hard war, a long war, a bloody war, a costly war', but he also committed the country to manufacturing whatever was needed for victory.

This was the promise put into practice on Pantelleria. After the industrialised destruction by American bombers came the heavy industry of American reconstruction. Giant American bulldozers swiftly remade Pantelleria's wrecked aerodrome into a mile-long airstrip for Allied bombers and fighters to use. Over in Malta, planning for the next step in the Mediterranean campaign, they built a brand new airfield on Gozo, from scratch, in ten days flat.

Now 30 Commando got ready to take part in the Allied assault on Sicily, Operation HUSKY. They were reinforced and reorganised. Lofty Whyman was promoted to sergeant, Harry Lund to corporal. Fair-skinned Dunstan Curtis's eczema had flared up in the African heat and he had returned to the more temperate UK, being replaced as commanding officer in Algiers by Lieutenant Commander Quintin Riley. Others had arrived by ship from Liverpool in late June; John Hargreaves-Heap brought more

---

*   In 1942 President Roosevelt had promised an annual production of 60,000 aeroplanes (rising to 125,000 in 1943), 45,000 tanks (rising to 75,000 in 1943) 20,000 anti-aircraft guns (rising to 35,000) and 8 million tons of shipping, rising to 10 million tons.

Royal Marines to reinforce 33 Naval Troop and Josh Ward, late of 3 Commando, disembarked the entire 34 Army Troop, with Paddy Martin-Smith from 12 Commando joining them in Algeria to replace an injured subaltern.

The most notable addition to the Technical Wing of the intelligence Commandos was swarthy Jim 'Sancho' Glanville, who had been involved with secret services in Yugoslavia and Iberia. He was the dynamic character whose knowledge of German commando activities in the Balkans had given Ian Fleming the seed of the idea of an intelligence assault unit. Enterprising Sancho Glanville was now reinvented on Sicily as an acting sub lieutenant RNVR in the Special Service Brigade. Since he had not had time to go to naval college at Greenwich, Glanville's fellow RNVR officers in the Technical Wing, Peter Orton and 'Paddy' Davies, had much to teach him about naval dress, discipline and deportment.

The triangular island of Sicily, at the toe of Italy's boot, is one of the most invaded islands in history. After Egyptians, Iberians, Phoenicians, Trojans, Greeks, Carthaginians, Romans, Goths, Vandals, Byzantines, Arabs, Normans, Spanish, Bourbons and Italians, it was the turn of the Americans and British. The Western Task Force landed General Patton's Seventh Army in the Gulf of Gela, and the Eastern Task Force took Montgomery's Eighth Army into the Gulf of Noto. As before, the US and UK forces (who now included the Canadians) went in separately. This Allied invasion of south-east Sicily on 10 July 1943 was even bigger than TORCH. But HUSKY's 2,000 ships, 4,000 aircraft, and 150,000 men could not escape Murphy's Law. The COPPs reconnoitring the beaches took 70 per cent casualties (including five dead officers) before anyone set foot on land. A decoy C-47 aeroplane, loaded with dummy paratroopers and pyrotechnical devices to simulate a non-existent attack, crashed in flames after a firework went off prematurely, killing all on board including the chief camouflage officer. The gusting winds scattered American paratroopers of

1 Commander Ian Fleming RNVR in Room 39 at the British Admiralty. As personal assistant and 'fixer' to both Directors of Naval Intelligence between 1939 and 1945, he knew many secrets and created a special force, 30 Assault Unit, to 'pinch' enemy intelligence and technology.

2 On 19 August 1942, Ian Fleming went to observe his intelligence assault unit in action for the first time in Operation JUBILEE, the Combined Operations cross-Channel raid against Dieppe. It was a disaster: hundreds of Canadian soldiers died.

3 Soon after Dieppe, Lord Louis Mountbatten, the director of Combined Operations, invited his cousin, King George VI, on a morale-boosting visit to COHQ in London.

4 Admiral John Godfrey was the Director of Naval Intelligence who gave Fleming his job and became the model for James Bond's fictional Secret Service boss, 'M'.

5 The Allies at first lagged behind the Axis technically, so 30 Assault Unit's mission was to 'pinch' advanced German technology for British Naval Intelligence. To crack enemy codes and decrypt their messages, the British needed to get hold of the sort of kit seen here in the vehicle that General Heinz Guderian used to command and control Panzer Blitzkrieg. The typewriter at bottom left with visible keyboard, lamp board and three removable wheels is actually an Enigma Geheimschreiber or encoding machine.

6 The tough British Commandos in 30AU earned their green berets by passing arduous training courses at camps like Achnacarry in Scotland.

7 British destroyer HMS *Malcolm* en route for Algiers, packed with American troops plus a team from 30AU for Operation TORCH, 8 November 1942.

8 'The Algiers boys': six of Ian Fleming's commandos returning from their exploits in North Africa in December 1942. L to R: Cpl Leslie Whyman, Marines Leslie Bradshaw MM and Ken Finlayson, Sgt John Kruthoffer, Marines Paul McGrath and Jack Watson, all survivors of Dieppe.

9 Marine Sandy Powell standing guard with his trusty Bren gun as 30AU men uncover a camouflaged V-1 rocket-launching site in Normandy on 18 June 1944.

10 German officers surrendering to 30 Assault Unit outside the Kriegsmarine headquarters at Octeville, Cherbourg, on 24 June 1944. Note the '30' flash on Major John Hargreaves-Heap's shoulder (far right).

11 Sergeant Paul McGrath DSM (squatting, second right) with part of his section of X Troop, 30AU, on their advance through Germany in 1945, looking for secret weapons and intelligence targets.

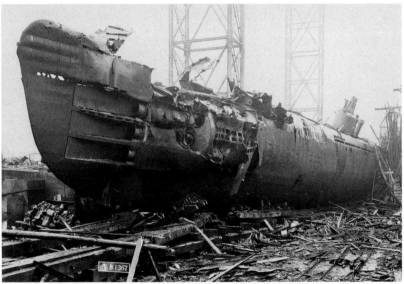

12 Lt-Cdr Patrick Dalzel-Job RNVR of 30AU in the first German midget
submarine captured by the Allies, on the Albert-Bapaume road in France,
9 September 1944. The mass-produced BIBER or 'Beaver', nine metres
long with two 21-inch torpedoes, was a last minute development in the
Kriegsmarine's desperate efforts to stave off defeat.

13 An official Nazi photograph, classified *geheim* or secret, of Allied bomb-
damage to the Deschimag shipyard in Bremen. Found by Marine Bon Royle
of 30AU, it shows a Type XXI electric submarine that was quieter and could
stay far longer underwater than earlier models, but which came too late to
win the war for Germany.

14 Captain Peter Huntington-Whiteley was the first Royal Marine officer to lead Ian Fleming's commandos in the field. The grandson of Prime Minister Stanley Baldwin survived the Dieppe raid and campaigns in North Africa, Sicily and Italy, as well as the D-Day landings, only to be killed in Dieppe on 12 September 1944, aged 24.

15 Actor meets author in 1962: Sean Connery with Ian Fleming on the set of the first Bond film, *Dr. No*. 'The person who plays Bond has to be dangerous,' Connery once remarked, 'If there isn't a sense of threat, you can't be cool.'
16 Ian Fleming and his wife, Ann, being served drinks by their housekeeper Violet at their home Goldeneye in Jamaica, where Fleming wrote all his James Bond books. It is also the setting for his brilliant, semi-autobiographical short story about 30AU, 'Octopussy'.

the 82nd Airborne over a thousand square miles of Sicily. With them jumped the famous news photographer Robert Capa, who was left hanging in a tree all night. In a subsequent wave, panicky Allied naval gunfire shot down dozens of their own planes, killing sixty US pilots and crewmen and eighty-one paratroopers.

The British airborne landing, Operation LADBROKE, was another ghastly failure only redeemed by the heroism of individuals. Sending 2,000 men by glider to capture the key Ponte Grande bridge near Syracuse was a bold and innovative plan, but such an assault had never been done before at night and there was no time for the 1st Airlanding Brigade to train. General Eisenhower himself looked up from Malta to watch the Allied Dakotas and Albemarles towing the gliders overhead in the moonlight. The wind, the dust, the friendly fire, the distortions of perspex windscreens and the novelty of night-flying made some pilots think the Italian flak was a lot closer than it really was, so many of the American C-47 'tug-planes' pulling the gliders released them too early. Around seventy gliders crashed into the sea. Some troops struggled ashore or were picked up by boats, but more than 300 men drowned. Out of two entire Airlanding battalions, only a single platoon of South Staffordshires managed to get to the vital bridge, take and hold it, fighting until their ammunition was exhausted. Soon after they lost the bridge, the Royal Scots Fusiliers retook it. Montgomery said the fact that the enemy had not destroyed the bridge saved him seven days.

30 Commando went ashore in Sicily near Cape Passero, with Eighth Army's XXX Corps, just behind the assault wave. The Italians had been lulled into thinking attacks only came on dark nights, but HUSKY surprised them on a bright moonlit one. Sancho Glanville's first target was an onshore German coast-watcher radar sweeping an area south-west towards Malta. In the brief firefight with the Allies, the German defenders blew the self-destruct charges,

destroying the control and display cabin. Glanville, accompanied by two ex-policemen, Walsh and Morgan, found the young Kriegsmarine lieutenant lying dead with several of his ratings. In his greatcoat pocket were his detailed notes of the long radar course he had just passed, and the handbook of the Telefunken T-39 Würzburg set, identical to the one pinched at Bruneval.

Another section's landing, though only lightly opposed, was a muddle. Their Royal Navy Reserve captain took them cautiously through choppy water to the wrong beach in a Landing Ship Tank (LST) whose 20-mm Oerlikons banged away at the few machine-guns and mortars on shore. Their fifteen-hundredweight Bedford truck drove off the bow ramp of the landing craft into water deep enough to stall the engine completely, so the seven men had to push it ashore with a tow from a friendly jeep. Small arms were popping, explosions going off. While marines Prince and Royle stripped the engine down, dried the carburettor, greased and repaired it, the others hared off to find what they could. After a quick skirmish with some Italians, Corporal 'Duke' Ellington captured and brought back a three-ton open truck in good working order. They later met up with their CO, Quintin Riley, and Martin-Smith joined them with the news that his party had captured an intact RDF station further down the coast, with all its operational documents, including a complete set of the ciphers and frequencies of the Italian air force's homing beacons for the months of July, August and September. Taken 'by hand of officer' to the RAF in Malta, this pinch enabled the Northwest Africa Tactical Air Forces to exploit the Italian beacon system themselves, using the enemy's own guidance to help them reach and hit their targets. Bon Royle's party took on a pill-box housing a Breda 13.2-mm machine gun. The Italian survivors were as eager to surrender as the men on Pantelleria, which seemed a pretty good start. Royle slept the rest of the hot and sticky first night in a British glider that had crashed in an almond grove. Nearby, a named, numbered wooden cross marked the grave of a previous glider passenger.

30 Commando left two corporals to guard the radar stations and moved on north towards Pachino and Syracuse, but when they eventually came back, they found both stations had been utterly destroyed. A sapper officer, outranking the NCOs, had blown up all the transmitters, receivers and towers, because they were 'interfering with fire-control'. Word came to Quintin Riley, in a villa that had belonged to a Fascist and which he had commandeered at Pachino, that the Special Raiding Squadron (SRS), an SAS unit led by Paddy Mayne, had gone ahead and landed in the naval base at Augusta. Already aggrieved that 30 Commando had not been able to go into Syracuse with Eighth Army, Riley now dispatched Red Huntington-Whiteley and Sancho Glanville in the Bedford lorry with a bunch of marines to get there fast. They entered the city with Scottish soldiers of the Black Watch, and were annoyed to see graffiti already painted on buildings: 'Captured by the SRS'.

It was incredibly hot. The port of Augusta had been bombed by the RAF, shelled by the Royal Navy and raided by the SAS men. Rats ran through ruins that stank of shit and dead bodies. In a stuffy office they discovered an Enigma machine with a plug board. Blows from a sharp instrument had damaged its rotors, but not destroyed them. Inside the naval air base, they found a range of bizarre acoustic instruments for detecting aircraft, including giant ear-trumpets manufactured by the Instituto Galileo Galilei in Florence, wired up to dials and devices that showed altitude, speed and direction. They seemed to indicate that the Italians had not yet acquired radar technology and that their allies the Germans were not sharing its secrets with them.

'Somebody coming, sir.' Challenge and counter-challenge. Password and response. There was an aggressive stand-off among the acoustic horns as Sancho Glanville was questioned by Major Humphrey Quill (whom we last saw in Iceland in 1940). The two men would later become friends and work together in Fleming's

Commando unit in 1944, but it did not start well. 'What the bloody hell do you think you're doing, getting in everyone's way?' 'I am from 30 Commando, following my commanding officer's orders.' 'Do you have any training in intelligence?' 'I have operated with three organisations that I am not allowed to name,' said Glanville.

Quill, who had been the staff officer (Intelligence) Levant in Alexandria for two years, asked Glanville whom he had been dealing with and Glanville, who had worked at one time or other for the Political Warfare Executive, SIS and SOE, was able to drop some satisfactory names, including that of Duncan Curtis, whom Quill had met in Bône four months earlier. Both men agreed it didn't matter who got what as long as the kit went back to the right people in Malta.

Quill was operating pretty much off his own bat. Having helped with coastal information for HUSKY, he was determined to take part in the actual operation and had put together a party of five other officers from Alexandria (including two Italian-speaking RNVR lieutenants, Croxton and Martin Solomon, who ran Quill's Italy and Sicily section) to collect intelligence and advise on a series of raids leapfrogging along the coast. Scrounging two jeeps, they had got passage to Malta and thence to Avola in Sicily, and had beaten 30 Commando to a Y listening station at Pachino where they discovered documents proving the Italians had penetrated British Naval Cipher No. 3, the Convoy Code. The last of Quill's party to turn up in the Augusta airbase's hall of acoustic horns was another fluent Italian-speaker, Lieutenant Commander Llandaff Rodd RN from the Combined Services Detailed Interrogation Centre at Alexandria, whose father James Rennell Rodd had been an outstanding British ambassador in Rome.

The 30 Commando men were sorting and packing stuff in Augusta naval base when a major of the Royal Marines Police appeared, investigating looting. Some men caught with stolen property were claiming to be from 30 Commando. Could he therefore please search their lorry? Rodd was furious when several personal items he was missing were found in the 30 Commando lorry. Huntington-Whiteley questioned all the marines but no one admitted anything. Everyone understood that 'requisitioning' items for the unit was standard wartime practice – after all, 30 Commando's official remit was to 'pinch' things from the enemy. But it was disagreeable if there was a thief inside the unit, stealing from his mates. There would be further indiscipline and truculence later among the marines of 30 Commando: punch-ups, careless discharge of firearms, rebukes from US General Matthew Ridgway for wandering around shirtless or selling captured enemy pistols to American GIs for cash. There was also a scam with currency. Some of the men tried to pay Sicilians with British 'Military Authority in Tripolitania' banknotes (valid only in Africa), insisting they were legal tender because they were in lire and centesimi.

Sicily seemed to encourage lawlessness. Rodd's eldest brother Francis, Lord Rennell of Rodd, was in charge of Allied Military Government of Occupied Territory (AMGOT) on Sicily, a job he had done before in Italian East Africa. Rodd had two Civil Affairs deputies, one British, one American, who had very different styles. The British, working from their imperial experience, favoured 'indirect rule' through established indigenous elites, and understood the necessary evil of employing elements from the old regime's security structure. The American deputy, however, Lieutenant Colonel Charles A. Poletti, an Italian-American former lieutenant governor from New York, worked with darker forces. Harold Macmillan commented in January 1944 that '[Poletti] is "the boss" of Sicily and just loves it. The Sicilians seem to enjoy it up to a point. I think they feel rather proud that one of themselves should have made it in America.' Poletti's personal interpreter, driver and *consigliere* was the gangster Vito Genovese, a man wanted for murder in America and who was an old friend of the Sicilian mobster 'Lucky' Luciano. Many of the new Sicilian mayors that Poletti installed were Mafia. Norman Lewis, author of *The Honoured Society*, a study of the Mafia, described the war's legacy in 1963: 'A golden age of new power and prestige followed with the Allied occupation of Sicily, secretly abetted by the Mafia. Presenting themselves as devoted anti-Fascists, the "men of honour" – as they prefer to be known – wormed their way into the good graces of the occupation authorities, and were soon in business as never before.'*

Important lessons were being learned for intelligence assault units in the field. Quill's makeshift unit managed to do well on Sicily, finding, for example, Italian navy documents hidden in the Mellili caves, because they included fluent Italian speakers who knew something of the culture and could follow up on information received. But, like 30 Commando, Quill's men got themselves into trouble for taking things without consent or proper clearance. They had no large vehicle, so they seized a derelict Italian fire engine from an abandoned airfield and cut off the top of its water-tank to make a capacious storage place for documents and equipment. When Admiral Andrew Cunningham, the Commander-in-Chief, Mediterranean, was wrongly informed that this vehicle was stolen from a *naval* dockyard rather than an airfield, he blew his top. The fire engine was removed and Quill was summoned to Malta and put under virtual arrest for three weeks. Quill only got back to Sicily in time to get into Messina with the Americans.

---

* US Naval Intelligence first dealt with the Palermo-born Mafioso, Charles 'Lucky' Luciano, in early 1942, while he was in prison in upstate New York. They initially wanted Italian-American patriotic muscle to help prevent sabotage and espionage in the New York docks following the mysterious fire on 9 February 1942 that destroyed the French liner then being converted at Pier 88 on the Hudson River into the US troopship *Lafayette*. Four Italian-speaking officers from New York's Third Naval District later went ashore in HUSKY with lists of Sicilian contacts supplied by the New York Mafia. For his assistance to the war effort, Luciano was freed from jail early in 1946 and deported to Sicily.

30 Commando took their booty from Augusta back to their new HQ. Down on the beach below the Capo Murro di Porco, where Paddy Mayne's Special Raiding Squadron had knocked out two coastal batteries on the first night, the bodies of more men from the 1st Airlanding Brigade were slowly being washed ashore. 'We buried them daily, marking and recording the graves. It was hard work as the ground was very rocky, not much soil cover, and bodies tended to fall apart after fairly prolonged immersion in the water.' Quite a few corpses had the tops of their heads missing, either sheared off in the glider crash or possibly trepanned by machine-gun fire. Their empty skulls reminded Bon Royle of lavatory bowls. Sicily in July was very hot and dry and brown. The malarial grey villages with Fascist slogans painted on the walls were full of dust; even mosquito-breeding water was scarce and welcome. The sweetish sickening stench of putrefaction and the buzzing of flies and bluebottles became a constant background hum because the superstitious peasants would not bury the dead for fear of *mal occhio*, the evil eye. They averted their gaze from corpses. There were so many, and not all from indiscriminate bombing. 'The men over here have changed,' the melancholy and perceptive Ernie Pyle wrote at the end of the Tunisian campaign to his readers back home in the United States. 'They are rougher than when you knew them. Killing is a rough business. Their basic language has changed from mere profanity to obscenity.'

US General George S. Patton liked to use obscene language in his shrill pep talks to soldiers. His high voice urged them to kill, not to fool around with prisoners, because the only good German was a dead one. In the early days of the invasion of Sicily, meeting stiff resistance from German and Italian troops, some in the US 45th Division took Patton at his word. At Biscari airfield Captain Compton ordered a firing squad to execute forty snipers who had surrendered, and Sergeant West killed thirty-six prisoners with a Thompson sub-machine gun. The British reporter Alexander Clifford witnessed other mass murders of captives at Comiso.

Lieutenant Colonel McCaffery of the US 3rd Division, who had been verbally ordered to shoot looters, emptied three clips of his .45 automatic pistol into a crowd of Sicilians who were scooping up liquid soap in a factory at Canicatti, killing men, women and at least one child. A month later, visiting a field hospital on Sicily, General Patton saw among the sick a shocked, trembling soldier who admitted to no wounds but 'nerves'. Patton slapped him, knocking his helmet off. 'You ought to be lined up against a wall and shot,' he shouted at Private Paul G. Bennett. 'In fact I ought to shoot you myself right now, God damn you!' As the three-star general pulled his ivory-handled revolver from its holster, Colonel Donald Currier, commander of the 93rd Evacuation Hospital, ushered him away from the sobbing soldier, still shouting, 'Get that coward out of here! I won't have those cowardly bastards hanging around our hospitals. We'll probably have to shoot them some time anyway, or we'll raise a breed of morons.' The reporter Noël Monks had just parked his jeep at the hospital. In his 1955 autobiography Monks wrote, 'We were walking towards the main hospital tent when General Patton emerged. He was shouting and gesticulating to a worried-looking army doctor and several nurses. We distinctly heard him shout: "There's no such thing as shell shock. It's an invention of the Jews."'

The Eighth Army got held up on the plains south of Catania when the Hermann Göring Division dug in on the slopes of Mount Etna and along the River Gornalunga, and the German 1st Parachute Division blocked the main road to Messina. A lorryload of 30 Commando was racing to get to Gerbini airfield when they got caught up in the front-line fighting. Marine officers have a Marine Officer's Attendant or MOA, the equivalent of a military 'batman' or servant, (called a 'flunkey' by his mates). Glanville's MOA and dispatch rider, Walsh, was blown off his motorcycle by a German shell, losing his steel helmet, but not his life. They all ended up in a trench with the 8th Durham Light Infantry, dealing with the wounded, sharing their cigarettes and fighting off attacks. As they were shelled again, a friendly Geordie saw Glanville feebly scratching at the side of the trench to deepen it. 'Ah see ye've nivver worked down a mine, sor,' he remarked, and furiously dug Glanville a safer niche.

When they got back to base Quintin Riley observed that this was not the best way to proceed. In future they must obtain clearance from the Eighth Army's tactical HQ, which Montgomery liked to keep forward of his main headquarters. Riley took Glanville up to TAC HQ to meet Montgomery's head of intelligence, scholarly Brigadier Edgar Williams, known to all as 'Bill', formerly a junior research fellow at Merton College, Oxford. The slight and bespectacled Brigadier Williams collated multiple sources of intelligence for Montgomery, including Rommel's signals from ULTRA, to help predict what the enemy were likely to do. Williams cleared 30 Commando to work in the Eighth Army sector in return for the promise that any captured documents affecting the army would be turned over to his people, and that any Italian civilians caught attempting to cross lines would be turned over to the military police. A pass from the Eighth Army was now added to the 'Mountbatten pass', a card signed by the chief of Combined Operations.

At Lentini, only a few miles from where Glanville failed to dig a better hole, an SOE officer, Malcolm Munthe, was also on the front line. Munthe, 'Callum' to his friends, spoke fluent Italian. After various extraordinary adventures with MI(R) and SOE in Finland, Norway and Sweden, Munthe had been sent to 'Massingham', the SOE detachment in North Africa, and thence to Sicily. His job for SOE's No. 1 Special Party was to infiltrate agents behind the Italian lines to link up with anti-Fascists and cause havoc and subversion to help the Allied cause. Now he was trying to get a wireless operator, a second lieutenant dressed as a peasant and carrying forged papers, across the front line into enemy territory. This young man (whom Munthe called 'Donaldbain' because his family asked that he not be identified) set out with two Italian agents to infiltrate Catania, still under siege by the Eighth Army. But he was captured by the Germans and his basket was examined: the melons were filled with explosives, his wine bottle was a concealed bomb. Not being in uniform, 'Donaldbain' was deemed to be a spy and saboteur.

The Germans interrogated him in vain. He refused to give the name of his unit or his contacts in Catania. They threatened him with death and showed him the Royal Carabiniere Regiment firing squad. No luck. They made him dig his own grave, but he turned that into a joke, getting down into it to make sure it fitted, wriggling and widening at the shoulders so he would be comfortable. The Germans promised to commute the death sentence if he talked. He would not. They stood him at the foot of the grave and at the top of his voice he cursed the Nazis and sent his love to his mother. '*Feuer!*' ordered the German officer. Not an Italian rifleman moved. '*FEUER!*' the Nazi screamed. The firing squad did nothing, but the German officer drew his pistol and shot the young British soldier dead.

Later the Italian sergeant in that stubborn firing squad came over to the Allies. 'Only a man who was very sure of his cause would die bravely like that,' he told Munthe. 'I would like to join you.'

One of 30 Commando's coups was getting into the Trapani naval base at the western end of Sicily. After La Spezia in northern Italy, it was the Regia Marina's largest base with an arsenal. The Allies had originally feinted west to keep the 15th Panzer Division, who were stationed not far from Trapani, away from the real landings and the fighting in the south-east and centre of the island. Two officers, three NCOs and a dozen marines from 30 Commando drove a jeep, the fifteen-hundredweight truck and four motorcycles from Syracuse to Agrigento and then followed the coast towards Trapani. Nearing their objective, they halted. On their left were the salt pans and the sea with the prison island of Favignana rearing up, and ahead a road through vineyards with signs saying *ACHTUNG MINEN!* They were wondering how to tackle this problem when a confident fourteen-year-old schoolgirl approached. She did not beg for *pane, biscotti* or *carammelle* like the skinny small boys in shorts who were everywhere in Sicily, but offered to ride in the lead jeep and guide them through the minefields. Peter Huntington-Whiteley drove with Jim Glanville in the passenger seat and the girl between them, while Corporal Lofty Whyman rode in the back with the Bren, the truck following a safe 'cable' (200 yards) behind. As they zigzagged cautiously through the mines, Glanville thought of the crossing of Grimpen Mire in *The Hound of the Baskervilles*. Safe on the other side, at Paceco, an Italian coast defence battalion put their hands up and Glanville told them to make a heap of their weapons and await the Americans. They drove straight through to Trapani naval base by the harbour. Nothing had been demolished and the stores and maintenance department for servicing underwater weapons were still intact on Monte Erice. Now it was time to bring in an expert from the Admiralty's Department of Torpedoes and Mines, Lieutenant Commander Ashe Lincoln, whom we first met when Winston Churchill ordered an investigation into magnetic mines in 1939.

Lincoln had not got off to a good start in his attachment to 30 Commando. When he first met them in Algiers, he showed Quintin Riley his Admiralty orders governing circumstances under which the unit should be put at Lincoln's disposal. Riley was not pleased and Lincoln thought the other man autocratic. Worse was to follow over a matter of religious observance. Riley was the son of the noted Anglo-Catholic Athelstan Riley, and insisted that everyone should kneel during morning prayers. Lincoln said he respected Riley's religion, but that he expected equal respect for his own, and as a Jew he would not kneel. 'My God, I hate all Jews,' said Riley. 'That is a pity,' replied Lincoln. 'You will have to tolerate this one as we have to go through a campaign together.' But eventually the two men worked together well, and became friends.When Lincoln reached Trapani naval arsenal to inspect the hoard of weapons, he had a wound in his left hand and his whole arm in a sling, so Marine Jock Finlayson had to help him:

We went to a factory or warehouse where sea-mines were stored; hundreds of them; beautiful rows of big round ones. Lt Cdr Lincoln was one of the select band of naval officers whose task was to unravel the latest dirty tricks and defuse German sea-mines etc and who must have ice-cold nerves. All afternoon I was assisting him getting bits off, and quite petrified, my vivid imagination expecting booby traps or time-pencils blowing us and Trapani sky high . . . I was mightily relieved when Lt Cdr Lincoln said he had all the bits of mechanism of interest to Naval Intelligence.*

As 1943 went on it was becoming clearer that Italy was losing the war. One Italian army had been destroyed in Russia in January, another captured in Africa in May, and now in July Sicily had been invaded. On 25 July Benito Mussolini fell from power in an Italian military and monarchist *coup d'état*. King Victor Emmanuel of Italy nominated Marshal Badoglio as the replacement military figurehead for Il Duce who had made such an unfortunate pact with the Führer. Badoglio kept up the façade of the alliance with Germany, but in August began secret negotiations with the Allies in Lisbon and Algiers to seek an armistice. As the Axis began to crumble, the strategy of the Germans in Sicily altered.

* 'The latest German pressure mines charged with the new Hexogen explosive' are what Giuseppe Petacchi brought over to the wartime Allies, for money, in *Thunderball*. Hexogen was the German name for the powerful military explosive that the Americans called cyclonite, the Italians T4 and the British RDX (Research Department Explosive).

Oberkommando Wehrmacht (OKW) was determined there should be no repeat of the dramatic collapse in Tunisia. Field Marshal Kesselring's men were ordered to fall back in successive lines and escape from Sicily across the Straits of Messina to Calabria in the toe of Italy.

The German officer in charge of defending the Straits of Messina was an eccentric show-jumping colonel called Ernst-Günther Baade who spoke excellent English and liked to wear a Scottish kilt with a large bone-handled dagger. He assembled a vast array of anti-aircraft guns and barrage balloons to protect the fleet of 120 lighters and barges organised by Fregattenkapitän Gustav von Liebenstein to ferry the Panzer Grenadiers, the 1st Paratroop Panzer Division Hermann Göring and the 1st Parachute Division by half a dozen routes across the narrow straits. Between 1 and 11 August 1943, 12,000 Germans with 4,500 vehicles and 6,000 tons of ammunition, fuel and stores got across. By 17 August, when the Allies entered Messina, 27,000 more German soldiers, 12,000 more tons of stores and 5,500 more vehicles (including 51 tanks and 163 guns) had been evacuated with almost no casualties in the brilliantly effective Operation LEHRGANG. Four crack German divisions lived to fight another day and kill many more Allied soldiers in mainland Italy, and the Italians also safely withdrew 63,000 men, 226 vehicles, 41 guns and 12 mules. The Allied command had missed a huge trick. They failed to use the strategic air forces that had pulverised Pantelleria, their navies didn't shell the ferries and the armies didn't land men on the other side of the straits to cut the escapees off.

The German evacuation was happening right in front of 30 Commando and they could do absolutely nothing about it. They found it disillusioning to think how incompetent or impotent their own top brass were. One small compensation was finding a German communications truck that had come off a bombed road outside Messina and gone over a cliff, killing its occupants, but not catching fire. It turned out to be a travelling Y station that had been intercepting and deciphering Eighth Army messages. The commandos searched the vehicle, picked the dead men's pockets, and packed it all off to the intelligence section of TAC HQ, who pronounced themselves 'very satisfied'.

The Americans and British raced each other to get into Messina first, and General Patton won the prize. But it turned out to be a Sodom's apple, bitter ashes. The town was wrecked, most of its citizenry fled, and what was left was noisome and dangerous. As naval parties started clearing the port, hauling up a depth charge that someone spotted in an anchorage, a massive explosion obliterated half a mole and a truckload of men; the mine was fitted with a pressure-release fuse, which meant that when you pulled it up to the surface it went off. Divers now had to go down and defuse 270 more, each one by hand. Messina's streets and buildings were also infested with square Teller mines. The British Naval Officer in Command (NOIC) at Messina was a large man whose face was bumpy with mosquito bites. Seeing that Humphrey Quill's band was doing the same job as 30 Commando, he put Quill in charge of 30 Commando's searches for intelligence material in the Italian naval HQ and other buildings. Glanville just managed to stop one marine from switching on a nice radio set that was connected to a stash of TNT under the floor. Pressing, pulling or lifting anything was dangerous when so much was booby-trapped. Light switches, door handles, lavatory cisterns, safes, cupboards, pictures, haversacks, bottles, weapons and other items that might tempt looters could all be wired to trigger an explosion. Meanwhile, German artillery lobbed shells across the Messina straits to slam into crumbling buildings.

30 Commando set up a base at Villa Ella near Milazzo early in September. As people moved about their missions, the unit's stores, kit and gear were piled up under a tarpaulin near the house. It was still very hot and dry and it was probably a carelessly discarded cigarette butt that started the fire, though some claimed it was sabotage. The commandos' personal possessions, clothing,

bedding, mortars, ammunition and explosives all blazed up. Everyone retreated with their personal weapons and took cover behind walls as the house burned down. After the conflagration, a passing squaddie from the Pioneer Corps (whose job was basically digging trenches and making roads) picked up a blackened .36 grenade and, for a laugh, shook it by his ear as if it was a duff clock. It blew his head off. He was among the last of the 13,000 who were killed in the invasion of Sicily in 1943. It always puzzled Ken Finlayson that a professional Royal Marine like him should survive every kind of danger, shot and shell, while this poor devil of a non-combatant was picked to die. That night, as they slept in the open, the weather broke into unrelenting rain.

More bad luck dogged them when they finally reached mainland Italy, trying to land at Salerno in Operation AVALANCHE on 9 September. Their landing craft got stuck on a sandbank, could not be kedged off and was only freed by a large wave from a huge explosion. When they finally got up the tortuous road to the naval HQ, clouds of smoke through the roof and windows showed that somebody had already torched all the papers. Everyone had cheered too soon at the news that the Italians had surrendered on 8 September; in fact the German 16th Panzer Division were defending Salerno even more fiercely. There was heavy shelling and sniping. In order to help the land forces of Fifteenth Army Group trapped at the beachhead, the US and the Royal Navy had to get in close to bombard the German positions with their big guns.

The opening pages of Norman Lewis's *Naples '44* portray panic, ineptitude, cowardice and chaos at Salerno, as does the first chapter of Donald Downes's arresting book *The Scarlet Thread: adventures in wartime espionage*. The forty-year-old Downes was one of the original, maverick OSS agents – not right-wing, probably gay – who had burgled the Francoist Spanish embassy in Washington DC. He had also helped infiltrate armed parties of former Republicans from North Africa into southern Spain where many were captured or killed at Malaga. Disembarking at Salerno on 9 September 1943 involved clambering down a manila-rope scrambling net, flapping from the rolling side of a big ship, into a small landing craft far below. Waiting to go, Donald Downes heard a scream: 'I saw a Colonel in mid-air, head down with his gadgets hanging before him, falling for the steel deck of the next landing barge. I heard the thud.' Downes eventually got ashore at Paestum with the 36th (Texas) Division, which had not been in combat before. He watched their anti-aircraft guns shooting down their own planes, peered at two corpses roasted to blackened crackling in a burned-out bulldozer, and witnessed the major he had befriended die violently next to him.

The Germans had also developed a new weapon, a radio-guided, armour-piercing, air-to-sea 1,400-kilogramme bomb, the Ruhrstahl X-1, which the Luftwaffe (who launched it from a Dornier 217K-2 bomber from 18,000 feet) called the Fritz-X. This was first used on 9 September 1943 to punish the deserting Italians. Two missiles punched through the battleship *Roma*, breaking her in two and drowning 1,255 men including Admiral Bergamini. On 11 September the American cruiser USS *Savannah* was disabled; on the 16th the famous British battleship HMS *Warspite*, a veteran of Jutland, Narvik, Crete and Cape Matapan, was hit, fresh from taking the surrender of the main Italian fleet at Malta. One of three X-1 missiles penetrated six decks before blowing a hole in the hull. Other ships sunk or disabled off Salerno included the cruisers HMS *Spartan* and USS *Philadelphia*.

Blasts on land assailed 30 Commando as the city of Salerno wobbled between the two sides. The German counter-attacks were fierce, and reinforcements had to be parachuted in and fleets of bombers diverted. The explosion of a near-miss mortar round permanently deafened Quintin Riley in one ear and destroyed the nerves of their sergeant major who went home badly 'twitched'.

At Salerno in September 1943 they never knew either where the German snipers were lurking or whether the Americans might shoot or bomb them by mistake. Operation AVALANCHE went, in the slang acronyms of the day, from SNAFU (Situation Normal: All Fucked Up) to FUBAR (Fucked Up Beyond All Recognition) and back again before it settled.

10

Invasion of the Islands

On 12 September 1943 30 Commando were once again at action stations on Landing Craft Infantry (Large) 249, approaching the island of Capri. They were nervously expecting enemy opposition when they began to hear the town band playing 'It's A Long Way to Tipperary'. The mayor himself was at the Marina Grande to greet the flotilla, a small man in a big top hat. After their twenty-five-mile voyage from the explosions and gunfire of Salerno, the festive scene had the surreal quality of *Alice in Wonderland*. They half wondered if Gracie Fields, who was among the many writers and artists with villas on the resort island, might appear.

The ship had two ramps either side of the bow, down which came Riley, Glanville, Paddy Martin-Smith and eight Other Ranks of 30 Commando. Intelligence had reported, but not yet deciphered, enemy signals coming from Capri, and it was their job to sort them out. The main body of 2,500 Italian troops stationed on Capri had surrendered at the armistice, but the mayor told the British commandos that while there were no German soldiers on the island, there was still a force of three dozen hard-core Italian Fascist soldiers under Colonel Salverini in the fort at the top of the island. It was their wireless signals that Intelligence had picked up.

That very day, 12 September 1943, a dramatic *coup de main* was taking place on mainland Italy. At Gran Sasso, high in the Abruzzi mountains, SS Colonel Otto Skorzeny and his paratroopers landed by glider to rescue Il Duce Benito Mussolini from his captivity in the Hotel Campo Imperatore and fly him to Vienna. While Marshal Badoglio and King Victor Emmanuel were calling for all Italian civilians and servicemen to join the Allies and to resist the Germans, Mussolini was set up as the head of a German-controlled puppet state in northern Italy, Repubblica Sociale Italiana (RSI), the Italian Social Republic, with Marshal Rodolfo Graziani, 'the Butcher of Ethiopia', as his minister of defence. Italy was now in a civil war between those who were pro-Allies and those who were pro-Axis.

Early in the morning of 13 September, 30 Commando commandeered a lorry and made their way up to Anacapri, climbing a cliff to reach the parapet of Colonel Salverini's fort. Surprised at their ablutions, the Italian garrison surrendered. Salverini was arrested elsewhere by Paddy Martin-Smith. The commandos found and dismantled the Capri wireless transmitter. In Salverini's safe were Italian codes, including one secret one that had not been handed over as it should have been under the terms of the Armistice, a list of Fascist party members in Naples who wanted to continue fighting, and dossiers on all the leading personalities of the island.

Most famous among them was the Swedish physician Dr Axel Munthe, the father of Malcolm Munthe. Axel Munthe was not on the island at that time, but his son had accompanied 30 Commando on this trip in order to requisition his father's house for the Allies. Munthe, who married an Englishwoman, had in 1929 published a book in English, *The Story of San Michele*, that became an international romantic best-seller, translated into forty-five languages. It told, among other things, how as a student in 1875 the author had sailed from Sorrento to Capri, climbed up the Phoenician stairs to Anacapri, become captivated by the ruined chapel of San Michele and, through caring for birds and animals and sick people, achieved his dream of restoring the buildings to beauty. According to the Fascist dossier, Axel Munthe was the illegitimate son of His Britannic Majesty King Edward VII. This fantasy rather surprised his eldest son, who knew better. When 30 Commando went with Malcolm Munthe to his father's famous house, they were impressed by the Villa San Michele's stunning view over the harbour and the blue bay. Among the litter of antiquities, Etruscan pots, Roman marble and Greek statuary, Quintin Riley got hold of the visitors' book and ruled off a new section, which he headed *September 13, 1943 – Liberation by the English*. 'What about the Scots?' asked Malcolm Munthe, indicating the kilt of his regiment, the Gordon Highlanders. All the commandos signed their names.

The mayor of Capri laid on a banquet where Rear Admiral Anthony Morse, Flag Officer, Western Italy, joined them for Caprese wine and song. Morse was setting up his headquarters on Capri, requisitioning the comfortable villa of Mussolini's daughter, the glamorous Edda Ciano, with its spectacular views and push-button devices in every room. Morse gave his blessing for 30 Commando to conduct further operations in the Bay of Naples, where American raiding parties were already active. In his autobiography, *A Hell of A War*, Lieutenant Commander Douglas Fairbanks Jr describes how they bluffed their way to the capture of the island of Ventotene, where the Germans had a radar station and Mussolini's Fascists kept a prison. Malcolm Munthe was in the harbour at Capri when Fairbanks offloaded from the American destroyer USS *Knight* three dozen of Mussolini's former prisoners, some of whom had been locked up for seventeen years.

Munthe had some liberating of his own to do. In this vital period when Italy was trying to free itself from Mussolini's regime and the alliance with the Nazis, the writer who mattered most to him was the philosopher Benedetto Croce, who represented liberal politics and freedom of thought and was, to Munthe, 'the greatest anti-Fascist in all Italy'. In 1883 the adolescent Croce had lost both his parents and his only sister in a massive earthquake on Ischia; himself injured and trapped long in the ruins, he had kept despair at bay by thinking about the universe. In the First World War Croce stayed coolly impartial when other writers were drawn into recrimination and hatred. Now the great writer was in danger of being taken hostage by the Germans or Mussolini's Social Republic. Hitler's special forces had staged a daring rescue of Benito Mussolini, and Munthe was determined that Allied special forces would rescue Benedetto Croce. The philosopher had moved from his home in Naples to escape Allied air raids and was living across the bay in the Villa Tritone, a handsome house perched on a clifftop in Sorrento.

On the night of 14 September 1943 a launch provided by the Regia Marina, the by now pro-Allied Italian Royal Navy, set out to get him. On board were the mayor of Capri and Adrian Gallegos, a half-English, half-Spanish SOE officer who had been earmarked as a guerrilla leader in 1941 if the Germans invaded Spain to attack Gibraltar, and who now worked as Munthe's naval assistant with SOE's secret flotillas in the Mediterranean. When they tied up their launch at Sorrento's fishing port, they could see the pale villa in its garden on the cliff up to their left. In the twilight Gallegos and the mayor made their way up to the villa, hugging the side of the road, alert for German troops, grateful to reach the dark garden. As they entered the Croces' sitting room, anxious faces turned towards them. In the dim candlelight, the family just saw Gallegos as a uniformed man with a pistol on his hip and a Thompson sub-machine gun in his hands. But Gallegos spoke fluent Italian and took Signora Croce aside to tell her what his mission was. Though they had already received anonymous threatening letters from Fascists and found a mine floating below the villa, she said he would have a hard job persuading her husband to leave.

Gallegos found Croce working on Dante by candlelight in his study. His white hair was cut short and a large book lay open on the table between them. When the soldier passionately urged the philosopher to leave, he answered serenely, 'I am an old man. I do not like the Germans but I am not afraid of them. Do you know as a fact that they are planning to capture me?' Gallegos assured him he had reliable information. 'No, I shall remain here,' said Croce. 'I would not want the people of Sorrento to think that I am afraid.' Gallegos pleaded that time was running out. Eventually, but reluctantly, the other conceded. At nine in the evening Croce left for Capri with his two youngest teenage daughters, excited to be eating sandwiches in the open launch. The next night, hearing that Germans had surrounded the villa, Malcolm Munthe went in another boat to collect Croce's wife and remaining daughter.

Croce was asked by an English officer for the names of 'dangerous persons and Fascists' in Sorrento, but the philosopher told him that after refusing to collaborate for so many years, he was not going to start now. Soon afterwards on Capri, the film star Douglas Fairbanks Jr watched an American sailor stumblingly reading Shakespeare to one of the Croce teenage daughters. She did not speak the language at all but wanted to hear what the poet's words sounded like in English.

Lieutenant Commander Douglas Fairbanks Jr USNR was part of a US navy tactical deception unit known as the 'Beach Jumpers' and he had come to Capri, along with a group of OSS agents led by Frank Tarallo and Henry Ringling North, on the destroyer USS *Knight*. Also aboard was the Californian novelist John Steinbeck, author of *The Grapes of Wrath* and a future winner of the Nobel Prize for Literature. For the last seven months of 1943 Steinbeck was a war correspondent, sending dispatches to the *New York Herald Tribune* which were collected fifteen years later in the book *Once There Was a War*. Steinbeck disparaged them then as 'half-meaningless memories of a time and of attitudes which have gone forever from the world, a sad and jocular recording of a little part of a war I saw and do not believe . . .'

One of them – 'SOMEWHERE IN THE MEDITERRANEAN WAR THEATER, *October 15, 1943*' – is about 30 Commando, and is clearly a version of what happened on the night of 17/18 September, when Glanville and Martin-Smith set off from Capri in their landing craft with seven men to investigate the torpedo works at the Baia peninsula. Steinbeck's piece, headlined 'The Lady Packs', began:

There is a little island very close to the mainland near Naples which has on it a very large torpedo works, one of the largest in Italy. When Italy had surrendered, the Germans took the island, mined it thoroughly, and ran the detonating wires under the water to the mainland, so that they could blow up the torpedo works if it seemed likely to be captured. The Germans left a few guards, heavily armed, and they also left an Italian admiral and his wife as a sort of hostage to the explosives planted all over the little island. To a small Anglo-American naval force a curious order came. One single torpedo boat was to take on some British commandos, who were to go ashore in secrecy, cut the wires to the mainland, kill the German guards, and evacuate the Italian admiral and his wife.

Steinbeck was not actually with the commandos that night, but he *had* been on a night run in the early hours of 14 September aboard a US patrol boat taking Quintin Riley and a group of commandos across from Capri in an abortive search for a secret wireless transmitter. So the American writer had seen and met 30 Commando, who do not seem to have taken to him. Martin-Smith's log described Steinbeck as a 'fat, red, blotched man', and Glanville indicated, without any more detail, that Steinbeck's 'behaviour' was 'objectionable'. The commandos would not have warmed to his description of them, either:

The celebrated commandos, the great swashbucklers, took their time in arriving. In fact, they arrived nearly at dusk, five of them, which to their mind is a large military force. And these were very strange men. They were small, tired-looking men who might have been waiters or porters at a railway station. Their backs were slightly bent and their knees knobby and they walked with a shuffling gait. Their huge shoes, with thick rubber soles, looked far too large for them. They were dressed in faded shorts and open shirts, and their arms were an old-fashioned revolver and a long wicked knife. Their leader looked like a weary and petulant mouse who wanted more than anything else to get back to a good safe job in an insurance office with the certainty that his pension would not be held up. These five monsters came shambling aboard and went immediately below decks to get a cup of tea and slice of that cake which tastes a little like fish.

As Steinbeck relates the short story, the commandos went across the waters in the dark to the island and got a rubber dinghy ready. The captain of the motor torpedo boat asked how long it would take to cut the wires, kill the guards, and bring out the admiral and his wife. An hour, said the commando officer. The guards and the wire wouldn't take long, he added, but 'the admiral's wife will need time to pack. She doesn't know we're coming. She won't have her things ready.' In his story, the dinghy was back in an hour, with no shots, no lights, no noise. 'A little slender woman was helped over the side, and then a quite stout admiral in a beautiful overcoat, although the night was warm.' Two of the commandos then rowed the dinghy back to the island. The captain of the motor torpedo boat was impatient with the further delay and questioned one of the men who had brought back the admiral and his wife.

'Accomplish the mission?' 'Yes, sir, there were eight guards, not seven.' 'You didn't take them?' 'No, sir.' He fingers the steel hilt of his knife, almost apologetically. 'What have they gone back for?' 'The lady's trunk, sir. Quite a large one.'

The real-life admiral's name was Eugenio Minisini and his wife did in fact have many pieces of luggage, though the torpedo works were not on an island, there were no German guards to assassinate and no dramatic wires to snip, as in Steinbeck's telling. Minisini was the head of Italian naval underwater engineering, working on a new 'magnetic pistol' (a kind of proximity fuse) for torpedoes as well as designing submersible assault craft and midget submarines, the field of technology in which Italy led the world. He was a valuable prize for 30 Commando, telling them exactly where his blueprints and documents were stored so they could go back and retrieve them a few nights later.

Marines Schermuly and Mares, two ex-policemen from 30 Commando, combed Minisini's offices, while others explored the brilliantly lit tunnels that led from San Martino to Baia and the torpedo ranges on Lake Fusaro. Minisini revealed that the Germans were doing important work on experimental torpedoes at the industrial works of Silurificio Whitehead SA at Fiume.

Quintin Riley alerted the Admiralty underwater technicians to come to Ischia.

The Allies were alarmed by the potential linking up of Italian and German research and development on underwater explosive technologies because the Italians led the world in a field where every other combatant nation had had problems with malfunctioning torpedoes, faulty pistols and so on. When Italy surrendered it mattered very much who got hold of this Italian technical expertise. After the 8 September armistice, not all the naval commandos of Decima Flottiglia MAS, the men who put the submarine technology into action, were joining the new and pro-Allied Italian Co-Belligerent Navy. Led by their commander, the dedicated Fascist Junio Valerio Borghese, who had signed a special treaty with the German navy on 12 September, many of them continued to fight on as bullyboys for Mussolini's Social Republic, this time on land. Their new badge was a Roman 'Xa', topped by a skull with a red rose in its grinning teeth.*

Seizing Minisini seemed to be a good piece of British work, with no help from the Americans, especially not from OSS. 30 Commando were not too keen on the OSS. They had come across some of their Italian agents in a sailboat rashly trying to infiltrate Naples in broad daylight. Riley, Glanville and the other officers agreed on 18 September that 'the intelligence we had been receiving from the OSS was not only valueless but in some cases dangerous, in that certain reports seem to have been planted by enemy sources'. 30 Commando passed Admiral Minisini on to Rear Admiral Anthony Morse's intelligence branch on or around 20 September, and soon afterwards the Americans pounced.

---

* J. Valerio Borghese's book about his wartime exploits, *Decima Flottiglia MAS*, was translated into English in 1954 as *Sea Devils* and stops abruptly on the day of the armistice, 8 September 1943. At the end of the Second World War, fighting a losing battle against Tito's troops and Communist partisans, Borghese was rescued by OSS officer James Jesus Angleton and driven to Rome in an American uniform.

According to an OSS Report of 10 March 1944 sent to General Donovan:

Admiral Minisini arrived in the United States on October 21, 1943 at the instance of the Office of Strategic Services. He was followed by a group of 12 selected Italian engineers and technicians whom OSS had brought to this country as authorized by Admiral Minisini and who arrived December 17, 1943 together with 40 tons of technical ordnance material which was necessary to facilitate their work in this country.

It was a brilliant US stitch-up. General Bill Donovan had got together with the Secretary of the Navy, Frank Knox, to try and finesse the surrender of the Italian navy and to capture their technical secrets. Donovan knew Mussolini's replacement, Marshal Pietro Badoglio, of old, having visited him on campaign in Abyssinia in 1935. Eager to distance themselves from the Germans and to cement the new alliance, the Italian authorities were only too keen to trade their technology with the Americans, and OSS field teams like the 'Macgregor Mission' led by Tarallo and North were there to facilitate it. The need to find out about the German guided missile that hit USS *Savannah* galvanised the process.

Donovan himself doubtless played a key role in pinching Minisini. The Medal-of-Honor-winning General turned up at the Salerno beachhead in late September 1943 expecting to eat K-rations and sleep in a foxhole with his helmet on, but found himself instead in a comfortable bed with sheets in the Hotel Luna on Amalfi, once a monastery founded by Francis of Assisi, but now entirely commandeered by the OSS. Donovan met all the OSS agents around the Bay of Naples including the ones who were handling the Italian defectors. Minisini and his Italian submarine engineers all ended up at the American Naval Torpedo Station at Goat Island, Newport Bay, Rhode Island, working on improving American underwater weaponry. This wholesale removal of foreign scientists and technicians in 1943 is important because it became the template for Operation PAPERCLIP in 1945, when many German technicians – especially rocket scientists like Wernher von Braun – were accepted into the USA without being scrutinised for Nazi war crimes.

The USA pinched Minisini, Germany pinched Mussolini, and the UK got the idealist philosopher Benedetto Croce. The SOE officers who rescued Croce went on to other adventures. Adrian Gallegos was captured by, and escaped from, the Germans several times in Italy, Germany and Austria. Malcolm Munthe was severely wounded by a German mortar on Sunday 6 February 1944 at Aprilia on the road to Rome, and took no further part in the war. The friend who was with him was killed instantly. He was Michael Gubbins, the head of SOE's eldest boy.

Another of 30 Commando's important targets was the Y listening station at Licola, ten miles north of the torpedo works on the Baia peninsula. On a deliberately noisy armed reconnaissance on the night of 18/19 September, Sancho Glanville took sixteen officers and men of the unit in their landing craft (their guns bulwarked with sandbags) up the coast from San Martino, aiming to test enemy firepower and then plot the sources of the gun flashes on the map. Machine-gun fire from the landing-craft's 20-mm Oerlikons started a lively fire in an enemy petrol dump at Cuma, but attracted heavy machine-gun fire from the defenders at nearby Licola. A 50-mm German PaK anti-tank shell passed straight through the landing craft's engine room and out the other side; metal fragments wounded two matelots and two marines, and they realised how difficult it would be to land from the sea. Some of the men who had not been let in on the purpose of the trip grumbled at an expedition they saw as pointless 'flag-waving'.

A land approach worked better. Five NCOs and seven marines landed north of Torregaveta and made for Monte Cuma where they had started the fire. Cumae, as it was called in classical times, was the site of the earliest ancient Greek settlement in Italy, where the prophetess known as the Sibyl once lived in a cave and wrote her prophecies on palm leaves. The bay of Naples is dominated by Mount Vesuvius, the volcano whose eruption on 24 August 79 AD destroyed the Roman city of Pompeii, and it is thought now that the Sibyl's volcanic cave may have been filled with subterranean fumes, which caused her visions. Lake Avernus (Lago d'Averno) nearby was believed by the ancients to give access to the Underworld, the realm of the god Hades. The god Apollo offered the Sibyl a thousand years of life if she would become his lover; she accepted but forgot to ask for youth as well as life, and over the centuries shrank and dwindled so much that in time she was tiny enough to fit in a bottle, where she lived wizened and wailing, longing to die.

30 Commando inspected the Sybil's caves but found no intelligence material. Then they were approached by two bright Italian boys aged fourteen or fifteen, partisans called Pietro and Peppino, who had armed themselves with Italian army carbines and were anxious to lead the commandos back to their village at Licola. Upon questioning, the commandos thought they seemed reliable and took them on as scouts to liaise with civilians. But as they approached the German Y station at Licola, the boys, instead of doing what they were asked to do – a quiet reconnaissance and report back – went boldly up to the German garrison and frightened them by saying that a large force of British commandos in green berets was approaching through the woods. The Germans panicked, set the building and its papers alight and fled. When 30 Commando arrived, the boys were trying to put out the fires, and many books, papers and operational documents stuffed into a central-heating furnace were safely extracted, scorched but legible. The German station had been eavesdropping on Allied army, navy and air force communications, and it was useful (if alarming) to learn what they knew. There was also a complete run of *A.H.M.*, the German armed forces gazette *Allgemeine Heeresmitteilungen*,

from January 1942 to date. Pietro and Peppino (whose surnames were never recorded) were just two of the many thousands of Italians who aided the Allies. In time the Italian partisans would keep seven German divisions pinned down, and in the north the partisans made German forces collapse and surrender around Genoa, Turin and Milan.

The war was also being fought further east in the Mediterranean, 500 miles away on the other side of Greece in the Aegean Sea, spattered with small islands that seemed ideally suited to commando operations – but 30 Commando's deployment of a small unit there involved them in a disaster.

The Americans saw the Aegean as a distraction, but both Adolf Hitler and Winston Churchill were obsessed with it. In April 1943 when Operation MINCEMEAT planted on a corpse left to wash ashore in Spain false information suggesting that the Allies were going to invade Greece instead of Sicily, it only confirmed the Germans' fears, and made them more determined to reinforce the Aegean. On 26 July Hitler forecast that the Allies would 'shortly begin landing operations against our strong line in the Aegean, Peloponnese–Crete–Rhodes, and against the west coast of Greece with Ionian islands . . . Turkey's neutrality is at present beyond question, but needs continuous watching.' Hitler was right to the extent that Churchill longed to get the Aegean in his strategic portfolio. If the Allies seized the island of Rhodes (a project that never quite materialised, code-named Operation ACCOLADE), its airfields could dominate the fourteen islands of the Dodecanese. Churchill wanted to draw neutral Turkey into the war on the Allies' side. ('Tell Turkey Christmas is coming!' he advised his diplomatist Anthony Eden.) If only he could control the Dardanelles and choke off German supplies, thus helping to relieve Russia . . . The old First World War fantasies that a brilliant sideshow in the east might deliver success and avoid slaughter on the Western Front still flickered on the horizon.

By August 1943, when Churchill travelled on the *Queen Mary* to the Quebec conference and then to the USA to badger Roosevelt, the Allies had not yet won the war, but Nazi Germany had probably lost it. The balance had tipped in favour of the Allies in the Battle of the Atlantic, and after the showdown with Russia at the Battle of Kursk on the Eastern Front, Germans losses became overwhelming. But Britain was losing its status too. Somehow in 1943 the baton of power and strength passed invisibly but irretrievably from the slowly dying British Empire to the awakening American giant; the USA, by now the senior partner in the Alliance, would increasingly call the shots. The biggest (though unspoken) threat was that the Americans might turn their backs on fighting the Germans in Europe and concentrate all out on the Pacific war against the Japanese. Eisenhower's Americans were prepared to go into mainland Italy in 1943, but there was no way they would go to Rhodes in the Aegean. 'God forbid I should try to dictate, but not one American soldier is going to die on that goddamned island,' US army chief of staff General George Marshall recalled saying to Churchill. The Aegean would be a British battleground only.

Rhodes was a Greek island held mainly by Italian troops under the beady eye of a smaller, tougher German garrison. When, after days of 'negotiating for peace with a rope around their neck,' Italy finally surrendered on 8 September 1943, the Allies had hoped that Italian soldiers everywhere would come over to them and turn their weapons on the Germans. But the German army had long prepared for this eventuality. On an agreed code word, ACHSE (Axis), the Germans acted swiftly and ruthlessly, disarming and threatening to shoot any Italians who lifted a finger against them. (There were 400,000 German soldiers in Italy.) B. H. Liddell Hart observed that in Rome, 'As the Italians' deepest wish was to cease fighting, they made their surrender to the Germans in the absence of the Allies.' But this was not always easy to arrange.*

The former Axis allies were already fighting intermittently on Rhodes when Major Lord Jellicoe of the SBS, Count Julian Dobrski of SOE and a signaller, Sergeant Kesterton, parachuted in to try and persuade Admiral Inigo Campioni to resist the Germans. It was Dobrski's first parachute jump, and he suffered a compound fracture of his thigh, though he carried on bravely interpreting through gritted teeth.

On 13 September Churchill telegrammed to General Sir Henry Maitland Wilson, Commander-in-Chief Middle East: 'The capture of Rhodes by you at this time with Italian aid would be a fine contribution to the general war. Let me know what are your plans for this. Can you not improvise the necessary garrison out of the forces in the Middle East?' In the event, the 7,500-strong German garrison seized Rhodes on 14 September and imprisoned 40,000 Italians before any Allied reinforcements could arrive. Jellicoe, Dobrski and Kesterton escaped, but Admiral Campioni was executed by the Germans six months later.

General Wilson's planning staff for Aegean operations, Force 292, was doing its best with scarce resources. 'We have occupied Castelrosso [Kastellorizo] island' he cabled London on 14 September,

and have missions in Cos [Kos], Leros and Samos. A flight of Spitfires will be established in Cos today, and an infantry garrison tonight by parachute. An infantry detachment is also proceeding to Leros. Thereafter I propose to carry out piratical war on enemy communications in the Aegean and to occupy Greek islands with Hellenic forces as opportunity offers . . . [T]he 10th Indian Division, partially equipped, is the only formation immediately available.

---

* Louis de Bernières's novel *Captain Corelli's Mandolin* depicts the real-life German massacre of thousands of Italian soldiers on the Ionian island of Kefalonia in September 1943.

But the scrappy war that followed in the south-eastern Aegean, with the ineffective use of special forces, including 30 Commando, was more like the disastrous Norway campaign in 1940 than the big amphibious operations that were becoming the Anglo-American mode. The Royal Navy did deploy six cruisers (four of which were damaged in the fighting) but mostly used smaller vessels (including Greek, Polish and Italian ones) like destroyers (six sunk, four damaged), submarines (three sunk, four damaged) and coastal force craft: motor torpedo boats, motor gun boats, minesweepers and motor launches (of which eleven were sunk and damaged). Because the Aegean war shaded into an established covert world, there were also unusual vessels like sailing caiques from the Levant Schooner Flotilla.

Since 1941, A Force in Cairo had been the Middle East HQ of MI9, the British secret service dedicated to the succour of Allied personnel on the run in enemy territory: escaped prisoners of war, shipwrecked sailors, downed airmen, straggling soldiers and refugees. MI9's escape lines from Greece ran through the Aegean and were co-ordinated from the west coast of Turkey by Lieutenant Commander Noël Rees RNVR, a vice consul at Izmir (Smyrna) but also the descendant of a long line of Levantine merchants, one of whom had revictualled Nelson at his own expense. Rees had set up a clandestine naval base near Çesme in Turkey, opposite the Greek island of Chios, where all sorts of caiques and fishing vessels and smugglers visited unmolested. There were arrangements with other villages and sheltered coves all down the Turkish coast where boats could hide. Rees was helped in all this by John Godfrey's excellent choice for naval attaché in Istanbul, Commander Vladimir Wolfson RNVR. Both men were awarded military OBEs for their work in the Aegean. By 18 September a motley collection of British forces had taken over several Dodecanese islands, including Kastellorizo, Simi, Kos, Astipalea, Leros, Samos and Ikaria, and the tiny squad of 34 Army Troop of 30 Commando was plucked out of the holding section to join them.

All of the Greek islands seemed to have women dressed in mourning black living in small whitewashed houses. Some Italians garrisoned on the islands wanted to fight the Germans, but most were reluctant and just wanted the war over. Just as Norway had seen a mixture of Territorials and newly formed special forces, in the Aegean there were Indians, Irishmen, Geordies and Kentishmen among the British infantry shipped in from Malta, but there was also a strong salting of assorted warriors from Raiding Force HQ at Haifa in Israel. Jellicoe's Special Boat Squadron (SBS) had three detachments of five patrols with twelve men in each, including the amazing Danish Viking warrior, Anders Lassen, the first man to climb aboard the Italian *Duchessa d'Aosta* when SOE daringly hijacked the ship at Fernando Po in West Africa in January 1942. The superb LRDG were also there with two squadrons (one composed of New Zealanders and the other a mixed bag of Rhodesians and Britons), fresh from retraining at the Mountain Warfare Training Centre at Cedars, a ski resort near Bcharre in Lebanon, for reconnaissance and partisan work in Europe's mountains. The 'Greek Sacred Squadron', an elite unit from the Hellenic army, was also defending home territory in the Aegean.

The 30 Commando unit in the Aegean, 34 Army Troop, was led by twenty-seven-year-old Captain Tom Belcher of the South Staffordshire regiment. The other men deployed were Lieutenant E. R. Phillips RNVR, Staff Sergeant Wilkinson, Corporal John Bancroft, and Privates Colin Ashton, Derek Levy, Francis McDaid the Bren-gunner, Frankie McLellan and John McDiarmid from Dunoon in Argyll. McDiarmid subsequently wrote about what happened to them on the island of Leros, although at the beginning of his account he has no real idea where he is or even what date it is. He has just found himself, with the others, on a black caique crewed by three tough British sailors and a bearded naval officer. The more boyish-looking naval officer was Lieutenant Martin Solomon RNVR, one of the men who had appeared on Sicily working with Humphrey Quill. Solomon was not a desk-bound intelligence officer: he had won one DSC for commanding Leigh-on-Sea cockle boats at Dunkirk in 1940, and another for taking supplies into besieged Tobruk with his motor torpedo boat, MTB 260, in 1942. He would also get an MBE for his Aegean work.

They moored at an unnamed Greek island and camouflaged the boat from German reconnaissance planes, or *shuftis*. Belcher and Solomon went ashore to find out what the Italian naval garrison were doing. They returned with an Italian admiral and a captured German flier whose Messerschmitt had been shot down by a South African Spitfire from Kos. In the cold night McDiarmid saw the irony of Derek Levy, a German-speaking Jew, sharing his cigarettes, his conversation and even his blanket with a sergeant of the master race committed to his extinction. He smiled at them both asleep, side by side like brothers.

Phillips and Solomon disappeared with the Italian admiral, and the others went on to different islands, including Naxos and Paros. McDiarmid saw the Greeks as a hardy, hairy people who used donkeys for transport and communicated up in the mountains by whistling. There were still priests in whitewashed churches with long beards and black robes and when McDiarmid dropped his trousers in a village outhouse, he was embarrassed to find women and children gathered to stare at him curiously.

Looking south from Kalymnos the commandos watched the aerial attacks on the RAF flying field at Antimachia on the island of Kos, five miles away. With more than 300 bombers, dive-bombers, fighters and transport planes available to them, the Luftwaffe's X Fliegerkorps gained air superiority. The nearest Allied planes had to fly hundreds of miles from Cyprus or North Africa and then back again, and there was no aircraft carrier. This too was reminiscent of Norway, where the successes of the Luftwaffe swung the campaign. The dramatic intensity of the German air attack on Kos was designed to terrify the neutral Turks (not far away) with the destructive power that could be visited on Turkish cities should they go over to the Allies. McDiarmid learned that the Germans valued their pilots. Some British SBS men rowed out to rescue a German airman who had parachuted into the sea after his plane was shot down. They were on their way back to land with him when a German Heinkel floatplane touched down on the water and taxied towards them. A machine-gun was pointed at the British boat; the Germans wanted their wet pilot back. He clambered on to the German float while the SBS men sat with their hands up in the rocking rowing boat, waiting to be machine-gunned. But the pilot just stuck out his arm, shouted '*Heil Hitler!*' and took off. 'Well organised,' commented an SBS bloke. 'Not like us.'

The Germans invaded Kos by sea and by air on 3 October 1943 and the Brandenburgers (German commandos) took it the next day, seizing the last airfields. 30 Commando retreated north from Kalymnos, sailing at midnight on 4 October. At 4 a.m. they landed on the island of Leros, which would become a graveyard for many British soldiers. As they brewed up by the water's edge at dawn, Belcher told his men not to worry about the expected bombing. He was lucky that way, he said. He'd been in several blitzes back home and escaped every time unharmed.

'I've had a scout around and I've found a safe place nearby, OK chaps?'

There was a peculiar slapping sound, the noise of running feet as Italian sailors scattered at the sight of German planes approaching on a dawn raid.

'Chaps, follow me!' Belcher shouted and set off running parallel to the water's edge towards a pile of stores with the others at his heels. McDiarmid stood rooted looking for his Bren gun.

'For fuck's sake, Jock, come on!' Derek Levy yelled.

'I can't find the Bren!' The aeroplanes were very audible now.

'There it is!' Bombs began to fall; houses were collapsing. 'We'll make it uphill!' Stukas machine-gunning from crooked gull wings released their bombs as they pulled out of shrieking dives. Levy and McDiarmid lay down flat whenever they saw one falling. After

200 yards they jumped into a hole containing a South African from the LRDG.

'Give me the gun!'

'Come on, I want a go!'

Their tracer bullets arced through the sky. When the raid was over, the South African went off to join his mates and Levy and McDiarmid walked downhill to the jetty. The harbour side was full of rubble, with stores scattered all about. Two sombre medical orderlies emerged from a bombed building carrying a stretcher and supplies, and one said, 'Your mates have copped it. Ran into a stick of bombs.'

'Where are they?'

'Taken away.'

'Brave bastards.'

'Poor buggers.'

McDiarmid recalled his 'curious insensitivity' at the news: 'I was alive, the sun was warm and the sky was blue.'

'Let's sit down and have a smoke.'

They sat alone on the jetty, chain-smoking untipped Greys from a broken carton of green packets and flicking the butts into the water to fizz out. Derek Levy spoke first:

'If everyone's been killed, I'm now senior man in the unit.'

'Sure. Senior of two.'

'If everyone else has been killed, I'm now a King's Corporal.'

'Yeah, yeah. What do we do now?'

'We'll have another smoke.'

The sun was rising bright on the white houses and it felt unreal. All their mates were dead and they had no one to turn to for orders. As a unit of two with no intelligence to look for and no idea how to find it, they decided they would become guerrillas and go and fight the Germans in the hills when they invaded Leros.

'Do I have to lug this Bren gun, Derek?'

They picked up some American M1 carbines lying about, liked their lightness, and found some ammunition to go with them, abandoning the Bren on another pile.

'Food now.' They filled their packs with boxes of rations.

'Cigarettes now.'

'We'll take as many packets as we can.'

So they had a final smoke and set off, plodding, uphill, weighed down with tins of food and packets of fags, to become *banditti*. Over the ridge, however, they met a dozen SBS men whose young officer asked, 'Where are you chaps going?' McDiarmid let Levy do the talking. The officer listened to their story and saw they were a bit bomb-happy. 'You'd better tag along with us,' he said, kindly. Within hours they were being bombed again by Stukas, out in the open. They were bombed many, many more times in the next five weeks on Leros. McDiarmid learned that his courage was average, compared to many others, but at least he never fouled himself: unlike some others, he had that under control. Derek Levy became a runner for Colonel G. L. Prendergast, one of the founders of the LRDG. The Aegean marked a glorious final hour for the New Zealand Squadron of LRDG. Their fathers' generation had been quiet heroes at Gallipoli, and now their sons fought and died like Spartans among islands that Odysseus knew. The dead included their thirty-four-year-old commanding officer, Lieutenant Colonel Jake Easonsmith DSO, MC, killed in action on 16 November. Their losses were grievous but they took a lot of the enemy with them. One LRDG patrol, hidden on Kithnos, spotted a large convoy carrying some 2,500 German troops, and radioed its position, size, speed, air cover and possible destination. The Royal Navy destroyed it the next day, with only ninety survivors.

Some days after their landing on Leros and the German bombing raid, which McDiarmid thought only he and Derek Levy had walked away from, Private McLellan showed up. He had in fact survived the stick of bombs and now narrated what had happened to the others. Belcher and McDaid had been killed by blast; Ashton had his backside completely blown away; Bancroft got shrapnel in his guts and died in two days; Wilkinson's feet were shattered, might have to be amputated. Then McLellan lifted his shirt to show his own back, covered with the blackheads of hundreds of bits of grit and dirt blasted into the skin. Around 10 November 1943 a sergeant drove up to their position in a jeep, asking if there were any commandos there.

'Sergeant, I'm one', said McDiarmid. Levy and McLellan also stepped forward.

'Three. Is that all?'

'Yes!' The SBS officer approached, and the sergeant saluted.

'Sir, all Commandos have to be at the jetty by 7 p.m. tonight.'

'Fine, sergeant, I'll see to it.' They said goodbye to the SBS men they had been with and left Leros two days before it fell to a German onslaught. On board the destroyer HMS *Fury*, heading for Alexandria, the remnants of Section 2 of the Army Troop drank blessed rum and gave thanks to their lucky stars and to Lieutenant Martin Solomon RNVR, who had traced them and made the arrangements to evacuate them. The Germans were already executing Italians in the Aegean, and there were fears that 30 Commando were particularly at risk because of Hitler's order of 18 October 1942 that all commandos should be shot out of hand.

As it happened, the young Dane who had done the three killings on Sark that triggered Hitler's order, Anders Lassen of the SBS, was on Leros at the time. He paired up with Solomon and after their fighting retreat from Leros the two men continued raiding German-occupied Greek islands, eventually helping to free Greece from Nazi rule. In October 1944 they liberated, and briefly ruled, Salonika, but Major Anders Lassen was shot and killed by a German-Ukrainian unit pretending to surrender at Lake Commacchio on 9 April 1945. Lassen was only twenty-four years old when he died. To his three MCs for gallantry was added a posthumous VC.

N

Yugoslavia, the kingdom of the Serbs, Croats and Slovenes, had declared itself neutral in 1939. After April 1941, however, when German forces occupied the country, it became a ferocious, internecine war zone. Croat nationalists (Ustase) started ethnic cleansing against Serbs and other minorities, the partisan fighters resisted the Germans, and outside the country, Yugoslav exiles squabbled among themselves. Britain tried to square this circle by both supporting the monarchy (constitutional but ineffectual) with words and supplying the partisans (Communist but effective) with arms.

In late September 1943 Quintin Riley wanted to move the 30 Commando unit from Capri to Bari in eastern Italy from where he could go across the Adriatic to help the anti-German partisans in Yugoslavia. He felt he needed a doctor to go with him, and ended up with a cheerful scruff of a Surgeon Lieutenant called Harry Richardson Gray who had simply come over to Capri on a twenty-four-hour leave with an assistant beach master from Salerno. Riley and Gray had a few drinks in the *piazzetta*. Riley said he was hoping to be in the Yugoslav islands and explained that 30 Commando was only about thirty strong, but he could certainly find a use for a medical officer. Of course, the medic might have to be left behind to look after any serious casualties if they were overrun by the enemy. Gray said that he'd like to come along.

Harry Gray pulled strings with contacts and finally ended up with 30 Commando in the villa they had taken over in Torre a Mare, six miles south of Bari on Italy's Adriatic coast. 'Doc' Gray started doing basic medical checks on the 30 Commando personnel and found many were suffering from dysentery and malaria. He ordered hospital stores from Malta and, setting himself up as welfare officer to the men as well, went to the NAAFI and Expeditionary Forces Institute (EFI) at Bari and drew full rations for the unit of tobacco, spirits, beer and 'nutty' or confectionery, as well as thirty-litre carboys of wine for the officers. He would provide this sort of essential care and maintenance for the unit till the end of the war.

A small party of six men from 30 Commando went over to Yugoslavia in a couple of motor torpedo boats loaded with arms, ammunition and medical stores as gifts for the natives. The aim was to link up with Brigadier Fitzroy Maclean of SOE and offer their help as raiders to Tito's Communist partisans. Sancho Glanville spoke Serbo-Croat and was keen to get back in the game, having identified some useful intelligence targets including the Whitehead torpedo factory at Fiume, the port and torpedo station of Pola, and shipyards at Trieste and Monfalcone. The crossing of the Adriatic to the island of Vis off the Dalmatian coast of Croatia took about eight hours. When they landed the partisans gave clenched fist Communist salutes and fired their guns a lot, but were shifty about their exact allegiances. Bon Royle, speaking only Italian, found that everyone hated the Germans first, and each other second.

The British boats went on to other islands, Hvar, Brac and Korcula, where they camouflaged themselves close inshore against German spotter planes. Glanville met Maclean at Korcula before setting off for Tito's HQ on the mainland. But things did not go well for him there. The future Marshal Josip Broz Tito was a Communist metalworker from Zagreb; his intelligence service had found out about Glanville's past, including his Croatian sympathies, and he was accused of supporting Tito's rival, Draža Mihailović. 30 Commando were barred from working in Yugoslavia, and in October 1943 Brigadier Maclean asked them to return to Bari. There Colin Gubbins told Quintin Riley that no one could go to Yugoslavia without the approval of the SOE office in Cairo, and Tito himself. Unfortunately, someone like Glanville who knew too much about the country, spoke the language and had a background in intelligence would not be welcome. In his SOE file in October 1941 Glanville was noted as having 'very pro-Croat sympathies . . . bordering on the fanatical', which 'might easily antagonise the people who are doing the real work'. He was seen as unquestionably loyal, but also as 'quite likely to "put his foot in it"'. Dunstan Curtis also questioned Glanville's judgement and said that 'alongside all his virtues he packed a pig-headed and arrogant certainty of his own rightness'.

The few guns that 30 Commando had shipped seemed like a drop in the ocean given the actual needs of Tito's partisans, who were usefully holding down more than twenty German divisions in Yugoslavia. SOE's answer was to use Axis weapons and ammunition captured from the Germans and Italians on Sicily. Over a dinner at Bari on 16 October 1943, Colin Gubbins ordered one of his officers, Donald Hamilton-Hill from the Cameron Highlanders regiment, to go to Sicily the next day, talk to the British and the Americans and get all the enemy arms he could across the Adriatic to Yugoslavia by Christmas.

With OSS help, Hamilton-Hill obtained fifty US trucks. By pulling strings, twisting arms and working flat out for two and half months, his team managed to catalogue, inspect, service, pack and transport by sea and road some 7,000 tons of captured German and Italian equipment for the Yugoslav partisans, including several heavy field artillery pieces, 40,000 rifles, 2,500 light automatics, 1,000 heavy automatics, 20 million rounds of ammunition, hundreds of thousands of hand grenades, 400 tons of Italian service uniforms and 250 tons of mule feed. Thus Britain helped Tito to power in Yugoslavia.

N

The lesson that 30 Commando learned in the eastern Mediterranean was a bitter one. Lives could be frittered away if you didn't have enough people in the right place, good lines of communication and clear goals. An admirable soldier called John Coates (who was later caught and tortured in Hungary as an SOE officer) briefly spent time with 34 Army Troop and recalled 30 Commando as 'a curious, mixed bunch of people, very interesting folk', but he put his finger on its management problem by adding that unpredictable deployments made it 'a somewhat chaotic sort of unit'. They were an *intelligence* assault unit, and were supposed to be used intelligently, not wasted as cannon fodder.

In 1944, however, the major Allied focus would shift back to north-west Europe and preparations for the biggest military invasion in human history. Once again re-organised and re-equipped, 30 Commando would go on to their finest achievements in the closing scenes of the Second World War.

11

Freeing the French

On 12 February 1944 General Dwight Eisenhower, Supreme Commander of the Allied Expeditionary Force, received his orders for Operation OVERLORD: 'You will enter the Continent of Europe and, in conjunction with the other United Nations, undertake operations aimed at the heart of Germany and the destruction of her armed forces.'

The Allied code-breakers were gearing up for the big battle, too. On 5 February 1944 the world's first digital electronic computer, Colossus, started work at Bletchley Park. Invented by the Post Office engineer Tommy Flowers, it helped to break the highest-grade German ciphers (known as 'Tunny'). Messages sent and received by Hitler and the German High Command were now encrypted by German Lorenz twelve-wheel teleprinter machines that made the old Enigma machines look primitive. To reconstruct the configuration of these new Lorenz wheels, Flowers had built a machine that could read and compare punched-paper teleprinter tapes at 5,000 bits a second, searching for a unique matching scan. It was electronics, not mechanics, that did the trick, using thousands of Osram GT1C argon-filled relay valves as switches. Mechanical metal-contact switches could only manage a thousand operations a second, but thermionic valves could achieve millions. The successor machine, Colossus Mark II, using parallel processing, increased the speed to 25,000 bits a second, meaning that five times as many messages could be broken, in a fifth of the time.

Special forces were assisting in another technological race. On Sunday 20 February 1944 a sausage of plastic explosive planted by Captain Knut Haukelid of SOE and the Norwegian Resistance in the bilges of the Norsk ferry *Hydro* holed and sank the vessel and sent thirty-nine drums of precious deuterium oxide, 'heavy water', destined for Nazi scientists, to the bottom of Lake Tinnsjø, 200 fathoms deep. The Germans needed the heavy water to build an atomic bomb, and though the act of sabotage killed fourteen Norwegian civilians, it scuppered Nazi chances.

The forthcoming assault on German-held Europe marked a turning point for the IAU. Commander Ian Fleming was insistent about that: 'Forget anything that happened in the Med,' he told Sancho Glanville. 'You can't behave like Red Indians any more. You have to learn to be a respected and disciplined unit.'

The origin of their transformation was a turf war between the NID and Combined Operations. Colonel Robert Neville RM of Combined Operations Planning (who had played a big part in the original Dieppe raid) came out to inspect the unit in southern Italy and made it clear that in his view the whole shooting match should be taken over by the Royal Marines. Ian Fleming would not hear of it. Nevertheless, a major reorganisation ensued. The unit was given a new name and a new insignia, and the old structure of 33 Navy Troop and 34 Army Troop was scrapped, together with the base at Amersham.

The new name was 30 Advanced Unit or 30 Assault Unit or 30AU, and they had their own shoulder patch: '30' in light blue on a naval dark blue square. A cornucopia of kit matched the new responsibility: Staghound and Humber armoured cars, armoured troop carriers and jeeps for transport, better wireless communications, a wide range of explosive devices. 30AU's three new troops, named (like naval gun turrets) A, B and X, contained about forty men each, plus an HQ Troop to handle signals and intelligence. They were billeted at Littlehampton on the south coast of England, and the fighting men were all Royal Marines, many of whom had been through commando training at Achnacarry.

'Sandy' Powell remembered his two month course there in the winter of 1943/1944 as punishingly 'horrible'.

30AU's new commanding officer was Lieutenant Colonel Arthur Woolley, formerly CO of 47 Royal Marine Commando. A photo taken in May 1944 shows the eleven uniformed Royal Marine officers of 30AU in their green berets, posing stiffly against the barbed wire fence of a Sussex field spattered with daisies. The seated five (Colonel Woolley front and centre) perch identically on wooden chairs, left knee over right leg, right hand over left forearm; each has a walking stick, a moustache and a fierce look. The back row includes the three clean-shaven troop commanders: Captain Peter Huntington-Whiteley (A troop), Captain Geoff Douglas (B Troop) and Captain Geoffrey Pike (X Troop). The Royal Marine wing were meant to provide the muscle and firepower of the unit and protect the intelligence-gathering brains (the old 36 Technical Wing). These RNVR officers, the intelligence collectors at the heart of the enterprise, were now safely transferred out of the grip of Combined Operations into an ad hoc division in Naval Intelligence, NID 30, newly created for the purpose by Ian Fleming.

But as a naval intelligence-gathering unit, 30AU also came under the ultimate control of Admiral Sir Bertram Ramsay, Allied Naval Commander Expeditionary Force, the man who eventually got the invading forces across the Channel to Europe. His HQ was at Southwick House, near Portsmouth. 30AU was actually the responsibility of his Assistant Chief of Staff, Intelligence. Admiral Godfrey's successor as DNI, Edmund Rushbrooke, had unsuccessfully lobbied to get the post for Humphrey Quill, the NID officer who had taken Iceland and knew the unit from Sicily. Admiral Ramsay chose instead Captain John 'Ginger' Lewes, who had won the DSC for evacuating men from Dunkirk. Captain Lewes was supposed to confirm 30AU operations with local military commanders, but of course 30AU also had direct radio links to NID 30 in the Admiralty, which would give rise to some friction.

After five years of committee meetings at the heart of the secret world, Fleming understood how to negotiate bureaucracy. A quarter of a century later Godfrey was struck by how well he had steered his IAU through the corridors of power. 'For such a novel enterprise it is essential an officer of drive and imagination of the highest order is supervising matters at headquarters, and looking after the 'Whitehall front . . . ' Setting up NID 30 within the Admiralty was astute, because 30 Commando was too small to fit the new definition of a commando unit (which had to be 600 strong), and with this arrangement Fleming retained some control over picking personnel and selecting targets.

Into NID 30 came a lot of RNVR officers with specialist technical expertise like Lieutenant Alexander Ionides and Lieutenant Guy Postlethwaite, underwater weapons experts from HMS *Vernon* in Portsmouth, Lieutenant Commander Patrick Dalzel-Job who, after his stint in Norway in 1940, had been involved with the X-craft miniature submarines that crippled the German battleship *Tirpitz*, and Lieutenant Commander Tony Hugill, who had a first in chemistry from Magdalen College, Oxford. Hugill had done secret Government work on protection against war gases from 1939 to 1940 and then served in the 'Wheezers and Dodgers', the Directorate of Miscellaneous Weapons Development, developing the 'Hedgehog', an anti-submarine weapon that fired spigot mortar bombs ahead of a ship. When he was summoned to the Admiralty in 1942 to meet Fleming and Godfrey ahead of his posting to Lisbon as naval attaché, Hugill had noted Fleming's 'melancholy, compelling sort of face and . . . brisk, dégagé but kindly air', but saw Admiral Godfrey as 'thunderous'.

Ian Fleming made Lieutenant Commander Robert Harling RNVR the liaison between the Admiralty's NID 30 and 30AU (and in *Thunderball* named the Nassau Commissioner of Police after him). Some of the marines thought of Harling merely as 'Fleming's head boy', but Harling was a remarkable man, and no pushover, as his comments on Fleming indicate. The black propagandist Sefton

Delmer, encountering Harling for the first time in Fleming's NID office, described him as 'a young man with the laughing, big-eared, long-nosed face of a mediaeval court jester and the shrewd appraising eyes of a physician'. Harling later revealed what he thought of Fleming: 'terribly lazy all his life except for during the war at the Admiralty . . . His capacity for work [then] was phenomenal and he was terribly good, a really fabulous Personal Assistant to the DNI.' In his view, though Fleming was 'fantastic at the job of coordinating, directing, organising the unit', he never really wanted to go into action with them. William Stephenson, the man who in 1940 coordinated British and American secret intelligence activities, claimed in his dotage that Fleming had come top of a wartime secret agents' course at Oshawa in Canada, but this was pure fantasy, itself probably inspired by the Bond novels.

According to Harling, Fleming 'always loved hearing about things – sex, war, personalities, danger – from other people, but . . . shied away from experiencing it himself'. Fleming's evocation of James Bond at the gambling tables in *Casino Royale* – 'he liked being an actor and a spectator and from his chair to take part in other men's dramas and decisions, until it came to his own turn to say the vital "yes" or "no" ' – suggests he was aware of his own semi-detached state. Harling thought Fleming 'avoided really becoming involved with people' in sexual matters too: 'he always had to experience everything at second hand. Once you've grasped this properly you've understood the books, everything.' Harling saw this as 'curious', though surely it is part of the writer's condition. The astute Joan Bright Astley, sometimes squired around wartime London by the 'very attractive' but 'melancholy' Fleming, made a similar comment to Harling's. She thought Fleming 'loved the world of the imagination more than he loved the reality'.

The NID 30 office was a windowless, stuffy room in the Admiralty Citadel where the NID night duty officer kept a bed with a grey blanket. It was a small, bleak place: just two tables, two telephones including a scrambler, three chairs, two cupboards and a filing cabinet. The RNVR officers would drop in, smoking furiously, when they were in London. They worked under different names at home and abroad and were pretty much in charge of their own destiny: according to Dalzel-Job, 'NID 30 prepared the list of "Targets", and the same people became 30AU in the field.' The administrative assistant for NID 30, a bright and efficient civilian, Margaret Priestley (later Bax) whom Fleming always called 'Miss Priestley', said that when a lot of officers crowded in, the NID 30 office looked like the cabin scene from the Marx Brothers film *A Night at the Opera*.

Sancho Glanville and his colleagues in NID 30 worked for months in that office compiling the important 'Black Books', lists of naval targets across north-west Europe. These were not just German naval bases and establishments, because the lists were compiled in response to queries from the other services and ministries as well as the Admiralty's. One 300-page volume listed the names, addresses and details of every German manufacturing company supplying the Kriegsmarine. The JIC set up the British Intelligence Objectives Sub-Committee (BIOS) to co-ordinate targets and personnel, and the Americans set up a similar organisation, the Field Information Agency Technical (FIAT). Slowly, naval and military intelligence was turning towards the large-scale acquisition of German scientific, technical and industrial secrets, and 30AU would be among the most effective operatives in the field.

Littlehampton was a sleepy seaside town in Sussex with a long bare beach where the RNVR officers practised pistol shooting and sometimes joined the marines of 30AU on commando training speed marches. The marines had their own skills and capabilities. 'Sandy' Powell was a Bren specialist who grew very fond of his light machine-gun, which he called 'Betsy' after Davy Crockett's flintlock rifle of the same name. He could strip and reassemble it in the dark and, to ease the spring and prevent jamming, usually loaded the thirty-round curved box magazine with one or two fewer .303 bullets than recommended. If you fired ten magazines in short steady bursts the barrel became red hot, but it could be changed in five seconds and while the new barrel was at work, you cooled down the old one with your water bottle. Or if need be by pissing on it.

From Littlehampton everyone was sent off on different specialised courses: at Holmrook Hall in West Cumberland, men were trained in bomb disposal, mine clearance, disarming booby traps and handling the fuses, detonators and different explosives they would need when opening safes and blowing hatches. Sergeant Paul McGrath of A Troop had a memorable stay. A local wrestling champion who hated the marines started a brawl in a pub, and McGrath decked him with a single punch; but at a dance, McGrath also fell for a lovely 'Lumberjill' from the Women's Timber Corps in her green beret and green jersey. (They would revisit Holmrook Hall on their sixtieth wedding anniversary.) John Brereton, Bert Morgan, Bon Royle and Jim Smith were sent to the HQ of the Army Film and Photographic Unit at Pinewood Studios to be taught how to take good shots with the compact, rugged Zeiss Contax II, the camera favoured by journalists like Robert Capa because its wide-aperture lens made best use of available light. This was vital, enabling 30AU to photograph German equipment and machinery too awkward for them to salvage and transport.

Bert Morgan and Bon Royle were promoted to lance corporal and corporal respectively in the Intelligence section and sent off to Manchester College, Oxford, home of the ISTD, NID 6, to work on 30AU's targets in Normandy. (Admiral Godfrey commented that 30AU's success was partly due to Fleming making full use of Naval Intelligence resources, not least the ISTD.) Retired senior officers in cardigans and glue-stained trousers showed them how to make accurate, three-dimensional, scale models of their targets built up from strips of wood stuck on to reinforced blow-ups of aerial reconnaissance photographs. Postcards, brochures, holiday snaps, oblique views, low-flying shots and even stereoscopic photographs gave perspective, proportion and height. These meticulous models were built in sections that could be stored and moved safely in wooden cabinets, then taken out and ingeniously assembled.

Colonel Woolley enjoyed the drama of gathering the men round when he unveiled an elaborate model of 30AU's key target in Cherbourg, the Kriegsmarine HQ at Villa Meurice. He proudly pointed out the forts, the quarry with the tunnels underneath, and where on their air intakes the 'beehives' or shaped charges might need to be placed. But the next day, the entire unit was summoned to the British Legion hall in Littlehampton and locked in under armed guard. Woolley was hopping mad. A couple of the lads had boasted to their landladies about their task in Normandy and word got back to Field Security. *'Jesus Christ! What can I do?'* exclaimed Woolley, thus supplying the unit with a comic catchphrase for when anything went wrong

Operation OVERLORD, the invasion of north-west Europe, was a huge military-industrial undertaking. In the lead-up, from 1 April to 5 June 1944, the Allied air forces flew over 200,000 sorties, dropped 195,000 tons of bombs on railways, factories, power stations and fuel depots and lost 1853 aeroplanes and crews. The cost was high for the French: 15,000 civilians were killed and more than 19,000 injured.

OVERLORD's three-week assault phase, the Normandy landings, code-named NEPTUNE, was on an awesome scale. Its architect, Admiral Sir Bertram Ramsay, described it truthfully in his Order of the Day on Tuesday 6 June 1944 as 'the greatest amphibious operation in history'. It was twice as big as the HUSKY landings of 1943, up till then the world's largest. Nearly 7,000 vessels of all sizes transported, protected and supplied the 150,000 Allied/United Nations soldiers who reached the far shore on the first day. The Kriegsmarine's warships and submarines could do almost nothing to prevent it; the German sea mine, so terrifying in 1939, had been dealt with by hundreds of minesweepers from a score of flotillas clearing ten wide channels called the 'Spout' that ran from the gathering point (code-named 'Piccadilly Circus') south of the Isle of Wight as far as the Bay of the Seine, so the Allied Task Forces could reach their beaches safely. A gross of tug boats hauled concrete caissons to make a two-square-mile 'Mulberry' harbour off Arromanches. Overhead flew 11,500 Allied aircraft, identified by the three white stripes on wings and fuselage, whereas the Luftwaffe could muster only 300 planes. By the time NEPTUNE ended on 30 June, 850,000 men, 148,000 vehicles and 570,000 tons of stores had been landed in France, and over a 100-mile front, a million and a half men were fighting to the death.

30AU were just a tiny part of this armada. They had been split into three forces with separate targets. First to land and first into action was PIKEFORCE, Geoffrey Pike's X Troop, under the overall command of Major Alan Evans, landing on D-Day itself on Juno Beach. Their target was straight inland: the great radar station at Douvres-la-Délivrande. Second to land was CURTFORCE, led by Dunstan Curtis, with two other naval officers and nineteen marines; they landed at Arromanches on Gold Beach on D+1, the day after D-Day, 7 June. Third came the main body of 30AU, WOOLFORCE, led by Colonel Woolley, comprising A and B troops, who landed on Utah Beach on D+4, 10 June. Their target was Cherbourg, at the top of the Cotentin Peninsula.

Geoff Pike drew himself up to his full height of six feet four inches and addressed X Troop: 'X the unknown quantity – here we go,' he said. It raised a smile. X Troop got into the lorries taking them to their pre-invasion 'Cage' at Southampton. All across southern England and Wales, thousands of vehicles were moving tens of thousands of men into secure holding camps near their embarkation ports, where they had to wait for days. It reminded Tony Hugill of his first corps camp with the Oundle cadet force: 'The same smell of grass trodden down under the sun, the same toughness in the meat, the same latrines.' They were instructed to write final letters home, to be sent only if they did not come back. On Sunday 4 June PIKEFORCE boarded the converted Kiwi liner TSS *Monowai*, together with men from the Canadian 3rd Division, and finally sailed a day later. Pike was amazed by the incredible sight of the English Channel full of ships.

Around 6.00 a.m. on the sixth day of the sixth month, in sight of the French coast where the Germans awaited them, they clambered awkwardly down rope nets into the smaller assault landing craft for the bumpy eight-mile ride to land. When sailors leant over to say goodbye and good luck, it seemed 'hellishly final' to Pike. In the grey early morning, the noise became horrendous. The cruiser *Diadem* and eleven destroyers began bombarding the coast to knock out the German strongpoints covering the beaches, and smaller landing craft hammered away with Oerlikon cannons and heavy machine-guns. Most alarming of all were the Allied rocket ships, heavy tank landing craft racked with nearly a thousand five-inch-diameter tubes, pointing at forty-five degrees, that could fire up to two dozen salvoes of sixty-pound explosive rockets. When these whooshed off, forty at a time, a roaring sheet of flame made the blast-blackened landing craft bounce in the water and devastated a great swathe of land on shore. The Germans responded with their own incendiary *Wurfgerät* rockets as well as mortars, shells and machine-gun fire. Pike saw another landing craft take a direct hit; wounded men floundered in the water. Everyone felt frightened of the beach ahead, crouching cold and wet in the landing craft. Pike worried most about letting the side down, 'knowing half my troops had been under fire before and I had not. You don't forget this sort of thing; nor do I forget the man beside me, Jim [Sancho] Glanville . . . who had seen a lot of war in the Mediterranean. He was an extraordinary man because he never seemed to be frightened but just interested in what was going on.'

At 8.35 a.m. their landing-craft ramp dropped down on the Nan Red sector of Juno Beach at high tide. They dashed across the sand to shelter by the edge of the promenade of St-Aubin-sur-Mer. No one got a scratch. Rockets had set the beachfront houses ablaze, machine-guns were chattering, and Pike saw men from 41 Commando being hit as they went down their ramps, slithering off to drown in the shallow water. To their left, 48 Commando were taking a terrible pasting. To their right, a Fort Garry tank was lurching about blindly with its flail blown off, crushing wounded men who could not crawl away. Marine Don King saw Glanville pointing with his walking stick at a butterfly: 'Look! A Black-veined White. You don't see many of those at home.'

Royal Marine Bill Powell landed on the same beach from a different landing craft, which by the time they reached Normandy stank of diesel and vomited cocoa. On board, they had each been given a copy of the personal message from General B. L. Montgomery, the commander-in-chief of the Twenty-first Army Group, which began, 'The time has come to deal the enemy a terrible blow in Western Europe' and ended 'And good hunting on the continent of Europe.' They had been given a big swig of navy issue rum, and suddenly Bill Powell saw a large White Ensign on a mast and a naval officer in a duffel coat apparently walking on the water. It was Ken Hudspeth, the skipper of the British miniature submarine *X-20*, holding on to the air induction mast and pointing the way forward through a cleared channel. Their landing craft or LCI(L) had two ramps at the bow that reared up and then bowed down, and the marines floundered ashore through chest-high water with weapons above their heads.

'The beach was indescribable,' remembered Powell, 'bodies everywhere, some dead, some wounded, others just shattered with it all. Equipment was strewn around. Yells, shouts and orders added to the mêlée.' Powell was the barbed-wire cutter, and he flung himself onto a tangle of wire, intending to snip his way through. Too late he spotted that the wire held yellow triangles with black skull and crossbones marking a minefield, and crawled swiftly back out again. Soaking wet, crusted with sand, he ran through a breach in the sea wall and got to a French street where Canadian soldiers were going door to door winkling out German snipers. Dreadful screams came from a burning house. Powell and a Canadian soldier ran across to find three middle-aged French civilians beating out the flames on two charred and smoking bodies. Barbecued flesh and burned cloth came away with their flailings. Powell babbled but nobody understood him. He and the Canadian looked at each other and ran away from the repugnant smell. Crouched in a doorway, the Canadian drew a packet of Sweet Caporal from the breast pocket of his soaked tunic, lit two and passed one over. Bill Powell had never smoked in his life, but he tremblingly sucked that cigarette down to a red spike. Throughout, the two Allied soldiers never said a word to each other. By 9.45 a.m. the two halves of PIKEFORCE had rendezvoused at the church and were off on foot, south towards Tailleville, en route to their objective, the radar station at Douvres-la-Délivrande.

War was bashing and grinding its way through the lives of civilians trying to get on with agriculture in Calvados country. Amid explosions, you could hear cows lowing to be milked. Evans was talking to Pike just as a French peasant bicycled past; a sudden German sniper's shot dropped the man dead and his bike clattered to the ground. The British officers dived on to their bellies and started crawling through the cornfield. Behind the town were undulating fields ringed by thick summer hedges, good defensive terrain for hidden German riflemen, machine-guns and mortars. Progress through this *bocage* was erratic. The Allied tanks had to deal with a battery of 88-mm guns and then a clutch of eighty fused rockets before they fought their way into bomb-damaged

Tailleville. The defenders of the German HQ ran up a white flag to indicate surrender but then, as the Canadians emerged from cover to take it, sneakily opened fire on them. After that, Allied troops were in no mood to take prisoners.

The night-time fireworks along the coast were spectacular: ack-ack bursts, caterpillars of orange-red tracer, star shells falling bright. The unit bivouacked for a long night in some German trenches, waiting for a counter-attack that never came. In the morning Marine Fred Farrington approached Major Evans on behalf of his mates.

'Permission to grow beards, sir?'

'Certainly not!'

They made their way on foot across fields towards the target at Douvres-la-Délivrande. The 130-foot-tall Siemens Wassermann tower had been damaged by naval bombardment on D-Day but the main radar control station to the south sprawled mostly underground, ringed by barbed wire, mine-fields and well-camouflaged defences. This was a hard nut that would take ten days to crack. They decided to wait for CURTFORCE with the vehicles.

N

Dunstan Curtis, the leader of CURTFORCE, is disguised as 'Roger' in the book that Lieutenant Commander J. A. C. Hugill DSC, RNVR wrote about 30AU in Normandy soon afterwards. *The Hazard Mesh* was aptly described on the jacket blurb as 'like no other war book yet published . . . a personal record . . . written in a vivid and vigorous style'. It is rather like something the twenty-four-year-old poet Captain Keith Douglas might have written had he not been killed on D+3 near Tilly-sur-Seulles. The literate and sometimes acerbic Hugill is keen 'to observe and report on what [we] were feeling, as we lived and worked and fought' but he is also security-minded enough not to put in certain details of what NID 30 and 30AU actually did. W. J. R. Gardner of the Naval

Historical Branch described it as 'a useful illustration of what *can* be written quite soon after the event without apparently incurring the wrath of the authorities'.

Tony Hugill had a bantering, sarcastic relationship with Dunstan Curtis but saw 'something truly Elizabethan about him, in the most admirable sense . . . with that small beard and moustache . . .' Hugill was also impressed by the single-minded Lieutenant Guy Postlethwaite, RNVR:

Face him with the problem of getting two torpedoes on to a truck, with only one man and a boy and a toothbrush to do it with and he will get the torpedoes there and will reappear perspiring with his hair on end, and grease all over him, and bleeding from about fifteen different abrasions, but radiant with happiness . . .'

The CURTFORCE convoy of freshly waterproofed vehicles, including a wireless truck, lorries, scout cars, jeeps and sidecar motor cycles, all fitted into two tank landing craft that formed part of Flotilla 16 in Squadron V of Force L from Felixstowe. Hugill told his marines, whom he considered 'a pretty poor lot, as Marines go', to sleep with a clasp knife handy in case they had to cut their way through the camouflage netting draped over the vessel. They landed early on D+1. Offshore, a crowd of ships, barges, landing craft, rhino ferries and amphibious vehicles, or DUKWs, bumped and collided. The French coast looked just as it did in the low-level oblique photographs. Every now and then there was a big flash and clouds of smoke and a noise as sappers cleared Gold Beach of mines. Tanks crawled up a hill, and drums of petrol were unloaded as a top priority. Hugill noticed how widgeon and teal flying low over the water looked like black tracer bullets. One ramp went down too early and a lorry slid irrevocably into ten feet of water. Their landing craft nosed ashore and ground on to the coast of France, and CURTFORCE drove through shallow water, splashing one marine's trousers. 'Why can't you drive more fuckin' careful, Lofty? Shakin' me off into the fuckin' oggin.'

The Dorsets and Hampshires had taken the beach the day before and there were still some dead bodies lying about stiffly. The 30AU men drove inland to Meauvaines to meet Curtis. He wasn't wearing a helmet because he thought it made him look 'moronic', but when warned about snipers he got smartly back into his scout car. The men camped in a grassy, high-walled orchard with mossy apple trees and a stone well at Crépon, near the spot where Company Sergeant Major Stanley Hollis of the 6th Green Howards had won the only VC awarded on D-Day. Hugill describes how they went to look at the local manor, a 'minor Luftwaffe HQ' hastily abandoned after a scuffle. Blood lay mingled with carrot and potato peel on the kitchen floor, there was a dead body in the garden, and the corpse of 'a huge Alsatian bitch' lay across the back door. There were abandoned rifles and helmets and uniforms everywhere, German pin-up photos, loaves of bread and empty bottles. Hugill was sickened by what he felt hung on the air,

a kind of macabre foulness, a smell not only of blood and bad drains . . . It is a sort of dingy-brown, Irish-stew smell which you find wherever Germans have lived. Said Roger: 'You're imagining things. It's just the soap they use and the cigars they smoke.' It is more than that. It is an aura that only the German leaves in a place he has inhabited, and I hate it.

WOOLFORCE, the last contingent of 30AU to arrive, on D+4, learned a basic infantry lesson the hard way: *Use your spade to make a shelter – dig in or get hurt*. On their first night in Normandy, near Sainte-Mère-Église, a German aeroplane flew low overhead and Patrick Dalzel-Job heard a bang and 'a peculiar fluttering noise in the air'. Nothing happened for a second, 'then the whole field was lit by sharp flashes and explosions'.

The German plane had dropped at least one early model of cluster bomb, the two-kilogram *Sprengbombe Dickwandig*. The first bang Dalzel-Job heard would have been the submunitions canister opening, spilling out three-inch bomblets whose outer shell sprang into four wings attached to the arming spindle, and the 'fluttering' sound was the bomblets rotating through the darkness, winding themselves up to explode their half pound (225 grams) of TNT on the ground. Shards of jagged shrapnel whizzed viciously outwards, killing three men and wounding twenty-one. There were two marines named Wright near Patrick Dalzel-Job. One of them, Corporal Leo Wright, grunted, clutched his throat and fell dead, the other, Dalzel-Job's MOA Bill Wright, rolled in agony on the ground, reaching for his back. Dalzel-Job pulled up his servant's battledress blouse and found a piece of shrapnel had hit the metal centre-piece of his army braces, bruising the skin badly but not penetrating it. Bill Wright cheered up: the 'grass-cutter' had his name on it, but not his number.

Bon Royle and Lofty Whyman were experienced enough to dig themselves a slit trench at the bottom of a ditch where the ground was softer and to line it with bracken. They were talking to Captain Geoff Douglas when a plane flew over and the 'curious shirring and whistling sound' of the bombs made them dive for cover quicker than their officer. Royle recalled the German anti-personnel bombs not as 'butterflies' but projectiles the size of a two-inch mortar round, with fins at one end and a striker plate at the other to make sure the bomb blasted its shrapnel far and wide rather than being safely smothered in soft earth. Many of the wounded were in B Troop, including Captain Douglas who was hit in the legs and 'Duke' Ellington (now sergeant) who lost several teeth and a testicle. Bon Royle watched helplessly as a twenty-year-old Anglo-Argentine marine called Lennard Bentley faded away before his eyes, dying from internal bleeding no one could staunch. Of the three RNVR underwater weapons experts, George McFee was untouched, Peter Young was put out of action for two months, and a bomb fin through the heart killed Lieutenant Alexander 'Rusty' Ionides.* Flight Lieutenant David

---

* In *The Times* of 5 June 2009 Lieutenant Ionides's daughter Anthea May

Nutting RAFVR, the Air Technical Intelligence officer attached to 30AU, found a deep shrapnel gouge in the handle of his Smith and Wesson .38 service revolver after the bombing. When the time to demobilise arrived, he felt sad to hand in the gun that had saved his life.

As first revealed in the Oslo Report at the beginning of the war, the Germans had long been working on rocket technology. CROSSBOW was the code name for the Allied campaign against German long-range ballistic missiles, and Flight Lieutenant Nutting's job was to make sure the unit reached their CROSSBOW targets swiftly. In August 1943 the Allies had bombed the remote island of Peenemünde on the Baltic coast, 130 miles north of Berlin, site of the German research and development centre where Walter Dornberger and Wernher von Braun were using slave labour to build rockets, but the bombing had not stopped the programme, merely moved it to Poland. At Sottevast, south-east of Cherbourg, the German Todt organisation had built a large bunker and launch site for long-range V-2 rockets, and they had also set up a series of camouflaged platforms across Normandy from which mobile teams from *Flakregiment* 155 could fire V-1 flying bombs as well.

Patrick Dalzel-Job asked to join a heavily armed group led by Sergeant Paul McGrath that was pushing fifteen miles beyond the American bridgehead at Omaha Beach. They were escorting Nutting to investigate and confirm a possible launch site for the V-1 flying bomb near Neuilly-la-Forêt. A concrete lane led to a dummy farmhouse hiding a semi-underground firing control room. Turf had been laid over the concrete bases and sockets for the legs of portable ski ramps to launch Fieseler 'doodlebugs' or flying bombs at Bristol and south Wales. Nutting and Sergeant

---

Ionides remembered being nine years old on one windy wartime day when her mother came back from work as a council architect. 'She opened the telegram, put her hand up to her throat and said, "Oh. He's gone. I never expected this." '

Major John Brereton rolled back turf, measured and photographed while some armed marines kept guard and others probed the ground with bayonets. That evening an RAF Hurricane flew the notes and photographs back to London. The next day, near Valognes, they examined a fuelling point for the bigger A4 rocket that the British called the V-2, testing it for hydrogen peroxide, which German technicians used to fuel faster German aeroplanes and submarines.

Just a week after D-Day, early on Tuesday 13 June 1944, the first of over 8,000 V-1 flying bombs landed in east London. These 'buzz-bombs', which sounded like a farting motorcycle until the engine cut out and they fell in awful silence, killed over 6,000 British civilians and injured nearly 18,000. It was bad for morale: though British and American propaganda insisted that Allied heavy bomber raids were wrecking German industry, pounding its factories into rubble and burning its laboratories, the enemy was still inventing new 'retaliation weapons' (*Vergeltungswaffe*). The bigger, faster, stratospheric V-2 rockets would start hitting Britain three months later. The V-2s killed fewer people in total but their individual impact was more devastating; carrying a ton of explosive, they dropped faster than the speed of sound from fifty miles up, unheard and unstoppable. (As Thomas Pynchon expressed it in the first chapter of his 1973 novel, *Gravity's Rainbow*: 'Them fucking rockets. You couldn't adjust to the bastards. No way.') But at least the commandos' foray meant one site was down, and they had discovered how the Germans camouflaged their weapons.

N

PIKEFORCE's main objective, the fortress at Douvres-la-Délivrande, had reinforced concrete emplacements housing a big Luftwaffe *Funkmeßstellung* or radar station, code-named DISTELFINK, with its own generator for light, power and air-conditioning, a Wassermann early warning tower to pick up planes more than 150 miles away, two intermediate-range Freya radar sets to warn of hostile aircraft and shipping and another pair of radars, the short-range, gun-laying Würzburg-Rieses. Together they formed a section of the electronic shield of the 'West Wall' protecting Germany, one of nearly a hundred radar sites strung out along the coast of northern France and Belgium.

In electronic warfare methods of attack and defence co-evolve. On D-Day, all the German radars in Normandy that had not been shot up by fighter-borne rockets and cannonfire were jammed by two squadrons of aeroplanes from 100 Group of British Bomber Command, carrying Mandrel sets whose broadcast 'noise' obliterated the real signals. Meanwhile, two British deception operations, TAXABLE and GLIMMER, conjured up ghost images of armadas heading away from the real landing sites towards Dieppe and Boulogne, far to the east. Dr Robert Cockburn created a sixteen-mile-square radar reflection that seemed to move steadily across the Channel by getting a squadron of eight planes (each with three navigators on board) to fly in a tight oblong pattern, dropping twelve bundles of electronic chaff a minute. As this 'Window', composed of lengths of concertina-folded reflective foil, fell through the air, it bounced back the radio pulses of the German sets, thus creating the simulacrum of a large invasion fleet on their screens.

The siege of fortress Douvres-la-Délivrande inside its minefield lasted many days and had elements of farce. A tank shell fired from the Black Watch regiment on one side bounced off the curved concrete roof and caused a return of fire from an English battery on the other side. Someone managed to stop it before anyone got killed. The Royal Navy Forward Observation Officers, who theoretically had the ability to summon huge naval bombardment from miles away, couldn't get through by wireless to their ships, and had to withdraw, under sniper fire. The Germans inside the radar control station, a mixed bag from the German Air Force Signals Regiment No. 53, and men from the 716th Division and the 192nd Panzergrenadiers, hunkered down in their bunkers, determined not to surrender. They were only finally driven out on 17 June by a menagerie of mine-clearing, petard-throwing Armoured Vehicles, Royal Engineers (AVREs) and determined infantry. Brigadier John Durnford-Slater of the Special Service Tactical HQ observed the final attack.

No enemy movement was to be seen above ground, but when we stood on a mound outside the perimeter, a heavy and accurate machine-gun fire was opened on us. The artillery put down smoke and No. 41 Commando came through wire in perfect formation. They threw grenades down all the alleyways and slits which led to the underground passages and soon the Germans had had enough.

A few 30AU men were in there, chucking No. 36M grenades. Woolley had withdrawn PIKEFORCE and X Troop to join him further north in the American sector, so only Sancho Glanville, Sergeant Spong, Lance Corporal Morgan and marines Webb and Booth were there to see five Allied tanks knocked out in the final smoky attack. In the end, 250 Germans and six officers came out with their hands up. As Glanville's handful of men set about their job searching the two-storey underground building, he was irritated by the mob of unauthorised looters, many of them officers, who came swarming in looking for trophies, drink and cigarettes. Glanville got Lieutenant Colonel Palmer of 41 Commando to post sentries, but still some things were lost, and after an exhausting siege with fifteen Allied casualties, the signals intelligence haul from PIKEFORCE's main target was small but useful: a set of wheels for the German air force Enigma machine and a cryptographer's pad with various workings on it

Hugill and Postlethwaite, however, who were moving along the coast, struck gold as they found and dismantled radar sites first at Arromanches and then at Pointe et Raz de la Percée at the west end of Omaha Beach. Hugill shaved in captured Vichy water there, which 'frothed a little on the face flannel'. German

Funkmeßstützpunkt (radar installations) IGEL and IMME yielded valuable intelligence that had to be taken back to England 'by hand of officer'. According to Glanville, this included a list of 'all German radar installations in NW Europe, giving the designation of each set, its wavelength, polarisation, pulse repetition frequency and aerial display', and the Admiralty rated it as 'most valuable' in helping to jam the system. 30AU were really coming up with the goods, fulfilling Ian Fleming's original vision of them as intelligence commandos.

Since the beginning of the Battle of the Atlantic, Naval Intelligence had been usefully interrogating captured U-boat crewmen. For OVERLORD, Captain Lewes instituted a new unit, the Royal Navy Forward Interrogation Unit (FIU), whose job was to find and question Kriegsmarine personnel either before or soon after they entered the prisoner-of-war cages. Taking the work into the field was a good idea because in the immediate shock of capture people would often say much more than they would after incarceration. The FIU worked directly with 30AU in intelligence-gathering and translation, but their particular role was to get useful information from prisoners and their papers back to the Admiralty. The former journalist Lieutenant Commander Ralph Izzard RNVR was in charge of the interrogators, using his idiomatic German to extract new technical information from enemy matelots who were made to feel that he knew everything already. Izzard's German-speaking team included twenty-eight-year-old Lieutenant Brian Connell RNVR and twenty-nine-year-old Captain Charles Wheeler RM, who both went on to distinguished broadcast journalism careers with ITV and BBC respectively. These interrogators attached to 30AU came across something novel in Normandy that summer. The German navy tried a new, last-ditch tactic after their U-boats and *Schnell*-boats failed to stop the invading forces. They sent out sabotage swimmers from the 'small battle units'

or *Kleinkampfverbände* to blow up Allied ships. Ralph Izzard was photographed at Courselles questioning one such captured 'human torpedo' who seemed to be little more than a stroppy teenager.

✗

The primary aim of the British Second Army after D-Day was to fight for Caen, and the first objective of the US First Army was to capture the port of Cherbourg. Since the naval HQ there was 30AU's principal target, 30AU went along with the Americans. They had to be careful patrolling near nervous and inexperienced US troops who tended to shoot first and ask questions afterwards.

Bon Royle carried a US-made Garand M1 rifle, and in the American sector he was always sure of finding the black-tipped, armour-piercing .30-06 ammunition that he found best for *bocage* fighting because it could punch through an earth bank. Royle thought the US artillery and US airborne troops were very good but many of the American infantry – especially in the 90th Division – were undisciplined, poorly trained and above all, not properly led. Panicky and bullying officers did not help to make good soldiers of their men. There was a general disrespect for the dead that appalled the Royal Marines. British battlefield practice was to bury all corpses quickly, marking the spot for later parties to exhume, identify and inter in military cemeteries, but American 'grave registration' was sometimes erratic. Bodies abandoned in the road were squashed cartoon-flat by the heavy vehicles that crowded the narrow lanes. Even their own dead were left lying there to be picked up a week or two later by PoW work parties. Tony Hugill talked to some US doctors taking wounded men back to England from Utah Beach. There was, they said, a high percentage of casualties among their troops with shellshock – which they called 'anxiety neurosis'. Hugill reckoned that British front-line troops were less prone to it. They weren't necessarily braver, just less hysterical.

The Germans had flooded the marshy middle of the peninsula; the land in the north, rising towards Cherbourg, was a little drier, but everywhere was pestilential with mosquitoes that summer, with everyone scratching at bites. The German fighting withdrawal was hard and ruthless. Small Norman towns like Valognes and Montebourg were smashed by both sides' shellfire and bombing. In the countryside, tanks could not manoeuvre through fields blocked by high-banked thick hedges without the help of armoured bulldozers. Infantry had to use 'fire and movement' tactics, taking cover from German mortars, machine-guns and snipers. Crawling through the cowpats of dairy farms, you came across the swollen bodies of cattle blown up by mines. It might be rich soil for farmers, but for soldiers it was either dust or mud.

30AU lost two men on 24 June. One was a young marine called Frank O'Callaghan who had become famous after moving into a new billet at Amersham. Having drunk a skinful of ale, the boy, nicknamed Paddy, had to get up in the middle of the night. He groped his way to the lavatory in the dark and was enjoyably 'easing springs' when he heard his new (but soon to be ex-) landlady asking 'What are you doing in my wardrobe?' Paddy O'Callaghan was the last man crossing a hedgerow gap when a bullet got him in the leg. He bled to death, aged nineteen, from a mangled femoral artery.

The next day, 25 June, was a bad day for 30AU. On the southern outskirts of Cherbourg, their commander Colonel Woolley was wounded in the head by an 88-mm shell-splinter off a Sherman tank, and Major Evans had to take command. Snipers wounded two other men in A Troop. Worse, the medical orderlies who went to tend them were deliberately targeted. One was killed, the other shot through the knee. This enraged the men, and one crime led to another. When three German riflemen surrendered, an NCO from 30AU shot them dead with a burst from a light machine-gun. It was a wet day in the aftermath of a great storm, and one witness told me he saw their blood flowing in the rainwater. An officer came around the corner just after and the NCO and several marines were RTU'd.

When asked about this incident, one former marine I talked to became very distressed even though he had nothing to do with it and it had all happened sixty-five years before. The memories of war can linger for a lifetime. When some of the 30AU Association gathered in Cherbourg for the fiftieth anniversary of the liberation, it proved too much for the former marine who, five decades earlier, had been instructed by Major Hargreaves-Heap to guard the Naval Intelligence map of Cherbourg with his life. On the anniversary trip this marine started getting flashbacks, ending up in a psychotic episode where he struggled ferociously with the French ambulance men whom he thought were German soldiers.

The map the marine had to keep safe was the 1943 third edition of a War Office town plan of the port of Cherbourg, marked up in blue and brown ink. The blue ink showed all the Kriegsmarine establishments, booms and wrecks, while the brown showed lines of sea mines across the harbour entrance and along the quays and other mines around the arsenal, together with their firing points and electrical leads. German Konteradmiral Walter Hennecke had prepared the whole of Cherbourg for systematic demolition. The naval Headquarters, 30AU's key target which overlooked the harbour, lay between two forts on the heights of Octeville. The Villa Meurice and the Fort d'Octeville were connected by underground galleries, and according to British Naval Intelligence, in October 1943 at least 400 men 'in field grey uniform with naval insignia' were reported as stationed at this HQ.

In March 1944 Hitler had designated Cherbourg as one of the key 'fortified areas' (*feste Plätze*), operational sites strong enough not to surrender even if surrounded. (Indeed, La Rochelle, Lorient and St-Nazaire held out until the end of the war.) The hills that crowned Cherbourg were honeycombed by a network of pill boxes, strong points, tunnels, bunkers and fortresses built in and around the old Vauban forts. When American aircraft swooped down to bomb and strafe them, they did more damage to their own troops in blue-on-blue mishaps than to the bunkers. The Allies sent eighteen ships to shell the embedded gun batteries at Cherbourg, but were biffed back by accurate German gunfire – the battleship *Texas*, the cruiser *Glasgow* and the destroyers *O'Brien* and *Barton* all retreated damaged.

Cherbourg was taken not from the sea but from the south by land: as usual, the infantry had to do the dirty work. There were savage fights for the Redoubte des Fourches and the Fort du Roule. German flak gun duelled with American howitzer. Men threw themselves at defences of reinforced concrete: two Medals of Honor were won at Cherbourg by GIs who rammed pole charges, fifteen-pound satchels of TNT on the end of ten-foot sticks, through the embrasures of enemy bunkers and who knocked out an 88-mm gun and two machine-guns with rifle- and hand-grenades. Hugill described dead Germans, 'a beastly greenish-yellow waxen colour', lying unburied along the verges of the roads to Cherbourg.

Generalleutnant Karl-Wilhelm Dietrich von Schlieben had received a special *Führerbefehl* when he was promoted to Cherbourg Fortress Commandant on 23 June 1944:

Even if the worst comes to the worst it is your duty to defend the last bunker and leave to the enemy not a harbour but a field of ruins . . . the German people and the whole world are watching your fight; on it depends . . . the honour of the German Army and of your own name.

On 26 June the three troops of 30AU joined the 39th Infantry Regiment from the 9th Infantry Division of US Army's VII Corps in the land assault. They heard the thunderous explosions of demolition echoing up from the port below as the Kriegsmarine set about methodically wrecking the harbour.

The German naval HQ was a large underground complex of tunnels quarried in the rock. Some German prisoners of war revealed that General von Schlieben himself was inside. After he had twice refused offers of surrender, two anti-tank guns were brought up to blow down the tunnel doors. A few ringing, smoky shots, some bursts of machine-gun fire and a few grenades thrown down the ventilation shafts, and the 800 officers and men inside surrendered. A lieutenant came out with a white flag, which he dipped limply in the cloying air. Tall, flabby-faced General von Schlieben came out of the shored-up tunnel in his black helmet, his pathetically new Ritterkreuz or 'Knight's Cross' (a last-minute German morale-booster dropped by parachute with hundreds of others), prominent at his throat, his *feldgrau* greatcoat spattered and stained with mud. Hennecke was behind him in his dark blue cap with gold braid and Nazi eagle. Their last messages to German Seventh Army recorded their destruction of the records and coding machines, and complained about the cowardice of those who had surrendered earlier. Now the disdainful general had to submit to the humiliation of being photographed and filmed for American newsreels, and learn the joy of K-rations.

'We took some amazing prisoners,' remembered Bon Royle.

The first bunch looked like nothing we had ever seen before and, after trying all sorts of languages on them, it turned out they were [conscripted] Georgians from Holy Mother Russia . . . Details in their paybooks were entered in Cyrillic script. After that we were no longer surprised as Poles, Rumanians, Balts and the U.N. itself fell into our bag.

There was a smell of hot men and high explosive in the tunnels. The wounded were evacuated and the diesel-generated air-conditioning restarted. 30AU men spent two days hunting for data in this dingy underworld, sifting right down to incinerator ash, not finding very much beyond routine intelligence. But there was a lot to loot, including extensive stocks of wine and spirits and souvenirs in the shape of German pistols and cameras to take away.

The photographer Robert Capa and the reporter Ernie Pyle saw a little street-fighting as they went with the 9th Division on their way to liberating the Cherbourg military hospital where 250 wounded men from the US 82nd Airborne Division were being held. While Pyle interviewed the freed prisoners, Capa made for the wine cellar, but was too late:

Every soldier of the 47th Infantry had his arms, jacket and pockets bulging with precious bottles. I begged one of them for just a single bottle, but he laughed and said, 'Only if you're Ernie Pyle.' With the next soldier, my approach was different. I asked him for a bottle for Ernie Pyle and he parted with it willingly. Soon I had collected my loot of Benedictine and brandy.

Across the city, the brothels opened and the wine flowed for the Ninth Division. Civilians were creeping back with hand-carts. The huge German arsenal down in the port surrendered the next day to a psychological warfare van with a loudspeaker. The garrison inside had clearly been listening to *Soldatensender*, the British black propaganda radio service run by Ian Fleming's friend Sefton Delmer, which demoralised the German defenders with a mishmash of truth and lies about amazing new Allied weapons. 'I cannot surrender,' said Generalmajor Robert Sattler, 'my orders are to fight to the last cartridge. It would be different if you could prove to me that our position is hopeless. If you could, for instance, fire one of those phosphorous shells . . . '

The docks were crunching with glass, and explosives had smashed through the pens for German *Schnellboote* or fast attack boats, 'large, cavernous, cathedral-like structures'. It was a scene of surreal violence. Tony Hugill describes how 'great reinforced concrete walls 10 and 15 feet thick had been shattered. Irregular lumps of concrete 100 cubic feet in volume had been blown 100 yards.' Vast girders lay torn and twisted like paper spills. A barge in one of the wrecked pens was still aflame, 'filling the air with dense, smarting smoke'.

N

30AU regrouped in a group of villas at Carteret, on the west side
of the Cotentin Peninsula, in countryside reminiscent of Dorset,
with a view of the Channel Island of Jersey ten miles away to the
south-west. But Carteret seemed damp and dour, with disagreeable
cooking by an oily corporal and the men bored and restless. The
haul from their main target at Cherbourg had been a let-down
compared to the information about radar that 30AU men had
found at Arromanches and Raz de la Percée or the discovery of
the V-1 and V-2 sites, and these were men of action who did not
enjoy keeping still. More generally, there was a natural feeling of
anti-climax after the adrenalin of the D-Day landings and the first
actions in France. Now the Allies were contained by the Germans
in Normandy, and the men were fretting to go onwards. Naval
officers like Hugill did not like being billeted with the marines *en
masse*; he thought they were like tiresomely dangerous children,
always breaking or setting fire to things, wandering into minefields
or getting into other scrapes from which they had to be extricated.

Perhaps partly due to this general state of discontent, Hugill
was not happy with his superiors either. Ian Fleming came to visit
his private army in July 1944, wearing his blue No. 1 dress uniform
with the three gold rings and green stripe of a commander RNVR.
In *The Hazard Mesh* Hugill gives a notably sour initial account of
how Fleming 'honour[ed] us with a visit':

We none of us liked him much. He was one of those very superior
professorial type R.N.V.R.s who got their claws into Their Lordships
early in the war and have kept them in ever since. As our proprietary
deity he felt himself entitled to demand offerings of Camembert and
libations of captured cognac of the better sort (But my dear feller this
stuff's undrinkable!) from time to time. He also interfered with us on a
high level . . . X [Ian Fleming] arrived and we fed him to the best of our
ability. We sat on the verandah sipping some cognac which he described
as passable. He shot a line about the dangers of life in London. He
enlarged on the imminence of V.2 . . . While we were talking one of the
marine sentries reported that a pilot had baled out of an allied aircraft
in trouble and landed in the sea. Roger [Dunstan Curtis] immediately

leaped to his feet and began casting about for means of getting him in. X said: 'Roger, it's no use your rushing around indulging in air/sea rescue work. That's not what you are paid for.' Roger turned to him in a fury and replied: 'For heaven's sake forget that bloody green stripe for a little. I only hope you find yourself in the drink by yourself one day. Then you'll think differently.'

Ironically, Dunstan Curtis had just presented commando fighting knives to six Frenchmen in Carteret on Bastille Day 1944 to honour them for rescuing an RAF pilot from the sea and helping him escape via Spain to eventual freedom.

But twenty-five years later, after the world-famous creator of James Bond had died, Tony Hugill wrote differently about Fleming's visit to Carteret. By this time, Hugill, who in real life had become managing director of Tate & Lyle in the Caribbean, had appeared under his own name in chapter 4 of the last James Bond book, *The Man with the Golden Gun* (1965), where he is a useful 'Mr Fixit' at a sugar estate in Jamaica: 'The top man at Frome is a man called Tony Hugill. Ex-navy. Nice man. Nice wife. Nice children. Does a good job. Has a lot of trouble with cane burning and other small sabotage – mostly with thermite bombs brought in from Cuba.' In the late 1960s Hugill's account of Fleming was more sympathetic:

He wanted to see the Crossbow Sites (the places from which the V.1's were intended to be fired) and I know he wanted to see how we were. Surprisingly, it seemed, our casualties were relatively few, and at this time only one officer and two ratings or marines had been killed, and a handful wounded. We had captured in a German H.Q. some Polish vodka, with which we plied him, but – with justice – he suspected it. (It had a headache in every tot.) We also had some vin ordinaire which – we agreed with him – was extremely ordinaire. But when he belly-ached about the brandy (I admit it was only Three Star) I became very angry and abusive and had to be shushed down.

It is easy to assume he was less abrasive in the 1960s in part because Ian Fleming the author had given him the accolade of immortality in his fiction. Fleming was viewed sardonically by a lot of people – Sancho Glanville, for example, called him 'the egregious Fleming, who always claimed to know everything' though Hugill came to think that Fleming's armour of arrogance was just a protection for an unhappy soul.

However, there is another, more positive, recollection of Ian Fleming's behaviour that evening, and it comes from the men, not the officers. Hugill's mention of casualties and of Fleming wanting to 'see how we were' in the later account is interesting in this context. It seems that Fleming did have an argument about the level of casualties with Lieutenant Colonel Woolley at Carteret. Marines serving the officers' meal reported the dispute between the two men to their mates and, according to them, Fleming did not think the numbers of dead and injured were 'relatively few', but too high. Although almost none of the ordinary marines in 30AU ever met or spoke to the distant Commander Ian Fleming, many gained the impression that the top man had their interests at heart, whereas Hugill's private diary recorded a growing ill-feeling against the commanding officer Fleming argued with, Lieutenant Colonel Woolley. 'The marine wing hums with mutiny,' Hugill wrote on 20 August 1944. 'Unless he's got rid of, one of his own troops will shoot him in the back in action.'

The time at Carteret was just a lull before they geared up for the great drive on occupied Paris. 'Then came the break-out,' wrote Bon Royle, 'and things became exquisitely fluid just as we liked it.'

12

Breakthrough

Generaloberst Friedrich Dollmann, commander of Seventh Army, died in his bathroom on 28 June 1944. Was it a heart attack, or did he kill himself to escape a Nazi court martial for losing Cherbourg? Spitfires shot up a German staff car on 17 July and wounded Generalfeldmarschall Erwin Rommel. On 20 July Adolf Hitler narrowly escaped the blast of a bomb placed by German conspirators under a conference table in the Wolf's Lair at Rastenburg, and began a vicious purge of everyone implicated in the plot. Some 5,000 were put to death; Rommel was forced to commit suicide by cyanide, Admiral Canaris was hanged at Flossenburg and his Abwehr organisation taken over by Heinrich Himmler's SS, and the execution of Generalleutnant Erich Fellgiebel, the chief signals officer, upset German secret communications. On 25 July, the biggest crack of all appeared in the military edifice supporting the Third Reich: the Allies broke out of their containment in Normandy.

Operation COBRA started with a massive Allied onslaught from the air: over a thousand heavy bombers pounded the German tanks and infantry east of Saint-Lô. Some of the bombs landed in the wrong place, killing 126 Americans (including Lieutenant General McNair) and wounding nearly 600. But the Germans were far worse hit, with concussed survivors left wild-eyed and babbling. The line in the south-west of the Cotentin peninsula crumpled before the American First Army's armoured divisions and low-level attack aircraft. General 'Blood-&-Guts' Patton thrust towards Brittany.

30AU was in the thick of it, riding the American mechanised

wave. Lieutenant Commander Ralph Izzard was with Patton's Third US Army in its drive on Brest, in a Humber 4 x 4 Heavy Utility car with two US liaison officers. One of them, Angus Thuermer, was a journalist who later went on to serve twenty-six years in the CIA. Like Izzard, Thuermer had been a correspondent in Berlin, reporting grim events like Kristallnacht and the invasion of Poland for the Associated Press. In December 1940 Thuermer had managed to scoop an interview with the famous English comic author P. G. Wodehouse, at the time held captive in a former lunatic asylum in Upper Silesia where he kept busy writing, longhand, a novel (called *Money for Jam*) in a padded cell. Wodehouse, deadpan, told Thuermer that he was becoming 'a great admirer of the German potato'. This interview, published in the *New York Times*, led to Wodehouse's undeservedly infamous broadcasts on German radio, where his ironic descriptions of the delights of internment were misread as treachery by the humourless.

Izzard remembered how General Patton, 'true to form', wreaked an 'appalling' amount of pointless destruction, flattening towns and villages before entering them and 'smashing every church tower and steeple' lest they harboured snipers. Flame-throwing tanks were sent in advance of the men to scorch the streets before they passed through. When they got to Vannes, Patton was ordered to turn round and head east to help trap a German army in the Mortain–Falaise pocket. Patton was relying on more than his mystic sense of history. He now had an 'indoctrinated' US intelligence officer, Mervin Helfers, and a British Special Liaison Unit (SLU) feeding him fresh ULTRA intelligence.

30AU scattered into small parties and got on with forward reconnaissance and capture on their own initiative. Mobile and well armed, they often went in ahead of Allied troops. Patrick Dalzel-Job first went south-east to try and slip around Caen, the old Norman city where William the Conqueror is buried, now reduced to rubble by Allied bombing and tank and infantry fighting. On 9 July, the day the Germans finally withdrew, Dalzel-Job was picking his way through the ruins when he met what he thought was a group of French labourers. One of them turned out to be Staff Sergeant Maurice Bramah of the British Glider Pilot Regiment, who had recently emerged from hiding in a wine barrel after an amazing series of escapes. His Horsa glider carrying medical supplies had crashed at Villers-sur-Mer early on D-Day; he survived it only to run into a German patrol who shot him three times and left him for dead. Bramah somehow dragged himself to a nearby farm where the French Resistance got a midwife to nurse his wounds in a safe house. Acting on a tip-off, a squad of Germans burst in and Bramah killed three of them with a Sten gun, survived a German 'potato-masher' grenade by upturning a bed as a shield, then escaped from the first-floor window by clinging to the telephone wire.

30AU's ability to move freely in the French countryside and connect with the French Resistance was partly due to the linguists the unit had recruited. Dalzel-Job had teamed up with Charles Wheeler from the Forward Interrogation Unit. One day Wheeler was in the garden of a château near Bréhal when an American soldier in a passing truck shouldered his rifle and casually shot the Frenchman Wheeler was talking to. He died in Wheeler's arms; his widow and family were hysterical with grief. Dalzel-Job remonstrated with the Americans, 'but many of these men were very simple-minded and they were only behaving as they would have done when hunting deer at home in the States – anything seen through the trees was there to be shot'.

Geordie Jim Burns of A troop remembered coming back from reconnaissance and meeting an American vanguard unit head-on. The Americans believed anyone coming in the other direction had to be the enemy and, levelling their guns, tried to arrest the motley band of intelligence-gatherers in their jeeps and lorries, who they thought couldn't be British, with their non-matching uniforms and caps. Some 30AU men had got navy badges on army khaki *and* were carrying US weapons. Were they disguised Germans trying to sneak through their lines? But when an ordinary GI casually called a British officer 'buddy', a young marine jumped out of a lorry and grabbed the hapless American by the front of his jacket. 'Listen here, BUDDY', he snarled, 'when you speak to a Royal Marine Officer you address him as 'Sir' AND you stand to attention!' Curiously, this helped persuade the Americans that they were, in fact, authentic 'crazy Limeys'.

So 30AU were cautious around Americans, but they also needed a degree of scepticism with the French. 'Everywhere the collaborators attempted to ingratiate themselves with the Allied soldiers as soon as we arrived', observed the war correspondent Alan Moorehead. The D-Day landings had upset the ecology of occupation; Frenchmen who had been doing business for years with Germans who at least paid promptly were not necessarily overjoyed by a *libération* that unleashed chaos and petty theft. Some who eagerly embraced the Allies were just seeking protection from their own neighbours with scores to settle.

'Collaboration', said the historian Henri Michel, 'is a kind of epidemic that spares no one', though Michel distinguished between the daily chronic infection where people just tried to get on with their life and work in a country occupied by foreign troops and the virulent fever of active collaboration that deranged about one per cent of the population. The summer of 1944 was not a good time to be outed as a collaborator: many women who had consorted with Germans – *collaboration horizontale* – were paraded with shaved heads by angry men whose own humiliating compromises would not bear scrutiny. Tony Hugill hated seeing one woman dragged through Rennes, 'shorn, tarred and feathered, and bleeding'. Across France, some 20,000 women had their heads shaved, and around 7,500 '*collabos*' were summarily executed. 'We were never sure what these chaps had been up to', said Bon Royle. 'We met any number of civilians wearing FFI armbands, French Forces of the Interior, a sort of *maquis* or partisan.' From 1941 de

Gaulle's Free French provisional government in exile had been trying to unify those who resisted German rule into one great Resistance movement. From 1 February 1944, *les Forces françaises de l'intérieur* (FFI) became de Gaulle's name for all the French resistance bands.

Patrick Dalzel-Job described how his squad proceeded through occupied country:

I led the way myself in Fraser's jeep, and the scout-cars followed at twenty-five yard intervals, on alternate sides of the road where possible. I preferred the jeep as leading vehicle, in spite of its lack of protective armour, because we could see clearly in every direction from it and could reverse or manoeuvre very quickly out of trouble, especially with Fraser's ability to drive very fast backwards; also, it was easy to dive into the ditch from the jeep if needs be. We carried the lightweight, semi-automatic .300 US carbines, which were handy and effective weapons at short range. It was the responsibility of the rather heavier gunned and armoured scout cars to cover our withdrawal if we came under fire.

'Wherever Germans showed any inclination to stand and fight they got all the fighting they wanted,' said Bon Royle. 'We had the firepower and we were quite ready to use every bit of it.' One way of telling if the Germans wanted a scrap was whether they wore their steel helmets; bare heads were often a sign of submission.

Tony Hugill was in Lannilis with some jeeps and men from A Troop when a Frenchman told him that 1,500 Germans were holed up in a radar station near St Pabu. He knew there must be big Luftwaffe radar stations in the north of Brittany covering the flight paths of Allied bombers towards the U-boat bases at Lorient and St-Nazaire, and thought they ought to have a 'dekko' at the place. '*Pas de quartier!*' shouted a bloodthirsty old Breton. They met a funeral cortège of sobbing women following the four coffins of young men tortured and shot by the Germans at St Pabu, and the white-bearded mayor of the village told them there were 400 Germans in the radar station. Tony Hugill determined to try and bluff them out by pretending he was with a big force, reasoning that a beleaguered German garrison surrounded by locals who hated them might want to surrender to regular Allied forces. If he was right, all to the good, if wrong, at least he wouldn't be alive to face the court of inquiry. Lieutenant Alec van Cleef, the other officer, agreed to hang back but keep a vigilant eye open. Hugill was going to go with his usual bodyguard, a young marine, but Sergeant Paul McGrath stepped forward, carrying his usual Thompson sub-machine gun. 'I'm coming with you, sir, and you too,' he said, pointing to Marine Sandy Powell holding his Bren-gun. Hugill nodded. They crawled up to a ridge to peer at the Luftwaffe radar station: two armed sentries on the gate and the heads of the crews manning three 2-cm Flakvierling guns whose four barrels could pump out hundreds of rounds a minute. Hugill tied a not very clean white handkerchief to the barrel of his American carbine. Then they stood up together. Safety catches off.

It was a 300-yard walk to the gate, but it felt like miles. Hugill's mouth was dry and he was all twisted up inside. The steady step of the two men just behind braced his quailing spirit. By rights the cheerfully aggressive Paul McGrath should have been an officer by now, because he was a born leader. He had completed the Officer Cadet Training Unit course successfully aged eighteen, but he had fallen foul of the major who was second-in-command and who told him to apply again later. An excellent NCO, he had lost a stripe once for punching a marine who didn't move fast enough and he would lose one again for thumping a senior German officer. But he was the man you wanted in a tight corner. At a watery-bowelled moment, Mac was staunch. 'By God, you've got guts, Tony, you have,' he muttered to his officer, and Hugill was grateful because he had never been so frightened.

The helmeted sentries waved them forwards. '*Öffnen Sie die Sperre!*' shouted Hugill, and they opened the gate. He sent for the Kommandant who was apparently at lunch. It was twelve noon by his watch.

'Where did you learn German, Englishman?'

'I've been to Germany several times before the war.'

'How did you like it?'

'It's all right.'

After five minutes the Luftwaffe Kommandant appeared, with four officers and a bodyguard of about ten armed men, all ominous in helmets. He gave a Hitler salute. Hugill made no answering gesture, just demanded their surrender.

The Kommandant refused. He was accompanied by two other Luftwaffe officers, a Kriegsmarine sub lieutenant and a hard-bitten Artillerieoffizier from the Afrika Korps who stared at Hugill with angry contempt. Only the sub lieutenant spoke any English, so their talk was a mixture of English and German.

'How many men have you?'

'We cannot say. How many have you?'

'I may not say.'

'We will not surrender to a small force.'

'I am the representative of a large force. If you do not surrender to me, I will return and call for an air bombardment, for *Kannonen* and *Panzer*. You had far better give up now. *Eure Lage ist hoffnungslos.*'

'You surely do not suppose we should let you leave here alive.'

The long silence of their impasse was broken by a burst of gunfire and a reply from the other end of the German strongpoint. Worried for their safety, someone in the waiting-and-watching party had started shooting at the camp. The Kommandant sent some of his bodyguard, at the double, to stop it from his end and McGrath coolly mounted the blockhouse to wave his arms and bellow an order for the bloody idiots to cease fire.

The Germans seemed keen to avoid trouble. Hugill pressed his advantage, telling the Kommandant sharply that if he did not return to his people in half an hour, they had orders to bring in the bombers and the artillery. That did it. A heated discussion took place and the diehard Afrika Korps man was overruled.

'All right. We will come with you, if we may keep our weapons.

But you must protect us from the French terrorists. We want your main body to take charge of us. We do not trust the French not to snipe us, unless we surrender to a larger force.'

Hugill and the officers left the radar station and went and stood about thirty yards outside the gate. As the Kommandant left, one of his men surreptitiously slipped him a grenade. Van Cleef the RNVR signals officer came to say some American 'tank-busters' were on their way. They sat down for a smoke and some stilted talk.

'Germany is winning the war.'

'Well, it's been a long war, five years.'

'Not too long for us, we can take it.'

'So can we.'

When coffee was produced from the German side, Powell says that he took one sip of the ersatz acorn brew and spat it out. A German pointed his Schmeisser machine-pistol at him but Powell and McGrath turned their weapons towards him with a steely look and he walked away. Another German smiled, and said of the coffee, '*Nicht gut.*'

The first Americans eventually turned up and abrasively demanded surrender, but the British told them, 'We've done that. It's all settled.' The interpreter told the Germans that America was the richest country in the world. They would be well looked after and well fed as prisoners, with the best doctors in the world. The German officers asked permission to fetch some clothes.

'You don't need clothes. We provide you with clothes.'

'I should prefer my German uniform to American clothes, however good.'

Sandy Powell tapped the Kommandant on the arm. He put out one empty hand, and then, shamefacedly, the other, holding the grenade he had been playing with behind his back. Now the 300 Germans lined up to put their helmets and weapons in a pile.

Elation was followed by shaky exhaustion and a tension headache. As Hugill and van Cleef wolfed down a K-ration each,

Powell came up with a bottle of wine from which Hugill drank gratefully, thirstily. He smoked a most enjoyable cigarette as he watched the line of buses fill up with the prisoners whom he had managed to bluff. The white-bearded mayor shook the hand of everyone in the unit, the *curé* blessed them and all the people of the village shouted.

Hugill was awarded the DSC and McGrath and Powell the DSM.

Four years' occupation brought out the best and worst of France. In January 1943 Pierre Laval set up a right-wing paramilitary organisation, *la Milice française*, whose 10,000 active members worked hand-in-glove with the German authorities in the repression of Jews, troublemakers and 'terrorists'. A few French fascists actually hero-worshipped the Nazis, among them the smooth Paris-based aristocrat, Guy Glèbe d'Eu, Comte de Marcheret, who used his charm and languages to help catch enemies of the Third Reich, working for the *Sicherheitspolizie und Sicherheitsdienst* (Sipo-SD) in its Kommando Paris building on Rue des Saussaies. When, very near the end of the war, a group of young FFI fighters came to the capital in search of weapons, Guy Glèbe d'Eu posed as an English officer called 'Captain Jack' and promised to show them a garage full of arms and ammunition. It was a trap: Hauptsturmführer Friedrich Berger of the French Gestapo and a squad of German soldiers were waiting, and all thirty-five were shot under the chestnut trees of the Bois de Boulogne.

The massacre happened on 16 August 1944, one of the last desperate moves by a failing regime. Encouraged by the advance from Normandy and the news of more Allied landings in the South of France, Paris was rising. Four years of occupation when German soldiers had walked unarmed around the city as uniformed tourists were coming to an end: hearing that the German Seventh Army was surrounded and being smashed in the

Mortain–Falaise pocket west of Paris, senior Nazis began stealing away eastward out of Paris with their loot. There were depots crammed with the French furniture and valuables removed by what was called *Dienststelle Westen* or the *Service de l'Ouest*. The 'service' in question meant the pillage of 4,000 Parisian homes and the packing up of 40,000 tonnes of furniture and fittings ready to be sent off to Germany. The Dépôt de Bassano in the rich sixteenth district of Paris, near Nazi headquarters, held some of the most beautiful of the stolen artefacts. How to get it all out in time? Soon stealth was replaced by panic. Automobiles and bikes were stopped and commandeered by Germans in the street. Resistance-inspired strikes broke out across the capital.

There is an old joke about German obedience to authority: 'There will never be a revolution in Germany because the police would not allow it.' In Paris, on the other hand, an alliance between the FFI and the 20,000 armed police was crucial to the uprising which began on Saturday 19 August 1944. Two thousand gendarmes inside the Prefecture of Police held off three German tanks on the Île de la Cité with small arms and Molotov cocktails made by Madame Curie's son-in-law, Frédéric Joliot-Curie. Desperate messages were sent to the Allies to parachute in arms or come to the rescue as barricades went up across the streets and small battles were fought across the city. A brief Sunday ceasefire soon broke down, but the Germans were losing control of the streets and were forced to retreat into key strongpoints. On Wednesday 23 August Hitler ordered mass executions, the demolition of the beautiful bridges across the Seine and the destruction of the city, but the new German military commander of Paris, monocled General von Choltitz, was civilised enough not to obey his Führer. The Allied command did not want to turn a great city into a battleground either. They had originally intended to bypass Paris in pursuit of the German army, but the FFI uprising forced their hand. American General Omar Bradley granted the Free French – General Philippe Leclerc's 2nd Armoured Division or *Deuxième division blindée* – the honour of liberating Paris on Thursday 24 August.

N

It was only thanks to some nifty footwork by Colonel Woolley that 30AU's WOOLFORCE were able to go into Paris with the *2e DB*. Woolley had to get a message to the rest of WOOLFORCE to hurry to the gathering point – they were delayed partly because the marines of X Troop had somehow managed once again to explode a petrol cooker and set fire to their billets. WOOLFORCE began gathering itself at Rambouillet, some twenty-two miles from the south-west edge of Paris.

Glanville saw 'a column of cars containing war-correspondents . . . apparently waiting to start for Paris'. The journalistic stars were all there, including the renowned Hungarian photographer for *LIFE*, Robert Capa, who would talk his way on to a French tank, named *Teruel* and manned by Spanish Republicans, by declaring that he too had been in the civil war, '*y yo soy uno de vosotros*' ('And I am one of you'). 'The Trio' of top reporters from the British press were there together, schoolmasterly Christopher Buckley of the *Daily Telegraph*, bespectacled Alexander Clifford of the *Daily Mail* and compact Alan Moorehead of the *Daily Express*. Making a nuisance of himself trying to supply what he called 'gen' was the heavily bearded and heavy-drinking American novelist Ernest Hemingway of *Collier's,* carrying an automatic pistol (quite against the Geneva Conventions) on the belt he had taken from a dead German with its old Prussian slogan *GOTT MIT UNS* ('God is on our side'), happily playing the guerrilla leader to a dozen FFI youngsters, and eager to enter Paris, 'the city I love best in all the world'. The melancholy American Ernie Pyle, now sporting a black beret on his bald head, caught the atmosphere of that sunny summer's day in his book *Brave Men*, in the chapter which begins 'I had thought that for me there could never again be any elation in war. But I had reckoned without the liberation of Paris . . .'

On Friday 25 August Pyle was stunned by the 'pandemonium of surely the greatest mass joy that has ever happened'. The matter-of-fact reporter, lyricist of the ordinary, found this extraordinary event hard to write about; he felt 'incapable', 'inadequate' to describe the tide of emotion as they were 'kissed and hauled and mauled' by frantic men, women and children 'until we were literally red in the face'. There seemed to be flowers everywhere: the women were all 'brightly dressed in white or red blouses and colourful peasant skirts, with flowers in their hair and big flashy earrings. Everybody was throwing flowers.' And yet above the happy din he could still hear sporadic explosions, sniper shots and the rattle of machine-guns. Celebration and killing danced together in an ecstatic *fête folle*.

When 30AU's X Troop, now about seventy-five strong, drove with Leclerc's *2e DB* column through the Porte d'Orléans, cheering, joyous crowds greeted them in the wide avenue later renamed Place 25 Août 1944. But Colonel Woolley thought it was too early for frivolities. At Place Victor Basch they turned west and headed straight for the Pont Mirabeau, where there were barricades to negotiate. On the other side, between the right bank of the Seine and the Bois de Boulogne, they entered the sixteenth *arrondissement*, the wealthy and fashionable district which had become the administrative centre of Nazi occupation and collaboration. The Military Command of Occupied France was at the Hôtel Majestic in Avenue Kléber, the Gestapo established in and around Avenue Foch, the head of the SS, General Oberg, lived in Boulevard Lannes, and the Palais de Chaillot in the Trocadéro Gardens had been draped in swastikas for grand Nazi ceremonies and Wagnerian concerts.

Here too was one of 30AU's targets, the French HQ of the German navy, the Oberbefehlshaber des Marinegruppenkommandos West. The Kriegsmarine had taken over the Rothschild estates bordering the Bois de Boulogne. Opposite his beautiful honey-coloured villa, the Château de la Muette, the Baron de Rothschild had built, in 1931, a complex of big-windowed, modernist flats. Ten years later the Kriegsmarine requisitioned much of the *quartier*, including both the château and this squat, five-storey block, which they painted in camouflage green and flanked with two fortified bunkers facing the forest. At the Porte d'Auteuil, woolforce swung north up the Boulevard Suchet heading for their first target. It was ominously quiet. The house at 2 Boulevard Suchet was empty, but from the other side of the road, over the Jardin de Ranelagh, they heard gunfire coming from the golden Rothschild château. A burst of 30-mm cannonfire bounced off the sloping side of Bon Royle's scout car, tracer flaring, and as he and Bert Morgan dived over a wall, Spandau bullets chased them. 30AU took up positions and there was a vigorous exchange of fire. For two hours, in the laconic words of Marine Bill Powell, 'We had a bit of a ding-dong with the Hun.' 30AU's Staghound armoured cars raced down the boulevard firing their cannons, and Captain Geoff Pike, Sergeant Major Harry Lund and the marines of X Troop pressed forward the attack. At last the Germans raised the white flag – perhaps word had got through that General von Choltitz had surrendered five hours earlier. Colonel Woolley mustered all his men together in the boulevard to look like a big force, and met the senior German officer to arrange terms. 'Out came the Jerries,' remembered Bon Royle, 'throwing their arms on to a heap at the roadside while I collected their paybooks. They kept coming and coming in an endless stream until there were several hundred of them.' In fact, 560 officers and men were surrendering to fewer than four score; it was a triumph for 30AU, and the Rothschild château was theirs.*

---

* Today the Château de la Muette is the headquarters of the Organisation of Economic Cooperation and Development (OECD). Carved in a stone plaque inside the new George Marshall conference centre beside it are words from

30AU handed over the German weapons to people with FFI brassards or to the more responsible-looking of the French civilians who swarmed out when the gunfire ended. The FFI promised not to shoot or injure the Germans and marched them away. Whether that pledge was kept, once out of earshot, is not known. Many disarmed and captive Germans were attacked by mobs in Paris, some injured and others killed.

Royle enjoyed a lavish (if cold) bath in a millionaire's octagonal tub carved from jade in the château. Someone else found sides of pork and bags of onions and started a fry-up. Pike deserved a celebration, and according to his obituary he did it in style, being 'the first Allied officer after the liberation to drink in the bar of the Hotel Ritz in the Place Vendôme'.

The world-famous hotel had actually been 'liberated' earlier that afternoon by the armed civilian Ernest Hemingway. The author of *The Sun Also Rises* and *For Whom the Bell Tolls* arrived in a convoy of jeeps carrying French FFI partisans, American officers, and numerous bottles. They crossed the Pont de Sèvres, went through the sixteenth *arrondissement* – dodging the odd sniper – to the Arc de Triomphe, down the Champs Elysées to the Travellers Club for champagne, on to the Café de la Paix in the Boulevard des Capucines for more of it, and eventually pulled up at the back entrance of the Hôtel Ritz in Rue Cambon. When Hemingway declared he had come to liberate the place, the manager Claude Auzello said, 'Leave your gun by the door and come in.' Hemingway walked up to the bar and asked for yet more champagne. Nobody really knows which bar it was, but the Ritz has subsequently renamed the little one by the Cambon

---

a speech by President George W. Bush on 13 June 2008: 'And in this building were written the first chapters of European unity, a story of co-operation that eventually resulted in institutions like NATO and the European Union, and the organization that carries the spirit of the Marshall Plan into a new century, the OECD . . .'

entrance the Hemingway Bar.* The manager was soon assuring Hemingway and the others that the Ritz had done its bit for resistance by keeping the very best wine, the *premiers grands crus classés A,* safe from the Germans. 'We saved the Château Cheval Blanc!' he said happily. 'Well, go get it' said Hemingway, and the heavy, sweating writer slugged down the great Bordeaux like fruit juice.

Friday 25 August 1944 was a warm, lovely night in the gardens and streets of liberated Paris. Wine flowed like water, and grateful *parisienne* women were generous to the liberating troops, including some lucky 30AU Marines stationed near the green Bois de Boulogne.

N

There were other important Americans arriving by jeep and commandeering hotels in Paris. Four of them from the US Navy were attached to the intelligence-gathering 'ALSOS Missions' to Europe. *Alsos* was the Greek word for 'groves', as in olive or orange groves, and was the encryption of the name of General Leslie Groves who was running the Manhattan Project, then building the atomic bomb in the USA. The ALSOS Missions covered 'all principal scientific developments' by the Axis, especially the rate of German progress on their own atom bomb project. The sailors landed in a DC-3 and drove their jeep, full of rations and petrol, into Paris to the Ambassador Hotel and eventually settled in the Royal Monseau on avenue Hoch. There the team grew to seventy-five, and the hotel chef turned American C- and K-rations into *cordon bleu* cooking. By November 1944 ALSOS had managed to track down the nuclear scientists the Germans had assembled in Strasbourg. They would not talk, but Professor

---

* The Rue Cambon entrance to the Ritz is used by James Bond in the final chapter of *From Russia With Love* (1957). 007 downs a double vodka martini in the same bar before tackling 'toadlike' Rosa Klebb in Room 204.

Samuel Goudsmit of ALSOS went through the meticulous notes of Professor Carl von Weizsäcker and found out that the Germans had been unable to build a nuclear bomb, and were not likely to get one soon. They had not yet succeeded in producing a chain reaction and, as Captain Albert G. Mumma of ALSOS later explained,

We [the Americans] had three complete successful methods of making fissionable material going at that time. All they [the Germans] had was a graphite pile that was supposed to produce plutonium, and it hadn't been working very well. Then they had the heavy water project up in Norway, which, again, had been pretty well destroyed by the attack . . . So the Germans hadn't really made very much progress.

The Kriegsmarine HQ staff who fled westwards to Gerardmer left a treasury of clues behind them. Over the next month, Jim Glanville and the other RNVR officers in NID 30/30AU did their intelligence work, piecing together an outline of all the German naval establishments in the Paris area – over fifty addresses. In time they shipped many truckloads of documentary evidence and technical kit back to the UK. Their initial target list was often wrong: they had been told the supreme commander-in-chief of the German navy, Admiral Dönitz, stayed in the Château de la Muette, but actually it was used for submarine crew refresher courses; the most important German naval HQ was at 43 Avenue Maréchal Fayolle, further up off the boulevard Lannes, a large, floridly decorated, stand-alone villa belonging to an Argentine. Here were the coding areas, the teleprinters, and a concrete Kriegsmarine communications room with secure landlines to every major port and submarine base in France, Belgium and Holland as well as Berlin, Hamburg, Kiel, Cologne and Wilhelmshaven. They found plain language texts of cipher signals and all kinds of top secret documents that had been shredded, but not cross-shredded.

Bon Royle became bang-happy in the next four weeks in Paris, blowing over eighty safes with *plastique* and fuse, using detonators he scrounged from the hundreds of potato-masher grenades littering the grounds of the Rothschild estate. The majority of the safes he blew revealed little, but the job was fun. At night he went to the Boulevard de Grenelle, which had everything a tired soldier needed. His last effort was a large Fichet safe, for which he used a previously unknown German demolition charge and an unfamiliar fuse. The resulting explosion knocked him for six and nearly brought the whole house down around his ears.

Elsewhere Paris began to show its harder face. People demanded food and resented British soldiers not sharing their meagre rations. The FFI began taking hefty bribes from collaborators to 'forget' the past. The black market started to fill up with pilfered US army stores and the brothels had new customers, American rear-echelon troops, loud and lewd, sprawling drunk in streets where better-disciplined German soldiers had been forbidden even to smoke. Prices rose like the crime rate; petty politics started again. *Libération* freed no one from old sins and new grudges.*

The 30AU officers managed to trace German navy wireless transmitters, the training centres for German radio operators and the suppliers of radio and radar parts and sets. They went to the Hotchkiss factory at Levallois and found twenty-two truck-loads of 10.5 cm ammunition for naval anti-aircraft guns in a railway marshalling yard. Now their discoveries became technologically interesting: a novel sextant, an unusual eight-bladed propeller, pieces of a completely new sort of steel, and some very large tubes whose purpose they did not understand. They interrogated scientists and businessmen who worked in small boat-building,

---

* In *From a View to a Kill*, Ian Fleming writes that James Bond had cordially disliked Paris since the war: 'Since 1945 he had not had a happy day in Paris. It was not that the town had sold its body. Many towns have done that. It was its heart that was gone – pawned to the tourists, . . . pawned to the scum of the world who had gradually taken the town over. And, of course, pawned to the Germans.'

in precision optics and in the manufacture of liquid oxygen, a low-temperature, unstable propellant which the Germans called *A-Stoff* or *Sauerstoff* and had moved to their V-2 rocket sites in special bowsers. The first of the V-2s, devastating *Vergeltungswaffe* or 'revenge weapons', would be fired from The Hague and hit Staveley Road, Chiswick, west London, in the early evening of 8 September, while the 30AU men were still working in Paris.

The fragments of the mosaic that the 30AU officers were assembling revealed three things of major importance. First, the extensive German research and development of new technologies; second, the way in which they were dispersing their production facilities; and third, a significant change in strategy and tactics. The Kriegsmarine had turned away from big ships – there were to be no more *Tirpitze*s. Half of Germany's steel was going towards constructing improved U-boats (Types XXI and XXIII) that could run deeper and go faster than before, and because of the ingenious *Schnorkel* (Snorkel) air-breathing system which could be used while U-boats were still submerged that came on stream in May 1944, they would not have to surface to recharge their batteries and get fresh air. This work was going on in the industrial heartland of Germany, in the shipyards of Bremen, Danzig, Emden, Hamburg and Kiel. Once 30AU had fought their way into Germany, these would become vital targets too.

The new submarines needed better defences against aircraft, so German scientists were developing anti-radar coatings and radar detectors that could poke above the waves like a periscope. German technicians were creating more devastating sea mines and more intelligent torpedoes that could home in on the sounds of a ship, however rapidly its captain might change course to escape. 30AU followed a paper trail to the Torpedo Arsenal West at Houilles, a German assembly and servicing site covering 25,000 square metres of the former Hispano-Suiza aircraft factory, much of it underground in former mushroom-growing cellars. The retreating Germans had tried to blow it all up with mines, but there were still cranes, lathes, drills and stacks of spares, hundreds of seven-metre-long torpedoes, and a Siemens charger for the electric varieties. Digging through the wreckage, they unearthed steel filing cabinets full of new blueprints. They went on to St Cloud and Fort Cormeilles and found six types of firing pistol and seven different types of torpedo, including acoustic homing GNATs, pattern-running, area-searching and independent-bearing types as well as an experimental wire-guided model, all of which brought British boffins hurrying over the Channel from the Department of Torpedoes and Mines.

The technical news they were gathering was grim. Though Paris was liberated, the greater war was far from over. Admiral Dönitz was now favouring an intensification of the use of mines and a change of tactics in submarine warfare through the introduction of 'small battle units', *Kleinkampfverbände* or K-bände as they were officially designated on 20 April 1944. These units (commanded by Konteradmiral Helmuth Heye) were essentially a German copy of the Italian Decima Flottiglia MAS and the Japanese Ko-Hyoteki attack groups. They had begun deploying frogmen, human torpedoes, *Seehund* midget submarines, and indirectly guided explosive *Sprengboote* in sometimes semi-suicidal missions. Over fifty men came from the Waffen-SS; at least one torpedo was steered by an eighteen-year-old criminal released from the cells to undertake the lethal task.

Patrick Dalzel-Job was in Rouen on 31 August when he got an 'Immediate and Top Secret' message from the Admiralty. The Germans had a new kind of assault craft for use against Allied shipping in the Channel, based somewhere between Dieppe and Le Havre. These were believed to be midget submarines, and the enemy would probably be trying to take them overland to Germany. Dalzel-Job went to Dieppe and worked his way west towards German-occupied Le Havre via Étretat, which he was pleased to liberate on 2 September. He then sent out small parties of French-speakers to scout for sightings of special craft. It was a confusing trail to follow because V-1 flying bombs on low-loaders and other covered vehicles were also on the roads. On 6 September a reliable report came in that eight midget submarines had left Fécamp a week earlier, heading north-east towards Germany in a convoy of low-trailers with canvas screens, pulled by big lorries that had difficulties on some corners because the submarines were nine metres long.

Dalzel-Job and Alec van Cleef were following a trail from Abbeville towards Antwerp in Begium when they heard that something significant had been found behind them in France, shot-up by Allied aircraft and left by the side of the road between Albert and Bapaume. They raced back by jeep to find a one-man midget submarine called a *Biber* or 'Beaver' resting on a burned-out trailer. It weighed over six tons, had an Opel car's petrol engine, an aluminium alloy conning tower with six armoured glass windows, and carried two G7e torpedoes. Photos and specifications were flown back to the Admiralty in London and a fortnight later the *Biber* was at Gosport in Hampshire, being closely examined by Commander Bill Shelford of the submarine establishment HMS *Dolphin*. He reckoned it was just a German clone of the unreliable British Welman mini-sub *W-46*, which had been captured by the Germans at Bergen in Norway in November 1943.

Le Havre, Calais, Brussels, Ghent, Antwerp, Liège, Malmédy, Bastogne, Luxembourg. By 12 September 1944 American, British and Canadian soldiers had raced to the borders of Germany, and the Normandy armies linked up with Allied forces advancing from the south of France. On the Eastern Front, Soviet armed forces pushed forward hundreds of miles, killing and capturing over half a million *Wehrmacht* troops. The Third Reich was facing its final, apocalyptic battle, and 30AU would be part of it.

But one man would not be going with them to Germany. Captain Huntington-Whiteley, the leader of the first squad of Ian Fleming's intelligence assault unit at Dieppe, known affectionately as 'Peter' or 'Red', was dead. Tony Hugill said the news came like 'a blow in the face'. Tall, red-haired Herbert Oliver Huntington-Whiteley, grandson of Stanley Baldwin, had been through the hardships of North Africa and Italy and was the best of the troop commanders. Patrick Dalzel-Job remembered him sitting on the edge of a camp-bed, strumming a banjo and quietly singing Edward Lear nonsense to himself: '. . . *They danced by the light of the moon.*' The men recalled how he had walked upright among them as they crawled through the *bocage*, saying cheerfully, 'Keep your heads down, lads.'

'Red' was killed while taking a surrender in Le Havre on 12 September. A mob of diehards came round the corner spraying bullets at those parleying by the white flag, their own German *Kamaraden* as well as the tall, spare figure of Huntington-Whiteley. They buried the young officer alongside Marine Geoffrey Shaw in Sanvic Communal Cemetery; Dunstan Curtis was upset to learn from the cross on his grave that he was only twenty-four.

Two 30AU men, Jim Feeley and 'Doc' Livingstone, were captured in Le Havre shortly afterwards, but fared better, freed twenty-four hours later when their captors surrendered in their turn. Feeley and Livingstone made themselves some money, too. Many Germans had picked up leaflets dropped by the RAF urging them to surrender, and the two men profited cheerfully by adding what seemed like personal certifications on the leaflets, charging 200 francs a go. They blew it all in Paris on wine, women and song.

'I've been trying to find some Free French girls,' went the joke, 'but they all seem to belong to this here Resistance Movement.' One marine from what Ian Fleming once called 30 Indecent Assault Unit informed his officer, 'I've had three fucks – if you'll pardon the word, sir – since we got to Paris.' 'They must have been very low women.' 'Not at all, sir. One of them even had a *boudoir*.'

13

Operation Plunder

Hands up! Open your hands! Halt! Who goes there? Give me your papers. Sit down! Stand up! [First phrases in German]

DON'T be sentimental. If things are tough for the Germans they have only themselves to blame. They made things much worse for the innocent people of the countries they occupied.

Instructions for British Servicemen in Germany, 1944

There must be no fraternization! This is absolute!

US Army Pocket Guide to Germany, 1944

In late February 1945, 30AU were gathered at Genappe in Belgium, near the battlefield of Waterloo, to prepare for the push into Germany. Thinking at the NID was focused on the threat from the new and more powerful generation of German submarines and from the Kommando der Kleinkampfverbänder's torpedo-men and midget submarines, one of which Patrick Dalzel-Job had come across on a road in France. These would be among 30AU's principal targets as they finally penetrated the heartlands of the enemy.

They were also dealing with yet another reorganisation. While the founder of the unit, Commander Ian Fleming, was escaping the hard winter by travelling on NID business to Australia – seeing Alan Hillgarth (chief of British Naval Intelligence in the Eastern theatre) in Ceylon and his brother Peter (head of Strategic Deception) in India on the way – a new CO had succeeded Colonel Woolley. The man who led the drive on Paris had moved on after making a speech to the unit at Littlehampton that left at least one commando unimpressed. Woolley held up before the men the white cross of his DSO on its crimson and blue ribbon and rousingly declared 'You won this!' 'Yes,' thought the marine, 'but you're the bugger that'll be wearing it.'

Colonel Humphrey Quill RM, who had clashed with 30AU in Sicily, became their new CO in November 1944. Formerly SO(I) Levant, the man in charge of naval intelligence in the eastern Mediterranean, he was a stickler for discipline. Quill brought in his own men to create what he wanted – as he defined it later, 'a high grade intelligence unit with signals communications so that small groups of one or two officers could search for targets or follow up local rumour or confirm data sent to us by the Admiralty'. In other words, the same kind of small fluid groups as in France, but this time with the advantage of a more mobile HQ and greatly improved signals. In Germany they would have access to a higher level of radio communications than before, the same systems as SIS and the Special Liaison Units (SLUs). The marines, in Quill's vision, were definitely 'of secondary importance' to the intelligence gatherers, effectively just the muscle 'responsible for providing drivers, communications personnel, and a bodyguard for each intelligence group'. Colonel Bill de Courcy-Ireland, a regular Royal Marine from 45 Commando who had been an Intelligence staff officer with Quill, took over the Royal Marine wing of 30AU, Dunstan Curtis stayed in charge of the Naval Wing, while Lieutenant Commander James Fawcett DSC, RNVR,* took over NID 30 at the Admiralty – he too had worked with Quill in the Mediterranean.

30AU now had around twenty-five officers (half Royal Navy, half Royal Marine) and 250 to 300 men. Though ready to splinter into smaller parties, they generally worked in seven teams of thirty men with eight vehicles apiece. A typical team would have a naval officer in charge, plus a technical officer or an attached scientist, a German-speaking officer from the RN Forward Interrogation Unit and a Royal Marine officer or senior NCO leading a section of

---

* Fawcett later became an international lawyer; one of his grandsons is the current Mayor of London, Boris Johnson.

well-armed marines with vehicles and, vitally, a W/T detachment. Most of the teams worked in Montgomery's Twenty-first Army Group area, but one was with Bradley's US Twelfth Army Group. Another would slide southward into the area of Devers's US Sixth Army Group and, at Tambach Castle, score the unit's greatest coup of the war.

⚡

Like the rest of the army at the end of a cold wet winter, 30AU were booted and gaitered, hung with packs and pouches, with the ubiquitous leather jerkin over muddy battledress. There were more berets than shrapnel helmets. Their first forays into the Rhineland, as German Army Group B retreated eastwards ahead of them, served as useful field training exercises for the teams and a testing-ground for kit, signals and procedures. Jim Besant went to Neuss and Krefeld; Patrick Dalzel-Job went to Duren, Hellenthal and into Cologne on 7 March; another team went to München-Gladbach, and Sancho Glanville to Saarbrücken. New members learned how to look out for snipers and road mines, and all of them began to get the hang of their improvised existence in the extraordinary chaos of the collapsing Third Reich. But there were problems too with the bureaucracies of their own side, some of whom saw 30AU as irresponsible cowboys.

Two years down the line, Fleming and Godfrey's ideas of intelligence-gathering commandos and 'target exploitation' had become widely accepted. The downside of this was that the machinery for dealing with the information afterwards had become cumbersome and disputatious – stakeholders like Combined Intelligence Objectives Subcommittee (CIOS) and Supreme Headquarters Allied Expeditionary Force (SHAEF) were wary of being bypassed and eager to see things first. There was also more competition to acquire stuff in the first place. Going into Germany 30AU was in a race with other predators and scavengers. The dung beetles of Enemy Equipment Intelligence

Branch (EEIB) and Technical Data Section (TDS) were beneath them, but TICOM and ALSOS were probably higher up the food-chain. TICOM was the Target Intelligence Committee, founded in October 1944, whose job was to discover everything about Axis signal intelligence, cryptography and cryptanalysis. By March 1945 TICOM had its own six target-exploitation teams ready to cross the Rhine – and later 30AU sometimes provided Royal Marines to protect them. ALSOS, as we saw in Paris, was the team of civilian scientists and counter-intelligence officers led by the vigorous Colonel Boris Pash sent to find everything that Italian and German scientists knew about nuclear fission and what progress they had made on building an atom bomb. (As already stated, they found the US had overestimated the competition – but they did eventually manage to capture seventy thousand tons of uranium and radium material.)

Then there were the T-Forces, cobbled together in the winter of 1944/5. As a longer-established Admiralty NID outfit, 30AU tended to see these army 'Target-force' units as no more than 'pongos' (army personnel) doing the job of security guards or mobile nightwatchmen. There was another reason to look down on their rivals. Although some in 30AU were no angels in this regard, Patrick Dalzel-Job alleged that T-Force 'guard-troops were often more interested in private looting than in securing enemy intelligence'.*

30AU for their part often rubbed higher authority up the wrong way. There was friction over, for example, captured documents. The Joint Chiefs of Staff ruled that all naval documents captured in the European theatre of operations should become the property of the British DNI, who would keep the US Navy Department informed through the Commander of US Naval Forces in Europe (COMNAVEU), Admiral Harold Stark. The documents were sent

---

* In his 2009 book *T-Force: the race for Nazi war secrets*, Sean Longden calls this suggestion 'unfair', and says the cap-badge rivalry was 'unjustifiable'.

to a central point, NID 24 at Bletchley Park, where officers from the various services of both Allies could examine them. But the glut of documents from Paris caused SHAEF to set up its own clearing house without consulting either the Admiralty or BP, leading to tedious rows.

Then, in February 1945, another layer of bureaucracy appeared when SHAEF G-2 created the Special Sections Subdivision to co-ordinate all Target or T-force operations (including those of 30AU) with the other specialist missions like TICOM, ALSOS, CIOS, the Consolidated Advanced Field Teams (CAFT), the Naval Targets Section Sub-Division (NTS), the United States Naval Technical Mission to Europe (US. Nav. Tec. Mis. Eu.), the US Strategic Bombing Survey, the British Bombing Research Mission, and so on and so forth. Brigadier Raymond Maunsell, formerly the head of MI5's Cairo branch, Security Intelligence Middle East, was put in charge of the new Special Sections Subdivision. On 12 March 1945, as 30AU was first venturing into the Rhineland, Major General Kenneth D. Strong, General Eisenhower's chief intelligence officer, sent Maunsell a memo which began, ominously:

I notice a number of cables have been received regarding the activities of the 30th Assault Unit.

As you know, this Unit and its activities have caused a certain amount of misgiving in the minds of the members of the CIOS (Combined Intelligence Objectives Sub-Committee). I hope that under the new organization the fruits of the work and activities of the 30th Assault Unit are being made available to CIOS and that there is no question of this organisation being by-passed.

Maunsell's American deputy, Lieutenant Colonel Francis Miller, thought 30AU, like any other CIOS team, should not be permitted near the front lines of the US Twelfth Army Group, but his reply to Kenneth Strong hid behind Captain Lewes at Naval HQ:

Captain LEWES has informed Brigadier MAUNSELL that he does

not approve of the use of 30th Advanced Unit personnel in combat operations. It is the policy of 'T' Sub-Division and of 'T' Force 12th Army Group that whereas 30 Advanced Unit *investigators* are welcome (as are all others) 30 Advanced Unit combat personnel will not be allowed to operate as a combat element of 'T' Forces.

On 16 March, back from a CIOS meeting, Maunsell wrote to Strong:

I have the assurance of [Captain Lewes] that the results of the work of 30 Advanced Unit are being made available to CIOS and there is no question of CIOS being bypassed.*

The 'Black List' or 'Black Books', compiled by Lieutenant Commander Fawcett and two WRNS from air photographs, ISTD information, PoW interrogations, SIGINT data and SIS reports, itemised the factories, firms and shipyards for 30AU's attention. (As war now occupied 70 per cent of the German economy, there were many targets.) This compilation was then broken down into geographical handbooks that mapped priorities by region to help the field-teams plot their advance through enemy territory. But even with all this detailed work, the addresses were sometimes out of date or the premises no longer standing.

Nazi Germany in 1945 was not in any sense a normal country. One third of the 600,000 German civilians killed by Second World War Allied bombing died in that final year of the war. Seven million people were made homeless by the raids of British bomber command and its leader, Air Chief Marshal Harris – 'Arthur Harris & Co, House Removers' as they were dubbed by British soldiers. A massive police state was crumbling from below

---

* A Canadian scientist in CIOS called Dr C. H. Noton seems to have been the source of the complaint about 30AU. If Ian Fleming heard about it, it is possible that the name Dr Noton may have later resurfaced in his imagination for the villainous 'Dr. No' in the novel of the same name. Certainly, when the makers of the first Bond film offered the title role of *Dr. No* to Noël Coward he replied with the memorable telegram: NO NO NO NO NO.

at the same time as it was systematically pounded by bombing from above.

'Be on your guard against "propaganda" in the form of hard-luck stories,' British soldiers were warned. The desperate people you met might be wearing stolen clothes or they might not even be German. There were over seven million foreign workers in Deutschland and few were volunteers: 2.8 million from the Soviet Union (with O for *Ostarbeiter* on their clothes), 1.7 million from Poland (marked P), 1.3 million from France, 600,000 from Italy. Absconders from forced labour joined deserters, evacuees, escapers, refugees, the homeless and the demented in a wandering army of millions of displaced persons or DPs, some of them organised into impromptu armed criminal gangs. On the one side there was still the stolid Germany trying to keep *Alles in Ordnung,* on the other a shifting Germany of the lawless and the helpless, pallid skulkers who came out at night, bundle-hugging scarecrows seen hacking pieces off dead horses strewn along the roads so they could roast them on fires in the woods. The motorised Allies were surprised how many horses were still used by the fuel-starved *Wehrmacht.**

When Patrick Dalzel-Job's jeep (with a captured, belt-fed, German heavy machine-gun mounted on its bonnet) drove in to Cologne on 7 March, his team found Germany's fourth-largest city nearly all wrecked and mostly evacuated. The Americans had fought the Germans who stayed behind, among them Himmler's *Volkssturm,* old men and young boys some of whom had only arm-bands for uniform (Russian officers called this mixture 'the stew': tough meat and green vegetables.) Some of those who resisted were blown to bits together with entire neighbourhoods because Americans

---

*   Various Bond villains – Le Chiffre, Drax, Goldfinger, Blofeld, etc. – emerged from the creative chaos of the war and particularly its end phase, when names, faces, places were being erased and remade, sides changed.

backed up their infantry with shelling, so a German teenager with an arm-band and an old Gewehr 98 rifle could indirectly bring down streets and houses round his head as American shells went astray and tanks butted through walls.

The rest of the German *Wehrmacht* had retreated to the east bank of the Rhine and destroyed the Hohenzollern bridge behind them. A few days earlier, 80,000 citizens had fled the last of the 262 air raids Cologne endured in the war. Water, sewage, gas, electricity, streets and houses were all smashed up; 40,000 people survived where half a million once lived; each citizen was the lord of 31.1 cubic metres of broken brick and shattered laths. Solly Zuckerman, the scientist who was the first to apply mathematical statistics to Allied bombing with his plan for the reduction of Pantelleria, visited the ruins of Cologne and offered to write a report for *Horizon*, the magazine edited by Ian Fleming's friend Cyril Connolly. It was to be titled 'On the Natural History of Destruction'. But Zuckerman was unable to finish the piece, and years later, all he could recall was the blackened cathedral sticking out of a jagged stony desert, and the memory of a severed finger he found on a heap of rubble.

Dalzel-Job was 'astonished' to find the civilian inhabitants of Cologne were friendly, and that they would, in conversation, give reliable information. Occupation at least meant an end to bombing and sensible Germans were obviously eager to ingratiate themselves with the new order, especially if it wasn't Russian. Suddenly it was hard to find anyone who had ever been a Nazi. Charles Wheeler, who rejoined Dalzel-Job in Germany, thought the fact that none of Dalzel-Job's teams ever lost a man killed or injured was attributable to his human gift for chatting up or 'button-holing' the locals in order to find out where the enemy was. His men penetrated their main target, the Schmidding-Werke in the northern zone of Cologne, without difficulty, apprehended the works manager and the chief engineer and found a new kind of mine as well as an amazing suitcase of research papers about rockets, guided missiles, jet-propelled aircraft and launching gear which the American naval officer Lieutenant Lambie took straight back to the SHAEF document centre at Versailles. Complete microfilms went to the Admiralty, and in ten days NID 24 had produced a 300-page translation of all the documents.

Dalzel-Job found a mobile team could move around in Germany much as they had in France, as long as they were constantly alert to danger. Things here were rarely what they seemed. A complete wreck did not always indicate total destruction: some factories had been carefully rebuilt underneath the camouflage of their own ruins.

※

All but one of the bridges over the Rhine, the great river that separated ancient Latins from the old Teuton tribes, had now been destroyed by the Germans. As the Allied armies pushed at the gates of Germany, an increasingly deranged Adolf Hitler in his Berlin bunker sent out a flying drumhead court martial to judge and execute four *Wehrmacht* officers he held responsible for failing to blow up the Ludendorff bridge at Remagen, thus allowing the US First Army to establish a bridgehead on the east bank of the Rhine. The enemy's human torpedoes and commando frogmen had also failed to destroy the bridge; before they had even set off, Sefton Delmer's London-based black propaganda radio station was slyly congratulating them in German on their 'heroic sacrifice', implying the mission was suicidal. In another desperate move Hitler replaced Gerd von Rundstedt as commander-in-chief of the German armed forces with Field Marshal Albrecht Kesselring, who had been leading the fighting retreat in Italy.

Operation PLUNDER, the crossing of the Rhine into the Ruhr industrial heartland on 23/24 March 1945, became a major media event for the 1.25 million men of Montgomery's Twenty-first Army Group. In the event the Allies built their own bridges across the Rhine. Thousands of Allied bombers and fighters kept the enemy at bay, bombing and strafing while the soldiers on the ground accumulated huge dumps of fuel, ammunition and vehicles at railheads. Artillery barrages from 5,000 guns accompanied the largest and longest smokescreen of the Second World War, a toxic, oil-based cloud under which landing craft full of infantry, together with hundreds of amphibious tracked vehicles known as 'Buffaloes', spearheaded ten crossings along a twenty-mile front. They were supported by two divisions of airborne troops – 20,000 men landing in 1,300 gliders or parachuting down from 650 Dakotas in the face of enemy flak. Close behind the 80,000 men of the first wave came thousands of military engineers with tons of bridge-building equipment, ready to construct seven floating pontoons across the Rhine, strong enough to take 40-ton tanks and a million more men in lorries and armoured vehicles.

Winston Churchill himself came to see the crossing and the airborne landings. Just as he had on the Siegfried line three weeks earlier, the prime minister enjoyed urinating into the German river. Some enemy shells fell near him, and General Alan Brooke honestly believed that the ageing warlord 'would really have liked to be killed on the front at this moment of success'. When his secretary, John Colville, came back from the other side spattered with arterial blood from someone else's wound, Churchill was thrilled, though he pretended to disapprove. 'Forward all on wings of flame to final victory', the Prime Minister wrote in Montgomery's autograph book on 26 March.

30AU men were among the first Britons to cross the Rhine on 23 March, the night before Montgomery's spectacular. Sancho Glanville's team of four officers and eight Royal Marines made the crossing further south, at Frankenthal, without fanfare, joined up with T-Force of US Sixth Army Group and immediately found themselves restricted. They were told they could not visit the plant of IG Farben at nearby Ludwigshafen until the CIOS team had finished. However, they did get into one 'Black List' target, turbine manufacturer KKK AG (Kühnle, Kopp & Kausch Aktiengesellschaft), because it was understood to be the place where the turbines for the new experimental T7 and T8 torpedoes were assembled and tested and so of prime naval interest.

What was special about these torpedoes was that they were powered by a revolutionary new fuel, hydrogen peroxide, code-named 'Ingolin'. (When used for aircraft and missiles, hydrogen peroxide's cover name was 'T-stoff', which derived from their old code name for it, 'Thymiol'. For ships the code name was 'Aurol', foreshadowing the name of the Bond villain, Auric Goldfinger.) 30AU teams had been hunting down this fuel in France and discovered two stainless steel railway tanks south of Dijon containing slightly deteriorated samples of hydrogen peroxide with a concentration of 83 per cent. They found the KKK offices and laboratories in utter chaos; combat troops had already gone through, looting carelessly, tearing all papers, drawings and files out of their cabinets and chucking them on the floor. It took three days to sort them all out, but a great deal of useful information was assembled before the inevitable row with T-Force and CAFT about whether it should be sent to SHAEF in Paris or the Admiralty in London. It was eventually decided that all documents taken from KKK which were of strictly naval interest, in the narrowest possible construction of the term, should be sent to the Admiralty, and all the rest – papers relating to raw materials, machining methods, production, etc. – should be returned to the plant in case the CIOS inspectors should wish to inspect them *in situ*. Glanville protested that the building was unguarded, but had to comply with the order. Such demarcation disputes made the inevitable mess and muddle of war even worse: the very next day, a US Army unit billeted in the building burned all the papers.

Luckily, Lieutenant Commander Mitchell RNVR of the SHAEF Japanese documents section, was allowed, bearing a CIOS pass, into IG Farben in Cologne. Even though he was really meant to be searching for evidence of German–Japanese cooperation, he helped 30AU get the information they needed by investigating what IG Farben had been manufacturing: German anti-radar devices and anti-ASDIC coatings, lightweight oxygen-producing equipment and special liquid fuels, all of great interest to the NID.

30AU had started well, but industrial production for the Kriegsmarine was dispersed nationwide, which made their task harder. Glanville's 30AU team reached Mannheim late on 29 March. Here their target was the successful German subsidiary of the Swiss electrical engineering firm Brown, Boveri & Cie, which made steam turbines and Büchi turbochargers for the German navy, switchboards for U-boats and the main electric motors for Type XXI and XXIII submarines. There was superficial damage from the fighting but the plant and machinery was mostly intact.

The big question that 30AU's forays into German factories and military establishments addressed was how the Third Reich had achieved its technological and industrial successes, and whether the Allies could profit from those advances before the evidence was destroyed. 30AU's discoveries were filling in the picture piece by piece. It was a mission after the heart of Ian Fleming, who had built up in pre-war London his unique library of books and papers about ground-breaking scientific and technical breakthroughs and inventions.

Patrick Dalzel-Job's team crossed the Rhine on a pontoon bridge built by Allied engineers near Xanten. Stewart Macpherson of the BBC described the scene:

Stretched across the bridge, and as far as the eye could see, were hundreds of tanks, lorries, carriers, bulldozers, ammo wagons, vehicles of every conceivable type, flooding across the river. Overhead, squadrons of Spitfires, Typhoons, Tempests, and Mustangs took their turn in patrolling – giving constant protection . . . just in case the Luftwaffe should dare interfere.

Then, together with XXX Corps of Dempsey's 2nd British Army, the 30AU men made their way north-east across the rolling farmland of the Hanoverian plain towards Bremen and the clutch of Kriegsmarine targets around the German Bight of the North Sea.

'Germany was full of surprises,' wrote Bon Royle. 'Because of the Allied air raids, German industry was scattered into small units over the whole country.' They made many diversions as they found wooden workshops, hidden beneath camouflage nets spread from the branches of the trees, making equipment for any of the armed forces, 'even for U-boats'. The team tried to miss nothing and Royle recorded several 'encounters with Jerry' as they searched. Sometimes farmers' barns held naval equipment evacuated from dockyards, 'boxes of torpedo gyros stowed alongside sacks of barley, shackles in the hen roost and lifebelts in the piggery'. On 13 April in Vechta the 30AU men found something different, a small prison containing what Dalzel-Job called some 'ordinary criminals, homosexuals and people under long sentences for listening to foreign radio broadcasts', whom they set free.

Other British troops only seventy-five miles to the east were finding far worse prisons. North of Hanover, some *Wehrmacht* officers came out under a white flag to warn the advancing British army that there was a typhus epidemic in what they identified as an SS-run camp in the sandy pine woods off the road to Lüneberg. On Sunday 15 April the first observers went in. They found 60,000 people, most of them Jewish, dying of hunger and thirst, disease and neglect in the concentration camp of Bergen-Belsen. The inmates were so far gone that 14,000 of them died *after* liberation, 2,000 from pathological overeating of Allied rations in their state of acute starvation.

The British army was unprepared, physically and psychologically. The place was so disgusting and the people inside so degraded that their would-be liberators often actually recoiled in a mixture of fear, anger and repulsion. Compassion for them took time to come because the Nazis had managed to reduce many of their victims to *Untermenschen,* wretched beings who seemed less than human. The chief medical officer of VIII Corps called Belsen 'the most horrible, frightful place I have ever seen', and described people dying en masse, dumped in death pits or just left outdoors. 'In the women's compound, in full view of the children's compound 50 yards away, we saw an enormous pile of naked dead women. It stretched about 60 yards by 30 yards.' Members of the British Army Film and Photographic Unit recorded these scenes in thirty-three rolls of film and more than 200 still photographs which horrified people in Britain.

April 1945 was the month of discovering murder and plunder. Further south in Germany, Patton's 3rd Army found Buchenwald, Ohrdruf and Kaiseroda in the same week. Ohrdruf was the first concentration camp encountered by American soldiers, on Wednesday 4 April 1945. It was mostly full of corpses and half-burned bodies; the SS had marched the survivors off to the larger Buchenwald ('beech forest') concentration camp, five miles from Weimar in Thuringia. The US Generals Eisenhower, Bradley and Patton all visited Ohrdruf on 12 April. German civilians as well as American soldiers were subsequently ordered to visit the camp where hundreds of dead bodies were left out on display: 'They may not know what we are fighting for, but they will learn what we are fighting against.' 80th Division American soldiers who had seen the camp showed little mercy shortly afterwards to the city of Erfurt.

The exhausted survivors from Ohrdruf found at the end of their forced march to Buchenwald a place where at least 17,000 people had died since the beginning of the year. 100,000 prisoners from all over Europe and Russia had been forced to work in munitions factories, with those who could no longer work killed out of hand. In a radio broadcast on 15 April, Edward R. Murrow, the European Director of CBS, described how when he entered Buchenwald 'an evil-smelling horde' surged around him. 'Men and boys reached out to touch me; they were in rags and the remnants of uniforms. Death had already marked many of them, but they were smiling with their eyes. I looked out over that mass of men to the green fields beyond where the well-fed Germans were ploughing . . .'

Other Germans had grown rich from the concentration camps. In the Kaiseroda salt mine in a village called Merkers, thirteen miles south-west of Eisenach in Thuringia, General Patton's soldiers came upon a Reichsbank official called Fritz Vieck trying to remove stacks of paper currencies from a steel vault 2,000 feet underground: nearly 3 billion Reichsmarks, 100 million French francs, 4 million Norwegian kroner, US$2 million, £110,000 sterling, as well as bundles of lira, pesetas and escudos. Also in the salt-mine vault were 100 tons of gold bullion, first reported in the newspapers as a cache of 4,000 to 5,000 gold bricks in twenty- or fifty-pound sizes, wrapped in grey bags and stacked in thirty rows. An official inventory indicated that there were '8,198 bars of gold bullion; 55 boxes of crated gold bullion; hundreds of bags of gold items; over 1,300 bags of gold Reichsmarks, British gold pounds, and French gold francs; 711 bags of American twenty-dollar gold pieces; hundreds of bags of gold and silver coins . . . ' Using the pre-1939 price of gold, US$35 per troy ounce, this treasure hoard was at the time valued at US$238.5 million (US$8.8 billion at today's prices.) Between 1940 and 1945, the Nazis deposited even larger sums of gold in Switzerland, amounting to US$378 million (or US$14 billion today), with the Swiss National Bank.

This is part of the reason why there was no shortage of money for the Third Reich to invest in scientific and technological advances. The gold was looted from the central banks of Austria, Belgium, Czechoslovakia, Danzig, Luxembourg, the Netherlands and Italy, or taken by force from institutions and individuals across Europe and North Africa. In the SS death factories it was broken with dental pliers from the jaws of dead Jews. It was shipped in rattling boxes of fillings, bridges and crowns to the Degussa refinery in Frankfurt to be smelted down with other stolen gold – jewellery, necklaces, spectacles, wedding rings – and then cast into solid, silent ingots.

N

On 12 April Sancho Glanville's 30AU Team 55 got new orders from SHAEF at Versailles for a mission in southern Germany. Originally they had been bound for Stuttgart, but Commander Hunzinger of SHAEF intelligence said that a 'naval intelligence target' had been discovered in Bad Sulza (liberated by General Patton's 3rd Army on the 11th) and asked 30AU to investigate. SHAEF was particularly keen to find out where 3/Seekriegsleitung (3/SKL or Abteilung Nachrichtenauswertung, the German NID) might have gone. Was there really, as rumour suggested, a secret 'National Redoubt' in southern Germany where the Nazis would make a last stand among the Alps? Hunzinger asked 30AU to take along an American officer, Lieutenant H. P. Earle USNR, of the Enemy Documents section at SHAEF, so he joined the Team 55 group of Glanville, Lieutenant Commander Bill Haynes, Lieutenant Jim Besant and Corporal Morgan, together with Marines Booth, Broad, Graham, Perry and Turner. The group had a jeep, a Chevrolet armoured car and a fifteen-hundredweight truck.

The 30AU men reached Bad Sulza on 17 April. It was a spa town whose sodium-rich waters were thought to be health-giving; hard by were the salt mines where the prisoners of war from Stalag IXC did forced labour. Their target was a former technical high school, which they found in a filthy and disordered state and investigated thoroughly. In a boarded-up cellar a number of interesting documents were hidden, including a charred letter with a list of the destinations to which the departments of the Seekriegsleitung or Naval War Staff had been evacuated. The people who had occupied the premises were signallers from 3/SKL, the Foreign War Navies section, and there were indications that 6/SKL, the meteorologists, had gone to Kaufbeuren.

Another subsection of the Seekriegsleitung was called 2 SKL/ KA: the meaning of that 'KA' suffix was not yet clear to 30AU, but they determined to track them down in their listed destination, somewhere called Tambach.

Some newly liberated French PoWs told Glanville's team that the German Naval Intelligence people had been in the high school but had since slipped on civilian clothes and vanished. However, they pointed out one man in a blue serge suit and a Bavarian hat with a feather in it: he was one of the German senior officers. They apprehended him, and he turned out to be an admiral in mufti.

At the time anti-German feeling among 30AU was running high. Not long after the shocks of Ohrdruf and Buchenwald, American troops had discovered the horrific Mittelwerk factory in the tunnels of an old gypsum mine in the Harz mountains where thousands of slave labourers from Nordhausen and Dora/ Mittelbau concentration camps had been worked in their striped pyjamas until they died of exhaustion, building deadly V-2 rockets on an endless conveyor system, components in at one end, complete missiles on railway wagons out at the other. It is unsurprising then that when one of the 30AU men, MOA Booth, got hold of the besuited and befeathered admiral, he turned to Sancho Glanville and said casually 'Shall I shoot him *now*, sir, or do you want to do it yourself?'

Lieutenant Earle took the material back to SHAEF; the others set out to find the apparent destination of the 2SKL/KA section of German Naval Intelligence, Tambach. They thought it was probably the village of that name down south near Ingolstadt in Bavaria, which had a naval base with a staging- and servicing-point for mines and torpedoes. 30AU's route to the autobahn took them past Buchenwald concentration camp. 'We were shocked,' wrote Jim Glanville, 'not only at the skeletons and heaps of corpses and the lampshades made of tattooed human skin, but at the polished brightwork and black-leaded furnaces in the crematorium, and at the carefully tended gallows and songbirds in their cages beside them.' The combination of cruelty and domesticity was particularly repellent.

✄

On 21 April, the day after Hitler's birthday, Feldmarschall Walter Model went for a short walk. As the ruthless commander of *Wehrmacht* Army Group B, which had fought its way back from France through Holland, he had seen his twenty divisions finally encircled and destroyed by the US First and Ninth Armies in the Ruhr pocket, with 325,000 of his troops captured, including twenty generals and an admiral. Whole German towns and villages had been destroyed, with thousands killed and injured, but Model – 'the Führer's fireman' – refused to surrender. Better to die for the Fatherland. He shot himself in a wood near Duisburg.

✄

On 22 April Dunstan Curtis's 30AU Team 10 helped capture the first purely naval intelligence target, Buxtehude, south-west of Hamburg. It was a bloodless victory, thanks to a few Germans who chose not to fight. Although many German naval officers were convinced Nazis, others were still *kaiserlich* ('imperial', or loyal to an older idea of the German empire) and many of their men were just reservists, essentially uniformed civilians. One of these, Oberleutnant zur See Karl Halaski, a parson and member of the Protestant 'Confessing Church' which had opposed Nazism since 1934, was in a small group who determined to surrender the town of Buxtehude peacefully. Halaski was adjutant to Konteradmiral Siegfried Engel, a man intelligent enough to realise the war was now unwinnable, but still determined to do his duty. As Engel studied maps showing the British advance, Halaski told him they would be hanged if they surrendered, but that would be a better fate than needlessly sacrificing other lives. Admiral Engel, who had been a guest of the Royal Navy before the war and understood the British mindset, did not try to dissuade Halaski, and another officer in charge of defending Buxtehude, Hauptmann Hans Haverkamp, a former secondary-school English teacher, quietly helped him set about disarming demolition charges on the bridges while pointing the Nazi fanatics in the wrong direction. There was some gallows humour. As the thunder of British artillery approached on 20 April, one sailor said 'Did you hear the salute for Hitler's birthday?' and everybody laughed. Hitler had ordered that every man fight 'to the last cartridge'; someone asked how they were expected to do that. Halaski said, 'Empty the gun and throw the cartridges away.'

21 April 1945 was a lovely spring day. The Germans did not retaliate to British firing, but one gung-ho Nazi, Leutnant Kaleu, was eager to bring up his anti-tank guns and start blasting away. Haverkamp promptly diverted his enthusiasm by sending him off to inspect all sectors in a motorcycle sidecar. Kaleu came back with a dent in his helmet from a machine-gun bullet, still roaring for action. Halaski (who knew his man) said 'Herr Kaleu, if we had some schnapps we could drink a toast to your heroic escape from a fatal bullet.' Kaleu sped off in the bike to fetch his stash of alcohol. They got him so drunk he fell asleep and could be quietly stowed in the barracks.

Early on Sunday morning, Admiral Engel went out to meet the British troops in the road. Halaski held the white flag and Haverkamp the English teacher did the talking. They had agreed beforehand that they would salute the old naval way rather than using the Nazi-style *Hitler-Gruß*. They offered the surrender, and asked for, and received, assurance of the safety of the city's population and protection of the female navy assistants. A time was agreed for British troops to come to the barracks where troops were waiting quietly, ready to lay down their weapons.

Curtis and a small contingent of 30AU's 'X' Troop were there. They escorted Engel home and Halaski went around various surrendered positions with a young British 30AU officer who spoke German. Halaski thought he could detect a Hamburg accent, and it turned out the young British officer had studied at the Gelehrtenschule des Johanneums, the city's oldest school. Though Halaski never names him, only one candidate from 30AU fits the bill: Charles Wheeler, who was born in Bremen on 26 March 1923, and grew up in Hamburg.

⚡

The long journey of Glanville's 30AU Team 55 via Stuttgart to the village called Tambach near Ingolstadt proved futile. Glanville decided that Schloss Tambach (Tambach Castle) near Coburg in Thuringia must be the target, so they drove back north almost to the place where they first started, using secondary roads to skirt places like Nuremberg which had been devastated by bombing, and steering clear of fighting. It was good to be mobile and well armed with plenty of ammunition in this land full of the tag-ends of fighting forces, stragglers and deserters, people who avoided the swift and powerful and preyed on the slow and weak. With many detours and improvisations they made their way north of Bamberg to the southern fringe of the Thuringian forest.

On the south side of the road to Weitramsdorf they came upon Schloss Tambach just before nightfall, so they could still make out a large seventeenth-century castle of pink stone with a dark slate roof. It was built in the form of a square letter U with two wings jutting south. Glanville and Booth walked around in the dusk, peering through the ground-floor windows. They could see bookshelves filled with files marked with the emerald green cross on a purple background, indicating a high security grading: *Geheime Kommandosache! Chefsache!* – the equivalent of the scarlet jackets of *Top Secret Ultra* files in England. They tried various doors until one opened. A surprised German naval rating raised his hands at the sight of Booth's tommy-gun and Glanville's drawn pistol. When asked who was in command the sailor replied 'Konteradmiral Walter Gladisch'.

Gladisch soon made an appearance with his colleagues,

Konteradmirals Kurt Aßmann and Arno Spindler. Now at last Glanville's unit learned the significance of the 'KA' suffix. The admirals explained that they were from the Kriegsgeschichtliche Abteilung (War Historical Department), who prepared historical records and papers on naval policy for the Oberkommando der Marine (Supreme Naval High Command), as well as classifying, storing and evaluating the German navy's archives. After November 1944 the naval records had been moved out of Berlin to save them from Allied bombing. The Germans had lost contact with their boss Admiral Karl-Georg Schuster, who had gone missing, believed captured or killed, on 8 April. Gladisch told the 30AU men that Admiral Dönitz was keen for the records to be preserved because they proved that the German navy had acted throughout the war in accord with humanitarian principles and the finest traditions of the sea.

When Glanville enquired exactly what was in the library, he was given a stunning piece of news about what 30AU had discovered. They told him the library contained the complete operational logs, war diaries, technical reports and administrative minutes of all German navy business from 1870 to date, a period in which there had been two world wars and three German navies, the Kaiserliche Marine (1870–1918), the Reichsmarine (1918–35) and the Kriegsmarine (1935–45).

Could this possibly be true? As a quick test question, Glanville asked for the detailed story of the fight between HMAS *Sydney* and the disguised auxiliary cruiser HK *Kormoran* off Western Australia on 19 November 1941 – and got it. A German admiral went away and came back with a fat file. Both ships had been sunk, but the Australian cruiser went down with all 645 hands – the biggest loss of life in the Australian navy – while most of the German crew had survived and were now PoWs in the Australian outback. According to the docket, in challenging the German raider, *Sydney* had come far too close to the *Kormoran* and so Kapitän Detmers was able to open devastating fire at under 1,000 metres, which in naval terms was point-blank range. It was not a pretty story, but the facts were there in the file.

Astonished, Glanville began to understand something of the value of his capture. But how on earth were they to protect it all? A Hungarian countess occupied one wing of the castle but the rest of the large building was vulnerable to attack. Armed bands of deserters and dispossessed were roaming the land; more pressing still was the danger of a deliberate attempt to destroy the evidence. The 30AU men had seen with their own eyes how desperate the SS was to destroy evidence and how fanatical and ignorant the Hitler Youth, grandiose ambitions now fatally thwarted, could be. Goebbels was spreading rumours of a clandestine resistance movement called *die Werwölfe* or the Werewolves, commandos leading a Nazi guerrilla insurgency.*

Glanville had no choice: he would need reinforcements if they were to hold on to the treasure they had won. Leaving Lieutenant Jim Besant the sole officer in charge, precariously supported by a few marines, he went off with his driver Marine Turner to find the American TAC HQ near Schweinfurt and get help from Patton's Third Army.

---

* Ian Fleming thought Werewolves was 'rather a spooky name'. He made Krebs, one of the villains in *Moonraker* (1955), a former leader of Hitlerjugend Werwölfe, with 'certain gifts which qualified him for the post of executioner and "persuader" to our merry little band.' These baddies also caught the imagination of other popular thriller-writers. In *Gimlet Mops Up* (1947) by Captain W. E. Johns, the 'King of the Commandos' is kidnapped and nearly killed by the Werewolves.

14

Getting the Goods

On Thursday 26 April 1945 at 4.40 p.m. an encounter took place near Torgau, about seventy miles south of Berlin, that both Moscow and Washington claimed was historic. Russian and American soldiers shook hands on the banks of the Elbe River, though they were soon to be opponents in the Cold War. Nazi Germany was now cut in two, its north severed from its south by the two Allied armies who had both advanced thousands of miles, one from the east, one from the west. Adolf Hitler, by now a half-insane troglodyte living on cake thirty-three feet below the Reich Chancellery, had foreseen this would happen, and put Großadmiral Dönitz in charge of the Northern Command Zone of Germany and Generalfeldmarschall Albert Kesselring in charge of Southern. In the fantasy bubble of Hitler's fetid bunker Dr Goebbels was still imagining a 'strategic pincer' movement by Dönitz and Kesselring bringing a 'second Waterloo' upon the Allies. In fact the severing of Germany into two parts clarified logistics for the Anglo-American armies. Montgomery in the north would seal off Denmark and Norway, clear the German coastline west of Lübeck and secure ports for supplies, while in the south, the Americans would advance into Bavaria and Austria and meet up with the Russians once more on the Danube.

Earlier the same day Bremen was captured in a two-pronged assault, a frontal attack west of the River Weser and a right hook from the east. Patrick Dalzel-Job's Team 4 entered the outskirts from the south-east, after the four infantry divisions of XXX Corps had already encircled the city. From Charles Wheeler and his other interpreter/interrogator Miles Cooke, Dalzel-Job had gathered information from civilians and prisoners about what lay ahead, and he had managed to slip the cumbersome leash of T-Force.

30AU's carriers and scout cars, bulky with lashed tarpaulins, ammo boxes, buckets and jerrycans, slipped past burning tanks and street debris and entered the area of government buildings around the massive Haus des Reichs office block. The marines, led by Captain Johnny Rose, grabbed a dozen Kriegsmarine officers from basements. Dalzel-Job left his support group here and headed west with the two scout cars of his recce group into the Altstadt, the old city area. Moving from corner to corner they came to the empty city square and looked across to the red brick front of Bremen City Hall. There was no firing, no sign of troops. Suddenly a German policeman popped his helmeted head out of an air-raid shelter and almost had it shot off. '*Bitte*,' he said with his hands up, '*die Stadt von Bremen* wishes to surrender; please will you come to the Rathaus, where the acting Bürgermeister is waiting?' Other civilians emerged cautiously from cellars and shelters. The atmosphere seemed friendly enough. Dalzel-Job, Cooke and Rose left the scout cars on guard in the square and went into an annex of the Neues Rathaus, an echoing red-brick building where an older man was standing, dressed formally in white collar, pin-stripe trousers and morning coat and, in some accounts, holding a top hat.

This was the deputy burgomaster, Dr Richard Duckwitz. His concern was for the lives and safety of his fellow citizens, especially the women and children, now living on short commons in shelters and cellars. This put him in conflict with the military, led by Generalleutnant Becker, who saw it as their duty to fight it out even if that meant reducing the city to rubble. Duckwitz asked Dalzel-Job to accept the formal surrender of the Hanseatic city of Bremen: its authorities and services would be placed at the disposal of the British army and they would do their best to get electricity, telephones, water, gas etc working again efficiently. Duckwitz introduced Dalzel-Job to Bremen's chief of police, Generalmajor Johannes Schroers, who controlled over 4,000 armed and uniformed men in the police, fire brigade and ARP. Could the Germans give an assurance there would be no sabotage? Most certainly: Schroers was adamant the police would take the strongest action against anyone who failed to obey the British authorities. (Later, Allied officers dismissed Duckwitz and appointed Schroers as Burgomaster because working with the police was seen as the most effective way to run civil affairs in occupied enemy territory.)

Dalzel-Job radioed British army HQ to report the city's surrender. 52nd Lowland Division was getting ready to shell the last positions held by the enemy in the city: General Becker was dug into the Bürgerpark and others were mounting a defence of Bremen docks. Shelling the shipyards would have been disastrous for 30AU's key naval targets, so Dalzel-Job set out with all speed to prevent it in a single scout car, proceeding in little dashes from cover to cover, making his way to the high, spiked gates of the Deutsche Schiff und Maschinenbau AG ('DeSchiMag') shipyard. But then the engine of the Humber scout car sputtered and stopped; they had run out of petrol. Worse, their radio contact with the other 30AU men was broken by Bremen's high buildings. Dalzel-Job spotted some German workers, commandeered a bicycle and tried to retrace his steps. The rubble-strewn road was rough and the pedals of German bicycles do not function quite the same way as British ones. A perfect sniper's target, he nevertheless managed to wobble through the obstacles to fetch the rest of his team. When they came back, the German worker was surprised to have his bicycle returned on a Bren-carrier, and the marine Dalzel-Job had left behind in the stalled scout car was happy to be relieved.

Now they opened the gates of the shipyard and found a naval bonanza: sixteen German submarines of the very latest type, and two German destroyers. 30AU caught all the directors and technicians before they could abscond, and spent hours going through the filing cabinets of technical plans. It was a clear night just before the full moon and the livid chiaroscuro made the dockyard of ships and submarines outside both strange and sinister. '*Links, rechts, links, rechts* . . . keep step you bastards!' Marching through crazed shadows, a lone Royal Marine chivvied along a party of German naval officers that he had found hiding in a basement, their clinking swords and medals gleaming in the moonlight.

The next day British troops captured the rest of Bremen. Generalleutnant Becker surrendered in the Bürgerpark and went into captivity with a defiant Nazi salute. Three separate bodies of British troops arrived, all with different orders to clear the shipyard. The last straw came when a staff officer from 52nd Division asked Dalzel-Job to sign a receipt for the sixteen U-boats. He got a marine called Ron Sutton to paint a large sign to hang on the gate saying that the shipyard now belonged to 30AU, annoying the other army personnel no end. Meanwhile, the forced labourers who had been freed broke into the warehouses full of alcohol looted from France: 'They were all just drunker than skunks, the whole bunch of slaves celebrating their liberation.'

Like the war itself, wartime leaders were passing away. White-moustached David Lloyd George was buried in Wales, remembered by most as the PM who led Britain to victory in the First World War, but by others as the corrupt old goat who might have become the British Pétain had the Nazis landed. Polio-crippled Franklin D. Roosevelt died at his house in Warm Springs, Georgia, at the age of sixty-three. Many who were not Americans mourned the US President who had committed the resources and fighting men of his country to liberate the world from Nazism. 'At Buchenwald they spoke of the President just before he died,' wrote Ed Murrow. 'If there be a better epitaph, history does not record it.' Big-chinned

Benito Mussolini died at the hands of Italian Communist partisans. Il Duce was hung upside down without dignity together with the bodies of his mistress Clara Petacci and other butchered Fascists, left dangling from the forecourt canopy of an Esso garage in Milan.

Adolf Hitler died in his Berlin bunker on Monday 30 April, the day after marrying his mistress Eva Braun and executing her corrupt brother-in-law. First the dog-handler Feldwebel Fritz Tornow had the distressing task of putting down Hitler's pet dog. In the toilets the man took a prussic acid capsule from its brass cartridge case and crushed it with a pair of pliers in Blondi's mouth; the alsatian bitch dropped dead in the reek of bitter almonds.

The new Frau Hitler sat on the flowered sofa in his private quarters. Her hair was dyed blonde and she wore a blue silk dress with white trimming and shoes with cork heels. Eva Braun crunched a cyanide capsule like Blondi's. Sitting beside her, the Führer put a 7.65-mm bullet from a Walther PPK pistol into his brain. Ian Fleming, never one to miss an arcane allusion, later made the concealable, semi-automatic Walther PPK police pistol the signature gun of James Bond.

Goebbels and Bormann watched aides pour petroleum over the two blanketed corpses in the garden. Russian shells were bursting all around; the final obsequy of a *Hitler-Gruß* was given from the shelter of the bunker stairwell. Seen through the crack in the door, the shrinking bodies seemed to wince and writhe in the flames and smoke.

Fire was the presiding fear at Tambach Castle, where Lieutenant Jim Besant had been left on watch while Glanville went for help; he had to stop anyone trying to torch the naval records. A great deal of petrol had been stockpiled for just this eventuality, but luckily the winter had been so cold, and the fuel-rationing so severe, that much of the tank had been siphoned off for heating and driving purposes. Besant got on well with the German admirals

– Gladisch the historian, Spindler the submarine expert, a bit stiff but interesting to talk to about the Zeebrugge blockade, and best of all Aßmann, with whom Besant could converse in Spanish. Besant soon discovered that the main danger to the archive was from the uniformed women in the castle, the German equivalent of the WRNS, the Kriegsmarine Helferin, who were led by a formidable character called Fräulein Andröde. She did manage to start a small fire in the library on his watch, but it was soon put out, without great damage. Marine Booth rudely suggested she should be given a good spanking for her arson attempt, but Miss Andröde was too beefy to go across anyone's knee. Besant thought she would have made a good concentration camp guard.

For the rest of the long night, Jim Besant kept himself awake with the ground coffee he had brought. He also managed to double his forces by identifying those German matelots who would unquestioningly obey the wishes of Großadmiral Dönitz, who had ordered the records to be preserved. Besant armed some of these loyal German sailors and sent them out on joint patrols with an equal number of 30AU marines, with strict orders to let no outsiders in and keep the ferocious women in their quarters.

Meanwhile Sancho Glanville had got through to Patton's HQ at Schweinfurt, reported to the chief intelligence officer, and sent an urgent message to the DNI, copied to Tony Hugill at Allied Naval Commander-in-Chief Expeditionary Force (ANCXF), describing the capture and asking what should be done with it. Third Army promised to send a company (i.e. 125 officers and men) to help guard the castle. Glanville and his driver turned the jeep around and headed back to Tambach, where there were further enjoyable discussions with the German officers about history, strategy and tactics, ranging over the battle of Jutland, the role of capital ships, and the best use of the submarine arm. The naval men of both countries bitched about the other armed services and shook their heads over shared problems with poor intelligence and expensive new gear that never quite worked.

The Admirals were most interested in our Commando shoulder flashes and wanted to discuss the value of the Commando raids – especially Vaagso, St-Nazaire and Dieppe and their operations in the Mediterranean. They did not consider the tactical or material results very important . . . but found the moral effect serious.

Glanville learned that 3 Commando's raid on Vaagso in Norway on 27 December 1941 had led to the German High Command's decision to keep 'adequate forces, including elite units' stationed 'at strategic points within easy reach of the coast' throughout Europe. It was a vindication of Churchill's early support for the Commandos. Just as he had envisaged, they had started 'a reign of terror' that had diverted good troops away to time-wasting guard duties.

N

Just after six o'clock on the day of Hitler's death, a deciphered radio signal from Berlin, printed out like a telegram, was handed to Dönitz at the new HQ at Plön in Schleswig-Holstein. This was the place to which the commander-in-chief of the German navy had moved the entire Oberkommando der Marine from Berlin eleven days earlier, one jump ahead of the Russians. When the message arrived, Dönitz was in conference with the minister of munitions, Albert Speer, the administrative genius who had regalvanised the German war economy since February 1942. Speer and Dönitz had become friends – and allies – while collaborating to achieve the more efficient assembly of new U-boats through mass production. Admiral Dönitz now read aloud a startling message from Hitler's secretary, Martin Bormann:

The Führer has appointed you, Herr Admiral, as his successor in place of Reichsmarschall Göring. Confirmation in writing follows. You are hereby authorised to take any measures which the situation demands.

Speer was a fitting audience because he was the man who probably gave Hitler the idea of making Dönitz his successor. Most people would have expected Hitler's deputy, Hermann Göring, to take over, but the fat Field Marshal had attempted a *coup d'état* a week earlier, and Hitler had stripped him of all his posts; Heinrich Himmler, leader of the SS, another powerful candidate for the succession, had been accused (justly) of trying to cut a deal via the Swedes.

Earlier that day Dönitz had met Himmler at Lübeck. Though neither knew that Hitler was dead, the black-uniformed SS leader was already acting like the head of state he was sure he would soon become. In his *Memoirs: Ten Years and Twenty Days*, written a dozen years later, Dönitz says he thought it was his, rather than Himmler's, duty to take on the leadership of Germany, because he could save more lives; but he had few troops, while Himmler had armed forces all over the country. By early evening of 30 April Dönitz was nevertheless the newly appointed head of the German government, and, in his own account, knew he must confront the head of the SS. Accordingly the two men met again around midnight.

Outside, Kriegsmarine and SS men squared up to each other. Himmler entered the building escorted by six armed SS men, but came into the office alone. Dönitz offered him a chair and sat down behind his own desk; the admiral says he had a pistol with the safety-catch off hidden among the papers on the writing desk. Himmler looked unprepossessing, a sweaty clerk in specs with a small head and a big bottom, but he was also a figure of monstrous and murderous power. Chief among his titles (held since January 1929) was Reichsführer-Schutzstaffeln, Head of the SS or 'Protection Squads'. The SS had grown into its own state and society within the National Socialist Third Reich, with its own police, the Gestapo, its own secret service, the SD, its own army, the 600,000 fighting troops of the Waffen-SS, its own doctors and 'racial scientists' and a successful economic empire that ruthlessly exploited the forced labour and slavery of 700,000 people in the 1,000 Konzentrationlagern (KZ, concentration camps) it ran.

But wealth and power can crumble fast. Dönitz handed Himmler the telegram from Bormann in Berlin: 'Please read this.' Astonishment was followed by deflation. Himmler went very pale. After a while he stood up and bowed. 'Allow me to be the second man in your state.' According to Dönitz, he told Himmler that there was no way he could make use of the Reichsführer's services.

In his fine book, *Hitler's Empire* (2008), the historian Mark Mazower questions whether there was any such 'dramatic' showdown between the two men and says that Dönitz's account is 'unreliable'. Certainly Dönitz was a convinced Nazi and adherent of Hitler, though in his memoirs he tried to distance himself from 'the inhuman side of the National Socialist system'. He claimed he was 'appalled' to find out about the death camps – as a busy naval officer he apparently had no idea what was going on. Yet the stain of the criminal system was everywhere. On 16 August 1942 an SS Brigadeführer ordered that hair combed and cut from women in concentration camps should be sold at 50 pfennigs a kilogram to make, among other things, 'hair-yarn socks for U-boat crews'. Russian troops found 7,000 kilograms of hair already bagged at Auschwitz in 1945.

But it cannot be denied that as leader Dönitz set out to save as many civilians as he could from the Soviet armies, who were using rape as an instrument of policy; naval evacuations and rearguard actions probably saved two million Germans from the Russians. He also wanted to preserve some German infrastructure and so stopped the deliberate demolitions. In early May, urged on by Albert Speer, he ordered that Hamburg should not be defended (the British were threatening to bomb, and Hamburg needed no repetition of Operation GOMORRAH, the horrific firestorm raids of 1943 that killed 30,000 people). Speer, like Dönitz, saw no point in smashing everything up. The armaments minister had long been determined to replace Hitler's policy of scorched earth (*Zerstörung*) with an alternative one of paralysis (*Lähmung*). He argued that destroying factories and plant was irrevocable: burying or hiding key components was more intelligent, because recovery would be quicker when the Germans got their territory back. Without Speer's and Dönitz's interventions, 30AU's work would have been much harder.

30AU entered Hamburg with the British army on 3 May and made straight for the waterside at Altona. The four biggest shipyards in Hamburg had built nearly a third of all German submarines in the war. The city did not smell as badly of death as Bremen, but there was a lot of wreckage and hundreds of craft had been scuttled or sunk. A mob of displaced persons was struggling to break into the naval stores and get at the high-grade rations for U-boat crews. A team fired a hammering burst from the twin Vickers machine-guns over their heads to get their attention. Now at least the looting could be organised more fairly.

At the Deutsche Werft AG shipyard 30AU discovered how submarines were put together. Bon Royle wrote:

U-boats were made in different parts of Germany like slices of sausage, brought to Hamburg by rail, put onto the slips, welded together, bits added, and then the outer skin put on. There were Type 21 and Type 23 U-boats, very effective and dangerous, full-size ocean-going vessels. Fortunately, they had had more than their fair share of bombing and the whole yard was a mess of drunken bits of U-boat, twisted girders, smoke-blackened sheds, etc. It was a pleasure to see it all.

In the large Blohm & Voss shipyard they found two heavily bomb-damaged submarines, *U-1408* and *U-1410*, lying on the jetty. These were not conventional submarines in form. Their forty-one-metre hulls were more fishlike and their exact functioning was mysterious because someone had cut out their turbine drives with a blowtorch and removed them. What were they trying to hide? The fifty-nine-year-old engineer Rudolf Blohm, who ran the yard with his brother, eventually admitted they were uncommissioned Type XVIIB submarines, each with one of the new Walter drives fuelled by hydrogen peroxide. They were capable of twenty-five knots underwater, far faster than anything the Allies had. The man who invented the drive, Dr Hellmuth Walter, could be found up in Kiel.

The Blohm brothers were Nazis and some of their wartime labour had come from the SS-run Neuengamme concentration camp by the old German Earth and Stone Works (*Deutsche Erd- und Steinwerke,* DESt) brickworks. This main camp near Hamburg and its many satellites in north Germany held over 100,000 prisoners from a score of countries. The camp also supplied labour to Carl Walther for the production of handguns; to Borgward, Continental and Volkswagen for vehicles and tyres; to Drager, who made gas masks, and to the IG Farben chemical works. There were no prisoners left in Blohm & Voss by 3 May because in April 1945, as the Allies advanced, the Germans were clearing concentration and PoW camps and moving half a million prisoners away from their potential liberators. Many died of exhaustion on forced marches; others who fell by the wayside were shot on the spot. One 30AU man told me what finding dead people face down in the mud with their hands tied behind their backs had made him feel about Germans: 'I still hate them,' he said. The overspill of movements was why Bergen-Belsen was so crowded: Himmler was trying to get rid of the evidence. One SS plan was to load thousands of prisoners on ships and then scuttle them in the Baltic. The *Athen* transported hundreds of people from the port of Lübeck to cram into the holds of the SS *Thielbeck* and the huge Hamburg–South America liner SS *Cap Arcona*, built by Blohm & Voss in 1927 and big enough to impersonate the *Titanic* realistically in a German film about the maritime disaster.

On 3 May 1945 *Thielbeck* and *Cap Arcona* did become death ships in Neustadt bay. But it was not at the hands of the SS. Tragically misinformed, four squadrons of Hawker Typhoon fighter-bombers from 83 group, 2nd Tactical Air Force, attacked the ships with rockets and bombs, believing the SS ships were full of SS men escaping to Norway. *Thielbeck* sank in fifteen minutes but *Cap Arcona* burned for hours. Many concentration camp prisoners in a final effort managed to jump overboard only to drown, and SS guards shot others swimming ashore. The beachside cemetery at Neustadt is a memorial to 7,000 victims; the true death toll may be twice that.

A joint 30AU/SAS party, acting as Brigade Reconnaissance Unit for the 5th Division in VIII Corps, arrived in Neustadt at 4.30 p.m. that day. Glanville's 1946 history of 30AU records, verbatim:

In the harbour the SS prison ship ATHEN was taken. This was found to contain about 6,000 prisoners for labour camps in NORWAY. They had been battened down for twelve days without food. Charts with annotations of operational value were taken from the CB room and passed to FOIC, KIEL. Two of the SS guards from the ship were summarily executed.

The same day, 3 May 1945, was also when Großadmiral Karl Dönitz, the new head of the German Reich, went back to school. He retreated north-west from Plön, past Kiel, up to Flensburg on the Danish border, and established his HQ in the Naval Cadet School on the south bank of Flensburg fjord, the place where he had first studied after joining the Kaiserliche Marine as a cadet in 1910. Marine-Schule Mürwik, known to German matelots as the 'Red Castle on the Sea', was (and still is) the central academy for the German navy. Dönitz needed a security blanket in the midst of Armageddon: the well-regulated home of his service tradition where, guarded by a special battalion of submariners led by U-boat ace Korvettenkapitän Peter Cremer, he hoped to keep things shipshape as his country collapsed into denial, physical squalor and an epidemic of suicides. At first the Großadmiral moved into the *Patria*, a 17,000-ton former Hamburg–America liner moored at the school's quay, but then he took over the large red-brick *Sportschule* for his offices. But his Flensburg government only lasted three weeks, and was little but a fantastic bubble.

On his way north late the day before, Dönitz had sent the supreme commander-in-chief of the German navy, Generaladmiral Hans-Georg von Friedeburg, together with Admiral Wagner and General Kinzel, to negotiate with General Montgomery at Twenty-first Army Group's TAC HQ at Lüneberg Heath. They were meant to offer the surrender of all German forces in north-west Germany on condition that the remains of the Heeresgruppe Weichsel, formed to hold the Red Army off Berlin, be allowed to retreat west and surrender to the British rather than the Russians. But in negotiations on 3 May Montgomery refused to talk about any German soldiers or civilians facing the Russians: that was a matter for the Soviets, he said. He had on display a large map with the giant advancing arrows of the Allies, and when von Friedeburg saw it and understood, 'apparently for the first time, the plight of the German armies on the various fronts', the German admiral broke down and wept.

Next morning Dönitz and Generalfeldmarschall Wilhelm Keitel authorised von Friedeburg to accept Montgomery's conditions for the north. Then he was to fly off to France and the SHAEF HQ at Reims to negotiate a separate surrender in the west and south of Germany, still trying to buy as much time as possible for Heeresgruppen Mitte, Süd and Südost to hold off the Russian 'Bolshevists'. At half past six in the evening, five German officers signed the instrument of surrender of all German forces and ships in Holland, north Germany, the Frisian islands, Schleswig-Holstein and Denmark, to come into effect at 0800 hours British Double Summer Time on the following day, Saturday 5 May 1945.

At that hour 30AU's Team 10, led by Dunstan Curtis, was ready to cross Second Army's 'armistice halt line' at Bad Segeberg, south of Kiel, with a force of 500 Allied men that included some jeeps full of 5th SAS, mainly Belgians, and elements of T-Force, led by Major Tony Hibbert of the Parachute Regiment. According to Sean Longden, Hibbert's verbal orders were to take Kiel before the Russians got there. Three days earlier Canadians from the British 6th Airborne Division had punched north from the Elbe crossing at Lauenberg to take Wismar on the Baltic just a few hours ahead of Soviet troops driving west. The Russians were untrustworthy allies; on his last day in Washington before he died, Roosevelt acknowledged that Stalin 'has broken every one of the promises he made at Yalta'. A joint Anglo-American–Russian force was to have entered Peenemünde, but Russian obfuscatory bureaucracy blocked any foreigners from the rocket site, because the Russians wanted the rocket scientists for themselves. Now Hibbert's job was to ensure the Russians were in no position to take any land north of the Kiel Canal. Intercepts from the Japanese embassy in Stockholm indicated that the USSR was planning to break the Yalta Agreement, seize Denmark, and control the Baltic.

The T-Force teams raced each other towards Kiel, barrelling past Germans who were too passive or dazed to react. The ceasefire had stopped planes flying, but they still had to dodge the wreckage of strafed and burned-out vehicles littering the road, evidence of the Tactical Air Force's previous sorties. By half past nine 30AU's jeeps and scout cars were entering Kiel, skirting west and heading north. Much of the city was damaged or destroyed: the last bombing by Mosquitoes of Bomber Command had only been three days earlier.

It was 10.15 a.m. when they achieved one of their prime objectives, entering and seizing the H. Walter KG company's works on the south bank of the Kiel Canal. Its handsome boardroom became their officers' mess, and it was a great moment when Dr Hellmuth Walter himself was arrested, along with Professor Kramer and other scientists and technicians. Walter, a flabby-cheeked man of about forty-five who had joined the Nazi Party in 1932, was a major capture for the British.

Walter had worked out that if you catalysed hydrogen peroxide, also known as dihydrogen dioxide for its chemical equation, H_2O_2, it would break down into oxygen and steam at high temperature. By adding another combustible fuel like ethanol to these expanding gases you got power as well as pressure – 'air independent propulsion' or 'closed-cycle propulsion'. He had patented the idea in 1925, when he was only twenty-five years old. Two impressive applications were the V-80 submarine and the Messerschmitt-163 jet fighter; the V-80 was the small prototype 'Walter boat' he built at Germaniawerft in Kiel in 1939–40. Previous to that, all submersible craft travelled relatively fast on the sea surface using diesel engines but much slower when once submerged and dependent on smaller electric motors – for example, the Kriegsmarine's Type VII U-boat made 17.7 knots on the surface using its 3,200 hp diesel engine, but only reached 7.6 knots submerged, using the 750 hp electric motor. Astonishingly Walter's V-80, driven by a Walter turbine using hydrogen peroxide, could achieve a speed of 28 knots (32 mph) underwater. The V-80 outstripped any submarine on the planet until the nuclear-powered vessels of the 1950s. The Walterwerk factory did not manufacture their own hydrogen peroxide: production was dispersed in the usual Nazi fashion. The biggest supplier was Otto Schickert & Co. at Bad Lauterberg; other factories could concentrate up to 500 tons a month at 83 per cent strength, stored in pure aluminium tanks 'passivated' with nitric acid. Most people know diluted hydrogen peroxide as an antibacterial agent and bleach – as in 'peroxide blonde' – but in higher concentrations it can be used as a propellant, although it is highly reactive and combustible and can only be stored in scrupulously clean aluminium, stainless steel or PVC.

Commander Curtis and Captain Pike later went to take the surrender of the port of Kiel from Konteradmiral Joachim von Gerlach at the huge bunker near the Tirpitzhafen naval base. German officers and ratings on duty and patrolling German policemen were permitted arms, but all others were to lay down their weapons. All shipping was frozen. It felt a little uneasy: the small British force was greatly outnumbered by the 25,000 Germans in uniform, some of whom were restless and sullen. Sergeant Paul McGrath reckoned that you had to impose your will before mutiny broke out, and so when a German naval officer truculently refused to do as he was told, McGrath punched him, hard. Striking an officer (even an enemy one) is a court-martial offence, but 'the conduct of the Royal Marine was subsequently held to be justified'.

The Walter factory consisted of a series of red-brick buildings with testing cells, laboratories, machine shops, drawing offices and record rooms. There were also two thick-walled bunkers, each holding ten twenty-ton aluminium tanks of hydrogen peroxide. A preliminary investigation revealed numerous torpedoes in various stages of completion, the entire stern of a Type XVII submarine coupled to a test brake, and many other interesting kinds of rig. Nothing seemed to have been actually sabotaged but in every case the combustion chambers of the engines had been removed, just as they had been from the U-boats at Blohm & Voss in Hamburg. Also, a great many of Walter's important papers and documents were missing, believed destroyed. Something was evidently going on.

Dr Hellmuth Walter himself seemed to talk freely, but only about generalities. He was grateful for the tea and coffee that 30AU pressed on him and his wife who had just had a new baby, their fifth child. He thawed enough to tell them how he had become a leader of industry in Kiel, forming his own company and eventually employing 4,500 people. His great dream had been speed, in the air or under the sea; since 1930 he had been working on aircraft for the Luftwaffe and vessels for the Kriegsmarine. He had helped Wernher von Braun with his rockets and the *Wehrmacht*'s V-1s. Hydrogen peroxide fuelled the piston in a cylinder that launched the V-1, and hydrogen peroxide drove the 'proportioning pumps' for the liquid oxygen and fuel of the V-2 rocket.

But when Walter was asked how exactly he used hydrogen peroxide and what the specific details of catalysts and combustion chambers were, he became vague or was reluctant to say anything at all. Since all the motors were missing or had had their vital components removed, there was no physical evidence to make up for his evasions. In fact Walter was in an awkward position: he was being pressured by the British and Americans and was terrified of the Russians, only forty miles away on the other side of Lübeck. Moreover he still felt bound to silence by the oath of secrecy he had given to the Nazis.

Early on the morning of Sunday 6 May, Dunstan Curtis had a second meeting with Konteradmiral von Gerlach. The German warned that news of the surrender terms had not reached everyone: soldiers north of the Kiel Canal were preparing for a last ditch stand: British troops would not pass without a fight. This was intolerable. Eventually von Gerlach telephoned Dönitz in Flensburg (with Curtis listening in) and the two Germans agreed to issue orders to the posts on the Friedrichsort bridge and to all commanders between Kiel and Eckernförde that a British detachment should be allowed to cross.

At eleven o'clock Commander Curtis, Lieutenant Commander Guy Postlethwaite and Captain Geoff Pike led a small convoy of vehicles with under three dozen men from 30AU across the bridge to the fortified promontory at Friedrichsort where there was a lighthouse and a radio station next to the mine-sweeping base. When the commanding officer surrendered, he was warned that he must obey von Gerlach's instructions and sabotage nothing. 30AU unit obtained full charts showing all the German minefields and all the mine-free areas from the Skaw tip of German-occupied Denmark east into the Baltic, a very useful acquisition, and then drove twenty miles north-west to capture the Torpedoversuchanstallt (TVA) or Torpedo Experiment/Trials Institute at Eckernförde. Guy Postlethwaite was left behind there with fifteen Royal Marines to set up an HQ and find out more about the German underwater experiments.

N

That Sunday in Northern France, talks of high strategic importance were being held between the Allies and the tatters of the Axis in a boys' school in Reims. The senior officers sent by Dönitz were trying to negotiate with General Eisenhower's team, but the lead delegate von Friedeburg had gone to pieces and Hitler's chief of staff, General Alfred Jodl, had to take over. The Germans still hoped they could somehow split the Allies, setting Americans against British or vice versa, and both of them against the godless Russians. But it wouldn't wash. For their part Eisenhower's team made high-minded appeals to German honour and sought to elicit a chivalrous capitulation. Finally, at 2 a.m. on Monday 7 May 1945, on a school exam table in the old ping-pong room, now plastered with maps and ablaze with *klieg* lights for newsreels, flanked on the right by his aide, Major Oxenius, and with von Friedeburg on his left, Jodl signed the Act of Military Surrender. American, Russian and French representatives of the Allies added their signatures, and the invited press scribbled and snapped.*

The last phrase of the surrender said: 'No ship, vessel, or aircraft is to be scuttled, or any damage done to their hull, machinery or equipment.' But it was too late for the German U-Boats in the Western Baltic: the code word *Regenbogen* (Rainbow) meaning 'scuttle all boats' had gone out on 30 April from Dönitz, following the naval tradition that ships and submarines should not be allowed to fall into enemy hands. Although the Allies ordered the instruction to be rescinded on 4 May, it spread by word of mouth and by radio. A total of 238 German U-boats were scuttled, half of

---

* Edward Kennedy of Associated Press broke the military embargo to get the world scoop of the German surrender on the AP wire at 09.36 EST on 7 May 1945. His SHAEF accreditation withdrawn for this crime, he was sent home and later fired by the news agency.

them Walter boats and the most modern Type XXIs and XXIIIs, whereas only 156 U-boats surrendered. When eleven Type XXI U-boats were taken to Lisahally in Northern Ireland, no one could work them properly because Dönitz had ordered all German submariners before the Armistice to destroy their operating handbooks. This would dash the Allies' hope of using them against the Japanese, but 30AU came to the rescue with nine Type XXI handbooks, unearthed at the Deschimag shipyard in Bremen.

The Russians demanded another, bigger, formal ceremony later on 7 May in Berlin, so that Marshal Georgi Zhukov, the bemedalled victor of the great tank battle against the Germans at Kursk, could sign on behalf of the Red Army. (Air Chief Marshal Tedder, Eisenhower's deputy, would sign too.) The German capital was still hazed with the smoke and dust of destruction; odd shots and explosions punctured the miasma. Accompanied by a Luftwaffe representative and once more by von Friedeburg for the Kriegsmarine, Hitler's chief toady from the army High Command, Wilhelm Keitel, still arrogant in his demeanour, with monocle and field marshal's baton, signed on behalf of the defeated. The unconditional surrender event finished at 22.43 Central European Time. At the lavish banquet afterwards Harry Butcher, Eisenhower's naval aide, got drunk on neat vodka while Kenneth Strong, Eisenhower's intelligence officer who had helped negotiate the Italian surrender, looked on in disgust. 'This was the second time I had taken an active part in capitulation ceremonies. Both brought home to me the futility and tragedy of war. Both I hated intensely. After the waste of the past years I felt they were curiously degrading to the victors, as well as to the vanquished.'*

---

*   Both German signatories, Jodl and Keitel, would be convicted of war crimes at Nuremberg in October 1946. After they were hanged, their bodies were cremated in the ovens of Dachau as an act of symbolic retribution.

VE Day, Victory in Europe day, 8 May 1945, signalled 'the greatest outburst of joy in the history of mankind' as Churchill wrote later: 'Weary and worn, impoverished but undaunted and now triumphant, we had a moment that was sublime.' But Ian Fleming was fretting in London. The bibliophile and collector wanted the cache of German naval records from Tambach badly. He was also afraid that they might fall into the hands of the Russians, believing that under the Four Power Division of Germany, Tambach would be in the Russian zone, the eastern part of Germany that would become the German Democratic Republic. (He was wrong about the line on the map – Tambach did not quite fall within the Russian zone – but he was right about the threat from Russia, which would be the backdrop to much of his fiction.) A couple of NID officers had been sent out from London to Germany to help secure the Tambach records, but had failed to achieve anything. In May 1945, therefore, Fleming flew out to see for himself.

He found Ralph Izzard, the expert Forward Interrogator, and the American Lieutenant Earle at the castle. It was Izzard to whom Ian Fleming made a typically off-beat suggestion that was also deeply serious: when Izzard got hold of the dozen top admirals in the German navy he should make each of them sit down and write a 10,000 word essay on 'Why Germany lost the war'. The results of this, and the Admiralty questionnaire that Izzard handed out, though often self-justificatory, were illuminating. Now at last Fleming got the chance to see with his own eyes what his intelligence unit had achieved. He was amazed at the size and comprehensiveness of the archive; with his intelligence background he could clearly see its potential importance. Of course, he became even more anxious to get 30AU's haul back safely to England. Strings had to be pulled, lorries and ships arranged.

Sancho Glanville, who had made the original discovery, seems to have played a central role in this, but gives no details in the account he wrote just after the war and, when approached in 1965 by Ian Fleming's first biographer, John Pearson, refused to 'disclose any information' unless Admiral Denning sent a written statement via the diplomatic bag of what he was allowed to reveal. Pearson's subsequent account is inaccurate, involving Fleming and Glanville driving to Tambach, finding an overexcited German admiral on the point of burning a huge pile of documents, and eventually prevailing on the latter to come back to London with Fleming and the entire German archives on a fishery protection vessel.*

By 1975 Glanville's attitude to disclosure had changed; the ULTRA secret had been revealed and the wall of official secrecy about the war was coming down, so Glanville was prepared to help Cecil Hampshire with his 1978 book *The Secret Navies*. He told Hampshire one very interesting story about a conversation he had with Fleming at the Admiralty not long after Fleming's visit to Tambach Castle. It must be borne in mind that Glanville did not like Ian Fleming; Denning noted with surprise how Glanville's post-war account of 30AU's activities made 'very little mention . . . of Ian [Fleming]'s connection with 30 Assault Unit . . . although I myself know how carefully [Fleming] fathered its development and activities'.

At any rate, according to Hampshire, Glanville, who had been 'nominated' to oversee '30AU['s] . . . responsibility for transferring the material intact to the Admiralty', was ordered back to London because Fleming had something to say to him. This was that Fleming

considered the [German] admirals to be a menace. They were, he said, solely concerned with plotting and planning the next war in line with their conduct after the treaty of Versailles. In best '007' style he thought they should be 'eliminated' and that Glanville was the man to do the job!

Glanville responded that he had not yet stooped to murdering prisoners of war.

---

* The German who actually came to London in May 1946 to help with the recovered documents was an Austrian Korvettenkapitan, Dr Peter Handel-Mazzetti, one of the two archivists of the German naval records.

Is this story true? Perhaps Fleming was verbalising his frustration with the rule-bound nature of life within a big, protocol-heavy organisation. Perhaps, now the war was coming to an end, he was starting to be seduced by a new kind of imaginative life where it was possible to sit behind an office desk and send off, at will, a secret agent with a licence to kill.

This sort of operation goes better in a James Bond book than in real life. In *For Your Eyes Only* (1960), some old friends of the head of the Secret Service have been cold-bloodedly murdered in Jamaica by Cuban gangsters working for a Nazi, and M now wants 'justice, or is it revenge?' He slyly manoeuvres his eager acolyte James Bond into actually suggesting it first: ' "These people can't be hung, sir. But they ought to be killed." '

Evidence that Ian Fleming was indeed exercising his imagination along these lines not long after the war comes from Denning's account of an early ''36 Club' dinner at the Junior Carlton.* A group of men who had all been in the wartime secret services were deploring the bland efficiencies of the modern intelligence business and regretting that real-life agents lacked the glamour and dash of those in novels:

Ian said the whole organisation wanted revolutionizing and he still saw a use for the traditional spy of fiction. Whereupon he imaginatively pictured the adventures he might have had in the last war given complete freedom and unlimited money. The exploits were not all that dissimilar to that of Bond . . .

But Ian Fleming's thought-experiment about murdering German admirals came to nothing. Hampshire's account concludes: 'Glanville, with a section of B Troop, duly set off for Tambach, and within a few days the business of cataloguing and packing

---

* 'Ned' Denning was the last DNI when the post was abolished in 1964, absorbed into the new tri-service Ministry of Defence where he became Deputy Chief of Defence Staff (Intelligence) under Kenneth Strong. There has been recent talk of re-establishing Naval Intelligence and the DNI.

the archives for shipment to London had been completed. In due course they arrived safely at the Admiralty.'

The other top men in 30AU still had a lot to do. Colonel Humphrey Quill arrived in Kiel, inspected the Walterwerk factory and questioned the reluctant Helmuth Walter. Early on 9 May, taking a German radio interception service officer with him in a Humber scout car, the CO of 30AU drove sixty miles north to the temporary capital of unconquered Germany, the enclave at Flensburg where Dönitz had just formed his new acting government, and where radio station *Reichssender Flensburg* was broadcasting the last messages and commands.

Accompanied by Dunstan Curtis, Brian Connell, Geoffrey Pike and an American officer, Captain A. G. Mumma, who had been with the ALSOS team in Paris and beyond, Quill met the officer commanding Flensburg, Kapitän zur See Wolfgang Lüth, and Dönitz's chief of staff, Korvettenkapitän Walter Lüdde-Neurath. They arranged for a conference the following day at Glueckstadt with senior officers of the Oberkommando der Marine. That night they stayed on board the SS *Patria*, crowded together with German naval officers who had lost their ships. They were the first British detachment to penetrate the inner HQ of the Kriegsmarine, but they were well fed and entertained and 'no untoward incidents of any kind occurred'. Indeed some Germans were still hoping they would be re-armed and join with the Allies in fighting the Russians.

At the meeting on 10 May 1945 Quill insisted upon, and duly received, a document signed by Admiral Otto Backenköhler, the chief of Kriegsmarine armaments, instructing all naval establishments to hand over to 30AU representatives (described as 'the unit under Herr Oberst Quel') all secret papers and material, whether already hidden or not. This was a vital open sesame, because many German navy establishments held that the order they had received not to hide or destroy any secret matter after 8.00 a.m. on 5 May did not apply to material they had hidden previously. Forty copies of this document, all signed by Backenköhler and sent to all team leaders, yielded results straight away at Eckernförde and especially at the H. Walter factory. A Kapitän zur See staff officer came down in person to tell Helmuth Walter that 'nothing whatsoever was to be withheld'.

'Then ensued a hilarious series of discoveries,' wrote Commander Jan Aylen, the senior engineering officer with 30AU who later rose to the rank of rear admiral.

The average rate of finding new weapons for the first fortnight was about two per day. Combustion chambers were retrieved from the bottom of flooded bomb craters. A case containing key torpedo data was dug up from a hole whose position had been revealed by the German Director of Torpedoes . . . At an outstation near Boseau on the nearby Plömer Zee, a sinister lake where midget crews, swimmers and other marine pests were trained, was found Walter's latest miniature, 25-knot, one-man U-boat which had been scuttled so successfully that the hull had collapsed under pressure.

The American Al Mumma took a shine to Geoff Pike, finding him 'a very enterprising young fellow . . . really full of beans'. Pike's marines discovered a whole trainload of Walter combustion chambers in a railway siding way up in the peninsula by the Danish border. He loaded all his vehicles on to the train and brought the entire haul down into Kiel. In the cab of the locomotive was Lieutenant Alastair Cameron RNVR, later professor of lubrication engineering at Imperial College, and stuck on the front of the engine was a big sign reading '30 ASSAULT UNIT'. 'They had all the combustion chambers,' recollected Mumma, 'not only for the Messerschmitt-163, but also for the launching mechanism for the V-1s, also for the proportioning system of the V-2s, also for the two types of submarines – the type XXI and XXVI submarines, which were of interest to us – as well as the torpedoes.'

N

The Germans were orderly people, accustomed to obeying superiors. As a realist, Winston Churchill knew the Allies had to begin by working with the existing hierarchy, no matter how little they liked it: 'The surrender of the German people should be completed through agencies which have authority over them,' he wrote to the Foreign Office on 14 May 1945.

I neither know nor care about Doenitz. He may be a war criminal . . . The question for us is, has he any power to get the Germans to lay down their arms and hand them over quickly without any more loss of life? We cannot go running around into every German slum and argue with every German that it is his duty to surrender or we will shoot him. There must be some kind of force which will give orders which they will obey. Once they obey we can do what we like to carry through unconditional surrender.

So the unreality of the Flensburg government was allowed to continue in its tiny enclave, four miles long and one mile wide, running from the Torpedo School to Glücksburg Castle. The new Cabinet met daily in a former classroom; typewriters clicked through reports and memoranda on getting Germany back on its feet and preserving 'the unity of our racial community'. German officers drove around in German staff cars, guarded by thousands of German soldiers from the army, navy and air force. But when Generalfeldmarschall Busch broadcast on May 11 that all German military and civilian authorities in Schleswig-Holstein were subordinate to him, it caused Allied annoyance. Worse, there were believed to be wanted war criminals inside the enclave: Heinrich Himmler was spotted, though he dodged out of sight and his presence was denied. The Nazi ideologue Alfred Rosenberg was arrested, drunk, hiding in the Flensburg hospital.

SHAEF decided to close Flensburg down and arrest the leaders, preferably without shooting. Operation BLACKOUT happened on 23 May 1945. Dönitz, Jodl and von Friedeburg arrived at the SS *Patria* at 9.45 for a ten o'clock meeting and were arrested on the hour. Meanwhile Royal Marines and two battalions of British troops with fixed bayonets and armoured support occupied the rest of the Flensburg enclave. Everyone was searched, and their possessions were looted; 6,000 people went into prisoner-of-war cages for grading and sorting. There was only one casualty. Generaladmiral Hans-Georg von Friedeburg, the head of the German navy, had been allowed back to his quarters to pick up one suitcase of possessions, and asked permission to go to the lavatory. After forty-five seconds his captors outside heard a groan that was more than costive. They broke down the door and found he had swallowed a phial of cyanide. His dead body in uniform was laid on the cot in his room; the rare Knight's Cross of the *Kriegsverdienstkreuz* with Swords, the one with the swastika in the middle, was pinched from around his neck. After that, all senior officers were stripped and closely searched again for suicide pills that might be hidden about their persons. It is hard not feel a twinge of sympathy for Großadmiral Karl Dönitz, who was found to be wearing eight pairs of underpants in case his weak bladder humiliated him in front of the enemy. Sergeant John Brereton of 30AU escorted Dönitz from Kiel to the PoW cage.

Heinrich Himmler was picked up almost accidentally the same day, in shabby clothes with a black eye-patch, claiming to be *Feldwebel* Heinrich Hitzinger of the *Geheime Feld Polizei* or Secret Military Police. After confessing his real identity he was taken to Barnstedt near Lüneberg. Around 11 o'clock at night, Dr C. J. Wells spotted something blue in his mouth and tried to get it out. Himmler bit down on the doctor's finger and jerked out of reach. He crushed the cyanide capsule between his teeth and then inhaled . . . With face contorted and veins bulging, the glassy-eyed *Reichsführer SS* crashed to the ground. 'My God! It's in his mouth! He's done it on me!' As they upended his body and slobbered his mouth in a bowl of water to try and wash out the poison, Himmler made horrible grunts and groans. Colonel Murphy and Major Whittaker scrabbled to grab his tongue to stop him choking, securing it with a clumsy needle and thread.

But the next morning, gravel-voiced Company Sergeant Major Edwin Austen recorded the last moments for a BBC microphone: 'After a struggle, lasting a quarter-of-an-hour, in which we tried all methods of artificial respiration, under the direction of the doctor . . . he died . . . and when he died . . . we threw a blanket over him . . . and left him.'

At last it was unconditional surrender. Now everything was up for grabs. Although Helmuth Walter had burned many documents, 30AU men were delighted to find complete microfilms of his work buried in the office coal cellar, and these were copied for London and Washington. In a safe they found a 16-mm film of the new secret weapons that Germany was working on, which had been shown to Hitler in his bunker before his death. One was a submarine that could lie on the seabed and fire a rocket with a warhead from under the sea – a forerunner of Polaris. Technical experts from all the intelligence agencies in the European theatre now started arriving at Kiel to see the riches 30AU were turning up. Walter was instructed to recommence his work, this time for the benefit of Allied spectators. Six hundred Germans were employed to complete his various weapons, devices and 'Ingolene' engines and demonstrate them to visiting VIPs from the UK and USA. In July 1945 top brass like the British First Sea Lord, Sir Andrew Cunningham, enjoyed the spectacle of a V-1 flying bomb shooting along its 150-yard launching ramp like a giant firework. Now they no longer had to fear them, the Allies could be impressed by the technical wizardry of Walter's lethal toyshop with its jet-driven explosive hydrofoils, radio-controlled glider bombs, remote-controlled tankettes, rocket-propelled 'sticky bombs', silent steam cannons, mine detonators and a new kind of big gun with a fuel injection system in the barrel to extend its range. There were also some ingenious deceptions: short-range torpedoes fired from U-boats being pursued by destroyers were not, in fact, attack weapons at all, but were designed to explode a canister releasing oil and bits of submarine kit and clothing, the sort of rubbish which would rise to the surface of the sea, and make the destroyers think they had sunk their prey and so give up the chase.

Commander Aylen of 30AU, together with Captain Mumma of the US Navy, spent seven months of 1945 investigating the works at Kiel. As engineer overseer, Aylen wrote the official report to the Navy's Director of Scientific Research in December 1945. Then the Royal Navy brought Helmuth Walter with his team and a quantity of plant over to England to continue his work in the Admiralty Development Establishment (ADEP) in the Vickers- Armstrongs works at Barrow-in-Furness. Now the Allies had their man and could capitalise on the products of his teeming brain.

Others were also after this knowledge. In July 1945 Dönitz asked to see Ralph Izzard. After his usual political speech claiming that only he could save Germany from Bolshevism, the Admiral revealed that some Russian officers had been to question him about the key men in his U-boat arm and the whereabouts of their families. Dönitz had given evasive answers, but it was his impression that the Russians were aiming for a fleet of 3,000 submarines and wanted to recruit German U-boat men: fifty captains, fifty engineer officers and ten constructors.

The two halves of 30AU's great captures in 1945 were actually connected, though this was not immediately apparent. When the blueprints and files from the naval archives at Tambach were finally sorted and studied, they were found to back up all the naval technology seized from the Walterwerk factory in Kiel and other shipyards. 30AU had hit a glorious home run. In August 1945 they were for the most part disbanded.

15

Aftermath

The end of the war in Europe did not mean the end of the Second World War. Fighting dragged on in Asia until the atom bombs destroyed Hiroshima and Nagasaki in August 1945. That July Sancho Glanville took a small 30AU squad to the Far Eastern theatre, and eventually found himself in Vietnam, hunting down Japanese radar technology and capturing a very senior Japanese naval officer – thus completing 30AU's hat-trick of Axis admirals. But the British and American forces in Saigon, welcomed at first by the Vietnamese people as liberators from the Imperial Japanese, ended up actually using captured Japanese troops with bandy putteed legs and long bayonets to suppress Vietnamese nationalists. Trying to restore colonialism in Indochina led to thirty ruinous years of guerrilla warfare and the eventual military defeats of France and the USA.

The new 'Cold War' started almost immediately after the Second World War finished. On 5 March 1946, three weeks before 30AU's last section was finally disbanded, Winston Churchill made his historic 'Sinews of Peace' speech in Fulton, Missouri. The seventy-year-old former prime minister (voted out of office in the July 1945 British general election) had embodied war since 1898 when he had charged with the 21st Lancers against spear-carrying Sudanese at Omdurman. Although he looked forward with hope to a united Europe and spoke with approval of the new United Nations Organisation, the main thrust of his speech was a warning against tyranny by the USSR. 'Nobody knows', he said, 'what Soviet Russia and its Communist international organisation intends to do in the immediate future . . . From Stettin in the Baltic to Trieste in the Adriatic, an iron curtain has descended across the Continent.' Churchill urged 'the Western Democracies' to stand together on the principles of the United Nations Charter.

The Cold War followed its inexorable logic. The USA determined to resist 'Soviet expansionism'; the USSR rallied all Communist parties against 'American imperialism' and absorbed free Czechoslovakia into a solidifying Soviet bloc. In 1948 came the Berlin blockade, and then the Berlin airlift to relieve it. After NATO was founded, the Warsaw Pact was formed in reaction. In the autumn of 1949 the Soviet Union got the atom bomb and Mao's Communists took China. The Soviet AK-47 assault rifle – the number one gun for guerrillas – went into mass production. Early in 1950 Senator Joseph McCarthy started his Communist witch-hunt in the USA and in June Soviet-backed North Korea invaded American-backed South Korea. Sixteen United Nations countries, including the USA and the UK, sent troops to defend the South, while the Chinese People's Army poured in to support the North. The proxy war between East and West lasted until 1953 and killed four million people.

Ian Fleming published his first James Bond novel, *Casino Royale*, in 1953. No wonder that James Bond started his fictional life as a creature of the Cold War, fighting the Stalinist terror of SMERSH. He emerged in the same year as Queen Elizabeth II's coronation and the British conquest of Mount Everest,* a neo-Elizabethan hero for an age when the British Empire was dissolving and Britain struggled to remain at the top table among the world leaders.

---

* Ralph Izzard covered the Himalayan story for the *Daily Mail*, despite *The Times*'s exclusive deal. 30AU's old Forward Interrogator got to Base Camp at 18,000 feet in tennis shoes, as recounted in his fine and modest 1954 book *The Innocent on Everest*.

After 30AU's pinch of Helmuth Walter and his secrets, Britain's initial intention was to lead the world in peroxide power. Walter's advanced-design, hydrogen-peroxide-powered Type XVIIB submarine *U-1407*, built by Blohm & Voss and scuttled by the Germans at Cuxhaven on the night of 6/7 May 1945, was raised by the Royal Navy after the war and recommissioned as a British vessel under the name HMS *Meteorite*. Following work at the Admiralty Experimental Station, Welwyn, two more High Test Peroxide (HTP) or hydrogen peroxide submarines, HMS *Explorer* and HMS *Excalibur*, based on Walter designs for the Atlantic Type XXVIW, were newly built for speed trials in the 1950s and achieved a remarkable twenty-five knots underwater.

What the British did not grasp straightaway was that the Americans had allowed them to have hydrogen peroxide-fuelled submarines because they had already seen the nuclear alternative. Captain (later Admiral) Albert Mumma* who, together with Commander Jan Aylen, oversaw the H. Walter factory at the end of the war, knew that the US Navy's Naval Research Laboratory had been working on nuclear power for submarine propulsion ever since March 1939. Mumma had been one of the ALSOS team chasing the Nazi atomic bomb and understood the potential of nuclear fission. He did not favour hydrogen peroxide because it was uneconomic:

It cost a dollar and half a kilowatt hour as against about six cents for the diesel. I knew that we could probably produce nuclear power at a maximum of maybe two or three times the cost of diesel power, not a factor of over 20 or 25. So that I was a nuclear enthusiast from those days

---

* Mumma was head of nuclear matters for the Bureau of Ships in Washington from 1947 to 1949, until he was replaced by the hard-driving Admiral Hyman G. Rickover, the father of the world's first nuclear-powered submarine, USS *Nautilus*, launched in January 1954. Rickover eventually let the British in on the secrets of nuclear submarines, and stood next to Lord Mountbatten when the Queen launched HMS *Dreadnought*, Britain's first nuclear sub, at the Vickers-Armstrongs yard in Barrow-in-Furness on Trafalgar Day 1960.

. . . The British wanted it, so they got Helmuth Walter and the type XXI submarine set-up and moved it to Britain.

What really scuttled hydrogen peroxide technology was the volatility of the fuel, which earned the new British submarines *Explorer* and *Excalibur* their nicknames *'Exploder'* and *'Excruciator'*. The dangers were dramatically illustrated when a leak from a twenty-one-inch Mark 12 HTP torpedo led to an explosion which sank the British submarine HMS *Sidon* at Portland on 16 June 1955, with the death of thirteen men. A decade after the end of the war, the glory days of H_2O_2 were over.* (An explosion of hydrogen peroxide leaked from a torpedo probably sank the Soviet submarine *Kursk* in 2000; the crude terrorist bombs on London transport that killed fifty-two people in 2005 also used it.)

Side by side with the work on hydrogen peroxide, the British had also been working on nuclear technology in a desperate struggle to catch up and get an 'independent deterrent'. Even though British scientists and technicians had helped the Manhattan Project to build the original atom bomb, the American McMahon Act of 1946 had frozen them out from all US nuclear secrets. But on 3 October 1952, off the north-west shoulder of Australia, Britain managed to explode a 25-kiloton bomb in an old warship on the ocean surface called HMS *Plym*, the first of twenty-one atmospheric nuclear tests that the British would hold in Australia and the Pacific up till 1958. The UK had joined the Cold War's nuclear club.

Helmuth Walter was also a pioneer in the air, contributing to the development of jets and rockets. At the end of the Second World War, all the Allies had been eager to capture the best Axis technicians in the field of rocket technology: some Nazi rocket scientists from Peenemünde ended up in Moscow helping the

---

* In the twenty-first century, with 'peak oil' and dwindling fossil fuels, some people are looking again at dihydrogen dioxide's possibilities.

Russians' long campaign to put the first man in space, while others like Wernher von Braun of the SS, Konrad Dannenberg and Arthur Rudolph who had used slave labour at Mittelwerk were creamed off by the Americans and eventually helped NASA land the first man on the moon.

30AU's pinch of Helmuth Walter was crucial to Britain's rocket technology and air industry: the very first gas-turbine jet-propelled aeroplane, launched in the summer of 1939, was a German Heinkel-176 that used a Walter liquid-fuel rocket engine. A later one that Walter designed and built for the Luftwaffe sent the single-seater Messerschmidt-163B Komet up at over 600 mph. This squat little fighter could reach 30,000 feet in two and half minutes, which amazed all those who saw it in 1945, though it had only five minutes' flying time before it had to glide down and land with an empty tank.

The British Ministry of Supply was anxious to incorporate such German engineering ideas into the Guided Projectile Establishment at Westcott and the Rocket Propulsion Group at Farnborough; the De Havilland Engine Company took forward Walter's ideas of combining piston, turbojet and rocket propulsion. Delta-winged jet-fighters like the Swallow, the Vixen and the Venom derived from Walter's Me-163, and the de Havilland DH 106 Comet also drew on Walter's ideas. This was the world's first commercial jet airliner to reach production, flying for BOAC in 1949. Alas, metal fatigue from the rivet-holes on pressurised windows eventually led to structural failure and two Comets tore apart in mid-air. Godfrey's brilliant naval attaché in Turkey, Commander Vladimir Wolfson RNVR, was killed on the first of these, flight 781, which came down near Elba on 10 January 1954. But the Comet was modified and improved enough to become the Hawker Siddeley Nimrod, the 'spy plane' that the RAF only phased out in 2010.

N

The third James Bond novel, *Moonraker*, was published in April 1955, two months before the real-life hydrogen peroxide explosion that sank the submarine HMS *Sidon*. In some ways an updating of John Buchan's *The Thirty-Nine Steps*, *Moonraker* can be read as focusing on the dangers Fleming perceived in British reliance on German scientists and German technology. Even in motor cars, British was best: 'The Bentley was going beautifully and [Bond] felt sure of holding the Mercedes.' The villain of this thriller is a wealthy self-made man (with red hair and a prognathous jaw) who is building a super-atomic rocket to protect Britain 'and give us an independent say in world affairs'. Sir Hugo Drax is paying for its development himself at a site on the white cliffs between Dover and Deal and says he will then give it to the nation. Drax, the surname of real-life Jamaican slave-owners, also plays on dihydrogen dioxide, the hydrogen peroxide that fuels his rocket. Drax had made his fortune cornering the market in coltan (columbite-tantalite), the refractory metal now so valuable in superconductors for computers and mobile phones, but previously used to resist heat in jet engines. To build his rocket, Drax is using fifty German guided-missile experts, the ones the Russians did not capture in the Second World War. His right hand man is a Dr Walter, who likes his name pronounced Valter. 'Scratch a German and you find precision, thought Bond.' Drax eventually turns out to be a camouflaged Nazi (whom Bond calls a 'Kraut'), Graf Hugo von der Drache, who served under the German SS Obersturmbannführer Otto Skorzeny; ten years on he is still secretly fighting the war against Britain, but on behalf of the Russians. His cruel aide-de-camp is called Krebs, whose name is perhaps taken from the German Nobel Prize-winning biochemist Sir Hans Krebs, but is also a hidden reference both to the German trawler *Krebs,* from which Naval Intelligence pinched an Enigma machine early in the war, and to the real surname of the German Communist double agent 'Jan Valtin', author of *Out of the Night*, the book Fleming had told his commandos to read.

Half English himself, Drax loathes the English: 'Too weak to defend your colonies, toadying to America with your hat in your hands. Stinking snobs who'll do anything for money.' To this Fleming counterposes his own lyrical and romantic patriotism, much of it bound up with the beauty of the Kent countryside. He knew the county well, having bought Noël Coward's house 'White Cliffs' at St Margaret's Bay, where he liked to watch the ships in the English Channel through a telescope. It was close to his favourite golf club, the Royal St George's at Sandwich, 'the best seaside golf course in the world' (lightly disguised as the Royal St Mark's in *Goldfinger*), the place where Fleming lunched on his last day on earth in August 1964.

Bond discovers the truth: Sir Hugo Drax's rocket 'Moonraker' with its warhead is not a patriotic enterprise, but a nuclear dagger aimed at the heart of London. With one bound, however, Fleming's hero James Bond and the plucky girl Gala Brand alter the rocket's trajectory, ensuring that the atom bomb destroys the fast Russian submarine, together with Drax and all his Nazis on board.

German wartime science, industry and technology were lifted lock, stock and barrel by the British after the war. They became key not just to British defence but British manufacturing. German scientists were soon at work in ICI, Pears and Yardley, and files released by the National Archives in the summer of 2007 indicate that some scientists and technicians did not come to Britain voluntarily. At the war's end, CIOS became BIOS, British Intelligence Objectives Sub-Committee. By the beginning of 1948, it had distributed a million copies of its 2,720 detailed reports on German industry to British universities, learned societies and trade associations so the nation could profit from German knowledge. There were 280 reports on chemistry alone. The Board of Trade drew together critical summaries of their investigations in fifty *BIOS Overall Reports*. The first seven were on German petroleum and synthetic oil, ship-building and marine engineering, timber, glass, the road system, agriculture, and rubber. There were others on things like aluminium foil, building, cameras, carbon paper and typewriter ribbons, clocks and watches, drawing pins, electroplating, fibres, fountain pens, gelatin and glue, jute, lead, magnetic sound recorders, motorcycles, pulp and paper-making, paper packaging, liquid-proof cartons, corrugated paper and fibreboard packing cases, printing, photo-engraving, photographic film, plastics, railway mainline booking ticket-printing machines, textiles, typewriters, vegetable parchment, wood pulp, etc. 30AU's pinch of Helmuth Walter and his Walterwerk factory was the forerunner of industrial espionage on a massive scale.

As more time elapsed, the sheer scale of 30AU's other great pinch, at Tambach, became apparent. Initially the Royal Navy was unforthcoming about how considerable the archives were. The figure of thirty tons appears in some accounts, and that alone seems like an impressive amount of paper. But at a 1973 conference held by the US National Archives, the researcher Howard M. Ehrmann tried to quantify the German Naval Archives at Tambach, and the answer seems to be at least ten times bigger:

How large a collection was this? I never really learned its size, whether expressed in cubic feet, linear feet, or weight in tons; but I have always understood that it was a considerable collection, larger than the captured German Foreign Ministry records reputed to comprise more than four hundred tons of documents.

According to Colonel Robert Storey, who assembled the documents to indict the Nazi regime at the Nuremberg International Military Tribunal, those German Foreign Office records in fact weighed 485 tons. So if the naval archives were even larger, they must have constituted an awesome weight of historical record. Rarely if ever can any country have captured so much of another country's past.

Sixty thousand files were initially shipped to London in many thousands of Munich beer crates. The bulk of the older material, some dating back to 1847, went to the care of NID 24 at Bletchley Park in Buckinghamshire, while thousands of files from 1935 to 1945 went into a basement in the Admiralty in London.

Frank Birch, head of the Naval Section at Bletchley Park, was immediately concerned about who would be getting their hands on the files. In a Top Secret ULTRA message to the Deputy Director of Naval Staff on 5 July 1945, he requested authorisation for the Historical Committee, including himself and Dr J. H. Plumb, later the eminent historian of the eighteenth century at Cambridge. He was most anxious to get hold of all cipher and signals intelligence material, 'a largeish number of volumes containing mostly but not exclusively P/L [plain language] signals. There are also extremely hot documents such as the American Swiss agents' papers dotted about the collection.' As long as 'any such material does remain in Admiralty my people must have access to it. They are, in fact, the only people who *should* have access to it.'

But all kinds of people were after slices of the information. Technical specialists wanted translations of material dealing with their narrow concerns: anti-radar materials, boilers, diesel engines, equipment shared with the Japanese, fuels, hydrophones, mines, Schnorkel improvements, torpedoes, water-cooling systems, welding, etc., etc. While a dozen German-qualified 'Writers Special' under Lieutenant Long tried to catalogue and index the collection (with another twenty translating), and a team of Americans under Lieutenant Shelley were microfilming the documents with Recordaks for the US government, the files were also being combed through by a team of German-speaking Special Duties (Linguist) WRNS, looking for evidence of war crimes.

Too many cooks spoil the broth. In an exasperated memo of 21 July, Commander Geoffrey Tandy wrote: 'The situation in respect of the Tambach Archives is almost farcical.' Top of his list of seven competing parties was 'a) *Cdr. Fleming* who has been given liberty to do as he pleases . . . ' The NID set up the Captured Document Library (short title CDL) in August 1945 to organise the enormous task. Its main customers were the Admiralty Divisions and Technical Departments, the US Navy, Naval Intelligence and the GC&CS (now being called GCHQ) and other British ministries. Its functions included receipt and safe custody, registration and duplication, screening for security and subject matter, promulgation of accession lists and synopses, and exploitation, study and research.

A committee, under the DNI, but chaired by Captain G. E. Colpoys, met fortnightly for the rest of the year to iron out any problems with users or the material itself. In Block D, for example, 'the lately arrived Tambach Archives [the last ten to twelve tons] have been stored in Room 70 and 82b and they occupy the whole of this space as the crates were so heavy and unwieldy that we could not store them more than three crates high.' Colpoys's final plea, on 6 December 1945, was that the library 'not be divided and dispersed but housed in one collection' so that 'its contents may at all times be available for reference and study'.

The work went on. One Wren later recalled her excitement at discovering in the archives the memos of Admiral Raeder describing his meeting Vidkun Quisling in December 1939, which pointed to the German conspiracy to invade Norway. Raeder's personal files, together with the minutes of Hitler's conferences with the commanders-in-chief of the German navy, became key prosecution evidence at the Nuremberg trials. As a result, Erich Raeder was sentenced to life imprisonment, and Karl Dönitz to ten years for the crime of 'waging aggressive war'.

In their final thrusts of the Second World War, Ian Fleming's commandos helped bring Nazis to justice at Nuremberg, and German technology to Barrow-in-Furness. By pinching the paper records, the weapons technology and at least one top scientist from Germany at the moment of its defeat, 30AU managed to get its hands on the software of the past and the hardware of the future. These were no small achievements for a hush-hush 'private army' of never more than 300 people who were not quite approved of by top brass.

*

In the second decade of the twenty-first century, Ian Fleming's Commandos have come back to life. In 2010 the United Kingdom Landing Force Support Group, based at Royal Marines Barracks Stonehouse, changed its name to 30 Commando Information Exploitation Group as a tribute to the original 30 Commando/30 Assault Unit. Their 'intelligence assault unit' functions are identical: the current military acronym is ISTAR: Intelligence, Surveillance, Target Acquisition, Reconnaissance – exactly the work of 30AU.

30 Commando, disbanded in January 1946, was re-mustered on a crisp, cold Monday morning, 13 December 2010. There was a spectacular inauguration parade by 450 bootnecks in their blues on the parade-ground of Stonehouse barracks in Plymouth, in front of the Commandant General Royal Marines, Major General 'Buster' Howes, when the new yellow and blue standard of 30 Commando Information Exploitation Group Royal Marines was consecrated, with the words of the Royal Marines Prayer: 'May our laurels be those of gallantry and honour, loyalty and courage.'

At the end of that bright day, there was beating the retreat with drums and bugles and a formal regimental celebration dinner in the Commando Forces Officers' Mess in the high-windowed hall of the eighteenth-century barracks. After the meal, the commanding officer of the newly renamed unit spoke. In scarlet mess dress, Lieutenant Colonel Matt Bradford-Stovin declared the instituting of a new tradition. He pointed to a vacant chair opposite him across the silver-laden table and said that at formal dinners henceforth there would always be a full place setting laid for one whom 30 Commando wished to honour, and he asked us all to raise a glass to the first such invisible guest.

Peter Jemmett, Bill Marshall, Paul McGrath, Bill Powell, Bon Royle and the other survivors of 30AU were unable to be present that night. But they still remember the man whom some called Red and others Peter, and they were there in spirit when the chairs scraped back and the new serving officers all stood and solemnly drank a toast to the Royal Marine who led the first 30AU unit at Dieppe and died at a moment of victory in France: '*Herbert Oliver Huntington-Whiteley!*'

N

Ian Fleming did not perish in combat and lived on for another twenty years. After the war he became the Foreign Manager of Kemsley Newspapers, on £4,500 a year plus £500 expenses, with two months' guaranteed holiday every year that he spent in balmy Jamaica escaping the British winter, writing a Bond novel a year. He was successful and lived well, but it did not make him happy. Perhaps it is Fleming's inner voice that speaks through James Bond's thoughts in *Goldfinger*, written fourteen years after the end of the war: 'I asked for the easy life, the rich life. How do I like it? . . . He had asked and he had been given. It was the puritan in him that couldn't take it. He had made his wish and the wish had not only been granted, it had been stuffed down his throat.' *From Russia With Love* betrays the same loathing of his over-indulgence: 'the blubbery arms of the soft life . . . were slowly strangling him'.

Ian Fleming died of congestive heart failure in August 1964, at the relatively young age of fifty-six, on his only son Caspar's twelfth birthday, thus repeating the tragic pattern of his own father's death so close to Peter and Ian's birthdays. Fleming's last, somewhat neglected, story, 'Octopussy', was published posthumously in 1966. Anthony Burgess rightly called it 'brilliant', and it reads like a back-handed tribute to 30AU as well as a valedictory parable from the author.

The central character of 'Octopussy', Major Dexter Smythe,

OBE, RM (Retd) is 'the remains of a once brave and resourceful officer', an alcoholic of the melancholy sentimental kind, afflicted with 'guilt over an ancient sin', now balding and fat and running to seed in the tropics. In his fifties, he has had two coronary thromboses but still smokes like a chimney and goes to bed drunk every night. '[U]nder the varnished surface the termites of sloth, self-indulgence . . . and general disgust with himself had eroded his once hard core into dust.' Just like Ian Fleming, he lives on the North Shore of Jamaica and he spends much time snorkelling in the warm water by his five acres, enjoying the brightness and danger of submarine life, which had also supplied some of the most vivid pages of *Thunderball*. Life underwater is the kingdom of his imagination: the submarine creatures are his 'people' – he has a scientific and experimental interest in his aquatic creatures and gives an octopus that lives there the pet name 'Octopussy'. He particularly wants to know if an octopus can eat a deadly scorpion fish and survive.

Smythe, like Fleming, has been able to retire to Jamaica because of what he did in the war. The fictional antihero of 'Octopussy' had joined the Commandos in 1941 and been seconded to Combined Operations HQ under Mountbatten where his excellent German had earned him 'the unenviable job of being advanced interrogator on Commando operations across the Channel'. In preparation for the defeat of Germany

the Miscellaneous Objectives Bureau had been formed by the Secret Service and Combined Operations, and Major Smythe . . . [was] told to form a unit whose job would be the clearing up of Gestapo and Abwehr hide-outs . . . They were units of twenty men, each with a light armoured car, six jeeps, a wireless truck and three lorries, and they were controlled by a joint Anglo-American headquarters in SHAEF.

In the course of his duties with MOB A Force, Smythe comes across a piece of paper that leads him to two thick bars of Nazi gold, hidden under a cairn near Kitzbühel. To preserve the secret, he shoots the mountain guide who took him there and drops his dead body down a glacier crevasse. Then he struggles downhill with the bars, each weighing 24 kilograms, a total of around 105 pounds. After the war, he takes his wife and the gold to Jamaica and lives off it, selling a slice each month to Chinese dealers.

Is this Ian Fleming's final sardonic self-portrait? – a sentimental drunk in Jamaica, living off the capital of his war, doling it out in chunks, each book a different slice from the bar of gold? Smythe's gold is said to be not 'good delivery', because the Nazis contaminated their Reichsbank bullion with the addition of 10 per cent lead, not detectable by eye. And perhaps Fleming's literary intelligence, as well as the cultural snobbery of his wife, Ann, and her friends, told him there was something suspect in the thriller genre too, that it was not the 99.99 per cent pure gold of proper literature.

James Bond appears in this short story as a *deus ex machina*. He arrives at Smythe's house in Jamaica from the Ministry of Defence with questions about activities in the Tyrol at the end of the war. The body of the murdered guide has been found as the glacier melted, with bullets in his head matching those from Smythe's service revolver. Bond has found out all about Smythe's gold deals. The jig is up.

And why has Bond bothered? Because Hannes Oberhauser, the mountain guide that Smythe killed, was a friend. Bond says, 'He taught me to ski before the war, when I was in my teens. He was a wonderful man. He was something of a father to me at a time when I happened to need one.'

So Fleming is in both drunken Smythe and young Bond, who like him has lost his father. He can see himself in the present, as a decaying old sinner, and in the past, as a cleansing hero. Now Bond becomes the quiet agent of death, informing Smythe that somebody will come to arrest him in a week, in effect telling the corrupt old man to do the decent thing with the bottle of whisky and the revolver in the library.

Perhaps, in the final moments of the story, when brandy-fuddled Smythe continues his risky experiment among the bright and dangerous denizens of the North Shore reef, making his last fatal attempt to see if Octopussy can eat the poisonous scorpion fish, he is returning to the commando days of his youth, dying as he executes his last intelligence mission.

Acknowledgements

Every lonely author in a cell relies on the generosity and solidarity of countless others. The genesis of this book took place in the Imperial War Museum in Lambeth, south London, when I attended the press view of the centenary exhibition *For Your Eyes Only: Ian Fleming and James Bond* on 16 April 2008. In a room of the exhibition dedicated to Ian Fleming's wartime naval intelligence career I first met Kathleen Kinmonth Warren, the eldest daughter of Admiral John Godfrey, as well as Major Iain Dalzel-Job, the son of Patrick. Some weeks later, while researching pictures for my previous book *Churchill's Wizards* in the National Archives at Kew, the Deputy Manager of the Image Library, Hugh Alexander, slid across the desk two volumes of 30 Assault Unit photographs. 'That's Charles Wheeler,' I said, pointing to a young man with thick dark hair standing behind a jeep in Normandy. I had spoken to Sir Charles Wheeler on the telephone about his wartime work as an interrogator of captured German navy personnel. The great BBC reporter had been a twenty-one-year-old Royal Marines captain when he landed in Normandy with 30AU on D-Day. 'What was it like?' I asked. 'Noisy,' he replied. I wrote to him about the National Archive photos but got no reply because he died that summer, aged eighty-five, on American Independence Day, 4 July 2008. They sang 'Let My People Go' at his memorial service in Westminster Abbey six months later, appropriately for the man who had reported the US Civil Rights movement so memorably on British television in the 1960s. The memorial was held on the same day as President Barack Obama's inauguration, and I sat behind the delegation from the Royal Marines among people from 30AU. Just back from Cairo, where I had met Freddie Townsend, one of the two founders of the 30AU old comrades' association, I could hand a note from him to the other one, Peter Jemmett. Mrs Dianne Fisher, the widow of CSM Gordon Fisher RM and the indefatigable secretary of the 30AU Association, was also there. Compassionate, practical, cheerful, she proved an invaluable source of contacts and information, loaning me her copy of the rare first edition of *Attain by Surprise*. When the 30AU association held their last get-together at the Union Jack Club in London on 2 May 2009, Dianne spoke of the maladies of age that were inevitably taking their toll of the old and the bold. This book would not have existed without her help, and the assistance of all the men listed in the dedication. Of course, the errors and omissions are all mine.

The author is also grateful for the help of Abebooks, Dr Mark Baldwin, Mr William Bland, Dr Jörn Brinkhus, Mr Mark Bolland, Mr Mark Burman, Mr Stuart Christie, the Churchill Archives at Cambridge, Professor B. Jack Copeland, Mr Jim Crone, Ms Eleanor Crow, Mr Rolf Dahlo, Ms Lucy Fleming, Professor M. R. D. Foot, Professor Barbara Goodwin, Mrs Kate Grimond, Mr Arnold Hargreaves, Dr Andrew Hodges, Mrs Fanny Hugill, Lieutenant Commander Miles Huntington-Whiteley, Mr J. N. Houterman, Mr Miles Izzard, Ms Sabrina Izzard, Ms Janis Jorgensen, Mr Zdzislaw J. Kapera, Ms Margie Kinmonth, Dr Ralph Kinmonth, Mrs Julia Korner, the Lilly Library at Indiana University, the London Library, Mr Julian Loose, Mr Andrew Lycett, Mr Peter McAdie, Mr Hugh Macdougall, Sra Patricia Martínez de Vicente, Ms Ana Mendes, Mrs Eleanor Michel, the National Archives at Kew, Mrs Judith Neillands, Mr Thomas Parrish, Mr John Pearson, Professor Paul Preston, Mrs Marianne Rankin, Dr Joel Silver, Mr Andrew Trimbee, Dr Paula Turner, who edited, set and corrected the text, Ms Kate Ward, Professor Wesley K. Wark, Lady Wheeler and Mrs Pat Wiegele-Dajani, the daughter of 30AU's Freddie Townsend, for the kindest hospitality in Cairo. As ever, I could not have got this book done without the cajoling, cosseting and mental clarity of my darling wife, the novelist Maggie Gee, who edited my drafts and Rubik's Cubed the structure. Our beloved daughter Rosa Rankin-Gee also helped, by telling me I was too slow and writing a book faster herself, a novella that went on to win the inaugural Paris Literary Prize in June 2011.

The author and the publisher are grateful to the following for the use of copyright material. Every effort has been made to trace or contact the copyright holders of material quoted in the text. The publishers would be pleased to rectify any omissions or errors brought to their notice at the earliest opportunity.

Major Iain Dalzel-Job for *From Arctic Snow to Dust of Normandy* by his late father Patrick Dalzel-Job. © The Executors of Patrick Dalzel-Job, 2005.

The Ian Fleming estate for: *Casino Royale*, Copyright © 1953; *Moonraker*, Copyright © 1955; *From Russia with Love*, Copyright © 1957; *Goldfinger*, Copyright © 1959, *For Your Eyes Only*, Copyright © 1960; 'From a View to a Kill', Copyright © 1960; *Thunderball*, Copyright © 1961, *On Her Majesty's Secret Service*, Copyright © 1963; *You Only Live Twice*, Copyright © 1964; *Octopussy*, Copyright © 1966. Reproduced with permission of Ian Fleming Publications Ltd, London, www. ianfleming.com. Non-Bond words, e.g. Ian Fleming's report on Dieppe, 1942 and 1961, and his introduction to *Room 3603* by H.M. Hyde, 1963, are Copyright © Ian Fleming Will Trust.

Mrs Veronica Gosling for *The Commander*, the 'autobiographical novel of 1940–41' by her late father, Robert Henriques.

Mrs Fanny Hugill for *The Hazard Mesh: a naval commander's personal narrative* by her late husband, Lt-Cdr J. A. C. Hugill, DSC, RNVR.

Squadron Leader David Colver Nutting MBE, RAFVR for *Attain By Surprise: capturing top secret intelligence in World War II*, which he edited in 1997 and 2003.

ACKNOWLEDGEMENTS

The John Pearson manuscripts, compiled for *The Life of Ian Fleming*, are courtesy of the Lilly Library, Indiana University, Bloomington, Indiana.

Once There Was a War by John Steinbeck (The Viking Press Inc., 1958, Penguin Books 1977, 1986, 1994, Penguin Classics 2000). Copyright © John Steinbeck 1943, 1958. Copyright renewed Elaine Steinbeck, John Steinbeck IV, and Thom Steinbeck, 1971, 1986. Reproduced by permission of Penguin Books Ltd (UK) and Viking Penguin, a division of Penguin Group (USA) Inc.

Source Notes

PROLOGUE

The excellent *Secrecy News*, an online publication of the Federation of American Scientists' Project on Government Secrecy, written by Stephen Aftergood, reported the suppression of *Operation Dark Heart* in September 2010.

Much of the official history of 30 Assault Unit is in the bound volumes from the NID now in the National Archives (TNA) at Kew in London. ADM 223/214 contains the narrative written by Lieutenant Commander Trevor James Glanville RNVR, assisted by Margaret Priestley, in 1946–7, plus significant addenda not in the copy at HW 8/104. ADM 223/500 and 501 have miscellaneous papers and target lists, ADM 202/598 and 599 contain photographs, and 30AU's unit diaries are in ADM 202/308.

Thirty years after compiling the history, Glanville was a prime mover in re-uniting the old comrades of 30 Assault Unit. The first London get-together of 30AU was at the annual Commando reunion on 28 April 1979 and their last, thirty years later, was at the Union Jack Club on 2 May 2009. Glanville assisted A. Cecil Hampshire in writing *The Secret Navies* (Kimber, 1978); the third and final part, 'Sailors in Jeeps' is about Ian Fleming's Commandos. He did a lot of work on his own autobiography but died in 1991 before completing it. Many of the papers he helped gather from thirty-three old comrades and the Public Record Office were pulled together by Squadron Leader David Nutting MBE RAFVR in the volume *Attain by Surprise: the story of 30 Assault Unit, Royal Navy/Royal Marine Commando, and of intelligence by capture* (David Colver, 1997; revised second edition, *Attain by Surprise: capturing top secret intelligence in WWII*, 2003). Two boxes of surviving papers from this project are in the Liddell Hart Centre for Military Archives at King's College, London, reference GB99 KCLMA History of 30 Assault Unit, 1942–1946. I have drawn on all these writings and on some survivors' memories.

The success of James Bond is undeniable: a survey of British crime/thriller writers in April 2011 found that Ian Fleming had outsold even Agatha Christie. The inaugural parade of 30 Commando is visible at: http://www.bbc.co.uk/news/uk-england-devon-11980837. Bond can be found thinking 'nostalgically and unreasonably' in chapter 24 of *From Russia With Love*.

1 DAY TRIP TO DIEPPE, 1942

Ian Fleming first wrote an account of the Dieppe raid for the NID's Weekly Intelligence Report in 1942. A 1961 version was published exclusively in *Talk of the Devil* (Queen Anne Press, 2008). From the copy kindly shown me by Fleming's niece (and editor of the volume) Kate Grimond, I drew the Lucian Truscott story and other details of what Fleming saw and heard that day. Hunter class destroyer descriptions come from Wallace Reyburn's *Glorious Chapter: the Canadians at Dieppe* (Harrap, 1943). The other reporters on the raid whose books came out in the same year, A. B. Austin, *We Landed at Dawn* (Gollancz) and Quentin Reynolds, *Dress Rehearsal* (Random House), are also valuable sources of colour and information. Churchill described Dieppe as a 'reconnaissance in force' rather than a 'Commando raid' to the House of Commons on 8 September 1942.

Dieppe features in Bernard Fergusson's history of Combined Operations, *The Watery Maze* (Collins, 1961) in the chapter tellingly entitled 'Trial and Error', and among other books consulted on Dieppe are Christopher Buckley's history, *Norway: The Commandos: Dieppe*, for HMSO in 1951, R. W. Thompson, *Dieppe at Dawn* (White Lion, 1956), Terence Robertson, *The Shame and the Glory: Dieppe* (McClelland & Stewart, 1962), Brian Loring

Villa, *Unauthorized Action: Mountbatten and the Dieppe Raid 1942* (OUP, 1989), Tim Saunders, *Dieppe* (Pen & Sword, 2005), Jim DeFelice, *Rangers at Dieppe* (Berkley Caliber, 2008) and Sir Martin Gilbert, *The Routledge Atlas of the Second World War* (Routledge, 2008). The radar expert was Jack Nissenthal and his story is told in James Leasor, *Green Beach* (Heinemann, 1975). The jacket Fleming wore on the raid was displayed at the Imperial War Museum in its 2008–9 centenary exhibition *For Your Eyes Only: Ian Fleming and James Bond*. Lieutenant Commander Peter Scott noticed the smell of hay, as recorded in chapter VIII of *The Battle of the Narrow Seas* (Country Life, 1945). Paul McGrath gave me a copy of his account of Dieppe, privately published in 1992, as well as a copy of John Kruthoffer's, when we first met at his home in March 2009. The problem with the pebbles is described by Hugh G. Henry Jr in *Dieppe Through the Lens of the German War Photographer* (After the Battle, 1993).

Churchill recounts the formation of the Commandos in chapter 12, 'The Apparatus of Counter-Attack, 1940', in *Their Finest Hour*, vol. 2 of *The Second World War* (Folio Society, 2002). For more on the army commandos I drew on Hilary St George Saunders, *The Green Beret* (Michael Joseph, 1949), Derek Mills-Roberts, *Clash by Night* (William Kimber, 1956), Lord Lovat, *March Past* (Weidenfeld & Nicolson, 2nd edition, 1979), Charles Messenger, *The Commandos 1940–1946* (William Kimber 1985, Grafton Books 1991), James Dunning, *'It Had To Be Tough'* (Pentland Press, 2000) and Tim Moreman, *British Commandos 1940–1946* (Osprey, 2006). John Parker's *Commandos* (Headline, 2000) used the Imperial War Museum interview with William Spearman (Accession no. 009797/08, reel 4) in which the former commando alleged that tied-up prisoners had been shot on Orange Beach at Dieppe. Will Fowler, in *The Commandos at Dieppe: rehearsal for D-Day* (HarperCollins, 2002), although not denying that defenders were probably killed in the heat of battle while trying to surrender, finds no evidence that any German soldiers were shot while tied up as prisoners. British wounded with their medical orderlies were also left behind on the beach; such a war crime would have been their death warrant. Both Parker and Fowler cite the Hitler order in full. Ross Munro's considered account of the landing he witnessed is in chapter XIII, 'Dieppe – Key to Invasion' of *Gauntlet to Overlord: the story of the Canadian Army* (Macmillan, 1946).

For the Royal Marines, see James D. Ladd, *Royal Marine Commando* (Hamley, 1982). For accounts of what happened in the mechanised landing craft, and all snatches of dialogue, I have drawn on the memoirs by Paul McGrath, John Kruthoffer and also Jock Farmer in *Jock of 40 Royal Marine Commando: my life from start to finish* (Shanklin Chine, 2007). Marine James Spencer's story was quoted in the anthology of personal experience edited by John Winton, *Freedom's Battle*, volume 1: *The War at Sea 1939–45* (Hutchinson, 1967). The Goronwy Rees quote comes from *A Bundle of Sensations: sketches in autobiography* (Chatto & Windus, 1960). I found the statistics on Canadian casualties in *The 1942 Dieppe Raid* (Veteran Affairs Canada, 2005), plus many other books, photos and memoirs concerning JUBILEE in the Library and Archives Canada, Ottawa, in October 2009. The nautical descriptions of M come from chapter 4 of Ian Fleming's *Moonraker* and chapter 12 of *From Russia With Love*.

2 THE GODFATHER

'China, Abyssinia, Spain, Czechoslovakia', Lloyd George's speech about appeasement, is quoted in *Keesing's Contemporary Archives* (hereafter *KCA*), p. 3292, section D. The naval statistics come from Brian Lavery, *Churchill's Navy: the ships, men and organisation*, (Conway Maritime Press, 2006), p. 9. 'To collect, classify and record' is from F. H. Hinsley, *British Intelligence in the Second World War* (5 vols, HMSO, 1979–90), vol. 1, p. 7. The single officer in the 'Movements Section' labours in Patrick Beesly, *Very Special Intelligence: the story of the Admiralty's Operational Intelligence*

Centre, 1939–1945 (Hamish Hamilton, 1977), p. 10. Franco's appeal to Mussolini for submarines is noted in Hugh Thomas, *The Spanish Civil War* (Penguin/Pelican, 1977), p. 739. Information on the Y listening service comes from John Pether's *Funkers and Sparkers* (Bletchley Park Report no. 17, 2000). Spotters' payments were recorded in *The Times*, 18 March 1940, p. 10, Col D. Bill Cordeaux's comment about 'shocking inefficiency' is in the Churchill Archives Centre's holding of the McLachlan/Beesly papers at MLBE/1.

Patrick Beesly's biography of Admiral John Godfrey is entitled *Very Special Admiral* (Hamish Hamilton, 1980). The founding of the JIC is described in Patrick Howarth's life of William Cavendish-Bentinck, the ninth Duke of Portland, *Intelligence Chief Extraordinary* (Bodley Head, 1986). Details of Field Security Police at UK ports come from Lord Hankey's Inquiry into SIS and MI5, as printed in Nigel West and Oleg Tsarev, *Triplex: secrets from the Cambridge spies* (Yale University Press, 2009), p. 220. Adolf Hitler's speech about 'the annihilation of the Jewish race in Europe' is reported in *KCA* p. 3427, section E, and his insulting phrase about Neville Chamberlain is recorded in Christopher Andrews's centenary history of MI5, *The Defence of the Realm* (Penguin, 2009), p. 205. Planning the invasion of Poland 'only three days later' appears on p. 29 of the *Fuehrer Conferences on Naval Affairs,* edited by Jak P. Mallmann Showell (Chatham Publishing, 2005). There is a good section on OB40 of the British Admiralty during the First World War in David Kahn's *The Codebreakers: the story of secret writing* (Weidenfeld & Nicolson, 1967), p. 266–97. 'The greatest Intelligence coup in history' comes from Patrick Beesly, *Room 40: British Naval Intelligence 1914–18* (Hamish Hamilton, 1982), p. 224. 'I learned anew, every day' is from Churchill Archives Centre MLBE 1/1. The Parliamentary activities of Lloyd George, Churchill and Eden are reported in *KCA* p. 3584, section B. For Godfrey's indebtedness to Reggie Hall, see Donald McLachlan, *Room 39: Naval Intelligence in action 1939-1945* (Weidenfeld and Nicolson, 1968), pp. 17–18.

The Flemings have their own bank. Details about the wealth and property of Ian and Peter Fleming's grandfather come from Bill Smith, *Robert Fleming 1845–1933* (Whittinghame House Publishing, 2000), pp. 27, 115, 145. Peter's reaction to his father's death is from p. 28 of the biography by Duff Hart-Davis, *Peter Fleming* (Oxford University Press, 1974), where Peter's 'preliminary canter' with Military Intelligence is noted on p. 208. Andrew Lycett (whose well-researched biography, *Ian Fleming* (Weidenfeld & Nicolson, 1995), is acute on his social milieu) cited his desire for weekly albatross delivery in the *Times Literary Supplement*, 30 April 2008. The description of Peter Fleming, 'a subtly comic figure . . . the pukka sahib' is from W. H. Auden and Christopher Isherwood, *Journey to a War* (Faber, 1973), p. 156. Ian Fleming recorded 'hero-worshipping my elder brother Peter' on the first page of his introduction to H. Montgomery Hyde, *Room 3603: the story of the British intelligence center in New York during World War II* (Farrar, Strauss & Co., 1962).

Details about the intriguing Alan Hillgarth come from his entry in the online *Oxford Dictionary of National Biography*, written by Denis Smyth. Godfrey's keenness on smart uniforms is mentioned in Brian Lavery, *Hostilities Only: training the wartime Royal Navy* (National Maritime Museum, 2005)p. 168. *Wavy Navy: by some who served* (Harrap, 1950) and *The R.N.V.R: a record of achievement* (Harrap, 1957) both by J. Lennox Kerr, with David James and Wilfred Granville respectively, describe life in the Royal Naval Volunteer Reserve, to which Brian Lavery's *In Which They Served: the Royal Navy officer experience in the Second World War* (Conway Maritime, 2008) is a good adjunct. The *RNVR Roll of Honour 1939–45* (Wave Heritage Trust, 2001) contains the names of over 6,000 officers and ratings from the British Empire who volunteered and perished. 'Well, there it is,' the Ted Merrett interview, conducted on 14 March 1965, is in the John Pearson papers in the Lilly Library of Indiana University at Bloomington.

3 TECHNOLOGY AND WAR

The Lilly Library owns the typescripts of the James Bond novels as well as Ian Fleming's unusual collection of scientific books, whose catalogue is online: http://www.indiana.edu/~liblilly/etexts/fleming/index.shtml. For more on Ian Fleming's book-collecting, see P. H. Muir, 'Ian Fleming: a personal memoir' in *The Book Collector* (vol. 14, no. 1, Spring 1965, pp. 24–33) and Joel Silver's entry in the *Dictionary of Literary Biography*, (*DLB*) 201, pp. 81–8. John Godfrey turning up in mid-July 1939 is noted in Mavis Batey's biography of the code-breaker Alfred Dillwyn Knox, *Dilly: the man who broke Enigmas* (Dialogue, 2009). The visit of Humphrey Sandwith, the man who ran the Admiralty Y service, to Poland with Alastair Denniston and Dilly Knox is described in Robin Denniston's book about his father, *Thirty Secret Years: A. G. Denniston's work in signals intelligence 1914–1944* (Polperro Heritage Press, 2007), pp. 118–20, although his name is mis-spelled there as 'Sandwich'. Ian Fleming's contribution to Section 17 of Naval Intelligence is described in the first chapter of McLachlan, *Room 39*. Lewis Mumford's view of the photograph is in *Technics and Civilization* (Harcourt, Brace & Co, 1934), p. 339, and the paradox that war stimulates the very inventions that the military then resist is on p. 95. The interview of 2 July 1965 with Sydney Cotton is among the Pearson papers in the Lilly Library. SIS agent Group Captain F. W. Winterbotham is famous for revealing *The Ultra Secret* (Weidenfeld & Nicolson 1974), but he also wrote another book about his spy work, *The Nazi Connection* (Weidenfeld & Nicolson, 1978), which touches on the RAF's possessiveness over aerial photography on p. 201.

Hitler's 'weapon which is not yet known and with which we could not ourselves be attacked' is reported in *KCA* p. 3736, section G. Admiralty detective work on enemy mining is described in the first two chapters of *Secret Naval Investigator* (William Kimber, 1961) by Commander Ashe Lincoln QC, with further details from Captain J.

S. Cowie's *Mines, Minelayers and Minelaying* (OUP, 1949). Winston Churchill's remark, 'about the lowest form of warfare', comes from the *Into Battle* volume of his collected speeches, p. 150. '45 British and neutral ships', see *Fuehrer Conferences on Naval Affairs*, p. 57.

Hugh Trevor-Roper's acerbic view of Claude Dansey is quoted in Anthony Read and David Fisher, *Colonel Z* (Hodder & Stoughton, 1984), p. 12. Sigismund Payne Best wrote *The Venlo Incident* (Hutchinson, 1950) and Louis Hagen edited and translated *The Schellenberg Memoirs* (André Deutsch, 1956). Nigel West's claim that Best and Stevens revealed a lot about British Intelligence is in his preface to an edition of Walter Schellenberg, *Invasion 1940: the Nazi invasion plan for Britain* (St Ermin's Press, 2000). For Ralph Izzard's adventure at Venlo, see 'Saved from Germans by Woman', *Daily Mail*, 12 November 1940. Professor R. V. Jones told the full story of the Oslo report in his *Reflections on Intelligence* (Mandarin, 1990), pp. 265–337. (It is depressing to contrast that salutary book with one written two decades later by a modern scientist who had exactly the same role in government service: Brian Jones, *Failing Intelligence: the true story of how we were fooled into going to war in Iraq* (Biteback, 2010)) The 'wholesale massacre of slave labourers' is from Captain F. Ashe Lincoln QC RNVR, *Odyssey of a Jewish Sailor* (Minerva Press, 1995), pp. 20–1.

4 THE PHILOSOPHY OF THE PINCH

Information on First World War 'pinches' comes from Patrick Beesly, *Room 40*, pp. 3–4, 265–6 and Kahn, *The Codebreakers*, pp. 268, 274. Bletchley Park's 'cinema and one mouldy café' is from recollections of Margaret Cordy, edited by Marian McGuire, in *Everyone's War*, no. 21, summer 10, p. 48. I attended the launch of Mavis Batey's biography of Dilly Knox at Bletchley Park in 2009. She talks to Michael Smith here: http://audioboo.fm/boos/312656-chatting-with-ww2-code-breaker-mavis-batey. The cover phrase, 'in the country', is mentioned by S. John Peskett in *Strange Intelligence: from Dunkirk to Nuremberg* (Robert Hale, 1981), p. 106. For the pinch by John Cairncross, the 'Fifth Man', see West and Tsarev, *Triplex*, pp. 193–4.

The online site uboat.net is a valuable source of submarine information, and the U-33 pinch is also described in chapter 8 of David Kahn, *Seizing the Enigma: the race to break the German U-boat codes* (Arrow Books, 1996), chapter 6 of Hugh Sebag-Montefiore, *Enigma: the battle for the code* (Folio, 2005), chapter 5 of Alastair Alexander, *Action Stations! U-boat warfare in the Clyde* (Neil Wilson Publishing, 2009) and Jak P. Mallmann Showell, *Enigma U-Boats: breaking the code* (Ian Allan, 2009), p. 34. Further information about Enigma machines is drawn from David P. Mowry, *German Cipher Machines of WW2* (Center for Cryptologic History, NSA, 2003), Hugh Alexander, *Cryptographic History of Work on the German Naval Enigma* (TNA, HW25/1), Patrick Mahon, *History of Hut Eight* (TNA, HW25/2), Gordon Welchman, *The Hut Six Story: breaking the Enigma codes* (Mark Baldwin, 2000), Stephen Budiansky, *Battle of Wits: the complete story of codebreaking in WWII* (Viking, 2000), plus *Action This Day: Bletchley Park from the breaking of the Enigma code to the birth of the first computer* (Bantam Press, 2001), edited by Michael Smith and Ralph Erskine, as well as many of the essays in *Colossus: the secrets of Bletchley Park's codebreaking computers* (Oxford University Press, 2006), edited by the admirable Professor B. Jack Copeland, who also edited *The Essential Turing* (Oxford, 2004). Details about Turing are also drawn from Andrew Hodges' fine biography *Alan Turing: the enigma* (Vintage, 1992). The historian Asa Briggs has written one of the most valuable memoirs of BP, *Secret Days: code-breaking in Bletchley Park* (Frontline Books, 2011).

Norwegian ship losses are recorded in *KCA* p. 3997A, and useful books on Norway in 1940 include J. L. Moulton, *The Norwegian Campaign of 1940: a study of warfare in three dimensions* (Eyre & Spottiswoode, 1966), Douglas C. Dildy, *Denmark and Norway 1940: Hitler's boldest operation* (Osprey, 2007) and Henrik O.

Lunde, *Hitler's Pre-emptive War: the battle for Norway 1940* (Casemate Books, 2008). The interesting essays in the volume edited by Patrick Salmon, *Britain and Norway in the Second World War* (HMSO, 1995), cover the subsequent resistance and Allied intelligence-gathering as well. '80 per cent of the high-grade iron ore' is from Showell, *Fuehrer Conferences on Naval Affairs*, p. 79. '130 tons of bombs and aviation fuel' is from Admiral Karl Dönitz, *Memoirs: ten years and twenty days* (Cassell Military Paperbacks, 2001), p. 81.

The inadequacy of British code-breaking and the superiority of German cryptology early in the war is cited in McLachlan, *Room 39*, p. 83; Hinsley, *British Intelligence*, vol. 2, p. 635; R. A. Ratcliff, *Delusions of Intelligence: Enigma, Ultra and the end of secure ciphers* (Cambridge University Press, 2006), p. 50; Kenneth Macksey, *The Searchers: radio intercept in two world wars* (Cassell, 2004), p. 77; David Kahn, *Hitler's Spies: German military intelligence in WW2* (Macmillan, 1978), pp. 215–17. F. H. Hinsley's account of warning the Operational Intelligence Centre is in *Codebreakers: the inside story of Bletchley Park* (OUP, 1994), ed. F. H. Hinsley and A. Stripp, chapter 10, p. 78, and the invasion 'by surprise' in volume 1 of *British Intelligence*, pp.115–25.

For the phrase Hitler 'has missed the bus', see *KCA* 3994 A and B. The tourist brochures and cruise photographs come from Churchill Archives, MLBE 1/1. 'Sweet Fanny Adams' is from D. McLachlan, *Room 39*, p. 413. Patrick Dalzel Job (who hyphenated his name after the war and is hyphenated throughout here) described his northern adventures in the first two chapters of his wartime autobiography, *Arctic Snow to Dust of Normandy: the extraordinary wartime exploits of a naval special agent*, (Alan Sutton, 1991, republished Pen & Sword, 2005). 'Wounding the still, dark surface' is quoted in Duff Hart-Davis, *Peter Fleming*, p. 224 and 'really do what you like' from pp. 229–30. Peter Fleming's papers are at the University of Reading and the MAURICEFORCE manuscript is MS 1391, box 28. Neville Chamberlain's 'quite impossible' is from the National Archives, CAB/65/7/1. 'Big yellow rats' is from Don Scott, *Polar Bears from Sheffield: a memorial to the Hallamshire Battalion of the York and Lancaster Regiment* (Tiger & Rose Publications, 2001), pp. 47–8. The descriptions of Colin Gubbins come from chapter 2 of *The Inner Circle: a view of war from the top* (Quality Book Club, 1972) by Joan Bright Astley, who also wrote *Gubbins and SOE* (Leo Cooper, 1997) with Peter Wilkinson, and from Donald Hamilton-Hill, *SOE Assignment* (Kimber, 1973), p. 10 and Captain W. R. Fell, *The Sea Our Shield* (Cassell, 1966), p. 60. Lieutenant Colonel Martin Lindsay wrote *Those Greenland Days* (Blackwood, 1932) and *Sledge* (Cassell, 1935), and Jonathon P. Riley the life of Quintin Riley, *From Pole to Pole* (Bluntisham Books, 1989). Charles Glasfurd's last smoke on the bridge is recorded in Lunde, *Hitler's Pre-emptive War*, p. 535.

Sir Harry Hinsley describes the failures of the Norway campaign in *British Intelligence*, vol. 1, pp. 137–42, and in Hinsley and Stripp (eds) *Codebreakers*, p. 78. The 'Narvik pinch', the seizure of *Polares* by HMS *Arrow*, is described in Kahn, *Seizing the Enigma*, p. 116, Sebag-Montefiore, *Enigma*, pp. 73–5 and the obituary of Alec Dennis is in the *Daily Telegraph*, 20 July 2008. In the National Archives at Kew, the 900 or so volumes, files and dockets from the old NID at the Admiralty are now to be found under ADM 223. Lieutenant George Pennell's trip to Orkney is in ADM 223/502, 'Security of Intelligence in Connection with Captured Ships'. Churchill's speech about Iceland is in *KCA* 4003A and Quill's account of the taking of Reykjavík in Operation FORK is in MLBE 1/16 in the Churchill Archives. Other details come from McLachlan, *Room 39*, pp. 265–8.

5 DOING DEALS

Admiral Darlan's promise to Winston Churchill is recorded in *Their Finest Hour*, p. 127. 'The Germans are only in the south of Paris' is from John Pearson, *The Life of Ian Fleming* (Aurum

Press, 2003), p. 118. Patrick Beesly personally facilitated Godfrey's wireless talk with Fleming in Tours, see *Very Special Admiral*, p. 158. Charles de Gaulle's wartime speeches are at www.france-libre. net. 'They bribed, cajoled and commanded', Brooks Richards, *Secret Flotillas, vol. 1: Clandestine Sea Operations to Brittany, 1940–1944* (Routledge, 2004), p. 26. Virginia Cowles's description of Bordeaux is from *Looking for Trouble* (Hamish Hamilton, 1942), p. 408. 'Cutting their run to the battle of the Atlantic by seven days' was cited in a talk, 'The War in the Atlantic', by Janet Dempsey at the National Archives on 3 September 2009.

The seizing of the French naval codes is recorded in Beesly, *Very Special Admiral*, p. 159, and on p. 40 of Charles Morgan's account of NID 9 and NID 17 in TNA ADM 223/463. David Brown, *The Road to Oran: Anglo-French naval relations, September 1939–July 1940* (Routledge, 2004) illuminates a sombre episode very well. 'Thoroughly dirty and ashamed' is from Colin Smith, *England's Last War Against France: fighting Vichy 1940–42* (Orion, 2010), p. 86. Churchill's parliamentary speech about Mers-el-Kébir, 'The Tragedy of the French Fleet', 4 July 1940, is in *Into Battle*, pp. 239–46, and the reaction to it is described by Harold Nicolson, *Diaries and Letters 1939–45* (Fontana, 1971), p. 97.

For '"Ardent sympathy" for the Axis' and the occupation of Tangier, see *KCA* p. 4110A. Spain 'near starvation', J. A. Fernández López, *Historia del Campo de Concentración de Miranda de Ebro (1937–1947)* (Miranda de Ebro, 2003), p. 91. 'I do not know how we shall carry on', Viscount Templewood, *Ambassador on Special Mission* (Collins, 1946), p. 16. Hillgarth's report, with the phrase about not snooping, is in TNA ADM 223/490. The Royal Marine Colonel Charles Thoroton ('Charles the Bold') succeeded the novelist A. E. W. Mason as 'Blinker' Hall's man in Spain in the First World War and features in Beesly, *Room 40*, pp. 190–200 and David Ramsay, *'Blinker' Hall: Spymaster* (Spellmount, 2008), pp. 247–51, which describes how he blocked Basque wolfram from getting to German steel works. 'Ian's decisive intervention' is in Lycett, *Ian*

Fleming, p. 110. Churchill's comments on Sir Andrew Duncan's letter are in the National Archives at ADM 1/9809 and the Juan March financial details in PREM 4/32/7 and T236/6154. The modern value of gold is calculated at the late 2010 price of US$1,300 per oz.

For 'most Americans against involvement in a European war', see Gore Vidal, *Times Literary Supplement*, 1 December 2000. 'The Norden bomb sight' is in Thomas F. Troy, *Wild Bill and Intrepid: Donovan, Stephenson and the origin of C.I.A* (Yale University Press, 1996), p. 54, and Alan Harris Bath, *Tracking the Axis Enemy: the triumph of Anglo-American naval intelligence* (University Press of Kansas, 1998), pp. 27–8. 'Lending a hose to a neighbour', see Ian Kershaw, *Fateful Choices: ten decisions that changed the world, 1940–41* (Penguin Press, 2007), p. 227. 'The most far-reaching . . . exchange of military secrets' is described in David Zimmerman, *Top Secret Exchange: the Tizard Mission and the scientific war* (Alan Sutton, 1996). Lord Lothian's aide-memoire to Roosevelt, 9 July 1940, is at http://www.nsa.gov/public_info/declass/ukusa.shtml.

'10-centimetre radars' are in Donald Macintyre, *The Battle of the Atlantic* (Macmillan, 1969), p. 148. There is a huge literature on radar in the Second World War but for the basic facts and concepts see J. G. Crowther and R. Whiddington, *Science at War* (HMSO, 1947), pp. 1–89; F. J. Wylie (editor), *The Use of Radar at Sea* (Hollis & Carter, 1952), pp. 1–35; M. M. Postan, D. Hay and J. D. Scott, *Design and Development of Weapons* (Longmans, Green & Co, 1964), pp. 373–430; Guy Hartcup, *The Challenge of War: scientific and engineering contributions to World War Two* (David & Charles, 1970), pp. 93–156; Brian Johnson, *The Secret War* (BBC, 1978), pp. 63–122; Colin Latham and Anne Stobbs, *Radar: a wartime miracle* (Sutton Publishing, 1996) and Paddy Heazell, *Most Secret: the hidden history of Orford Ness* (The History Press, 2010), pp. 67–102. The 'thyratron' is described in Barry Vyse and George Jessop, *The Saga of Marconi-Osram Valve: a history of valve-making* (Vyse, 2000), pp. 252–3. For the Japanese 'forced into kamikaze suicide tactics', see Jones, *Reflections on Intelligence*, p. 311.

'FBI had enquired', see TNA HW 14/45. Thomas Parrish, in *The American Codebreakers: the US role in Ultra* (Scarborough House, 1991) was one of the first to dig in this area. 'A free exchange of intelligence' is described in Bradley F. Smith, *The Ultra-Magic Deals: and the most secret special relationship 1940–1946* (Airlife, 1993), pp. 43–4 and Christopher Andrew's essay, 'The Making of the Anglo-American SIGINT Alliance', from *In the Name of Intelligence: essays in honor of Walter Pforzheimer* (NIBC, 1994), p. 99. On 24 June 2010, the US and UK governments released more information about their early signals intelligence collaboration: at http://www.nsa.gov/public_info/press_room/2010/ukusa.shtml see UKUSA Agreement Release 1940–56, 'Early Papers Concerning US–UK Agreement 1940–44', pp. 18–24.

Ian Fleming's involvement with Spain is in ADM 223/480 and 490 and further Goldeneye matters are in CAB 84/28/241. On escape routes through Iberia, see M. R. D. Foot and J. M. Langley, *MI9: escape and evasion 1939–1945* (Bodley Head, 1979), pp. 71–81, and for the Pat O'Leary escape line the website http://www.conscript-heroes.com. Before the war, MI5's first DSOs (defence security officers) abroad were in Cairo, Palestine and Gibraltar. The history section of the British Security Service website https://www.MI5.gov.uk contains 'The Battle for Gibraltar 1942–45', but the fuller, illustrated account of the fight against espionage and sabotage can be found in two volumes in the National Archives, KV4/259 and 260. A good description of the different British secret agencies based on 'the Rock' is in Desmond Bristow's autobiography, *A Game of Moles: the deceptions of an MI6 officer* (Little, Brown, 1993). See also Appendix E of Brooks Richards, *Secret Flotillas, vol 2*, pp. 669–88.

SIS work in Spain features in Keith Jeffery, *MI6: the history of the Secret Intelligence Service 1909–1949* (Bloomsbury, 2010), pp. 402–10 and Section V (counter-espionage) work in Kenneth Benton, 'The ISOS Years: Madrid 1941–3', *Journal of Contemporary History*, vol. 30 (1995) pp. 359–412; see also the obituary of Benton in Wolverhampton Grammar School *Old Wulfrunian News*, 2000. The Abwehr branch in Madrid (the biggest outside Germany) is described in Richard Deacon, *The Silent War: a history of western naval intelligence* (Grafton, 1988), pp. 140–3. Writing under his real name, Donald McCormick, the same author suggests on p. 107 of *17F: the life of Ian Fleming* (Peter Owen, 1993) that Fleming toyed with kidnapping Canaris in southern Spain. On Himmler in Spain, see Domingo Pastor Petit, *Espionaje: la segunda guerra mundial y España* (Plaza & Janés, 1990), p. 757. For the list of 6,000 Spanish Jews, see Jorge M. Reverte, 'La lista de Franco para el Holocausto', *El País*, 20 June 2010; Giles Tremlett, 'Franco gave list of Spanish Jews to Nazis', *The Guardian*, 21 June 2010. 'Not a hero but a pipsqueak' (*statt eines Heroen ein Würstchen*) is from *Hitler's Table Talk 1941-44* (Weidenfeld & Nicolson, 1953), edited by Hugh Trevor-Roper, p. 569. Paul Preston's essay, 'Franco and Hitler: The Myth of Hendaye 1940', appeared in *Contemporary European History*, vol. 1, no. 1, (March 1992) and other accounts of the meeting are in Ian Kershaw, *Hitler* (Penguin, 2009), p. 582 and two books by Stanley G. Payne: *Fascism in Spain 1923–1977* (University of Wisconsin Press, 2000), pp. 332–6 and *Franco and Hitler: Spain, Germany and WW2* (Yale University Press, 2008), pp. 90–5.

Juan March telling Alan Hillgarth 'the Spanish government would resist' is in the Churchill Archives Cambridge, MLBE 1/16 MISC. Dr E. Martínez Alonso's daughter, Patricia Martínez de Vicente, has written more about her father saving people from Nazi persecution in *La clave Embassy* (La Esfera, 2010). Gibraltarian construction work features in *After the Battle*, no. 21 (1978) pp. 15–23, and Admiral Godfrey's secret stay-behind cave is in ADM 223/464; Jim Crone has done further investigations at www. discovergibraltar.com.

On funding for Bill Donovan's trip see Gill Bennett, *Churchill's Man of Mystery: Desmond Morton and the world of intelligence* (Routledge, 2006), p. 257 and note 54. Alex Danchev edited

Establishing the Anglo-American Alliance: the Second World War diaries of Brigadier Vivian Dykes (Brassey's, 1990), where the Donovan trip is covered in pp. 24–65. Hillgarth's 25 March 1941 letter to Godfrey about the 'dangerous amateurish activities' of SOE is in the Churchill Archives. 'Bridled and delayed' is in McLachlan, *Room 39*, pp. 204–6. The 'Bodden beams' saga at the straits of Gibraltar also features in 'El Hatto', chapter 29 of R. V. Jones, *Most Secret War (The Wizard War* in USA*): British scientific intelligence 1939–1945* (Hamish Hamilton, 1978), pp. 254–9; Templewood, *Ambassador on Special Mission* , pp. 162–4; Ewen Montagu, *Beyond Top Secret Ultra* (Peter Davies, 1977), pp. 90–1; and Jeffery, *MI6* , p. 408. The clearest (and annotated) overview is Ralph Erskine's 'Eavesdropping on 'Bodden': ISOS v. the Abwehr in the straits of Gibraltar', in *Intelligence and National Security*, vol. 12, issue 3, July 1997, pp. 110–29.

6 THE COMMANDOS GET CRACKING

The statistics of French killed, wounded and captured in 1940 are from Alan Shepperd, *France 1940: blitzkrieg in the west* (Osprey, 2009), p. 93. Churchill's fight-back is in chapter 12 of *Their Finest Hour*. 'A ridiculous, almost a comic, failure' is from John Durnford-Slater, *Commando* (Kimber, 1953), p. 32. For 'the German modern war machine', see Admiral of the Fleet, the Lord Keyes, *Amphibious Warfare and Combined Operations* (Lees Knowles Lectures, 1943) p. 81. 'Silly old Roger Keyes' is from *The Diary of Sir Alexander Cadogan, 1938–1945* (Cassell, 1971), edited by David Dilks, p. 249. On NID 17 being set up 'to co-ordinate intelligence', see Hinsley, *British Intelligence*, vol. 1, p. 286. Ian Fleming's liaison with both 'C' and SOE is in TNA ADM 223/463. Professor M. R. D. Foot spoke frankly about the clashes between SOE and SIS in his ninetieth-birthday talk at the Special Forces Club, London, on 7 December 2009.

For the 'successful pinch of a month's keys' see Mahon, *History of Hut Eight*, p. 24. 'Godfrey sent Ian Fleming to talk to Dilly Knox' says Mavis Batey in *From Bletchley With Love* (Bletchley Park Trust, 2008), p. 6. That Ian Fleming was 'never indoctrinated into ULTRA' is stated by Nigel West in his *Historical Dictionary of Ian Fleming's World of Intelligence: fact and fiction* (Scarecrow Press, 2009), in the entry on Enigma, p. 67. The text of Fleming's plan for Operation RUTHLESS is from Mahon, p. 25, and the square-bracketed note is from McCormick, *17F*, p. 65. 3 Commando details are from chapter 1 of Durnford-Slater, *Commando*, and the George Herbert stories from Peter Young, *Storm from the Sea* (Greenhill Books, 2002), pp. 15 and 160. The cover of Robert Henriques's novel, *The Commander* (Secker and Warburg, 1967) shows a Mills bomb and a dagger. 'We shall fight on the beaches', Winston Churchill's 'Dunkirk, June 4, 1940' speech, is on pp. 222–3 of *Into Battle*. HM Submarine *Clyde's* movements can be traced on Naval-History.net, and Operation KNIFE figures in William Mackenzie, *The Secret History of Special Operations Executive 1940–1945* (St Ermin's Press, 2000), p. 54. David Stirling's 'pips' confession is in Andrew Croft's autobiography, *A Talent for Adventure* (Self Publishing Association, 1991), p. 159. Fairbairn and Sykes's dramatic entrance at Inverailort is from personal memories by Major R. F. 'Henry' Hall, on the BBC's website *WW2 People's War*, ID No: U1740845. Knut Magne Haugland's SOE file, HS9/676/2, is in the National Archives, and Major General Colin Gubbins wrote his recommendation for the DSO on 2/8/1944. The Gavin Maxwell walking backwards trick is in Hamilton-Hill, *SOE Assignment*, p. 23. Michael Calvert's demolitions and explosives are mentioned in Dunning, *It Had To Be Tough*, p. 91, and Pierre Lorain, *Secret Warfare* (Orbis Publishing, 1984), p. 154. For 'Splendid attack!' see Fell, *The Sea Our Shield*, p. 86. Lord Lovat's view of Roger Keyes is in his autobiography, *March Past*, p. 189, and chapter 9 of that book, 'The Brave Music of a Distant Drum' is a fine encapsulation of the Commando ethos. There is authentic footage of training at Achnacarry, Wrexham and

St Ives in the 1945 Admiralty drama/documentary propaganda film, *Commando: the story of the green beret*, on the Imperial War Museum DVD *The Royal Marines at War*. Stuart Allen's *Commando Country* (National Museums of Scotland, 2007) is the definitive study of Second World War commando training in Scotland. For 'Signallers looked on in despair', see Fergusson, *The Watery Maze*, p. 78, and Lovat, *March Past*, p. 211. For evidence that the Lofoten raid was 'concerted between the NID and the GC&CS', see Hinsley, *British Intelligence*, vol. 1, p. 337, and Hugh Alexander, *Cryptographic History*, chapter 2. For Alan Turing 'reading all February's back traffic', see David Kahn, *Seizing the Enigma*, chapter 10.

Ralph Izzard recounted taking the German officers out to dinner in a letter to John Pearson, 22 November 1965, now in the Lilly Library. From his obituaries – *Daily Mail* 8 December 1992, *The Independent* (by Jan Morris) 14 December 1992, *Daily Telegraph* 15 December 1992 – it's clear that Izzard was, as Morris wrote, 'most people's beau ideal of the old-school foreign correspondent.' He is fictionalised as Granville Jones in Tom Stacey's 1988 novel, *Deadline*, re-issued twenty years later as *The Man Who Knew Everything*, and there is a good account of him in Andrew Trimbee's book about journalism in Bahrain, *The Inshallah Paper* (Quartet, 2009).

For the Abwehrtruppen in Yugoslavia, see Fritz Kurowski, *The Brandenburger Commandos: Germany's elite warrior spies in WW2* (Stackpole Books, 2005), p. 48, and Montagu, *Beyond Top Secret Ultra*, pp. 92–3; their role in the capture of Athens is in George E. Blau, *The German Campaign in the Balkans – Spring (1941)* (Naval & Military Press, 2003), p. 111. The beginning of the idea of 'intelligence commandos' for the British is described in Nutting, *Attain by Surprise*, pp. 13–14, confirmed by T. J. Glanville's SOE Personnel File in the National Archives, HS 9/589, released to me under FoIA in 2009. Churchill writes about Pantelleria in *The Second World War*, vol. 3, *The Grand Alliance* (Folio Society, 2002), p. 47. Mountbatten's mission statement for Combined Operations is in Fergusson, *The Watery Maze*, pp. 87–8. For 'a good, clean battle', see Durnford-Slater, *Commando*, p. 85.

Flight Sergeant Charles Cox's account of his part in Operation BITING, a model raid for scientific intelligence, is in Latham and Stobbs, *Radar*, pp. 112–18; see also chapter 27 of Jones, *Most Secret War* as well as George Millar, *The Bruneval Raid* (Bodley Head, 1974), Ken Ford, *The Bruneval Raid* (Osprey, 2010). The Joint Intelligence Committee memo is J.I.C. (42) 223 (o) (Final).

7 MAPPING THE FUTURE

Godfrey's search for '*the* great authority on *any* subject' is in TNA ADM 1/10218, 21 June 1939, and his work with Tom Harrisson in ADM 223/503. For women geographers in the Second World War, see 'The 'Map-Girls' by Avril Maddrell, *Transactions of the Institute of British Geographers*, NS 2007. For Geographical Handbooks and the ISTD see chapter 13, 'Handbooks for Invasion' in McLachlan, *Room 39*, Beesly, *Very Special Admiral*, pp. 205–14 and Professor W. G. V. Balchin, 'United Kingdom Geographers in the Second World War', *The Geographical Journal*, vol. 153, no. 2, July 1987, pp. 159–80. 'Of course Godfrey was sacked' and 'a bit of a tease' are in the Saunders interview, 24 March 1965, Pearson papers, Lilly Library. For 'an unmitigated pest and bully', see Godfrey's letter to his wife Margaret, 27 July 1945, quoted in Beesly, *Very Special Admiral*, p. 297.

For 'improved Naval Cipher No. 5', see Jürgen Rohwer's essay, '*The Wireless War*', in Stephen Howarth and Derek Law, *The Battle of the Atlantic 1939–1945: the 50th anniversary international naval conference* (Airlife Publishing, 1994), p. 414. For an account of F-21 and the OIC, see David Kohnen, *Commanders Winn and Knowles: winning the U-boat war with intelligence 1939–1943* (The Enigma Press, 1999). For Axis submarines sinking ships in the Caribbean, see R. A. Humphreys, *Latin America and the Second World War, 1942–1945* (Athlone, 1982), p. 3.

President Roosevelt spoke about the 'secret map, made in Germany' in his Navy Day speech in Washington DC on 27 October 1941. The text is in *KCA*, p. 4867A. Fourteen Latin American republics were to be replaced by five 'vassal states', and he also claimed the Germans were going to abolish all world religions and establish an international Nazi church with *Mein Kampf* as its Bible and the sword and the swastika as its symbols. The concocted map is reproduced on p. 277 of *British Security Coordination: the secret history of British Intelligence in the Americas, 1940–45* (St Ermin's Press, 1998). Ivar Bryce admits monkeying with what was clearly a Lufthansa fuel-depot map on p. 65 of *You Only Live Once: memories of Ian Fleming* (Weidenfeld & Nicolson, 1975), and the document also figures in Max Paul Friedman, *Nazis and Good Neighbours: the United States campaign against the Germans of Latin America in WW2* (Cambridge University Press, 2005), p. 58 and note 50, p. 251, as well as in Thomas E. Mahl, *Desperate Deception: British covert operations in the United States 1939–1944* (Brassey's , 2001), pp. 55–6, 182.

Ian Fleming's desire to buy land in Jamaica is in Bryce, *You Only Live Once*, p. 74. Noël Coward told John Pearson on 22 May 1965 in the Savoy Hotel that Goldeneye was 'a perfectly ghastly house' built in the wrong place for the 'divine' view, and that the food was 'abominable' compared to what was on offer in the Bond books. Coward also said of Fleming, 'I loved him and he loved me.'

8 MAYHEM IN THE MAGHREB

For Roosevelt's broadcast 'messages of friendship for the French people', see *KCA* p. 5445A. 'Rehearsed in Belfast docks' is cited in *A Partial History of 135th Infantry Regiment*, www.34infdiv. org. 'Pretty rugged fellows', 'My God, I've been hit!', and the 'smouldering boxes' incident are all from Nutting, *Attain by Surprise* pp. 25–6. For 'trying to stop the blood-gush with his bare hands', see the BBC's website *WW2 People's War*, Robert Miller's article ID: A7590512. Fleming's 'exact account of what we were to look for' is in the Dunstan Curtis interview, 16 April 1965, in the Pearson papers, Lilly Library.

'The Almighty in His infinite wisdom' is invoked by Winston Churchill in *Secret Session Speeches* (Cassell, 1946), p. 81. 'If Admiral Darlan had to shoot Marshal Pétain' comes from Churchill, *The Second World War*, vol. 4, *The Hinge of Fate* (Folio, 2002), pp. 516–17. For the murder of Darlan and the execution of Bonnier de la Chapelle I have drawn on *KCA* p. 5525A; Alan Moorehead, *The End in Africa* (Hamish Hamilton, 1943), pp. 56–8; Douglas Dodds-Parker, *Setting Europe Ablaze* (Springwood Books, 1983), pp. 115–17; Robin Winks, *Cloak and Gown: scholars in America's secret war* (Harvill Press, 1987), pp. 183–4; and Tim Luckhurst, 'De Gaulle's Greenock Gambit', *Sunday Times*, 4 January 2004. On pp. 648–9 of his *Churchill's War*, vol. 2, *Triumph in Adversity* (Focal Point, 2001), David Irving makes much of Anthony Eden blacking out a short sentence in the account of a London dinner with Generals de Gaulle and Catroux on 8 December 1942 that he had dictated afterwards at the Foreign Office, and then writing in red ink beside it, 'Too secret to record.'

The 'Spektor' coding machine appears in chapters 12 and 21 of *From Russia With Love*. For the 'multi-turnover Abwehr machine', see Batey, *Dilly*, p. 155 and Peter Twinn, chapter 16 in Hinsley and Stripp (eds) *Codebreakers*. Ian Fleming's 16 September 1942 memo to Commander Richard Ryder which includes the reading list for Intelligence work is in ADM 223/214. 'Holy smoke!' is transcribed from my interview with A. G. Royle, 17 July 2009.

'Magnificent simplicity' comes from Ernie Pyle, *Here Is Your War* (Henry Holt & Co, 1943), pp. 172–4, and 'a wonderful place for clarifying the mind' from Alan Moorehead, *A Late Education: episodes in a life* (Hamish Hamilton, 1970), p. 249. The account of captured Italian limpet-mine-layers is from the interestingly gossipy book that appeared in the narrow window before Cold War security clamped down, *My Three Years With Eisenhower:*

the personal diary of Captain Harry C. Butcher, USNR, naval aide to General Eisenhower, 1942 to 1945 (Simon & Schuster, 1946), p. 191. For more on Italian frogmen, see also J. Valerio Borghese, *Sea Devils* (Andrew Melrose, 1952) and Paul Kemp's excellent *Underwater Warriors* (Caxton Editions, 2000), pp. 16–65. 'A little more of the turbot, waiter' comes from the official account of the British airborne divisions, *By Air to Battle* (HMSO,1945), p. 36. 'Money belts stuffed with notes' is in Hampshire, *The Secret Navies*, p. 189. The 'huddles with Dunstan Curtis' are cited in Nutting, *Attain by Surprise,* p. 42. The claim that SAS men were the first from Eighth Army to get through to First Army is in Johnny Cooper, *One of the Originals: the story of a founder member of the SAS* (Pan Books, 1991), p. 76. The characterisation of the Jeep's animal qualities is from Pyle, *Here Is Your War,* p. 234, and the description 'brown-skinned and white-eye-browed' from p. 182. 'A rather rakish and dishevelled boy scout' is from Moorehead, *The End in Africa*, p. 154.

'Grope as you go' is a phrase from the Royle interview, 17 July 2009. 'A Goyaesque muddle' is quoted by Julian Evans in *Semi-Invisible Man: the life of Norman Lewis* (Jonathan Cape, 2008), p. 220.

9 TESTING THE WATERS

'Layforce capture', Churchill's Operation WORKSHOP memo, 3 December 1940, is in *Their Finest Hour*, pp. 561–2, and the hope for 'practically unopposed landings' in *The Hinge of Fate*, p. 658. For 'the first time in history', see Sir John Hammerton (ed.) *The Second Great War* (Waverley Book Company, 1947), p. 2667. For the 'central control system for aiming the guns had been hit', see Butcher, *My Three Years With Eisenhower,* p.279. The Pantelleria papers of the Bombing Survey Unit are in the Baron Zuckerman of Burnham Thorpe archive at the University of East Anglia, Norwich, Boxes SZ/BSU/1–5. See also chapter 3 of John Peyton's biography,

Solly Zuckerman: a scientist out of the ordinary (John Murray, 2001).

For the first use of the term 'United Nations', see Brian Urquhart, *New York Review of Books*, vol. LVII, no. 13, summer issue, p. 42. In the invasion of Sicily, the COPP casualties are noted in Ian Trenowden, *Stealthily by Night: clandestine beach reconnaissance and operations in WW2* (Crecy Books, 1995), p. 61. The deaths 'including the chief camouflage officer' are mentioned in Thaddeus Holt's magisterial work, *The Deceivers: Allied military deception in the Second World War* (Weidenfeld and Nicolson, 2004), p. 323. The experience of the war photographer Robert Capa (born Endree Friedmann in Budapest in 1913), 'hanging in a tree all night', comes from his wonderful 1947 memoir of the Second World War, *Slightly Out of Focus* (Random House, 2001), p. 68. Carlo D'Este gives the figure of sixty US pilots and eighty-one paratroopers in his masterly biography *Eisenhower: Allied Supreme Commander* (Weidenfeld & Nicolson, 2003), p. 433.

'Made it in America' is from Harold Macmillan, *War Diaries: the Mediterranean 1943–1945* (Papermac. 1985), p. 352. Norman Lewis's take on the Mafia in his review of Danilo Dolci's *Waste* is quoted in Evans, *Semi-Invisible Man*, p. 482. For more on 'Lucky' Luciano and US Naval Intelligence, see Rodney Campbell, *The Luciano Project: the secret wartime collaboration of the Mafia and the US Navy* (McGraw, Hill, 1977); Appendix N, 'Unholy Alliance: the Luciano Connection' in Carlo D'Este, *Bitter Victory: the battle for Sicily 1943* (Collins, 1988); Ezio Costanzo, *The Mafia and the Allies* (Enigma Books, 2007); and Tim Newark, *The Mafia at War: Allied collusion with the Mob* (Greenhill Books, 2007).

Humphrey Quill describes reaching Messina in MLBE 1/16 at the Churchill Archives Centre. 'Prolonged immersion in the water,' is from Nutting, *Attain by Surprise*, p. 82. The change of language 'from mere profanity to obscenity' is noted by Ernie Pyle in *Here Is Your War*, p. 242. 'Killing men, women and at least one child', see Stanley Hirshson, *General Patton: a soldier's life* (Harper Perennial, 2003), pp. 372–9. 'A breed of morons' is quoted by Carlo

D'Este in *A Genius for War: a life of General George S. Patton* (HarperCollins, 1996), p. 534, and 'an invention of the Jews' by Noël Monks in his autobiography, *Eyewitness* (Frederick Muller, 1955), p. 195. The story of 'Donaldbain' is from Malcolm Munthe, *Sweet Is War – to them that know it not* (Gerald Duckworth & Co, 1954), p. 172–3. 'I hate all Jews', is from Lincoln, *Odyssey of a Jewish Sailor*, p. 29. Finlayson's worrying time in Trapani helping disarm mines is in *Attain by Surprise*, p. 105. The evacuation of '12,000 Germans with 4,500 vehicles' is in Hinsley, *British Intelligence*, vol. 3, part 1, p.95, and Operation LEHRGANG is described in d'Este, *Bitter Victory*, appendix I, pp. 606–9.

For the Salerno landings, see Des Hickey and Gus Smith, *Operation Avalanche: the Salerno landings 1943* (Heinemann, 1983) and chapter 5 of Colin John Bruce, *Invaders: British and American experience of seaborne landings 1939–1945* (Caxton Editions, 2003). Chapter 4 of Robin Winks's formidable study of OSS and CIA, *Cloak and Gown*, is entitled 'The Athlete: Donald Downes'. For more on Downes and the failed Operation BANANA in Spain, see David Baird, *Between Two Fires: Guerrilla War in the Sierras* (Maroma Press, 2008). It was Donald Downes who leaked (via Ernest Cuneo) the news of General Patton slapping two soldiers to the muckraker Drew Pearson, who published it in November 1943, thus breaching the 'gentlemen's agreement' that Eisenhower had reached with the press, according to Douglas Waller, *Wild Bill Donovan: the spymaster who created the OSS and modern American espionage* (Simon and Schuster, 2011), p. 281. For references to 'other ships sunk off Salerno' by the new guided missile, see Roger Ford, *Germany's Secret Weapons in WW2* (Spellmount, 2000), pp. 91–3, and David Porter, *Hitler's Secret Weapons 1933–1945* (Amber Books, 2010), p. 161.

10 INVASION OF THE ISLANDS

In *Rescuing Mussolini: Gran Sasso 1943* (Osprey, 2010), Robert

Forczyk is rightly sceptical about 'Rear Area Commando' Otto Skorzeny, whom he calls 'an ardent Nazi' and 'an accomplished and unabashed liar'. Having looted a handsome nest egg from the Reichsbank in April 1945 (cf. Mark Seaman, *Bravest of the Brave: the true story of Wing Commander 'Tommy' Yeo-Thomas* (Michael O'Mara Books, 1997), p. 224), Skorzeny went on to make himself useful to Western Intelligence and Allied military in the Cold War, as well as acting the hero to fascists in Franco's Spain. Charles Foley's best-selling *Commando Extraordinary: the spectacular exploits of Otto Skorzeny* (Longmans, Green & Co, 1954 and Pan Books, 1956), with an introduction by Major General Sir Robert Laycock and final chapters virtually dictated by Colonel David Stirling, uses Skorzeny as a kind of battering ram in the propaganda campaign to restore the SAS among British special forces.

Information about Capri and secretive operations in the Bay of Naples come from chapter VI of Nutting, *Attain by Surprise*, Munthe, *Sweet Is War*, pp. 170–1; Adrian Gallegos, *From Capri into Oblivion* (Hodder & Stoughton, 1959), pp. 22–7; Jeff Matthews, *Around Naples* website; Douglas Fairbanks Jr, *A Hell of a War* (St Martin's Press, 1993), pp. 205–6; John B. Dwyer, *Seaborne Deception: the history of the US Navy Beach Jumpers* (Praeger Publishers, 1992), pp. 36–7; and chapter 9 of Max Corvo, *OSS in Italy 1942–1945* (Enigma Books, 2005). George Allen and Unwin had published Benedetto Croce's *La Storia* in 1941, with the new title *History as the Story of Liberty*.

The claim that the American Office of Strategic Services (OSS) intelligence was 'valueless' is in Nutting, *Attain by Surprise*, p. 134. For further light on the murkier Cold War neo-fascist activities of J. Valerio Borghese, see Stuart Christie, *Stefano Delle Chiae: portrait of a black terrorist* (Anarchy Magazine/Refract Publications, 1984). 'Admiral Minisini arrived' is quoted in Charles T. O'Reilly, *Forgotten Battles: Italy's war of liberation 1943–45* (Lexington Books, 2001), p. 128. On US help to Italian freedom fighters see Peter Tompkins, 'The OSS and Italian Partisans in

WW2', *Studies in Intelligence*, spring 1998. (Before he wrote *The Secret Life of Plants*, Tompkins was in the OSS.) David Stafford's official history, commissioned by the Cabinet Office, *Mission Accomplished: SOE and Italy 1943–1945* (Vintage, 2011) paints the fullest picture to date of the British secret war in Italy, and is full of interesting characters and incidents. Visitors to Florence will learn surprising things about the Ponte Vecchio, for example.

The armoured division sent to Greece is mentioned in Hinsley, *British Intelligence*, vol. 3, part 1, p. 120. 'God forbid' is quoted in Andrew Roberts, *Masters and Commanders: how Roosevelt Churchill, Marshall and Alanbrooke won the war in the West*, (Allen Lane, 2008), p. 412. 'A rope around their neck' comes from Butcher, *My Three Years with Eisenhower*, p. 342, and 'in the absence of the Allies' from B. H. Liddell Hart, *The Other Side of the Hill: Germany's generals, their rise and fall, with their own account of military events, 1939–1945* (Cassell, 1948), p. 359.

The largely forgotten fighting in the Greek islands is the subject of Peter C. Smith and Edwin R. Walker, *War in the Aegean* (Kimber, 1974, rev. edn, 2008) and Anthony Rogers, *Churchill's Folly: Leros and the Aegean, the last great British defeat of WW2* (Cassell, 2003). Winston Churchill's own account is in *The Second World War*, vol. 5, *Closing the Ring*, chapter 12, 'Island Prizes Lost'. Dianne Fisher showed me John McDiarmid's hand-written account of what happened to him. There are pictures of Jake Easonsmith at http://www.cliftonrfchistory.co.uk/memorial/WW2/easonsmith.htm. 'The Royal Navy destroyed it' comes from Julian Thompson, *The Imperial War Museum Book of War Behind Enemy Lines* (Sidgwick & Jackson, 1998), p. 265. For the Danish warrior *par excellence*, see Mike Langley, *Anders Lassen VC, MC of the SAS* (Hodder & Stoughton, 1988) and Mogens Kofod-Hansen, *'Andy': a portrait of the Dane Major Anders Lassen* (Veterans of the Danish Fight for Freedom,1991).

The comment that T. J. Glanville was 'likely to "put his foot in it" ' comes from his SOE personal file in the National Archives,

HS9/589. Dunstan Curtis called Glanville 'pig-headed' in a letter to Humphrey Quill, dated 9 December 1947, which is filed in the bound volume ADM 223/214. '400 tons of Italian service uniforms' make their appearance in Hamilton-Hill, *SOE Assignment*, pp. 69–84. 'A somewhat chaotic sort of unit' comes from the Imperial War Museum taped interview with Dr John Coates which is quoted in Alan Ogden, *Through Hitler's Back Door: SOE operations in Hungary, Slovakia, Romania and Bulgaria 1939–45* (Pen & Sword Books, 2010), pp. 51–2.

11 FREEING THE FRENCH

'You will enter the Continent of Europe', Eisenhower's historic order, is quoted in the official military history, Major L. F. Ellis, *Victory in the West*, vol. 1, *The Battle of Normandy* (HMSO, 1962), in appendix 1 on p. 499. The speed of parallel processing: 'five times as many . . . in a fifth of the time', is one of the achievements of the great Post Office engineer, T. H. Flowers, as described in chapter 8 of *Colossus*, edited by B. Jack Copeland. Knut Haukelid described his sabotage in *Skis Against the Atom* (Kimber, 1955) and the action 'scuppered Nazi chances' according to Richard Rhodes, *The Making of the Atomic Bomb* (Simon and Schuster, 1986), p. 517.

Fleming's admonition, 'You can't behave like Red Indians any more', is quoted in Nutting, *Attain by Surprise*, p. 160, and the photograph of the Royal Marine officers appears on p. 166 of the same book. For the lobbying of Quill and the selection of Lewes, see Robert W. Love Jr. and John Major (editors), *The Year of D-Day: the 1944 diary of Admiral Sir Bertram Ramsay* (University of Hull, 1994), p. 15. John Godfrey's note about 'looking after the Whitehall front', dated 6 September 1970, is inserted in the bound volume ADM 223/214. The description of the notoriously short-tempered Godfrey as 'thunderous' is in '007 et . . . moi', the article about Ian Fleming that Tony Hugill wrote for the BOAC in-flight magazine

Welcome Aboard in the late 1960s. Robert Harling as 'Fleming's head boy' was a phrase used by Peter Jemmett in conversation in June 2010, and the description of him as a 'mediaeval court jester' comes from Sefton Delmer, *Black Boomerang: an autobiography*, vol. II (Secker & Warburg, 1962), p. 70. Robert Harling's obituary tribute to Ian Fleming appeared in *The Sunday Times* on 16 August 1964 and John Pearson interviewed Robert Harling on 11 February 1965. William Stephenson's fantastical claim that Ian Fleming excelled on a secret agent course in Canada (see Pearson, *The Life of Ian Fleming*, pp. 138–141), is definitively refuted by David Stafford, *Camp X: SOE and the American connection* (Viking, 1987), pp. 277–84. Joan Bright Astley talked to Lucy Fleming in *The Bond Correspondence*, broadcast on BBC Radio 4 on 24 May 2008. The 'Night at the Opera' parallel was drawn by Margaret Bax Priestley in 'NID 30: a personal memoir', dated 11 December 1993.

The bombing of France before D-Day, '200,000 sorties', comes from Ellis, *Victory in the West*, vol. 1, p. 109. The figure of '15,000 civilians killed' is cited in Anthony Beevor, *D-Day: the battle for Normandy* (Viking, 2009), p. 49. Geoffrey Pike's 'hellishly final' thoughts are put into the mouth of 'Bill Jefferies' in Lieutenant Commander J. A. C. Hugill, *The Hazard Mesh* (Hurst & Blackett, 1946), p. 31. The description of Sancho Glanville as insouciant amid danger is from Nutting, *Attain by Surprise*, p. 172. Dianne Fisher showed me Bill Powell's hand-written account of the landing; Powell was also interviewed in Charles Wheeler's fiftieth anniversary film *D-Day: Turning The Tide*, first broadcast on BBC1 TV on 5 June 1994. Tony Hugill handed out Montgomery's message of encouragement to the Marines in his LCT but held back Eisenhower's, because he thought its piety would not go down well. Jock Gardner's comment on *The Hazard Mesh* is from a letter to Mrs Fanny Hugill, 27 February 1997. Guy Postlethwaite 'radiant with happiness' is from Hugill, *The Hazard Mesh*, pp. 24–5, and 'macabre foulness' is on p. 25.

The bombing of WOOLFORCE near Utah Beach is described in chapter IX of Nutting, *Attain by Surprise*. Wright's 'name but not number' is from Dalzel-Job, *From Arctic Snow*, p. 122. The dope-sheets in the National Archives show that the first photographs that Sergeant John Brereton took in France were of the graves of three 30AU comrades, though the photos themselves are now missing. For more on V-1 and V-2 rockets see Michael J. Neufeld, *The Rocket and the Reich: Peenemünde and the coming of the ballistic missile era* (Harvard University Press, 1995) and Dennis Piszkiewicz, *The Nazi Rocketeers: dreams of space and crimes of war* (Praeger, 1995). The Atlantic Wall radar sites come from Alfred Price, *Instruments of Darkness: the struggle for radar supremacy* (Kimber, 1967), p. 200. The attack on Douvres-la-Délivrande, 'they threw grenades', is in Durnford-Slater, *Commando*, p. 195. The 'set of wheels' is mentioned in the document, 'Sigint Captures by 30AU' in TNA ADM 223/213. In the contemporaneous pencil diary he was keeping (quite against regulations), Tony Hugill records being delighted to hear in mid-June that their 'Arromanches job' was 'the biggest scoop of radar intelligence in the war', which had pleased the DNI, the Air Force and the Board of Admiralty. See also my introduction to the reissue of *The Hazard Mesh* (Faber Finds, 2011).

The identification of men 'in field grey uniform with naval insignia' was in the notes attached to the 30AU intelligence map of Cherbourg, now in the possession of 30 Commando. The setting up of 'operational sites strong enough not to surrender' is mentioned in Chester Wilmot, *The Struggle for Europe* (Collins, 1952), p. 324. Hugill describes the 'beastly greenish-yellow waxen colour' of corpses in *The Hazard Mesh*, p.50. The invocation of 'the honour of the German Army', in the Seventh Army war diary on 23 June 1944, is quoted in Robin Havers, *Battle for Cherbourg* (Sutton Publishing, 2004), p. 70. Robert Capa described his 'loot of Benedictine and brandy' in *Slightly Out of Focus*, p. 162. The excuse to surrender the garrison, 'one of those phosphorous shells', is mentioned in Delmer, *Black Boomerang*, p. 120. Hugill described the destruction of Cherbourg docks in *The Hazard Mesh*, p.52.

Ian Fleming's visit to Carteret is on p. 60 of *The Hazard Mesh*. He arrived with Robert Harling, ACOS (I), 'Ginger' Lewes, and the scientific adviser Professor Patrick Blackett, the head of the Admiralty's Operational Research department. Glanville's phrase 'the egregious Fleming' is from Nutting, *Attain by Surprise*, p.180. The scuttlebutt from 'Marines serving the officers' meal' came from the A. G. Royle interview in July 2009. Royle's 'exquisitely fluid' phase is quoted in Nutting, *Attain by Surprise*, p. 204. Hugill's diary of the later phase also records the pleasure and excitement of the drive into Brittany.

12 BREAKTHROUGH

The blue-on-blue bombing that killed 126 Americans, including Lieutenant General McNair, is described by Anthony Beevor, *D-Day*, pp. 345–7, and most graphically by Ernie Pyle in *Brave Men* (Henry Holt & Co., 1944), pp. 434–9. Former CIA man Angus Maclean Thuermer died at the age of 92 and his obituary was in the *Daily Telegraph* on 15 June 2010. His daughter Kitty Thuermer wrote about him here: http://peacecorpsworldwide. org/pc-writers/2010/09/17/a-writer-writes-kitty/online. Ralph Izzard's comments about destruction are in a letter to Mrs Fanny Hugill, 28 March 1987. For Patton and ULTRA intelligence, see Parrish, *The American Codebreakers*, pp. 223–9.

Sergeant Bramah's escape is described in *Slipstream*, the Parachute Regimental Association Central Scotland Branch news-letter, March 2006, pp. 2–3. Patrick Dalzel-Job describes the casual shooting of the civilian in *From Arctic Snow*, p. 135. For old collaborators ingratiating themselves with new invaders, see Alan Moorehead, *Eclipse* (Sphere, 1968), p. 99. 'Collaboration is a kind of epidemic' ('*une sorte d'épidémie qui n'épargne personne*') is from Henri Michel, *Paris allemand* (Editions Albin Michel, 1981), p. 114. (His sequel volume, *Paris résistant* (Albin Michel, 1982), is just as good.) The figure of 20,000 women's heads shaved is from Stéphane Simmonet, *Atlas de la libération de la France, 6 juin–8 mai 1945* (Editions Autrement, 2004), p. 66. Dalzel-Job's driving tactics are described in *From Arctic Snow*, p. 138. Hugill's bluff at St Pabu is in chapter 13 of *The Hazard Mesh*, in notebook 3 of the manuscript, Churchill Archives Centre HUGL 9 and in diary 4, 1–21 August 1944, CAC HUGL 4. He subsequently recommended both McGrath and Powell for the DSM.

The young resisters 'shot under the chestnut trees' are commemorated in Jean-Louis Goglin and Pierre Roux, *Souffrance et Liberté: une géographie parisienne des années noires (1940–1944)* (Association Paris-Musées, 2004), pp. 150–4. The Molotov cocktails made by Joliot-Curie are mentioned by Stephen J. Zaloga in *Liberation of Paris 1944: Patton's race for the Seine* (Osprey, 2008), pp. 55–9. Lt-Colonel Woolley's report to ACOS(I), 21 November 1944, in ADM 391/44, describes how 30AU got into Paris. His first plan was to parachute X troop directly on to a heavily defended racecourse in the west of Paris, where they would have been massacred. Tony Hugill's uncensored diary in August 1944 is frankly cynical about Woolley's ambitions to get a full colonelcy and to win the DSO. Ernest Hemingway's view of the city he loved is from the end of 'How We Came To Paris', in *By-Line: Ernest Hemingway* (Penguin, 1970), p. 354. Robert Capa describes 'Papa' Hemingway's freelance activities with the 4th Division approaching Paris in *Slightly Out of Focus*, pp. 176–188. Ernie Pyle's liberation of Paris is in chapter 34 of *Brave Men*. 'A bit of a ding-dong with the Hun' comes from a conversation with Bill Powell on 3 July 2009.

Geoffrey Pike's obituary was in the *Daily Telegraph* on 18 November 1997. For Hemingway and the Hôtel Ritz, see Michael Taylor, 'Liberating France Hemingway's Way', *San Francisco Chronicle*, 22 August 2004. On the German inability to build a nuclear bomb, see Samuel A. Goudsmit, *Alsos* (Henry Schuman, 1947), pp.68–71, and the reminiscences of Rear Admiral Albert

G. Mumma, 1st interview, 3 October 1986, held by the US Naval Institute. Descriptions of the intelligence finds in Paris are from Glanville's Report, 25 October 1944, in ADM 391/44. For more on the German 'small battle groups', see Lawrence Paterson, *Weapons of Desperation: German frogmen and midget submarines of WW2* (Chatham Publishing, 2006), p. 37; Paul Kemp, *Underwater Warriors*, p. 186; Ralph Izzard's Forward Interrogation Unit report, 17 November 1944, CAC MISC 31; and Hinsley, *British Intelligence*, vol. 3, part 2, chapter 59. The Naval Intelligence Division docket on the first German BIBER midget submarine, with the initial sighting report, Ian Fleming's order to 30AU to capture it and the subsequent technical examination, is TNA ADM 1/16836. The sexual information is from the fifth notebook of Hugill's diary, now in the Churchill Archives Centre.

13 OPERATION PLUNDER

The Bodleian Library in Oxford republished the 1944 Foreign Office *Instructions for British Servicemen in Germany* in 2007. 'You're the bugger that'll be wearing it' is from Nutting, *Attain by Surprise*, p. 222; 'A bodyguard for each intelligence group' is from Hampshire, *The Secret Navies*, pp. 233–4. On 1 June 2009 the US National Security Agency/ Central Security Service finally declassified and approved for online release TICOM's magnum opus, the remarkable and comprehensive nine-volume *European Axis Signal Intelligence in World War II*. Other TICOM reports were being released by NSA to the US National Archives and Records Administration as late as April 2011. The figure of 70,000 tons of uranium and radium materials comes from 'Boris Pash and Science and Technology Intelligence', an online article from the US Army Intelligence School at Fort Huachuca, Arizona. In a clear case of pot abusing kettle, Patrick Dalzel-Job accused T-Force of 'private looting' in *From Arctic Snow*, p. 162, and Sean Longden called that 'unfair and unjustifiable' in *T-Force*, pp. 318–9. The friction over captured documents is recorded in ADM 223/214, pp. 238–9, and the demarcation disputes between T-Force and 30AU in WO 219/1668.

'Tough meat and green vegetables' is from Anthony Beevor and Luba Vinogradova, *A Writer at War: Vasily Grossman with the Red Army 1941–1945* (Vintage, 2006), p. 323. Zuckerman's memory of 'a severed finger' is recorded by W. G. Sebald in *On the Natural History of Destruction* (Hamish Hamilton, 2003), p. 32. The bridgehead on the east bank of the Rhine is described in Derek S. Zumbro's first-rate history *Battle for the Ruhr: the German Army's final defeat in the West* (University Press of Kansas, 2006), pp. 102–6. For the suicidal mission of the river frogmen, see Paterson, *Weapons of Desperation*, pp.216–21. Field Marshal Lord Alanbrooke's observation that the PM 'would really have liked to be killed' is in his *War Diaries 1939–1945* (Weidenfeld & Nicolson, 2001), p. 678, and Churchill's thrill at his secretary's blooding is in John Colville, *The Fringes of Power: Downing Street diaries 1939-1955* (Weidenfeld & Nicolson, 2004), p. 577. Churchill wrote 'Forward all on wings of flame' in Field Marshal B. L. Montgomery's autograph-book, '*Ten Chapters: 1942 to 1945*' (Hutchinson, 1945), p. 25. The BBC man Stewart MacPherson recorded the squadrons of 'Spitfires, Typhoons, Tempests, and Mustangs' on 29 March 1945, as transcribed in Desmond Hawkins, *War Report: D-Day to VE-Day* (BBC Books, 1985), p. 272. The 'boxes of torpedo gyros' occur in Nutting, *Attain by Surprise*, p. 247.

The figure of 14,000 prisoners dying after liberation is from Ben Shephard, 'The medical relief effort at Belsen', in Suzanne Bardgett and David Cesarani, *Belsen 1945: new historical perspectives* (Valentine Mitchell, 2006), p. 37. For 'wretched beings who seemed less than human', see chapter 8, 'A Host of Corpses' in William Hitchcock, *Liberation: the bitter road to freedom, Europe 1944–1945* (Faber, 2009). The US journalist-turned-intelligence officer Ralph Ingersoll also recorded the feelings of disgust, hatred and shame stirred in him by visiting Landsberg camp in his book *Top Secret* (Harcourt Brace, 1946), pp. 254–61. The heap of bodies that 'stretched about 60 yards by 30 yards' is from the *Daily Mail*, 19 April 1945, quoted in the *Daily Mail* compilation book *Lest We Forget: the horrors of Nazi concentration camps revealed for all time in the most terrible photographs ever published* (Daily Mail, 1945), p. 13. The figure of '100,000 prisoners' is from *Buchenwald Camp: report of a Parliamentary delegation* (HMSO, April 1945), also cited in *Lest We Forget*, p. 7. Ed Murrow's account of his visit to Buchenwald is quoted in A. M. Sperber's fine biography, *Murrow: his life and times* (Fordham University Press, 1998), p. 249, and the complete text is also in *Reporting World War II: American journalism 1938–1946* (Library of America, 2001), pp. 625–9. The British and American reporters saw only a fragment of mass-murder. The great Russian reporter Vasily Grossman encountered larger killing-fields hundreds of miles to the east and wrote 'The Hell of Treblinka' in September 1944, now translated and annotated by Robert Chandler in *The Road: stories, journalism and essays* (New York Review of Books, 2010), pp. 116–62. Everyone knows there is a huge literature on the Holocaust, but to begin to comprehend the deaths of millions under both Nazism and Soviet Communism, see the incomparable *Blood Lands: Europe between Hitler and Stalin* (Bodley Head, 2010) by Professor Timothy Snyder of Yale University. To learn what the Allies knew about the Holocaust in 1942, see the reports of genocide in the *New York Times* in *Reporting World War II* and the essays by Richard Breitman and Norman J. W. Goda in *US Intelligence and the Nazis* (Cambridge University Press, 2005). For explanations of why so little was done about it, see *Why We Watched: Europe, America and the holocaust* (WW Norton & Co, 2008) by Theodore S. Hamerow. In his April 1945 pamphlet, *What Buchenwald Really Means*, the left-wing Jewish publisher Victor Gollancz tried to counter the hatred of all Germans induced by reports of the camps by pointing out that German citizens had also suffered and died there too.

'4,000 to 5,000 gold bricks' is from *KCA* p. 7125, 8 April 1945. The Merkers inventory: 'List of Money, Gold Bullion found in salt mine H-66850, Merkers, 8 April 1945', is appendix I in 'G-4 Functions in ETOUSA Operations', RG 331, NACP, cited in Greg Bradsher, 'Nazi Gold: The Merkers Mine Treasure', *Prologue* (NARA), spring 1999, vol. 31, no. 1. The Swiss National Bank figures of Nazi bullion received are from A. L. Smith, *Hitler's Gold*, 2nd ed., (Berg, 1996), p. 163. The Degussa refinery figures in Richard J. Evans, *The Third Reich at War* (Penguin, 2009), pp. 344–5. For post-war ramifications of such immense looting see *Nazi Gold: the London conference, 2-4 December 1997* (The Stationery Office, 1998).

'Shall I shoot him *now*, sir?' is from Jan Aylen's memoir 'Recollections of 30 Assault Unit', in *Naval Review*, October 1977/ January 1978. Trevor Glanville noted the 'songbirds in their cages' by the gallows in Nutting, *Attain by Surprise*, p. 260. The capture of Buxtehude is described by Karl Halaski, 'Uns war klar: wie spielten um Kopf und Kragen', *Buxtehuder Tageblatt*, 3 June 2000. Glanville's account of Tambach Castle is described in the Prologue and chapter XIV of Nutting, *Attain by Surprise*.

14 GETTING THE GOODS

The hoped-for 'strategic pincer movement' is from Joachim Fest, *Inside Hitler's Bunker* (Pan, 2005), p. 46, and 'the severing of Germany' from Kenneth Strong, *Intelligence at the Top: recollections of an intelligence officer* (Cassell, 1986), p. 191. Patrick Dalzel-Job describes venturing into Bremen in *From Arctic Snow*, pp. 161–8. The German side of the surrender is from Herbert Schwarzwälder, *Vom Kampf um Bremen bis zur Kapitulation* (Schuenemann CE, 1978), pp. 102–7. 'Gleaming in the moonlight' is from Jan Aylen, 'Recollections of Assault Unit No. 30', *Naval Review*, vol. 65, no. 4, October 1977, p. 317. 'Drunker than skunks' is from the Mumma reminiscences, US Naval Institute, 20 April 1987, p. 111.

The historian H. R. Trevor Roper, a wartime SIS officer, wrote the classic 1947 account, *The Last Days of Hitler* (revised ed. Pan Books, 1966). Morbid fascination also led me to the Security Service website, https://www.mi5.gov.uk/output/hitlers-last-days.html, as well as to Joachim Fest, *Inside Hitler's Bunker: the last days of the Third Reich*. The German title of Fest's book was *Der Untergang* and it was the basis of the celebrated Eichinger/Hirschbiegel film *The Downfall*, with Bruno Ganz as Hitler. An interesting article by the production designer and military consultant Andrew Mollo on the quest for authenticity in the movie is in *After the Battle*, no. 128, pp. 44–55.

'The forced labour and slavery of 700,000 people' is from Alan S. Milward, *The German Economy at War* (Athlone Press, 1967), pp. 155–61, and Hermann Kaienburg, *Die Wirtschaft der SS* (Metropol, 2003), p. 431. The figure of '7,000 kilos of hair' is from Edward T. Linenthal, *Preserving Memory: the struggle to create America's Holocaust Museum* (Columbia University Press, 2001), p. 212. Speer's strategy of hiding rather destroying is described in Milward, *The German Economy at War*, p. 185. Royle's pleasure at seeing U-boats destroyed in Hamburg is in Nutting, *Attain by Surprise*, p. 232. He discovered the official German photographs of earlier bombing raid destruction under the rubble of the shipyard. The tragedy of the *Thielbeck* and the *Cap Arcona* are touched on in CAB/66/65/61 and WO 309/1592. The summary execution of two SS guards is recorded by Glanville in ADM 223/214, p. 250.

The twenty-three days of the Flensburg government are described by Karel Margry in *After the Battle*, no. 128, pp. 2–34. 'The German admiral broke down and wept' is from Field Marshal Sir Bernard Montgomery's lecture, '21 Army Group in the Campaign in North West Europe, 1944–45', published in the *Royal United Services Institute Journal*, November 1945, p. 445. Montgomery records the German surrender in *Normandy to the Baltic* (Hutchinson, 1947), p. 277. Roosevelt's acknowledgement of Stalin's broken promises is cited in Barbara Tuchman, *The March of Folly: from Troy to Vietnam* (Abacus, 1985), p. 306. The fear that the Soviet Army might seize Denmark, and control the Baltic is in 'Operation Eclipse' in Gilbert, *Routledge Atlas of the Second World War*, p. 181; http://www.majorhibbertslog.co.uk/OPE02p1.html, and Sean Longden, *T-Force: The Race for Nazi War Secrets*, pp. 144–6. Rear Admiral Mumma records in his reminiscences that a deliberate Soviet palisade of obfuscation and delay prevented a joint Allied intelligence team getting into the Peenemünde rocketry site.

30AU acquired Dr Hellmuth Walter's large-size Nazi-style business card. On it, his principal title was *Wehrwirtschaft-Führer* or 'war economy leader', indicating high status in the Third Reich's military–industrial complex. Only in second place was he designated *Betriebsführer* or 'works manager' of H. Walter KG (*Kommanditgesellschaft*, 'limited partnership') of Kiel. Technical details about the advanced German submarines as well as the lists of surrendered or scuttled U-boats are on the useful site uboat. net. '500 tons a month at 83 per cent strength' is from the CIOS Evaluation Report no. 48, *Hydrogen Peroxide*, 2 June 1945. Paul McGrath was not punished for striking the arrogant German according to ADM 223/214. 30AU's provision of 'nine Type XXI handbooks' is from TNA HW8/37. Kenneth Strong's disgust at capitulation ceremonies is in *Intelligence at the Top*, pp. 211–12. 'Weary and worn, impoverished but undaunted' is from Churchill, *The Second World War*, vol. 6, *Triumph and Tragedy* (1953), p. 430.

The curious story about Ian Fleming wanting Glanville to eliminate the German admirals is from Hampshire, *The Secret Navies*, p. 257. Fleming imaginatively picturing the adventures he might have had is described in an undated note by Norman Denning, 'The Creation of Bond', in the Pearson papers, Lilly Library. The discoveries in places like the sinister Plömer Zee are from Aylen, 'Recollections of 30 Assault Unit' in the *Naval Review*, October 1977/January 1978. Mumma's reminiscences about finding the combustion chambers for rocket planes and submarines are from the US Naval Institute interview 2, p. 116. Churchill's view that 'once they obey we can do what we like' is from *Triumph and Tragedy*, p. 592. The death of von Friedeburg and Dönitz's pathetic 'eight pairs of underpants' are recorded in *After the Battle*, no. 128, pp. 21–5. For the death of Heinrich Himmler, see *After the Battle* no. 14, pp. 28–37. You can listen to Sergeant Major Austen's voice on the remarkable Oriole record of actualities, *The Sounds of Time, 1934–1949* (1949), compiled by Frederic Mullaly and narrated by John Snagge. The 'forerunner of Polaris' phrase is from Geoffrey Pike's obituary in the *Daily Telegraph*, 18 November 1997. Aylen and Mumma's report on the works at Kiel is ADM 199/2434 in the National Archives, Kew. Ralph Izzard's report on Dönitz's view of Soviet submarine ambitions in the Churchill Archives Centre under MISC 49.

15 AFTERMATH

Glanville's report on his activities in Saigon in 1945 is at the end of the bound volume ADM 223/214. When read in conjunction with SOE Indo-China file HS1/104 (and the benefit of hindsight) you get a sense of troubles brewing from the demise of empire. Churchill's 'Iron Curtain' speech at Westminster College, Fulton, Missouri is printed in full in *KCA*, pp. 7770–2. The weekly 'Diary of World Events' also points out it was deplored by two Labour MPs at home. (It does not state that at least one of them, Tom Driberg, was in the pay of the Soviet KGB.) Submarine work at the Admiralty Experimental Station, Welwyn, is described in TNA ADM 297. Mumma's view that the British wanted to develop hydrogen peroxide technologies and so 'got Helmuth Walter', while the USA was quietly following the nuclear route features in his recorded reminiscences for the US Naval Institute.

There is a large literature on Britain's quest for the atom bomb and the cancerous legacy of its twenty-one atmospheric tests in the Pacific and Australia, including Eric Bailey, *The Christmas*

Island Story (Stacey International, 1977); Derek Robinson, *Just Testing* (Collins Harvill, 1985); Denys Blakeway and Sue Lloyd-Roberts, *Testing Britain's Bomb* (Unwin, 1985); Joan Smith, *Clouds of Deceit: the deadly legacy of Britain's bomb tests* (Faber, 1985) and J. Haggas, *Christmas Island: the wrong place at the wrong time* (Minerva Press, 1997). The grisly paranoia of nuclear defence and attack is probed thoroughly in Peter Hennessy, *The Secret State: preparing for the worst 1945–2010* (Penguin, 2010).

There is much evidence that 'useful' Nazis were fast-tracked into the countries that wanted their scientific knowledge or technical skills. See Eric Lichtblau, 'Nazis Were Given 'Safe Haven' in US, Report Says', *The New York Times*, and 'Justice Department Censors Nazi-Hunting History', National Security Archive Electronic Briefing Book No. 331, both 13 November 2010. Books on the subject include Tom Bower, *The Paperclip Conspiracy: the battle for the spoils and secrets of Nazi Germany* (Paladin, 1988) and Linda Hunt, *Secret Agenda: the United States Government, Nazi scientists and Project Paperclip, 1945–1990* (St Martin's Press, 1991). The UK is not innocent in this matter. See Ian Cobain, 'How T-Force abducted Germany's best brains for Britain', *The Guardian*, 29 August 2007, and Stewart Payne, 'How Britain put Nazis' top men to work', *Daily Telegraph*, 30 August 2007.

There are more Krebses with sinister connotations: General Hans Krebs was Hitler's last Chief of General Staff, and a Russian-speaker who told the Soviet Army that Hitler was dead. He killed himself in the bunker. Another Hans Krebs, the founder of the Nazi movement in Czechoslovakia, was later executed for his war crimes in Bohemia-Moravia.

'The first seven BIOS reports' were listed in *Nature* 161, (13 March 1948), pp. 388–9. A list of industries and industrial processes pinched from the Germans is at www.openlibrary.org/BIOS. Howard M. Ehrman's wondering about the actual size of the German Naval Archives at Tambach is in *Captured German and Related Records: a National Archives conference*, edited by Robert

Wolfe (Ohio University Press, 1974), pp. 158–9. The Operational Archives Branch of the Naval Historical Center at the Washington Navy Yard, DC, has about 3,900 reels of microfilm of material from Tambach. See also Charles Burdick, 'The Tambach Archive – a research note', *Military Affairs*, vol. 36, no. 4 (December 1972), pp. 124–6. The figure '485 tons' is from Whitney R. Harris, *Tyranny on Trial: the trial of the major German war criminals at the end of WWII at Nuremberg, Germany, 1945–1946* (Southern Methodist University, 1999), p. xii. The Colpoys memo about 'the only people who should have access' and making the contents 'available for reference and study' is TNA HW8/37. The discovery of Admiral Raeder meeting Vidkun Quisling is in the BBC website *WW2 People's War*, article ID 2661581.

The trappings of success disgusted the puritan Scot in Ian Fleming. James Bond's complaints about 'the easy life, the rich life' are in *Goldfinger*, chapter 2, and 'the blubbery arms' envelop him in *From Russia With Love*, at the opening of chapter 11, which is entitled 'The Soft Life'. Anthony Burgess rightly described 'Octopussy' as a 'brilliant short story' in his admirable essay, 'The James Bond Novels: an introduction', which prefaced the Coronet reprints of Fleming's books in the mid-1980s.

Index

Lüth, Kptn.z.S. Wolfgang, 314
Lycett, Andrew, 88, 103n

Maaloy, 128–9
McCaffery, Lt Col George, 184
McCarthy, Sen. Joseph, 321
McDaid, Pte Francis, 209, 213
McDiarmid, John B., 144, 209, 210,
    211–14
McFee, George, 161, 169, 234
McGrath, Paul 'Mac': Algiers mission
    (1942), 148, 150, 151, 153; at Dieppe,
    4–6, 12, 13–16, 17; at Holmrook
    Hall, 225; investigates V-1 site, 235;
    post war, 331; sails to Algiers (1943),
    162; St Pabu capture, 254, 256–7;
    surrender of Kiel, 307
McGroarty, Pat, 53n
McLachlan, Donald, 44, 45, 103, 140
Maclean, Brig. Fitzroy, 216
McLellan, Frankie, 209, 213–14
Macmillan, Harold, 181
McNair, Lt Gen. Lesley J., 249
Macpherson, Stewart, 281
Madagascar, 149
Madrid, 85–6, 89, 97–8
Madura, SS, 81
Mafia, 181–2
Magdeburg, 57, 122
Mahares, 167
Mahon, A. P., 121
Maidstone, HMS, 163
Makeig-Jones, Capt. W. T., 48
Malcolm, HMS, 148–51
Mallorca, 24, 38, 85
Malta, 22, 83, 101, 102, 127, 175, 177
March, Juan Ordinas, 86–9, 100
Marcheret, Guy Glèbe d'Eu, Comte de,
    257
Mares (30AU Marine), 200
Marshall, Bill, 331
Marshall, Gen. George C., 18, 96, 206
Martin-Smith, Paddy, 178, 194, 195, 199
Mason, Prof. Kenneth, 137
Masterman, Sir John, 158
Maunsell, Brig. Raymond, 274–5
Maxwell, Gavin, 117

Mayer, Hans Ferdinand, 54–5
Mayfield, Brian, 114
Mayne, Paddy, 179, 183
Mazower, Mark, 300
Medhurst, AVM Charles, 133
Medmenham, 138
Menzies, Brig. Stewart (C), 51–2, 91, 107,
    133, 156
Merkers, 284
Merrett, Edward, 29, 39
Mers-el-Kébir, 83–4, 149, 150
Messina, Straits of, 189–90
Meteorite, HMS, 322
MI5: formation of Special Intelligence
    Units, 135; listening in on Germans,
    125; NID links, 27, 44; Rock of
    Gibraltar watch, 97; Twenty (XX)
    Committee, 158
MI6, 53, 133, 135, 145
MI8, 157
MI9, 97, 208
Michel, Henri, 252
Mihailović, Draža, 216
Miller, AB Robert, 151
Minisini, Adm. Eugenio, 200–3
Minorca, 38
Mionchinsky, Zlata, 127
MI(R), 37, 69–70, 114
Mitchell, Lt Cdr, 280–1
Mittelwerk factory, 286, 324
MO9, 113
Model, Genfeldm. Walter, 287
Molotov, Vyacheslav, 43
Moltke, Genfeldm. Helmuth von, 7–13
Monks, Noël, 184
Monowai, TSS, 228
Montagu, Ewan, 126, 141
Montgomery, Gen. Bernard L., 8, 177,
    185, 229, 272, 278, 279, 292, 304
Moorehead, Alan, 149, 162, 168, 252, 259
Morar, Loch, 118
Morgan, LCpl Bert, 178, 225, 238, 285
Morgan, Charles, 44–5
Morocco, 139, 149, 153
Morse, RAdm. Anthony, 201
Mortain–Falaise pocket, 250, 258
Moscow, 31